CIVIC ACTIVISM IN SOUTH KOREA

Civic Activism in South Korea

THE INTERTWINING OF DEMOCRACY
AND NEOLIBERALISM

Seungsook Moon

Columbia University Press
New York

Columbia University Press
Publishers Since 1893
New York   Chichester, West Sussex
cup.columbia.edu

Copyright © 2024 Columbia University Press
All rights reserved

Library of Congress Cataloging-in-Publication Data
Names: Moon, Seungsook, 1963- author.
Title: Civic activism in South Korea : the intertwining of democracy
and neoliberalism / Seungsook Moon.
Description: New York : Columbia University Press, [2024] |
Includes bibliographical references and index.
Identifiers: LCCN 2024003376 | ISBN 9780231211482 (hardback) |
ISBN 9780231211499 (trade paperback) | ISBN 9780231558938 (ebook)
Subjects: LCSH: Social movements—Korea (South) |
Political participation—Korea (South) |
Neoliberalism—Social aspects—Korea (South) | Democracy—Korea (South)
Classification: LCC HN730.5.A8 M67 2024 | DDC 303.48/4095195—dc23/eng/20240322
LC record available at https://lccn.loc.gov/2024003376

Cover design: Julia Kushnirsky
Cover photograph: Seungsook Moon

To Ben and our late fathers, Dr. Yonggoo Moon and Dr. Roger Caldwell

The democratic movement, then, is in fact a double movement of transgressing limits: a movement for extending the equality of public man to other domains of life in common, and in particular to all those that govern the limitlessness of capitalist wealth; another movement for reaffirming the belonging of anyone and everyone to that incessantly privatized public sphere.

JACQUES RANCIÈRE, *HATRED OF DEMOCRACY*

What is meant when it is said that we live in democracies? . . . what we call democracy is a statist and governmental functioning that is exactly the contrary: . . . the monopolizing of *la chose publique* by a solid alliance of State oligarchy and economic oligarchy. . . . We live in States of oligarchic law, in other words, in States where the power of the oligarchy is limited by a dual recognition of popular sovereignty and individual liberties.

JACQUES RANCIÈRE, *HATRED OF DEMOCRACY*

CONTENTS

ROMANIZATION OF KOREAN WORDS xi

ACKNOWLEDGMENTS xiii

Introduction: Democracy and Neoliberalism Examined Through a Lens of Civic Activism 1

Chapter One
The Development of "Citizens' Organizations" in South Korea 23

Chapter Two
Profiles of Three Citizens' Organizations 51

Chapter Three
Negotiating with the Market in Neoliberal South Korea 87

Chapter Four
Neoliberal Governance I: Collaborative Law and Policymaking and Undermining Grassroots Participation 124

Chapter Five
Neoliberal Governance II: Grassroots Participation Through
Private-Public Partnership and Undermining Civic Autonomy   153

Chapter Six
Refusing Neoliberal Governance and Pursuing
Prefigurative Activism   180

Conclusion: Reflecting on the Intertwining of Democracy
and Neoliberalism   202

NOTES   217

BIBLIOGRAPHY   263

KOREAN PRIMARY SOURCES   277

INDEX   283

ROMANIZATION OF KOREAN WORDS

For romanization of Korean words, this book follows "The Revised Romanization," instead of the McCune-Reischauer system, except for a name whose personal orthography is publicly known. Korean names of political leaders follow the Korean practice of writing a last name first and then a given name; a hyphen is used to link two syllables of a given name.

ACKNOWLEDGMENTS

This book was long in the making, and most of its initial writing was done during the Covid-19 pandemic when the whole world was locked down and people were confined to their homes and neighborhoods. After Spring Break in mid-March 2020, I completed the second half of the semester via online Zoom, in shock and disbelief about the rapidly escalating casualties of the pandemic in the United States. Fortunately, I was able to take an extended sabbatical leave during the following academic year (2020–21), generously supported by "the Laboratory Programme for Korean Studies" (AKS-2018-LAB-2250001), a five-year research grant from the Ministry of Education of the Republic of Korea and the Korean Studies Promotion Services of the Academy of Korean Studies. This research was also supported by a matching grant from the Dean of the Faculty Office at Vassar College. Reducing my teaching load by one course per year for two additional two years, the AKS grant enabled me to secure more time to work on this book. My home department, Sociology, provided me with small research grants from the Leslie A. Koempel Fund, created by a former faculty member there.

The global pandemic turned my life as a scholar into something akin to the monastic life of a nun/monk. Unable to travel and meet people in person, my life revolved around simple routines of reading, thinking, and writing; walking and resting; and eating and sleeping. I started a weekly zoom meeting with Martha Kaplan, my colleague in the Asian Studies Program at Vassar, to talk about our book projects and writing. I thank her for being a good listener and a supportive intellectual interlocutor during the lockdown. I also thank James M. Jasper for generously reading an earlier version of my book proposal and giving me constructive feedback without any personal connection other than being members of the imaginary cosmopolitan community of scholars. I thank Carter Eckert, Sun Joo Kim, and Paul Y. Chang, my colleagues in the Korea Institute at Harvard University, for reading a version of my book proposal and earlier versions of sample chapters and supporting the book project. I thank my six colleagues in the AKS research grant group: Aerin Chung at Johns Hopkins University; Gilsoo Han at Monash University; Kyungja Jung at the University of Technology, Sydney; Jaeeun Kim at the University of Michigan, Ann Arbor; Nora H. Kim at the University of Mary Washington; and Timothy Lim at California State University, Los Angeles. They shared valuable ideas and questions about an earlier version of chapter 3 during an online conference in June 2022, and seven of us shared collegial support for our individual book and article projects for five years from the summer of 2018. My special thank-you goes to Eric Schwartz, Editorial Director of the Columbia University Press, for believing in my project and guiding me effectively through the entire process of giving birth to this book. I also owe a special thank-you to two anonymous reviewers who provided me with meticulous and insightful feedback to strengthen this book.

There are more individuals who assisted me with their research support and personal support than I can list here. I am deeply grateful for the groups of staff activists, volunteer activists, lay members, and officers of the four citizens' organizations who shared their experience and ideas over time. In particular, I thank staff activists who provided me with electronic copies of Annual General Meetings of their organizations, which were all meticulous records of their activities and discussions, as well as valuable photographs. I thank Elizabeth Salmon, Social Science Librarian at Vassar, and Mikyung Kang, Librarian for the Korean Collection at Harvard-Yenching Library, for their reliable professional service. I thank my student research assistants, Sophia Choi and Yewon Kang at Vassar College and Jieun Paek at Yonsei University. I thank my niece, Jihee Kwak, for supporting my research with short notice. Last but not least, I am especially thankful to Ben, my life companion, who brought loving care and hilarious humor into my life while I worked on this book. Without his unexpected humor, sharing our passion for classical music, opera, and jazz, as well as cooking and sharing good food together, working on this book during the pandemic would have been much more difficult. These mundane activities became extraordinary, especially because he was recovering from life-threatening surgery and treatments during the pandemic. I also convey my special gratitude to my mother, Doseon Lee, an amazing and exceptional woman in her late eighties, and two sisters, Seungyon and Seunghee, for their unwavering trust in me and loving support.

CIVIC ACTIVISM IN SOUTH KOREA

INTRODUCTION

Democracy and Neoliberalism Examined Through a Lens of Civic Activism

> The wealth of the country is measured not so much by the quality, quantity and morale of its labor force, as by the country's attractiveness to coolly mercenary forces of global capital.
>
> —BAUMAN, *LIQUID MODERNITY*, 185

> I came to join the intern program/citizens education here because I have felt that there aren't many things I can do for myself in society. In college, I have heard a lot about "global leaders" and "reformative education" for talented individuals, but in reality I don't feel such identity or self-esteem *because society doesn't need us*. I feel such words are empty, and they turn me into a tool to be used.
>
> —WONHUI (EMPHASIS ADDED)[1]

> Numerous slogans we hear in college don't sound like they belong to the place of education. Popular majors among students are ones centered around *business management*. Of course, this is not just a problem in our country, but it has become the goal of entering a college. Until high school, we have been taught the *mindset of business management* at home and school. Then in college this continues, and it does not feel right. Yes, I get it; many students like myself have to work and make a living. But colleges are so commercialized, and they are only thinking about making money.
>
> —EUNHYE (EMPHASIS ADDED)

In the summer of 2015 I met Eunhye and Wonhui, two young women in their early and mid-twenties, respectively, while carrying out research that evolved into this book. They became involved in one of the "citizens' organizations" that are my focus here. Their words poignantly capture salient aspects of South Korean society that have been transformed by neoliberal globalization, especially since the 1990s. In a society in which wealth is based not on human labor but on the ability to attract globalized capital, even young people with college educations from "reputable" universities can feel that they are entirely expendable and find the popularized rhetoric of making young people into global leaders through reformative education hollow.² Although human labor of various sorts continues to be indispensable for enriching the quality of human lives beyond the generation of material wealth, the globalized neoliberal capitalist economy has heightened its vulnerability under the regime of "flexible labor" (*nodongyuyeonhwa*). The neoliberal transformation of South Korea is not limited to its labor market and the economy but has spread to its culture, including interactions among individuals in everyday life and their way of thinking about the self and the meaning of life. Eunhye's generation was born and came of age in the decades of rapid neoliberal transformation in democratizing South Korea and has been amply exposed to business management thinking at home and at school as a hegemonic framework to make sense of their actions and interactions. As a result, especially without much exposure to other ways of thinking and living, young people of her generation have learned to see themselves as "human capital" because labor is discredited, made more vulnerable, and culturally stigmatized (see chapter 3). To survive and prosper in the more precarious labor market characterized by "unlimited competition" (*muhangyeongjaeng*), their human capital and their education are important investment components. For young people with some critical consciousness, colleges appear to be one more place of business that sells commodities to those who can pay for them and prioritizes making money through efficient or corrupt transactions.

The lives of these two young women and others you will meet in this book were shaped by the global force of neoliberalism that the South Korean government actively embraced as a zeitgeist of the 1990s when the end of the Cold War elsewhere led to a global celebration of the "victory" of capitalism over communism.³ The triumphant West aggressively promoted the free market and footloose transnational capital as the source of prosperity and liberal democracy in the Third World and the former Eastern Bloc. Riding on the so-called third wave of democratization in the world, Kim Young-sam's civilian government (*munminjeongbu*: 1993–1998) pursued neoliberal globalization in the name of advancing Korea's economy, politics, and society. In particular, his government promoted the project of *Segyehwa* (worldification), a Korean version of globalization, as the source of more prosperity and recognition for the country.⁴ When the euphoria of globalization was upended with the Asian financial crisis (1997–98), the succeeding government of Kim Dae-jung (1998–2003) accepted the International

INTRODUCTION

Monetary Fund (IMF) rescue package and carried out further neoliberal restructuring of the economy.[5] The next "progressive" government, that of Roh Moo-hyun (2003–2008), signed the South Korea-U.S. Free Trade Agreement (KORUS FTA), bypassing democratic procedures and against massive popular resistance (see chapter 4). Ironically, during the decades of democratization in South Korea, the government controlled by progressive individuals and political camps, who were associated with the democratization movement of the 1970s and 1980s, neoliberalized the society before the "conservative" government took it further for the next ten years.

Neoliberal transformations of societies have taken place to varying degrees and through different paths around the world. Despite the common valid association between neoliberalism and a capitalist economy, in practice neoliberalism is never just about economic policy because the economy is organically bound to ruling a given population to provide the state with the necessary additional resources to run its essential apparatuses. It is also through contentious politics among different social groups, including various classes but not limited to them, that neoliberal economic policy is chosen and implemented willingly or forcefully, or a combination of both. The political nature of the neoliberal transformation is vividly illustrated globally by popular protests and movements against this process. In fact, after reemerging in the West as an ideology of economic policy in the 1970s, neoliberalism has evolved into "political rationality," a mode of ruling that has transformed not only the economy but also politics and culture around the world.[6] During the last two decades of the twentieth century, the United States as the promoter of economic globalization underwent its own neoliberal transformation through the ascendance of markets "as *the* normative model not only for business transactions but for virtually all aspects of economic, social, and political life."[7] In particular, neoliberalism has popularized the practice of governance by promoting the partnership among government, business, and civil society within the market framework. Combined with the existing logic of "rationalization" in modern society (à la Max Weber), neoliberalism has contributed to further intensify quantified accountability and professionalization for efficiency. It is compelling to examine how neoliberalism is related to democracy, both modes of ruling, in light of their ongoing entanglements. Neoliberal economic restructuring was globally promoted as an integral part of democratization or even as a precondition for liberal democracy. But in the aftermath of the 2008 global financial crisis, global discourse on the crisis of democracy has replaced the celebration of democratization and the consolidation of democracies, as authoritarian and populist politics has spread especially in the so-called mature democracies in the West and Japan.[8] In response, contemporary scholars have examined the relationship between neoliberalism and democracy. This book contributes to this inquiry from the angle of civic activism and how it has coped with the neoliberal transformation in South Korea.

By *civic activism*, I refer to activism practiced by individuals involved in "citizens' organizations" (*simindanche*) that emerged and spread as the vehicle for democratic social change in neoliberalizing South Korea. Comparatively speaking, civic activism pursued by "progressive" (*jinbojeok*) citizens' organizations can be seen as a Korean version of a social movement, critically responding to neoliberal globalization and yearning for an alternative world order. It is hopeful and redemptive to highlight collective movements and their spirit of struggle to solve serious problems generated and aggravated by neoliberal globalization.[9] However, such resistant activism is more complex than a one-dimensional opposition and protest against neoliberalism. In the face of persistent resilient neoliberalism even after the global financial crisis, such celebration and due recognition can obscure the intricate workings of neoliberalism.[10] Hence, in this book I address the following questions: "How does civic activism that is consciously oriented toward democratization negotiate with neoliberalism?" and "How and to what extent does neoliberalism enable civic activism and simultaneously undermine it?" Answering these questions requires an in-depth qualitative study of activism in South Korea and elsewhere. This line of inquiry illuminates why and how ordinary people as the citizens of a democracy have simultaneously resisted and accepted the neoliberal transformation of the economy, politics, and society. To examine the complex relationship between democracy and neoliberalism, I trace trajectories of activism coping with problems generated or aggravated by neoliberalism as it has profoundly transformed South Korean society, especially since the 1990s. The analysis of how civic activism has negotiated with neoliberalism in South Korea can shed light on the theoretical and empirical understanding of the complex and evolving relationship between democracy and neoliberalism in the world.

INTRODUCTION

HOW TO APPROACH DEMOCRACY AND CIVIC ACTIVISM

Drawing on Gabriel Rockhill's critical reflection on contemporary democracy, this study approaches democracy simultaneously as a value and as a product.[11] As a value, it refers to a mode of ruling characterized by *practices* of equality, self-determination, and participation of grassroots people in society. Although Rockhill does not mention practices, I emphatically highlight them through my focus on civic activism. As Jacques Rancière argues, grassroots people are those who do not have a natural entitlement to ruling such as wealth, superior capacity (of talent, wisdom, and knowledge), and firstborn or highborn status. Democracy as a value and a set of practices allows and even encourages ordinary people to rule because they are believed to be equal to those who have been considered to be qualified to rule.[12] This meaning of democracy as a value and set of practices converges on substantive democracy rather than procedural democracy. It also allows us to recognize the competing meanings and practices of democracy, rather than assuming it is a uniform entity that is linearly developing and spreading teleologically.

Democracy as a product refers to "a brand name for a product manageable at home and marketable abroad" that shows the primacy of its image over its substance.[13] The image reflects the *narrow instrumental view* of democracy equated with regular elections of political leaders and multiple political parties representing different social groups. Although these institutional arrangements are historically significant, since the Cold War era the United States, as a superpower/military empire, has forcefully promoted American-style democracy: that is, national governments that observe regular elections but promote and protect the dominance of big capitalist business in society, which could undermine substantive democracy.[14] Although lauded as pragmatic arrangements for practicing democracy in populous societies, these arrangements have repeatedly shown profound deficiency and failures in promoting democracy as a value—that is as a form of ruling by people as a majority—especially in societies in which money in the form of big capitalist business controls the functioning of electoral systems and political parties. As a result, existing democratic governments in reality have been plutocratic oligarchies rather than democracies. Yet the brand value of democracy as a product remains globally popular in the era of neoliberalism, and all types of governments in the world beyond the United States lay claim to being democracies.[15]

Civic activism is an important aspect of democracy as a value and as a set of practices. At an existential level, civic activism stems from the human capacity to imagine what does not exist and to turn that into a reality through collective endeavors. As Kathleen M. Blee points out in her qualitative study of activist groups in Pittsburgh, Pennsylvania, activists are "exceptions" rather than the norm. Using an analogy of poetry to routine speech, she considers the best face of civic activism as a vehicle to "transport us to another place, compel us to relive horrors and, more importantly, enable us to imagine a new society."[16] Before the global spread of democracy as a desirable form of ruling, exercises of this capacity were largely controlled by elites wielding political, economic, and cultural power. Historically, such elites mobilized those ruled to build and maintain an empire or a nation through secular and religious ideologies, as well as through material incentives and physical force. In democratic societies of the twenty-first century, "ordinary citizens" can act to turn their dreams about a better or different world into a reality. Yet, as Pierre Bourdieu argues, these ordinary citizens are not a homogeneous group but include diverse heterogeneous groups with power differences in terms of their possession and use of cultural, symbolic, social, and economic capital. Hence the dynamic of political participation in the context of civic activism becomes complex, which merits an in-depth qualitative study.

An additional complication is that not all voluntary and collective endeavors to create a better world are equally valid because the deceptively plain adjective "better" is loaded with moral values and judgment. As cult movements and white supremacist movements have shown, a better world for one can be a worse world or even no existence at all for another.[17] From a cynical angle, as Michael L. Gross documented, responsible citizens involved in morally inspiring activism are motivated not so much by lofty moral values as by competitive and parochial concerns.[18] Without idealizing activism but recognizing its actual and potential capacity, I define civic activism as a set of ideas and practices that *solve common problems and promote and protect public resources equally open to everyone for use*. Two features distinguish civic activism in its collective or individual form from other types of voluntary human actions: recognition of the equality of all human beings and their right to self-determination.

INTRODUCTION

CIVIC ACTIVISM AS SYMBOLIC ACTIONS AS WELL AS POLITICAL ACTIONS

During the past decade, social scientists have paid increasing attention to spontaneous militant street protests or internet-based activism as "new" forms of social movements that contest the destructive consequences of neoliberal globalization.[19] These studies shed light on novel features and emerging trends in opposition to neoliberalism, and some of them convey rich accounts of activism from the perspective of cultural sociology.[20] Yet they do not delve into the relationship between democracy and neoliberalism. Instead they assume that neoliberalism is external to these movements, and they overlook how neoliberalism as a hegemonic political rationality can be intricately intertwined with activism and social movements oriented toward democratization. The assumption stems in part from the emotional and existential need to identify resistance and explore alternatives to the enduring power of neoliberalism and in part from the narrow conceptualization of neoliberalism merely as an ideology and practices of economic policy.[21]

Compared to these studies of new activism, studies of the so-called old form of civic activism remain compelling for at least three reasons. First, although not as dramatic and spectacular as mass street protests and uncivil confrontations, civic activism in organized and enduring forms is critical to its reproduction and evolution precisely because of its stability and continuity. Second, civic activism in these forms has shown diversity within and across national societies and changes over time that deserve in-depth qualitative studies beyond formal typology and facile generalizations. As discussed in detail in chapters 1 and 2, citizens' organizations in South Korea are diverse and have developed distinct identities around democratizing social change rather than doing charitable activities. Such in-depth studies need to examine the extent to which civic activism negotiates with neoliberalism as a dominant ideology and set of practices for ruling in our time. Third, the distinction between new and old forms of civic activism is ambiguous and even trendy rather than substantive or definite, especially from the perspective of the social movement cycle; most social movements are institutionalized over time if they survive beyond their initial stages.[22] This suggests that the new and old forms reflect different cycles of social movements and civic activism at different stages of their development.

Using the cultural sociology perspective, I approach civic activism as symbolic actions, beyond political or strategic actions, that are imbued with moral meanings.[23] Instead of assuming civic activism as a given entity out there to be observed and discovered, I examine how it is constructed, contested, and negotiated among different social groups. By paying close attention to discourses and rhetorical frames generated over time by the citizens' organizations, I focus on ordinary people involved as lay members, paid staff activists or volunteer activists, and officers. Their discourses include various publications and other written texts, as well as in-depth interviews and conversations I conducted about their organizational and individual identities and activities. This focus on meanings and the interpretation of social actors involved in activism reveals complex ways in which neoliberalism as a dominant mode of ruling in the world is related to the workings of democracy.

This emphasis on civic activism as symbolic actions does not overlook its essentially political nature. As Charles Tilly aptly noted, because the state is the institution of ruling that has controlled the production, collection, and distribution of critical resources in a given society, civic activism almost always involves the construction and dissemination of claims and demands directed toward the state by negotiating with it and appealing to various social groups as its supporters; it is ultimately oriented to modifying power relations in society and to the distribution of major resources.[24] Yet in the process of articulating their claims and demands and reaching out to other social groups for their support, human beings need to make sense of their actions related to certain moral values.

For the analysis of civic activism using qualitative data I collected from four citizens' organizations, I use Pierre Bourdieu's theory of social space and political fields, which departs from the intellectual illusion that equates the theoretical concept of social class as a real class that mobilizes people to form groups for collective actions.[25] This break with objectivism enables us to see symbolic struggles that take place in different political fields where "what is at stake is the very representation of the social world." The point is not that there is no social class reflecting socioeconomic hierarchy, but that such a class, as Max Weber also pointed out, is neither an automatic source of solidarity nor a natural basis of mobilization.[26] Bourdieu conceives the social world as a multidimensional space constructed on the basis of principles of differentiation or distribution.[27] This means that social actors and groups of social actors are defined by their relative positions in a given space and are thus distributed in accordance with two factors: (1) "the overall volume of the capital they possess" and (2) "the composition of their capital (the relative weight of the different kinds of capital in the total set of their assets)."[28]

To elaborate, according to Bourdieu, there is an underlying rule of "the monopoly of the professionals" that governs the dynamic of political participation, which we can broadly conceive in a given social context. Civic activism would be a specific category of political participation. The rule reflects that, even in a formally democratic society, effective political participation is predicated on the mastery of such cultural or symbolic skills to use language and articulate claims and demands using a certain political rhetoric. As long as this symbolic competence is unevenly distributed among individuals and social groups, Bourdieu's theory suggests, political participation in democratic society also resembles a monopoly situation characterized by "the concentration of political capital" in the hands of a small number of professionals who possess or have access to "symbolic instruments for perceiving and expressing the social world." Defining political capital as a form of symbolic capital founded on belief and recognition, Bourdieu posits that this supremely free-flowing capital can be conserved only at the cost of unceasing work necessary both to accumulate credit and to avoid discredit.[29] He further points out that this group of professionals also monopolizes the production of politically effective and legitimate forms of perception and expression and that such monopoly is challenged only during a period of crisis. For groups of nonprofessionals, the relation between their interests and their capacity to express these interests determines the boundary between what is politically utterable or unutterable, and politically imaginable or unimaginable.[30]

The struggle among political professionals takes the form of a struggle over the symbolic power of making people see and believe, of predicting and prescribing, of making known and recognized, which is at the same time a struggle for power over the "public powers."[31] Politicians, and by extension professional activists and officers of civic organizations as political actors, owe their specific authority to the political field. The personal capital of fame and popularity is often the product of the reconversion of the capital of fame accumulated in other domains. The delegated capital of political authority is the product of a limited and provisional transfer of capital held and controlled by the institution and by it alone.[32] Similarly, the power of a discourse produced and disseminated by political professionals depends less on its intrinsic properties than on the mobilizing power it exercises.[33] These underlying rules highlight the importance of symbolic competence in political participation and in exerting political power over people in contemporary society. The power of the ideas that one proposes is measured not by their truth value but by the power of mobilization that they generate, that is, the power of the group that recognizes those ideas.[34] In chapters 3 through 6, drawing upon Bourdieu's theoretical insights, I discuss different ways in which civic activism negotiates with the market and neoliberal governance, which enables democratization and simultaneously constrains it.

NEOLIBERALISM AS A POLITICAL RATIONALITY OR A MODE OF RULING

In this book I expand and deepen the focus of empirical studies of neoliberalism from the angle of economic policy and restructuring to that of practices of ruling and social transformation in relation to democracy locally and globally.[35] Empirical studies of neoliberal globalization have aptly documented escalating economic inequality generated and aggravated by increasingly precarious labor and the lack of responsibility on the part of mobile transnational capital.[36] Empirical studies of activism and NGOs highlighted the problematic consequences of neoliberal economic restructuring on them, documenting how they were turned into instruments of outsourcing and privatization.[37] These studies, however, rarely engage in dialogue with broader and deeper critiques of neoliberalism as a political rationality advanced by theoretical studies. By bridging empirical studies of activism with theoretical studies of neoliberalism, I provide a more nuanced and grounded account of how and to what extent neoliberalism develops a contradictory relationship with democracy in South Korea—simultaneously enabling civic activism oriented toward democratization and constraining it.

Theoretical studies expand and deepen our understanding of neoliberalism by conceptualizing it as a mode of ruling rather than merely as an economic ideology and policy that has shaped and transformed not only our economy but also our politics, culture, and the making of individual subjectivities.[38] Although not using the concept of neoliberalism, Zygmunt Bauman developed a theoretical analysis of neoliberal society with the concept of "liquid modernity."[39] Drawing on Pierre Dardot and Christian Laval, as well as Wendy Brown and Zygmunt Bauman, I highlight their analyses of neoliberalism pertinent and relevant to South Korea in terms of the modus operandi of the nation-state and the construction of subjectivities. The following three points are particularly relevant. First, neoliberalism as a political rationality that guides practices of ruling has transformed how the modern state rules, from the exercise of its *sovereign power* over its internal population to the exercise of its *governance* over it.[40] This means that the state's power relies less on repressive or prohibitive law and hierarchical order and more on productive and pastoral power of orienting and guiding the conduct of its population in more diffused ways. An empirical example of this is the practice of governance, popularized as the partnership among government, business, and civil society; historically this partnership was not entirely new but became distinct. In studies of economic globalization that overlooked this transformation, the state's power is commonly misconstrued as declining and retreating. Instead of weakening and declining, political elites wielding the state's power in many societies in the West and elsewhere actively reorganized how to rule more effectively by embracing neoliberal political rationality. This sweeping grip of neoliberalism has been well documented by studies of how and to what extent both left-leaning and right-leaning governments in the world embraced it.[41] As discussed in chapters 4 through 6, the rise and spread of governance in local and national politics as a main feature of democratization in South Korea since the 1990s testifies to this ongoing neoliberal transformation of the state's power.

Second, in our neoliberal world, how does the state orient and guide the conduct of its population? It has adopted the logic of the financial markets and business enterprises. As a result, "both persons and states are expected to comport themselves in ways that maximize their capital value in the present and enhance their future value, and both persons and states do so through practices of entrepreneurialism, self-investment, and/or attracting investors."[42] This is how the ruling of a population is intricately interwoven with the ongoing evolution of the capitalist economic system. The financialization of capitalism has spread the following practices around the world and altered the lives of hundreds of millions of people: borrowing money to buy necessities and luxuries in the face of escalating and widespread employment insecurity, investing in oneself to enhance their value as human capital through health and fitness, as well as education and training to survive in competition or, better, to win in competition; turning debts that people accumulate into "financial products" through securitization, which people can buy for investment, and investing money to make more money and managing indebtedness through overworking and accounting to avoid financial enslavement. In the global proliferation of these common practices, states do not directly dictate to individuals but nevertheless have bolstered the underlying rules of the financial market and capitalism to strongly favor capital and big corporations. Pierre Dardot and Christian Laval point out the political nature of debt in neoliberal society thusly:

> Obviously, debt is an economic means of extracting and transferring wealth to lenders and, in the event of a risk of default, imposing the solution most advantageous to them. But it is much more than that. It is a formidable means of *government*. . . . Debt is one of the most effective weapons of political war.[43]

As discussed in chapters 3 through 6, all of these practices have grown explosively in South Korea since the 1990s through the proliferation of credit cards and various other loans, intensification of the popular fever for education and training to obtain credentials and certificates, and the immense popularization of practices of reinvestment (*jaeteqeu*) to become rich quickly.[44]

Third, closely related to the second point, the state has turned itself into a neoliberal actor in the process of directing its population through the logic of financial markets and business enterprises. Hence the punishment for going against the logic has become primarily economic for the state as well. Observing at the turn of the third millennium, Bauman wrote:

> Insubordinate governments, guilty of protectionist policies or generous public provisions for the "economically redundant" sectors of their populations and of recoiling from leaving the country at the mercy of "global financial markets" and "global free trade," would be refused loans or denied reduction of their debts; local currencies would be made global lepers, speculated against and pressed to devalue; local stocks would fall head down on the

global exchanges; the country would be cordoned off by economic sanctions and told to be treated by past and future trade partners as a global pariah; global investors would cut their anticipated losses, pack up their belongings and withdraw their assets, leaving local authorities to clean up the debris and bail out the victims of their added misery.[45]

As discussed in the following chapters, the state in South Korea, regardless of the ideological orientation of political leaders and their administrations, has been conducting itself as supporters and protectors of neoliberalism actively or reluctantly in the face of the actual and potential consequences just described.

THE RELATIONSHIP BETWEEN DEMOCRACY AND NEOLIBERALISM

This book includes significant contributions to theoretical and empirical studies of the relationship between democracy and neoliberalism. Theoretical studies of this relationship rely primarily on experiences in the West, including North America and Western Europe. A recurring theme revolves around the crisis of liberal democracy that has been "hollowed out," "depleted," or "eclipsed" by neoliberalism.[46] Empirical studies of declining democracy focus on the rise of authoritarian populism in the West.[47] Although some of the theoretical studies recognize the productive power of neoliberal political rationality, both theoretical and empirical studies tend to stress its destructive dynamic, which undermines democracy through the market logic that implodes the boundaries among the economy, politics, and the social and thereby destroys public things, institutions, and space. This undermining of the public is unmistakably present and has grown in South Korea, but the historical context of its democratization also highlights how neoliberal governance that restructured the state can facilitate participatory practices of democracy by generating political openings for nonstate actors. Although long-term outcomes of this facilitation are contingent on specific local contexts and their structural positions in the global economy and geopolitics, the experience South Korea shares with other non-Western societies illuminates the extent to which liberal democracy is intimately intertwined with neoliberalism, which tends to be obscured in Western contexts.

With some exceptions, theoretical studies highlighting neoliberalism as a destructive force external to democracy rely primarily on experiences and practices of democracy in the West.[48] Given the global spread of the neoliberal mode of ruling, theorizing the relationship between democracy and neoliberalism requires the expansion of its scope beyond the West. Empirical studies of neoliberalism expand the scope by documenting divergent responses of political elites and regimes in non-Western societies to neoliberal programs or divergent trajectories of neoliberal restructuring in connection with sociocultural factors and the timing of the implementation of neoliberal restructuring. However, most of these empirical studies do not fully engage in a theoretical discussion of the relationship between democracy and neoliberalism. Instead they discuss paradigms of political development or culturalism.[49]

In his comparative study of Argentina, Chile, Estonia, and Poland, Aldo Madariaga presents a more complex analysis of neoliberal resilience, focusing on the actors and coalitions that supported the establishment of neoliberalism and guarded its continuity over time.[50] Directly focusing on the relationships between neoliberalism and democracy in societies outside Western Europe and North America, Madariaga identifies political institutional mechanisms that link the successful development of neoliberal capitalism and its limitations on democracy. In critical response to the paradigm of political development that tends to assume a linear process toward a market democracy, some qualitative studies of societies in Latin America pay attention to the complex intertwining of neoliberalism and activism.[51] Building on these studies, I bring the theoretical discussion and a rich empirical study of South Korea together to identify the contradictory relationship between democracy and neoliberalism and elaborate on it.

My main argument regarding South Korea is as follows. Neoliberalism as a mode of ruling undermines (substantive) democracy by destroying common or public resources equally available for everyone to use; in addition, neoliberalism facilitates (substantive and procedural) democracy by generating political space for nonstate actors to participate in addressing and solving problems as long as this activism does not disrupt the core workings of neoliberal capitalism.[52] The intertwining of democracy and neoliberalism observed in civic activism in South Korea reveals the sophisticated work of neoliberal governance that urges us to move beyond the one-way direction of attributing the weakening of democracy to neoliberalism.

INTRODUCTION

This seemingly causal argument is shared by most theoretical and empirical critiques. However, the weakening of democracy allowed the ascendance of neoliberalism, as pointed out by Madariaga's comparative study of how different countries have fallen under neoliberal transformations to varying degrees. The weakening of democracy is not a theoretical and normative problem; it is a practical consequence of contentious politics among hierarchical social groups. Democracy as a value and its practices can be protected against political and economic elites, a numerical minority, only when diverse social groups form solidarity and become a numerical/political majority. My analysis of civic activism in South Korea shows that the presence of social groups and actors pushing for democratization is crucial. Their activism can turn neoliberal governance into democratic governance. When they encounter resistance, these social groups and actors need to join with other broad-based social groups to challenge the political and economic elites. In the absence of such pressure by the majority, democracy is weakened and the neoliberal transformation becomes stronger.

A theoretical implication of the intertwining of democracy and neoliberalism needs to be discussed in empirical studies in Asia, Latin America, the Middle East, and Africa, as well as in former communist countries in Eastern Europe and Central Asia. Unlike the West, where democracy as a branded product has been managed internally, most societies see the ostensible promotion of democracy as an integral aspect of neoliberal globalization. This is clearly reflected in the academic field of transitology and in the use of descriptive terms such as "democratic neoliberalism," "neoliberal democracy," and "neoliberal good governance."[53] This common experience compels us to recognize the enduring equation of the "free market" with liberal democracy and the subsequent "instrumentalization" of democracy in practice that stems from the period of the Cold War.[54] For many people in these societies, therefore, liberal democracy is not only a desirable political system promoting equality among citizens but also an ideological tool of the West to promote its dominant values and institutions, which are often supported by their own elites and conservative populaces. These values and institutions have prioritized the sanctity of private property and individual civil and political rights over the equality of social conditions in terms of basic welfare. This reality reminds us that liberal democracy is pursued, practiced, and contested in the global and local contexts of unequal economic, political, and social relations. Established power relations among social groups in society structure how the political opening generated by neoliberal governance can be used. In the case of South Korea, for example, neoliberal governance facilitated democracy in the form of a partnership between the state and professional activists of large advocacy organizations in drafting and reforming laws and policies. But these activists could not push beyond the hegemonic notion of democracy practiced around individual rights and freedom, which do not challenge the core logic of neoliberalism.

RESEARCH METHODOLOGY

To highlight the distinct patterns in the complex interactions between neoliberal governance and civic activism oriented toward democratizing social change in South Korea, I concentrated my study on three organizations: the People's Solidarity for Participatory Democracy (PSPD), two local branches of the Democratic Friends Society (DFS), and the Friends of Asia (FOA). While the English names of PSPD and FOA are what these organizations have used for themselves, that of DFS is my translation of their Korean name; for the two local branches of the DFS I also use English translations of their names, Goyang (GY) Branch and Northeast (NE) Branch. As discussed in chapter 1, in their conscious emphasis on democratizing social change, these citizens' organizations are differentiated from other volunteer associations that focus on charitable activities, common hobbies, or the economic interests of their own members. Although these three organizations broadly share an orientation toward social change, they are diverse in Korean civil society in terms of size, organizational structure, and activism issues and practices. PSPD is a large advocacy organization with a professional activist staff who deal with a broad spectrum of national issues but focus on monitoring the state and big business regarding the protection and support of social minorities. The two branches of DFS are feminist organizations of medium size that rely on volunteer activists and part-time staff to pursue the empowerment of local women and other local residents by addressing a range of issues. FOA is a small, local organization of volunteer activists (who are its members) and supporters (who are not its members), and their focus is on foreign migrant issues.

Given the history of the democratization movement in South Korea, the choice of these citizens' organizations deserves clarification. After South Korea replaced its military dictatorship with a procedural democracy, the democratization movement of the 1980s organically underwent differentiation from its coalition of factory workers, peasants, the urban poor, intellectuals (religious leaders, writers, artists, and students), and dissident politicians who came together under the broader category of people (*minjung*). Especially after the fall of communism, many activists searched for a different mode of activism and joined emerging "citizens' movements." This new form of movement embraced middle-class reformative activism within the liberal democratic system, whereas other activists adhered to a "people's movement" that focused on workers, peasants, and other marginalized social groups. This bifurcation did not represent a rigid dichotomy in practices; the two camps often worked together, and many progressive citizens' organizations have embraced aspects of the people's movement. I chose these progressive citizens' organizations (rather than the people's movement organizations) because they intended to represent all Koreans as citizens in accordance with the reality of democratization and were more conscious of their identities as vehicles of democratic change (see chapter 1). To be certain, as my analysis of civic activism shows, the largely middle-class orientation of the citizens' movement has constrained its activism, especially in the context of neoliberal transformation. However, this constraint illuminates rather than obscures the limits of liberal democracy as a brand or the instrumentalization of liberal democracy that marginalizes or excludes socioeconomic equality in terms of basic welfare.

I did not include the labor movement (unions) and other examples of the "people's movement" (*minjungundong*) that have dealt with urgent economic problems caused and aggravated by neoliberalism for the following reasons. From a broad perspective of state and society relations, these movements are important elements of citizens' movements oriented toward societal democratization, but their members have self-identified as workers/laborers rather than as citizens. Many scholars have described the differences between citizens' movements and people's movements.[55] This intriguing dichotomy reflects the narrow understanding of democracy and democratization, separating political and civil rights from economic rights in capitalist societies. A critical inquiry into this common perception would require another book-length study. My focus on the citizens' organizations, which have been self-consciously oriented toward democratization, further illuminates the problematic perception as an integral element of the contradictory relationship between democracy and neoliberalism.

In this book I rely on archival and field research I conducted from 2004 to 2020. Three rounds of major fieldwork were carried out from August 2004 to May 2005, from September 2009 to January 2010, and then the summer of 2015. Additional archival research was carried out in the summer of 2019 and from August 2020 to August 2021. During my long-term and short-term research, I collected in-depth interviews with members of PSPD, DFS local branches and its headquarters, and members of FOA. I interviewed fifty-seven members of PSPD, including nine staff activists and three officers; forty-six members in the two DFS branches and their headquarters, including fourteen staff/volunteer activists; and eighteen members of FOA, including two staff activists. To supplement this relatively small number of interviewees, I collected internet blog posts by FOA members and supporters. I asked these groups of lay members, activists, and officers semi-structured open-ended questions about their life stories with a focus on their involvement in these organizations. I interviewed them at various sites, including offices, cafes, and restaurants near these organizations as well as sites near their workplaces. Several were interviewed in their homes. Most interviews lasted for one to two hours, and several people were interviewed multiple times over a decade. Initially, I contacted these organizations and visited them in person, describing to staff or volunteer activists my interest in learning about their lay members' experience of joining the organizations and getting involved. I met members of these organizations through informal referrals and participant observation at regular and special gatherings for lay members, which ranged from lectures, movie or book discussions, and fund-raising events to street campaigns and social gatherings. For PSPD, a large organization with multiple staff activists performing various functions, I focused on interviewing staff activists who had been responsible for managing lay members. For the two DFS branches and FOA, local organizations with fewer activists, I interviewed as many activists as possible. Most of these interviews (about 90 percent) were tape-recorded in Korean with the interviewees' consent and transcribed in Korean for the remaining 10 percent of interviews, I took notes during the interviews and filled in some of the information after the interviews were completed.

I also collected various publications both in printed form and online. These citizens' organizations have kept extensive and detailed records of their activities, significant events and accomplishments, as well as their challenges and setbacks, in their newsletters, monthly house organs, annual proceedings of their general meetings, and special anniversary publications. PSPD has produced a wide range of publications documenting its history of activism, and the two DFS branches generated a detailed record of their activism since 2012. By taking advantage of the advanced internet infrastructure in South Korea, even a small local organization such as FOA generated an extensive online record of writings by its members and supporters. During the summer of 2019 and winter of 2020, when I conducted supplemental research on the three organizations, I obtained proceedings of the annual general meetings of PSPD and the two DFS branches. Because DFS proceedings since 2012 are particularly detailed in conveying not only factual information but also interactions among various groups involved in their activism, I relied on these documents to complement my interview data for recent years, especially after 2015. For FOA, I compiled the writings of sixty members and supporters about their experiences of activism by reviewing 509 blog postings from 2010 to 2020.

During my archival research, I compiled the *NGO Times* (see chapter 1) by skimming through the entire set of old newspapers available at the National Assembly Library and making notes and digital photocopies of relevant articles. I do not use extensively the *NGO Press*, a later and current version of the *NGO Times*, because it began publication after the formative years in the development of civil society in contemporary South Korea. These archival data as well as in-depth interview data provide the discourses on civic activism and identities I utilized for my qualitative analysis in this book.

OVERVIEW OF INDIVIDUAL CHAPTERS

Chapter 1, "The Development of 'Citizens' Organizations' in South Korea," discusses the historical context of citizens' organizations as they emerged and spread as a major vehicle of democratization in South Korea after its transition to procedural democracy in the late 1980s. It traces how the citizens' organizations were shaped by the confluence of democratization and neoliberal globalization, especially in the 1990s. They continued to evolve in the aftermath of the two major economic crises as "precipitating events" that generated activism/social movements; both the "progressive" administration (1998–2007) and the "conservative" administration (2008–2017) actively embraced the neoliberal logic of deregulation, privatization, and capital accumulation and promoted the market as the solution for an array of problems. Against this backdrop, this chapter identifies common features that distinguish the citizens' organizations from older volunteer associations in civil society: (1) financial and political independence from the state, (2) a focus on institutional and social change rather than charitable activities and services, and (3) grassroots participation. I argue that these common features constitute the moral codes of citizens' organizations, which work as the rhetorical framework for interpreting and assessing their activism and identities. I argue that the historical context illuminates the intertwining of democratization with the promotion of neoliberal globalization, which has been common to most non-Western societies that witnessed the so-called third wave of democratization. This shared historical experience is critical to deepening our understanding of the relationship between democracy and neoliberalism.

Chapter 2, "Profiles of Three Citizens' Organizations," discusses basic facts about the three citizens' organizations chosen for the in-depth qualitative analysis of civic activism: PSPD; two local branches of the DFS, Goyang (GY) Branch and Northeast (NE) Branch; and FOA. These organizations illuminate three distinct patterns in the interplay between neoliberalism and civic activism oriented toward democratization. I examine their differences and similarities in terms of their civic identities and activities in connection with the moral codes discussed in chapter 1. I also highlight underlying tensions between the normative ideals of citizens' organizations, which promote and pursue equality and solidarity, and their routine operations and daily experiences, which are affected by the larger social forces generating hierarchy and division such as bureaucratization, professionalization, and social status tied to education and cultivation. This attention to the local sociocultural context provides the framework for the discussion in the following chapters on how civic activism negotiated with neoliberalism as it facilitated and simultaneously tried to constrain equality.

Chapter 3, "Negotiating with the Market in Neoliberal South Korea," analyzes how the three organizations negotiated with the market as it became the dominant model for organizing human lives and governing people beyond being a tool for economic activities. Using qualitative data, I identify the common resistance of these organizations to market logic and their acceptance of pragmatic market practices. They resisted the neoliberal logic of individualization and profit maximization by developing and practicing communal social relations in their identities and activism.

At the same time, to pursue activism for democratization, they adopted, to varying degrees, such established market practices as monetary expression of membership, "marketing" to maintain their members and recruit new members, and accepting the consumerist sensibility of legitimizing fun and enjoyment as the source of motivation. This chapter also highlights how the market constrained the maintenance of paid activists and their reproduction.

Chapter 4, "Neoliberal Governance I: Collaborative Law and Policymaking and Undermining Grassroots Participation," focuses on PSPD and analyzes how and to what extent neoliberal governance enables and constrains civic activism pursued by the organization in dealing with problems generated or aggravated by neoliberal globalization. Using qualitative and archival data, I discuss how PSPD actively used political opportunities generated by neoliberal governance to pursue its activism centered around law and policy reform concerning social safety and welfare issues. In the process of cooperating with "progressive" governments, PSPD often mobilized the horizontal network of social movement organizations. Yet the content of law and policymaking and reform shows that such participation was allowed only as long as it did not seriously challenge the fundamental workings of neoliberal capitalism. The enabling condition of neoliberal governance also led to the reproduction of the hierarchical division of labor between lay members and professional staff activists and undermined active grassroots participation. As Bourdieu argues, asymmetrical access to and competence to use cultural/symbolic capital in policy and legal reforms reinforced the hierarchy and marginalized substantial grassroots participation.

Chapter 5, "Neoliberal Governance II: Grassroots Participation Through Private-Public Partnership and Undermining Civic Autonomy," focuses on the GY and NE branches (of DFS) and analyzes how and to what extent neoliberal governance enabled local volunteer activist women to pursue feminist activism and simultaneously constrained them. The repeated election of a former leader of PSPD to the Seoul mayoralty (2011–2020) spread neoliberal governance and increased the partnership between local governments and local DFS branches. The political opening generated by neoliberal governance enabled the branches to use resources of local governments to provide social services and to infuse them with their feminist views. These branches managed to maintain their political autonomy from government, but their growing financial dependence on government bureaucracies undermined their civic autonomy. This dependence was escalated by neoliberal restructuring of the economy, which spread employment insecurity and shrank their membership base. Consequently, the expansion of local feminist activism funded by government was accompanied by a growing disengagement with their local members and the decline of grassroots projects.

Chapter 6, "Refusing Neoliberal Governance and Pursuing Prefigurative Activism," focuses on FOA and analyzes how and to what extent its refusal to go along with neoliberal governance enabled its activism and constrained it. Dedicated to issues concerning foreign migrants, this local organization chose to be an outlier for both structural and ideological reasons. Structurally, as a small local organization, it was unlikely to receive sizable and stable government funding. Ideologically, it prioritized its pursuit of social movement and social change over partnership with government entities to secure more resources and expand its influence. On the one hand, this distancing enabled it to pursue its own grassroots and prefigurative activism of working with foreign migrants as if they are equal members in Korean society rather than treating them as objects of charitable services. On the other hand, in the face of the neoliberal challenge, the lack of resources subjected the organization to persistent financial precarity.

The final chapter, Reflecting on the Intertwining of Democracy and Neoliberalism, brings together empirical and analytical insights from the in-depth study of civic activism in South Korea in dialogue with existing theoretical debates on neoliberalism and democracy. Examining the contradictory relationship between democracy and neoliberalism from the vantage point of activism pursued by the citizens' organizations, I argue that neoliberalism not only undermines democracy as a value and a set of practices but also facilitates it by restructuring the state and generating political openings for participation and cooperation. Neoliberalism undermines the substantive aspect of democracy by shrinking or destroying public resources, institutions, and spaces that are equally open to everyone and are necessary to the equality of social conditions. At the same time it facilitates procedural and participatory practices of democracy by generating political openings under the rubric of neoliberal governance as long as these practices do not seriously challenge neoliberal capitalism. This contradictory relationship illuminates the limited conception of democracy in the global promotion of liberal democracy.

Chapter One

THE DEVELOPMENT OF "CITIZENS' ORGANIZATIONS" IN SOUTH KOREA

> Non-governmental organizations play a vital role in the shaping and implementation of participatory democracy. Their credibility lies in the responsible and constructive role they play in society. Formal and informal organizations, as well as grass-roots movements, should be recognized as partners in the implementation of Agenda 21. . . . With a view to strengthening the role of non-governmental organizations as social partners, the United Nations system and Governments should initiate a process, in consultation with non-governmental organizations, to review formal procedures and mechanisms for the involvement of these organizations at all levels from policy-making and decision-making to implementation.
> —UNITED NATIONS, AGENDA 21, IN REPORT OF THE UNITED NATIONS CONFERENCE ON ENVIRONMENT AND DEVELOPMENT, RIO DE JANEIRO, JUNE 3-14, 1992, 389, 390.

Coinciding with the global revival of nongovernmental organizations (NGOs), in the late 1980s "citizens' movement organizations" (*siminundongdanche*; or citizens' organizations: *simindanche*) began to emerge and spread in South Korea as a new vehicle of activism. This revival took place in the context of the global expansion of neoliberalism, which has transformed the nature of the state and its relation to society. Once South Korea acquired its coveted UN membership in 1992, citizens' organizations embraced NGOs as a common self-referential term, reflecting the influence of the UN. In 1998, The *NGO Times* sponsored a United Nations Development Programme (UNDP) conference to discuss cooperation between the UN and NGOs.[1]

Domestically, the citizens' movement organically grew out of the democratization movement of the 1980s, which brought workers, peasants, the urban poor, intellectuals, and dissident politicians together under the category of people (*minjung*) against the common enemy—military dictatorship.[2] Middle-class professionals, especially lawyers, professors, and religious leaders, served as leaders of the unified movement and gained moral authority for supporting workers, peasants, and other downtrodden people. In particular, numerous college students turned themselves into factory workers in solidarity with them (*nohakyondae*). Once the transition to procedural democracy was achieved, especially after collapse of the Communist Bloc, a growing number of activists departed from the minjung movement and accepted reform-oriented activism, working within democratic institutions rather than working for a radical revolution. The minjung movement has existed among workers (*nodongja*), farmers (*nongmin*), the urban poor (*doshibinmin*), and their supporters, but it was a citizens' movement that came to represent civil society revived through democratization. During the decades of democratization, citizens' organizations carved out a space for activism that promoted progressive social change and popularized such activism as a new ideal of civil society.[3] Citizens' organizations influenced other existing civil society associations to consider civic activism or social movement as one of their main activities and encouraged ordinary Koreans to see themselves as agents of social change.

This chapter provides a history of this development in the 1990s and the 2000s, when citizens' organizations witnessed rapid growth and then a relative decline in their societal influence.[4] This contemporary history needs to be understood against the backdrop of the neoliberal transformation of the world. I argue that the emergence and spread of citizens' organizations were enabled by neoliberal globalization, and this intertwining of democratization with neoliberalism compels us to examine how and to what extent governance as a major mechanism of neoliberalism promoted and then undermined democracy in South Korea. This contemporary history is followed by a broader discussion of state-society relations in traditional Korea. Although quite distant from the present, this historical comparison enables us to see contemporary civic activism in terms of the politics of status distinction tied to moral authority and cultural capital. As Bourdieu argues, the comparison between the middle-strata professionals of the late Joseon Dynasty and the professional middle-class leadership in citizens' organizations illuminates the enduring importance of cultural/symbolic capital in actual and potential politics of contention. The former were pacified by the political/cultural elite in the Joseon Dynasty who recognized their literary refinement, whereas the latter became active in sociopolitical change by using their cultural capital but reproducing hierarchy among citizens.

In this chapter I focus on how progressive citizens' organizations tried to democratize their relation to the state and their internal working by developing certain moral codes in the context of the transnational circulation of governance that the United Nations promoted regarding NGOs. The UN promotion of NGOs contributed to the legitimacy of newly emerging citizens' organizations as respectable social and political actors working for public issues in tune with the global trend. In their pursuit of democratization, citizens' organizations turned neoliberal governance into a mechanism of democratization by highlighting public interests and developing the following moral codes to establish and maintain their identities: (1) independence from the state, (2) diversity, (3) movements for institutional and social change, and (4) participation of grassroots or ordinary citizens. I adopt the term *moral codes* to recognize the profoundly moral nature of civic activism, rather than to evade or obscure it, because such activism is about imagining an ideal or alternative and turning it into a reality to improve a current situation, address a problem, or correct a wrong. Although each of these codes individually is not peculiar to South Korea, the heightened emphasis on the combination of independence from the state, activism for social change, and grassroots participation gives them a cultural flair as a South Korean version of civic activism.

The history of citizens' organizations in South Korea tells us how civic activism takes a particular form that was shaped by a local history of democratization intertwined with neoliberal globalization. It also shows the extent to which democracy as a product/brand can be substantiated by actors and social groups in the local context. This deeper and broader understanding helps us pay attention to the contradictory relationship between neoliberalism and democracy through the lens of civic activism. It also helps us avoid a hasty devaluation of citizens' organizations as an "old" form of NGOs that have become problems rather than solutions. This criticism has some merits, especially for large international advocacy organizations run by professional activists, which have become the dominant NGOs globally.[5] However, the focus on this type of NGO obscures local variations in civic organizations in a given period and changes in them over time. To move beyond a cursory typology and facile overgeneralizations, we need to conduct in-depth qualitative studies of various types of civic organizations over time. To reconstruct a nuanced history of citizens' organizations as a South Korean vehicle of civic activism, I rely on the discourse of "civil society" by the *NGO Times* (1993–2007) and secondarily on scholarly publications on the subject. As a collective self-representation in the making, civil society discourse was integral to the emergence and spread of citizens' organizations.

The *NGO Times* was a weekly paper published by leading citizens' organizations when the Kim Young-sam administration began civilian and democratic rule (1993–1998) after the end of military and authoritarian rule. Literally meaning citizens' newspaper in Korean (*Siminuisinmun*), it was intended to be a "representative newspaper for citizens' movements to foster wholesome civil society" and to provide the "major forum for recording collective representation and critical self-reflection of social movement organizations."[6] In 1996, the leading citizens' organizations (such as the Citizens Coalition for Economic Justice, the People's Solidarity for Participatory Democracy, the Citizens United for the Environment, and the Young Men's Christian Association) established the Citizens' Movements Information Center (*siminundongjeongbocenteo*) and began to publish the *Korean NGOs Directory* every three years and has published the *Korean Civil Society Yearbook* since 2002. The weekly was closed temporarily in 2007 due to a sexual harassment scandal involving the president of the NGO Times Corporation.[7] Under reorganized leadership, it was replaced in mid-2007 by the *NGO Press* (*Siminsahoesinmun*), which means civil society newspaper. This newspaper still exists online (www.ingopress.com) as a clearinghouse for information about civil society in South Korea.

INTERTWINING DEMOCRATIZATION AND NEOLIBERAL GLOBALIZATION IN THE RISE AND SPREAD OF CITIZENS' ORGANIZATIONS

In the aftermath of the Cold War (outside the Korean peninsula), globalization became equated with the spread of neoliberal capitalism and procedural democracy. This was a real-life example of democracy promoted as a product/brand. The World Bank promoted efficiency and anticorruption along with democracy when funding development programs, which led to neoliberal restructuring for many countries.[8] The "unholy trinity" of the International Monetary Fund (IMF), the World Bank, and the World Trade Organization (WTO) expanded neoliberal governance by reducing politics to a means to facilitate and even maximize capital accumulation.[9] In this context, the UN revived NGOs as major partners with governments and international organizations, and this idea resonated well with neoliberal governance. Initially defining NGOs as international agencies working on issues concerning human rights, the environment, humanitarian assistance, and economic development in the global South, the UN disseminated global standards concerning NGOs. The cooperation between the UN and NGOs as nonstate actors contributed to the spread of governance, which has altered the workings of the state from the "sovereignty" to a "partnership." Translated as "collaborative ruling" (*hyeopchi*), the concept of governance became popularized as a democratization of ruling that invites nonstate actors into policymaking, implementation, and decision-making.[10] Although governance is not inherently neoliberal, the specific economic and political context of its global spread has turned it into a major mechanism of neoliberalism as a mode of ruling. After all, international development the UN has promoted has been funded by the powerful transnational financial organizations—the IMF, the World Bank, and the WTO, which was re-created in 1995 by revamping the 1948 General Agreement on Tariffs and Trade (GATT). It is noteworthy that the UN's initial introduction of NGOs as its legitimate partners had been dormant during the Cold War. The 1945 UN Charter (Article 71) clearly mentioned it, but this partnership did not gain significant traction during the Cold War, when liberal democracy was narrowly "instrumentalized" as a regular election and capitalist economy against the communist systems in the Eastern Bloc.[11] NGOs gradually regained their role within a series of UN conferences on the environment from 1972 to 1992. It was not until the 1992 UN Conference on Environment and Development that NGOs were actively involved in preparing for the conference and participating in it.[12] This conference adopted policy statements concerning the role NGOs could play in designing, implementing, and evaluating programs and policies within the UN system. The global visibility of NGOs as a legitimate actor in national and global politics influenced the leading citizens' organizations in South Korea to adopt the term to mainstream their unfamiliar identities in Korean society.[13]

The popularization of the term *NGOs* in South Korea was well reflected in the discourse of civil society. In initially carving out civil society as a distinct sphere for citizens' organizations, the discourse tried to identify what types of organizations and activities were included in it. Their major publications, including the *NGO Times*, *Directory of Korean NGOs*, and *Korean Civil Society Yearbook*, conveyed a broader and looser boundary of civil society than scholarly publications focusing on citizens' organizations as the new segment of civil society. These nonacademic publications tend to use several key terms interchangeably with one another. The most notable term associated with civil society was *nongovernmental organizations* (NGOs; *mingandanche*).[14] This shows the underlying significance of transnational flows of ideas and practices to domestic social and political development. It is worthwhile to mention that civil society was defined as the sphere wherein NGOs were active and that this definition took advantage of this concept being globally revalidated by the UN. The NGOs in South Korea include an old type of volunteer associations that have existed since the premodern era; these range from religious and occupational organizations to charity-oriented and socializing organizations. It also includes the new type of volunteer associations oriented toward social change, which were interchangeably called citizens' organizations (*simindanche*), civil society organizations (*siminsahoedanche*), or citizens' movement organizations (*siminundongdanche*). As neoliberal globalization expanded the power of the market, the nonprofit nature of civil society was also highlighted. However, in contrast to Japan and the United States, the term *nonprofit organizations* (NPOs) was not as widely used as NGOs in South Korea, especially in the 1990s.[15] An emergent change occurred in 1998 when the NPO Support Act was established by the Kim Dae Jung administration shortly after Japan passed its NPO law. The popular usage of NGOs over NPOs reflects different degrees of dominance of the state versus the market over the society in a given time period. With the strong legacy of authoritarian rule in South Korea, where the developmental state dominated over volunteer associations and the market, NGOs became significant to civic identities of citizens' organizations. As discussed in later chapters, the focus on the state has been modified as the market has rapidly become dominant and has overshadowed the state in the process of the neoliberal transformation of South Korean society in the twenty-first century.

Another significant aspect of neoliberal globalization that influenced the rise of citizens' organizations in South Korea was the transnational circulation of advocacy organizations run by professional staff activists as a model of civic organization. As scholars of U.S. civic life have documented, this type of organization oriented to policy research and design multiplied and became dominant in the late 1960s after the identity-based New Social Movements promoted the empowerment of racial, ethnic, and sexual minorities.[16] Although not completely replacing traditional membership organizations with local chapters and federations, this advocacy type became a salient force in U.S. politics and civic life.[17] Not all advocacy organizations supported neoliberalism or functioned as its tool, but there is an elective affinity between the professionalization of activism and neoliberal governance. The professional focus on expertise and technical mastery, which is not inherently neoliberal, resonates well with the economic metric of efficiency and is incorporated into neoliberal governance to make the extreme dominance of markets and business models sensible and palpable. This convergence was keenly observed by Hui-yeon Cho, the leader of a major citizens' organization.

> Citizens' movements have played splendid roles in normalizing liberal democracy in South Korea. These roles were certainly progressive. However, paradoxically, this normalization can conform to the neoliberal restructuring of the world; democracy that we forcefully demanded to the authoritarian power and transparency we forcefully demanded to the economic conglomerate are values of globalization that transnational capital lauds. . . . The new neoliberal world order has promoted autonomy, deregulation, freedom, and flexibility in normalizing and idealizing its market mechanism. Those elites who have pushed for neoliberal globalization recognize that transparency and democracy are more beneficial to the workings of neoliberal market order and hence have supported and promoted democracy in the Third World.[18]

During the 1990s when South Korea was undergoing neoliberal globalization, the model of professional advocacy inspired leaders and activists of citizens' organizations pursuing democratization. As discussed next, leading citizens' organizations took this model for their organizations with cultural twists such as the moral codes.

DEMOCRATIC APPROPRIATION OF NEOLIBERAL GOVERNANCE

The transition to procedural democracy and the pursuit of substantive democratization during the past three decades has been closely intertwined with the spread of neoliberal governance in South Korea. The first civilian government under Kim Young-sam (1993–1998) actively embraced neoliberal restructuring of the labor market, deregulation, and privatization to differentiate its democracy from the authoritarian rule of the developmental state that had dictated the economy in the preceding decades (albeit less so in the 1980s). Pursued under the project of *segyehwa*, which was initially adopted as one of his policy goals in late 1994, the economic restructuring coincided with establishment of the WTO and the emergence of regional free-trade agreements.[19] In the aftermath of the Asian financial crisis, the government under Kim Dae-jung (1998–2003), a leading dissident who fought for democracy against the military regimes, was pressured to accept the IMF rescue package and accelerate the neoliberal transformation of Korean society.

Despite apparent differences in political orientations, the governments under both Roh Moo-hyun (2003–2008) and Lee Myung-bak (2008–2013) continued to adopt neoliberal globalization as an established way to pursue economic growth.[20] On the one hand, by enabling citizens' organizations to aspire to be a partner with the democratizing state, neoliberal governance generated a significant political opening for "progressive" (*jinbojeok*) social groups to push for democratization.[21] These progressive groups consisted of both the urban middle-class commonly associated with the citizens' movement and farmers, workers, and the urban poor commonly associated with the people's movement.[22] Although people's movement organizations were repressed by the state for their radical ideas and subsequently driven to keep their militant activism, these two movements managed to work together by building and maintaining a coalition.[23] The progressive groups paid attention to economic and societal democratization beyond the narrow definition of procedural democracy.[24] Such attention and following efforts turned democracy from a product/brand promoted through neoliberal globalization into democracy as a value and practices of equality, self-determination, and participation.

On the other hand, such a political opening did not automatically guarantee substantive democratization; citizens' organizations had to fight for it and forge their identity around their moral codes. They had to struggle for the basic civil right to assemble, express ideas, and join organizations. Taking advantage of this political opportunity, reform-minded professionals who were largely lawyers, college professors, religious leaders, and segments of former activists of democratization and labor movements established citizens' organizations as the vehicle for citizens' movements. The secretary of the Citizens' Coalition for Economic Justice (CCEJ), founded in 1989 as the first (self-consciously) citizens' organization, articulated that in democratizing Korea ordinary citizens would become the subjects of a social movement dealing with mundane issues to promote public interests. According to him, such ordinary citizens would be represented by a progressive, new middle class.[25] By recasting Koreans as middle-class citizens who could contribute to positive social change, the emerging discourse of civil society envisioned progressive citizens as members of the civil society; this was reflected in the Korean translation of the concept of civil society literally as citizens' society.[26] In a keynote speech at the 1994 Civil Society Organizations' Common Policy Council Meeting, Mun-gyu Kang, the secretary of the Korean Federation of YMCA, defined the citizens' movement as an autonomous volunteer movement to restore citizens' freedoms and rights and to look for alternatives to the status quo through actual practices. He also distinguished citizens' movements from other "political movements that aimed at gaining power to control the state" but recognized a necessity for citizens' movements to participate in "the state politics to achieve our goals."[27] These reformers and activists defined civil society as a public space where social movements were to be carried out to promote public interests. In comparison with liberal Western societies, the pursuit of private interests or the interests of specific groups were initially delegitimized.[28] The conscious emphasis on social change through ordinary citizens' involvement distinguished citizens' organizations from preexisting civil society associations, which have pursued leisure activities and conviviality, occupational interests, charitable activities for the less fortunate, and religious activities. However, this initial equating of progressive citizens' organizations with civil society quickly evolved and recognized other forms of organizations.

Moral Code of Independence from the State

Leaders of major citizens' organizations viewed their organizations as independent from the state but working with it to solve common problems and promote public interests. This ideal was particularly significant to the identity of citizens' organizations because of the enduring legacy of extensive and intrusive control over voluntary associations by the authoritarian state. It also reflected the UN's promotion of NGOs as a major partner to governments and international organizations. This moral code not only points to a significant shift from militant and oppositional struggle against authoritarian rule but also showed the agency of activists in appropriating the notion of neoliberal governance. Their independence (*dongnip*) from the state was necessary to function as "watchmen for democracy," which involved "monitoring, reporting, and publicizing what the government cannot or fails to do."[29] According to this view promoted by leading citizens' organizations, their activism was directed toward the government, including its actions tied to laws and policies. They also expected the government to provide them with conditions for promoting democratic citizenship education.[30] Wol-ju Song, corepresentative of the Citizens' Organizations Council, argued that such governmental support would be necessary precisely because citizens' organizations complement the government by offering comprehensive and professional alternatives and represent a broad spectrum of citizens.[31] Such a partnership meant constructively helping or complementing the government rather than merely criticizing and opposing it. This self-positioning reflected an expectation of goodwill from the democratizing state, but building such a novel relationship required difficult negotiations with the state over legal terms on the establishment of a new civic organization and its relationship to the state.

The independence of citizens' organizations from the government has two major dimensions: financial and political. The leading citizens' organizations early on paid keen attention to how to establish and maintain financial independence from the government. They started with changing legal and conventional practices. In early 1994, fifty-four organizations came together and formed the Civil Society Organizations' Common Policy Council.[32] First, they demanded elimination of special laws that allowed funding of progovernment or government-sponsored organizations.[33] This change would remove special favors given to these administered mass organizations (AMOs) and contribute to building a level playing field for citizens' organizations. Prior to democratization, these AMOs played active roles during elections and promoted and implemented the government's policies and programs.[34] In the beginning of Kim Young Sam's government, a majority of these AMOs were defined as "nonprofit corporations" that could receive financial support from the government that was unavailable to other volunteer organizations.[35] They received both funds for their routine operations from central and provincial governments and tax reductions, and they also used public facilities for free. Although this category of special laws has been removed, the conventional practices of AMOs have remained due to their political expediency during election times. Even the civilian government of Kim Young-sam was inclined to keep them for their utility as an efficient election machine. Around election time financial support for these organizations increased, and members of AMOs were mobilized to support the governing party's candidates in local elections. The Right Living Association had 124,000 members, the New Village Movement Association had 2.9 million members, and the Federation of Freedom United had 250,000 members. The last one, in particular, recruited its members from former employees of the Security Planning Agency.[36] Moreover, a new government-sponsored organization, Committee to Promote Wholesome Development of National Territory (*Geonganghan guktosaeop chujinwiwonhoe*), was established in 1993.[37]

Second, the leading citizens' organizations demanded revision of laws that restricted fund-raising activities, including the Collection of Donation Prohibition Law (*Gibugeumpum mojipgeumjibeop*) and an article on financial contributions in tax law concerning the corporations. This demand was in response to the conventional practice of allowing AMOs to raise funds despite the legal prohibition of such activity at the time. Legislated in 1951 during the Korean War, the Prohibition Law permitted soliciting donations only with the government's approval. As strange as it sounds, it was intended to protect individuals and groups from extortions during wartime. It was not until 2007 that the approval system was replaced by a registration system. Under this modified system, however, civil society organizations were still required to register with the state in advance of fund-raising efforts.[38] The citizens' organizations tried to replace this authoritarian control with a reporting system (*singoje*).[39] Regarding the tax law, until 2005, a civil society organization could not receive tax exemption for membership fees unless it was registered as a judicial person.[40] The persistence of government control over fund-raising even after democratization illustrated the enduring legacy of authoritarian rule. Although individual or business donations to progressive citizens' organizations remained uncommon in South Korea, the legal change toward more autonomy was symbolically significant.[41] This change would strengthen the civil rights of citizens' organizations and foster an institutional condition for increasing their financial autonomy.

In the decade of democratization, the state was also interested in exploring a new relationship with citizens' organizations. In 1994, the Ministry of Interior conducted a survey to assess public sentiments on government funding of civil society organizations, including citizens' organizations. Poll results ranged from enthusiastic support to suspicion, depending on the types of organizations and their relations with the government. Major government-sponsored organizations of the past welcomed the legislation on funding, whereas progressive citizens' organizations oriented toward monitoring state power were concerned about weakening their independence and moral authority. Traditional membership organizations (such as the Lions Club and Rotary Club) that had existed for a long time supported specific project-based funding. Responding to these diverse views, the ruling party (Democratic Freedom Party) conveyed a need to change the rigid perception that equated government funding with political dependence and becoming a government-sponsored organization.[42] It was not until the beginning of the Kim Dae-jung administration that the government announced its plan to expand financial assistance for all civil society organizations. In 1998, the government established a mechanism for project-specific funding through open competition in the Nonprofit Organization Support Act.[43] Yet the funding plan triggered an impassioned controversy among citizens' organizations for and against it. The opponents highlighted the undermining of political neutrality and the purity of citizens' organizations, and the proponents stressed pragmatic flexibility to balance independence from the government with the transparent use of governmental funding.[44] Supporters mentioned Germany as a model to follow where the government provides NGOs with funding through a neutral agency.

Government funding for NGOs in the West and Japan have been well-established practices, which ordinary citizens largely accept as an aspect of democratic governance.[45] The provision of these resources by the government for civil society organizations would be desirable and even necessary given that the state is the institution of ruling that administers the collection and distribution of critical resources. Government funding as a technique of ruling can promote democracy if its goal is to provide resources equally for various types of NGOs. The governments in Sweden and Norway have supported diverse mass-based organizations to promote the representation of various voices and socioeconomic interests to strengthen participatory democracy.

In the lack of such a tradition in South Korea, however, the controversy over the issue of government funding persisted. A survey of twenty-two major NGOs conducted in 1998 by the Asia Civil Society Study Center showed that most of these organizations relied on membership fees and financial contributions as the major sources of their revenue and therefore suffered from financial instability. As a solution to this common problem, these organizations listed the creation of a public fund for civil societies by the government and business (69.6 percent), their own fund-raising activities (34.8 percent), and indirect support through tax benefits (34.8 percent).[46] Similarly, the public perception of direct government funding of NGOs has been largely negative because of the enduring memory of AMOs funded and controlled by the authoritarian government and recent incidences in which both conservative and progressive governments withdrew funding opportunities from NGOs critical of their policies. In 2006, the Roh Moo-hyun government (calling itself "participatory government") denied funding opportunities to citizens' organizations that opposed the South Korea–U.S. Free Trade Agreement (KORUS FTA). Similarly, the following conservative government under Lee Myung-bak cut off project-based resources granted to various civil society organizations in the aftermath of the 2008 candlelight protests against U.S. beef imports. Some 1,840 organizations that joined the protests, along with some fifty organizations under the Korean Progressive Coalition, were blacklisted as "illegal and violent protest organizations." The list also included the Democratic Labor Party and other progressive political parties but excluded a few conservative organizations that actually used violence against progressive parties and organizations.[47] The following conservative government under Park Geun-hye withheld funding opportunities for citizens' organizations critical of government policy and showered progovernment organizations with such opportunities.[48] In addition, criticism of progressive citizens' organizations by conservative counterparts have commonly mobilized public suspicion of receiving money from the government (or business) to taint their moral authority.[49] Hence some leading citizens' organizations have not received any funding from the government since the NPO Support Act was enacted in 1998. Instead of this type of direct financial support, echoing the 1998 survey previously mentioned, leading NGOs preferred indirect support such as tax exemptions and tax benefits.[50]

Owing to the enduring legacy of authoritarian control of volunteer associations, political independence from the state was especially important to the civic identities of citizens' organizations. For several decades under authoritarian rule, the government had tightly controlled exercises of basic civil rights concerning the freedom of assembly, protest, and expression by requiring its approval. Approvals were needed for the establishment of a new organization, the publication of new periodicals, and public gatherings and protests. Even after the transition to electoral democracy, the problem of using the AMOs resurfaced during elections.[51] To strengthen political independence of their own and other civil society organizations from the government, the leading citizens' organizations demanded basic civil rights. In particular, they asked for replacement of the approval system with a registration system, which would increase their autonomy from the government.[52] I return to this discussion in chapter 2 with specific examples.

Initially, progressive citizens' organizations tried to maintain a healthy distance from the government even when they had a supportive relationship with it. The progressive government under Kim Dae-jung recognized the organizations as partners in their emerging democratic governance.[53] Yet in the aftermath of the Asian financial crisis that accelerated the spread of neoliberal governance under the IMF's structural adjustment package, his government neglected the economic and social democratization that these organizations had pursued.[54] In response, the Korean Citizens' Organizations Council, composed of eighty organizations across the country, held the National Citizens' Organizations Conference and discussed how to push forward what had been slow and inadequate reforms under his rule.[55] To maintain political independence, the council also kept its distance from a nationalist movement to save the country from the economic crisis that the government had initiated. Echoing the history of popular nationalist movements to save the country during times of crises, this movement aimed to mobilize ordinary citizens to join "the second founding of the nation" in the midst of the crisis. Despite a friendly relationship with the government, citizens' organizations were largely suspicious of such official initiatives for fear of damage to autonomous citizen's movements at the grassroots level.[56]

However, the healthy distance from government became blurred as a growing number of officers and staff activists of leading progressive citizens' organizations entered institutional politics through administrative appointments or elections. During the 1990s, a handful of professors who served as officers of the CCEJ were appointed to government offices because of their professional expertise. During the 2000s, a growing number of both officers and staff activists of the CCEJ became government officers.[57] There were differing views on this practice. A positive view argued that officers and staff activists ought to have the right to make a personal choice to run for public office or to be appointed, just like members of any other occupational group or as individuals. Moreover, they argued, citizens' organizations would need to create a milieu in which members could return and work with them after their political or administrative career. However, the prevailing public view was largely negative toward this revolving door between citizens' organizations and institutionalized politics.[58] Although civic activism is political by nature in a broader sense, conservative public opinion equated political independence and neutrality with the absence of any political participation in the government. Although those officers and activists entered politics as individuals rather than as members of civic organizations, their growing number and visibility became a liability for progressive citizens' organizations; they undermined the organizations' "political neutrality" or independence in the eyes of the public, especially the conservative public. I return to this controversy in chapter 2. The balance between the ideal of political independence from the government and practical partnership with it became complicated. During the Kim Daejung and Roh Moo-hyun governments, the growing proximity between the leading citizens' organizations and the government further polarized politics between the progressives and the conservatives and led to a backlash from conservative citizens' organizations.

The significance of the moral code of independence from the state is an effort to democratize the relationship between the government and citizens' organizations. In forging their independent identity from the government against the persistent legacy of authoritarian rule, citizens' organizations aspired to be equal partners with the government. I cannot overemphasize the importance of this shift in the history of state-society relations in the Korean peninsula. Throughout the twentieth century, Japanese colonial rule, the U.S. military occupation, the Korean War, and authoritarian rule during the Cold War established and maintained the state's strong position in relation to society. Hence the state was able to dominate and dictate to the populace and mobilize them for projects through the ideologies of nationalism, anticommunism, and economic development/modernization. By using political openings generated by neoliberal governance, citizens' organizations tried to establish democratic relations with the government.

Moral Code of Diversity

By the mid-2000s the growth of progressive political and social forces during the decade of democratization galvanized the consolidation of the "New Right." In particular, progressive voices and their visibility in national politics grew noticeably right before and during the Roh Moo-hyun government (2003–2008).[59] In 2004, conservative mass media and politicians who had ruled Korean society for decades brought together existing conservative voices by forming National Neo-Conservatism United (*Sinbosujuui jeongukyeonhap*). Vying for political control and grassroots appeal in the democratizing society, the New Right used trendy issues to court the differentiating public beyond anticommunism as its core ideology. Compared with the old conservatism, the New Right glorified the market as the source of individual freedom and prosperity in an era of neoliberal globalization. During the 2007 presidential election, the conservative camp mobilized the conservative populace around the theme of "a lost decade" under the two proceeding progressive administrations (1998–2008) and were able to elect Lee Myung-bak (2008–2013), a former executive of Hyundai, a leading economic conglomerate fostered by the authoritarian state.

Along with this rearticulation of conservative political and social forces, the initial local meaning of civil society as a sphere of progressive social movements expanded to include a wider range of civil society associations. In 2006, mirroring their historically new development, approximately 40 percent of all citizens' organizations were formed in the 2000s. According to the *2006 Korean NGOs Directory*, civil society encompassed the following organizations: (1) nonprofit organizations pursuing public interests, (2) nongovernmental organizations, (3) volunteer citizens' organizations pursuing public interests, (4) downtrodden people's organizations oriented toward radical and systemic social change, (5) government-sponsored organizations (*gwanbyeondanche*), (6) civil society organizations pursuing radical social change, and (7) interest groups pursuing their group interests by influencing the government.[60] Echoing democratizing pluralism, this broad list of civil society organizations included progressive social movement organizations, religious organizations, occupational organizations, and even government-sponsored associations. This ambiguous boundary is not peculiar to South Korea but mirrors an encompassing tendency in the category of NGOs that has been interchangeably used for civil society in other countries.[61] What is noteworthy in this Korean list is the distinction between citizens' organizations pursuing public interests (category 3) and NGOs (category 2). This suggests that NGOs refer to their original definition of international agencies working for human rights, the environment, and economic development, which need to be separated from domestic civic organizations. Along with this pluralistic expansion, the initial view of the middle class as agents of social change participating in citizens' organizations was expanded to include diverse social groups; that is, a citizens' movement refers to a broad movement of all Koreans, not just middle or downtrodden strata that had been tied to the citizens' movement and the people's movement, respectively.[62] Although these categories are broad and imprecise, they convey an underlying moral code of evolving civil society in contemporary South Korea: diversity. The list of civil society organizations above also highlighted the importance to civil society of public interests and social change as well as grassroots participation.

There was increasing diversity in activism that was pursued to promote public interests. According to the *2006 Korean NGO Directory*, there were 17,400 NGOs or civil society organizations.[63] Approximately one-third (5,556) of these NGOs were categorized as "citizens' movement organizations" and other volunteer associations pursuing "public interests." Public interests can be defined in multiple ways, but the discourse of civil society associated them with movements or activism for democratic social change through monitoring the powerful and supporting the marginalized and weak. As the single largest category of NGOs, the citizens' organizations were further divided into "civil society organizations" (1,336), "social service organizations" (1,030), "environmental organizations" (736), "cultural organizations" (549), "educational and academic organizations" (355), "organizations of the poor and local autonomy" (325), "women's organizations" (296), and "organizations of workers, farmers, and fishermen" (170).[64] Although this subcategorization is neither precise in terms of description nor analytical, it conveys various ways in which public interests were pursued: through legal and policy reforms, provision of social services, activism focusing on environmental issues, cultural issues, educational issues, women's issues, and activism by the marginalized and lower socioeconomic groups to promote their interests and concerns.

The significance of the moral code of diversity lies in the recognition of differences among organizations that coexisted with citizens' organizations in South Korean civil society. From their initial position of seeing themselves, who were associated with educated middle-class citizens, implicitly as privileged agents of democratization, citizens' organizations came to accept, at least in principle, different ways to get involved in volunteer associations and pursue different goals and meanings. This evolution was captured by the expansion of the agent of social change from the middle class to a wide range of social groups; it also suggested that citizens' organizations should democratize their relations with other types of organizations and potentially work together for common concerns.

Moral Code of Movements for Institutional and Social Change

In the process of diversification within civil society, the discourse of civil society maintained that civic activism for institutional and social change was a major feature of citizens' organizations. Chan-yong Jeong, the NGO ambassador to the UN, reaffirmed the role of "civil society organizations" as "monitoring and counterbalancing the power of the government, business, and other powerful groups especially when they abuse their power."[65] Echoing the ideal of partnership with the state in democratic governance, he highlighted the cooperation between citizens' organizations and the government in terms of policy development and implementation through debates beyond fixing problems generated by the government.[66] Jae-jeong Yi, former Secretary of Unification and a leader of citizens' movements, reiterated that citizens' organizations would exist to realize freedom, equality, and other democratic values and therefore were distinguished from traditional volunteer associations that pursue common hobbies and leisure activities.[67] In the following chapters, I detail how civic activism for institutional or social change was differentiated from traditional activism offering disaster relief, aid to the poor, and other urgently needed social services.

In the process of democratization, activism for social change through various means became popularized, which led to the formation of a new type of hybrid civic organization and the adoption of civic activism by existing organizations in civil society. Hybrid professional organizations were founded to pursue public interests and social change rather than to advance their own narrowly defined occupational interests. Examples include the Council of Doctors Practicing Humanism (*Indojuui silcheon uisa hyeobuihoe*), the Council of Democratic Press Movements (*Minjueollon undong hyeobuihoe*), and the Democratic Lawyers' Group (*Minjubyeohosamoim*). Their development was not uniformly smooth or tumultuous processes; it depended on what political taboos an organization transgressed in their identity and activism. The National Teachers' Union (NTU: *Jeongukgyojigwonnodongjohap*) is illustrative here in terms of pushing the boundary of democratization. Established in 1989, NTU was a new type of occupational organization that resembled other movement-oriented citizens' organizations. It dealt with larger social issues, such as democratization of education and society and reunification of Korea, and went beyond the usual occupational interests of teachers as government employees. Because of its name and identity as a union, it was persecuted by the democratizing government under Kim Young-sam. In deeply anticommunist Korean society, the NTU incited "red scare," and their movement for "genuine education" (*chamgyoyuk*) was accused of being "communist education." During the Roh Tae-woo administration (1988–1993), its 1,500 teachers were fired by the government, and Kim approved of their reinstitution only with the condition that they renounce their NTU membership. Under Kim Dae-jung's government, NTU finally became legal.[68]

Embracing the moral code, some traditional membership organizations with religious, nationalist, or consumer orientations modified their activities and goals. Cases in point include the Young Men's Christian Association (YMCA), Heungsadan, and the Central Association of Consumers Cooperatives, which paid growing attention to broader social issues beyond Christian activities, nationalist education, and consumer issues, respectively.[69] The YMCA was particularly interesting in this regard. Established in 1903, the YMCA is the oldest existing NGO with a large membership of over 200,000 and forty-five local chapters. It was a major actor in the Independence Movement during the colonial period and, as a result, was disbanded by the Japanese colonial government and restored after independence. In the process of democratization, it became a citizens' organization by building on its tradition of social engagement; it is officially a Christian organization but it has dealt with largely nonsectarian social issues, including the improvement of quality of life and the protection of social minorities.[70] Founded in 1913 by Chang-ho Ahn, an iconic nationalist leader, to achieve national independence and prosperity, Heungsadan has worked to build an "authentic democratic republic, where all national members are free and live well." After independence, it has focused on the civic education of young people. Since the late 1990s, it has incorporated civic activism for social change through a national unification movement, a transparent society movement, and an education movement, along with grassroots movements in local communities.[71] Established in 1983, the Central Association of Consumers Cooperatives initially focused on the purchase of safe agricultural produce directly from farmers. It expanded its attention to broad social issues important to local producers, such as collaborative childcare and health care, that went beyond the purchase of safe food.[72]

The significance of the emphasis on institutional and social change is that it questioned the age-old norm of charitable activities that volunteer associations around the world have performed to deal with a wide range of social problems and aspired to deal with deeper causes of such problems. Charitable activities stem from paternalism, which implies hierarchy and reproduces inequality among individuals and social groups, whereas democratizing activism for institutional and social change aspires to increase equality among individuals and social groups by digging deeper to solve problems rather than providing only temporary relief. Such aspirations recast ordinary people as citizens who are empowered to act and bring about long-term systematic change. This moral code also shows how far the revived UN ideal of NGOs as partners with governments and international organizations in the era of neoliberal globalization is being appropriated by citizens' organizations as a new vehicle of democratization.

Moral Code of Grassroots Participation: Internal and External Critique of Citizens' Organizations

The discourse in civil society recast diverse groups of ordinary citizens and grassroots people as agents of social change, emphasizing active participation in citizens' organizations as a vehicle for civic activism. This moral code was central to the democratic civic identity of citizens' organizations, but it has been the most challenging issue for these organizations. An enduring and growing gap between the ideal and the reality of grassroots participation has generated recurring internal and external critiques since the late 1990s. Critical self-reflection in the discourse of civil society was initially articulated around shortcomings of the dominant practices of large advocacy organizations, which focus on national politics and are run by professional staff activists. These leading citizens' organizations have been characterized by their Seoul-centered advocacy activities oriented toward institutional changes through law and policy reforms. As a result, they could neither build broad membership bases rooted in local communities nor focus on the everyday problems faced by local residents. To address these underlying limitations, civil society early on recognized a need to develop local movements addressing issues relevant to local residents.[73] In the aftermath of the IMF crisis, the civil society discourse articulated the problem of "citizens' movements without citizens," which has become a popular catchphrase used by both internal and external critics. In response, large citizens' organizations initiated some symbolic remedies; they reduced the numbers of their full-time staff and tried to focus on membership expansion campaigns by organizing cultural events, film festivals, arts exhibitions, and crafts markets that appealed to the wider public. These organizations also tried to modify the passive role of members primarily as financial resources by paying attention to mundane issues relevant to them and facilitating their active participation.[74] To understand the pressing concerns of grassroots men and women, the Progressive Network was created in 1998 to reach out to internet users, a rapidly growing constituency in South Korea.[75]

In connection with the moral code of grassroots participation, members of citizens' organizations who are volunteer activists (*jawonhwaldongga*) have been normatively or ideologically central to the civic identity and activism of citizens' organizations. Practically, their unpaid work could mitigate the lack of financial and human resources of citizens' organizations. However, in the actual practices of large advocacy organizations, volunteer members were often confined to auxiliary tasks that did not require professional expertise or experience. It was exceptional for volunteer activists to participate in citizens' organizations in an active, central, and continuous manner. A basic problem was the small numbers of volunteer activists. A 1998 survey of twenty-three NGOs conducted by the Asia Civil Society Movement Research Center found that all of the NGOs wanted to make active use of volunteer members but had difficulty securing a sufficient number of members. Among these NGOs, citizens' organizations recruited volunteers through newsletters and announcements in university programs for social engagements, whereas welfare service–oriented organizations used mass media, business firms, and other related organizations for recruitment. Of the NGOs surveyed, 30 percent had manuals on volunteer activities that managed members' information, relevant records, and activities journals.[76] It was not citizens' organizations but welfare service–oriented organizations that collaborated with the government that drew a steady stream of volunteer activism.[77] As citizens' organizations became better known and some universities created courses on volunteer social service, a growing number of college students spent their summer vacations volunteering in citizens' organizations. These students were motivated by the combination of gaining a course credit, meaningful vacation time, enrichment of their personal experience, and interest in citizens' movements. But given the temporary status of these students, with some exceptions they performed auxiliary work to support full-time staff.[78]

The internal criticism of a lack of active and sustainable grassroots participation in advocacy-oriented citizens' organizations expanded to the theme of citizens' organizations being in decline. This referred to the influence of such organizations on society as a whole. Relying on national survey data, the public influence of citizens' organizations peaked in the late 1990s and early 2000s and had declined since the mid-2000s.[79] In critical self-reflections, leaders and staff activists of leading citizens' organizations viewed community-based, small-scale organizations with active lay members as their corrective or alternative to large advocacy organizations focusing on national issues.[80] By the mid-2000s, some leaders of citizens' organizations reframed the problem of their declining influences as an opportunity to make a "turning point" in their style of activism. After establishing procedural democracy, they argued that the advocacy-type movement focusing on national politics became less compelling and they needed to find a new model of civic activism. The enduring focus on the state and monitoring its power to promote procedural democracy, basic rationality, and anticorruption was turned into an obstacle to facilitating active grassroots citizens' participation.[81] Echoing earlier critical self-reflection, critics of advocacy organizations again envisioned locally based grassroots movements dealing with mundane concerns that spoke to ordinary people and thereby effectively motivated them to participate in civic activism. Meanwhile, an officer of a leading feminist organization argued that the crisis was specifically that of leading advocacy-type citizens' organizations because other types of citizens' organizations had always been in crisis due to poor financial conditions, lack of personnel, and having small membership bases.[82] To establish institutional mechanisms to nurture grassroots and local movements and strengthen their long-term viability, leaders of citizens' organizations intended to establish a foundation named "citizens' activities support center." Such a foundation, they hoped, could begin with a few local branches in residential areas of potential success and expand across the country over time.[83]

Going a step further, some professional activists argued for a "new paradigm" of citizen's movements focusing on the individual citizen's agency rather than on expert-centered leadership tied to the organization. They considered small community-based local organizations as a complementary corrective to the dominant civic identity. Gwan-yeong Oh, an activist of Doing-Together Citizens' Action (*Hamggehaneun siminhaengdong*), pointed out that small community-based organizations addressing everyday issues that mattered to their own members were doing well.[84] This new paradigm was not quite new because such self-criticism has existed since the late 1990s, but in the face of the political resurgence of conservative forces the urgency to expand grassroots movements through direct communication with grassroots citizens became stronger.[85] This discussion developed into a theme of "democratization within the social movement circle," which involved moving away from the Seoul-centered, policy-centered advocacy organizations led by professionals and full-time staff members. This internal democratization focused largely on middle-class issues that could be corrected by reaching out to social minorities, including the working class and other marginalized social groups. Critics argued that leading citizens' organizations paid "symbolic attention" to such critical issues as irregular employment and economic polarization but did not really work on these issues as their primary focus.[86]

The significance of the moral code of grassroots participation is that it reminded citizens' organizations of what democracy would be about and why it would matter. As discussed in the introduction, democracy is a mode of ruling that enables the majority of ordinary people without much power, wealth, or social status in society to participate in all aspects of society with equality and self-determination. Grassroots participation is not only a normative ideal but a crucial practice through which ordinary people can solve common problems affecting their lives. Democracy matters because it is a radical vision of the practices of a good society.

As discussed previously, however, practicing this moral code is particularly difficult and challenging because we live in an era when knowledge, information, and professionalism are necessary and celebrated. Meritocracy legitimizes leadership and dominance by those who have merit, which is commonly understood as knowledge, experience, formal training, and other types of qualifications; whereas democracy is not about merit but about the equal worth of human beings in determining their own lives. There is an underlying tension between meritocracy and democracy that cannot be completely resolved. As analyzed in the following chapters, critical reflection on the moral code of grassroots participation shows a major challenge and tension in civic activism pursued by citizens' organizations in South Korea. I next consider the moral code of grassroots participation from a broader perspective.

CITIZENS' ORGANIZATIONS SEEN FROM A COMPARATIVE HISTORICAL PERSPECTIVE

From a comparative historical perspective, citizens' organizations as a dominant vehicle of civic activism in South Korea show a significant change in the way the ruled interact with the ruling elite controlling the state.[87] Citizens' organizations illustrate a democratic way for the populace to make demands on the ruling elite. This populace is not the entirety of the ruled but usually only the upper segment and their supporters; in democratizing South Korea the upper segment was largely an urban, professional, middle class who became leaders of citizens' organizations. In creating these civic organizations and promoting them as vehicles of civic activism, they envisioned themselves and other citizens as independent and cooperative partners of the state in democratic governance. According to the discourse of civil society, they were ideologically committed to active grassroots participation in their organizations, but in practice pragmatic necessity and the urgency of running a citizens' organization dealing with various national issues made middle-class professionals and professional activists the active participants. As Bourdieu argues and as I discuss in the following chapters, uneven access to and capacity to use cultural/symbolic capital continues to generate hierarchy among ordinary citizens. Although recurring criticism of leading citizens' organizations discredited them as "old" or "jaded" forms of activism, they have played a critical role in enabling educated middle-class leaders and their supporters to build a better world with their own hands and to institutionalize this effort rather than praying for divine justice and intervention or benevolent mercy from powerful elites. This development is historically significant because they popularized the moral codes of social change and participation in civic activism that were neither naturally nor readily accepted by conservative Koreans who had experienced political violence personally or had learned about it. We can grasp its significance more deeply through a comparative historical perspective on civil society in traditional Korea.

Studies of the historical roots of civil society in traditional Korea convey the dominance of commercial inclination over political rebellion or contestation for social change among a rising social group. They also show that the ruling elite in Joseon Korea contained a rising middle social stratum, by recognizing its civility in terms of literary cultivation.[88] During the eighteenth century, when the Joseon Dynasty's economy prospered through the growth of commerce and manufacturing and advances in agricultural technology, a growing number of government officials in the middle strata accumulated wealth through international trade (with China) and domestic commercial activities.[89] Positioned between landed aristocrats and the majority of commoner peasants, the core of this middle strata included lower-ranking scribers working for the central bureaucracy in the capitol and people with professional skills in translation, medicine, cosmology, law, and other areas of expertise necessary for the smooth functioning of the royal court and its bureaucracy. Despite their growing wealth and cultural capital enhancing their civility, this social group did not develop into a political force challenging the old order. A handful of them became critical intellectuals questioning the institution of the hereditary status system, but the majority of its affluent members became consumers enjoying imported luxuries and entertainment. Why? They accumulated their wealth through trade and commerce precisely because of their positions as state officials, therefore their economic base was too closely interwoven with the status quo to destroy it. In the precapitalist Joseon society, the state tightly controlled commerce, especially in the capitol, which was constructed to support the political elite and ensure the smooth supply of material resources necessary for ruling. The middle-strata officials were allowed to pursue these economic activities because the state did not pay them sufficiently.

Instead of political rebellion or social reforms, this growing group of wealthy merchants sought recognition from the ruling aristocracy of their rising social status in terms of literary cultivation and refinement. This local history is instructive of the complex dynamic of civility and cultural hegemony. Some of these middle-strata merchants became keenly interested in publishing their own literary works. During the eighteenth and nineteenth centuries, the group of translators produced scholars with literary talent and knowledge comparable to that of ruling aristocrats/scholars. Using their wealth and literary skills, they published collections of poems written by several hundred writers of the middle strata. While their works conveyed the common theme of their alienation from political power despite their wealth and cultivation, this emergent class consciousness was contained by the recognition of their civility by the ruling aristocrats/scholars. These elite members praised their writings and contributed their own works to those collections. Along with the consumption of luxury goods and entertainment, this recognition pacified middle-strata writers.[90] This historical example sensitizes us to the idea that a rising middle strata in changing economic and political contexts does not automatically challenge the ruling elite of their society. When they develop critical consciousness about the status quo, it does not automatically lead to demands for their participation in ruling; their political potential can be aborted by cultural recognition and other cultural activities that enhance their social status. It wasn't until the contemporary processes of democratization and then neoliberal globalization that the notion and practice of governance spread and a segment of the rising middle class of educated professionals turned their critical consciousness about the status quo into civic activism.[91] Using their interpretive agency, they appropriated governance as democratic practices of cooperating with the state to promote public interests. I return to this issue of civic activism and social status in South Korea in later chapters.

CONCLUSION

This chapter discusses a history of citizens' organizations constructed through the discourse of civil society. As a perspective of leaders and active participants in leading citizens' organizations, the discourse illuminates major moral codes of civil society that shape citizens' organizations as a main vehicle of civic activism: independence from the state, diversity, movements for social change through promoting public interests and social justice, and grassroots participation. The discourse of civil society initially equated civil society narrowly with progressive citizens' organizations oriented toward civic activism for institutional reforms and social change. However, as the conservative forces resurged and compelled citizens' organizations to accept plurality, the boundaries of civil society expanded to include diverse categories of volunteer associations. The historical significance of citizens' organizations in South Korea is that they were the first vehicles used by ordinary citizens to solve their common problems within the democratizing system. They recast ordinary people as actual and potential agents of social change as they routinely engaged through their connection to citizens' organizations.

The emergence and spread of citizens' organizations as well as their diversification convey the historical development in South Korea of civic activism as organized and sustainable activities in which ordinary citizens can partake. Citizens can make demands on political and economic elites to solve or address their common problems, democratizing the society further in the process. This was a significant historical development in South Korea that is often overlooked in the internal and external criticism of citizens' organizations. It is neither natural nor automatic that volunteer associations are founded for routinized and sustained civic activism ideally involving grassroots citizens.

However, the spread of citizens' organizations as a main vehicle of democratizing social change took place during the neoliberal transformation of Korean society. The discourse of civil society shows the active adoption by leading citizens' organizations of NGOs as being self-referential to legitimize their new identity. Although this term was revived by the UN in the context of neoliberal globalization, the civil society discourse turned neoliberal governance into democratic governance by appropriating it and linking it to public interests and social justice, which revolved around monitoring the powerful and protecting and supporting the powerless. The appropriation of governance promoted as democracy in the context of neoliberal globalization highlights the extent to which democracy as a product/brand is turned into democracy as a value and practices of achieving equality and self-determination. The UN promotion of NGOs as a legitimate actor in national and international politics gave citizens' organizations the respectability they needed as new entities in Korean society, but other core aspects of neoliberalism have impacted civic activism and identities in more complex and profound ways. In preparation for this analysis, in the following chapter I describe the three citizens' organizations I chose for this study: the People's Solidarity for Participatory Democracy, two local branches of the Democratic Friends Society, and the Friends of Asia.

Chapter Two

PROFILES OF THREE CITIZENS' ORGANIZATIONS

Citizen's power changes the world.
—PEOPLE'S SOLIDARITY FOR PARTICIPATORY DEMOCRACY

We are making a society where gender equality and social justice are realized.
—DEMOCRATIC FRIENDS SOCIETY

We want to become genuine neighbors to those who took long journeys to us.
—FRIENDS OF ASIA

These three mottos convey the ethos of civic activism in South Korea in the twenty-first century. In this book I focus on these three citizens' organizations; these mottos appear in their publications and guide their informal interactions for building, maintaining, and modifying their civic identities and activism. When I visited the People's Solidarity for Participatory Democracy (PSPD) for the first time in the summer of 2004, it was renting a building in Insa-dong, a town reinvented as a trendy folk village of traditional Korean arts, crafts, and food that catered to foreign tourists and domestic visitors. Situated in Seoul's old downtown, the four-story building overlooked crowded intersections and subway exits. Metropolitan bustling and cacophony became somewhat filtered as I stepped up to the second floor to meet Kong *gansa*, a staff activist, in a "philosophy café" named Zelkova Tree (*Neutinamu*).[1] After a brief conversation, he took me to a small reception desk on the third floor that was attended by a volunteer activist named Mr. Hong. Behind him were open office spaces and a few small rooms where full-time staff and volunteer activists worked. These spaces and the people in them reminded me of a newspaper company where journalists worked individually and in groups to accomplish their urgent tasks. This atmosphere of white-collar professionals working rather frantically captured PSPD's identity as a professional advocacy organization run by full-time staff activists. I revisited PSPD five years later in the fall of 2009; the organization had moved into a new building constructed in 2007, a few miles northwest of Insa-dong (figure 2.1). This five-story building symbolized its ceaseless hard work and determination in becoming a leading citizens' organization. During my visit in the summer of 2015, I noticed that the basement and the first and second floors had been remodeled to provide a multipurpose open space and a café to promote convenient use by members and local residents.

During my initial fieldwork between 2004 and 2005, I visited four local branches of the Democratic Friends Society (DFS) situated in the Greater Seoul region and chose two of them for this book: the Northeast (NE) Branch located in Seoul and the Goyang (GY) Branch in Gyeonggi

FIGURE 2.1. PSPD building, 2022 *Source*: Photo by the author

PROFILES OF THREE CITIZENS' ORGANIZATIONS

Province. They were two of the most actively run and oldest branches and were suitable for this study of organized civic activism over time. Reflecting the high population density of Seoul and the surrounding Gyeonggi Province, these branches were nestled in urban jungles of residential and commercial buildings.[2] There were some differences between them in terms of dominance of apartment buildings vis-à-vis traditional multiunit residences and single-family houses. The GY Branch was located in a residential city created by the government to disperse the bursting population of the capitol city in the 1980s. As a major urban residential development, the provincial city enjoyed more open green space and less population density than Seoul. Existing at the outskirts of Seoul, the NE Branch was in an area less densely populated and less overwhelmed by apartment buildings than newer areas of Seoul. Yet both branches had their small offices, auxiliary centers, and food cooperative stores in commercial buildings filled with shops catering to residents in their area (figure 2.2). These neighborly

FIGURE 2.2. GY Branch located in a busy commercial district, circa 2015 *Source*: Provided by GY Branch

locations conveyed their identity as a feminist civic organization that tried to reach out to local women as potential agents of social change. A majority of these local women were housewives with children. When I revisited these branches in 2009 and in 2015, they were still in similar locations, but the food co-op had been separated from DFS to increase its viability in the growing competitive market for "organic" and "environment friendly" food in urban South Korea.

In the fall of 2009, I met Ms. Jang, a founder of the Friends of Asia (FOA), in its modest single-story house in a provincial city just north of Seoul. Similar to the GY Branch of DFS, this small citizen's organization was situated in a residential city that the government built outside Seoul in the 1980s to disperse Seoul's bursting population. As a result of urban planning, the FOA house was nestled among large apartment complexes and commercial buildings separated by wide straight streets and parks (figure 2.3). As I entered its office, I felt as if I were visiting someone's private home because I had to take off my shoes and wear a pair of indoor slippers. There was a small library space and a larger multipurpose open space where FOA carried out its programs and events for foreign migrants who were married

FIGURE 2.3. FOA office, 2023 Source: Photo by Jihee Kwak

PROFILES OF THREE CITIZENS' ORGANIZATIONS

to Korean men or employed by small rural businesses. The space conveyed its civic identity as a small local organization that provided urgent services for vulnerable social groups. During my multiple visits, Jang introduced me to Mr. Kang, a part-time staffer working with her, and other members who were volunteering to teach the Korean language to foreign migrants who were mostly from other Asian countries. The volunteer teachers were a diverse group of largely local residents who were schoolteachers, graduate students, and white-collar employees. When I revisited FOA in the summer of 2015, it was still in the same place but Jang had moved on and Kang had been elected to lead the organization in early 2015.

I discuss the profiles of these citizens' organizations to convey their underlying commonalities as well as their differences and changes over time. This comparative discussion is thematically organized around the underlying moral codes that the discourse of civil society popularized for citizens' organizations in general (see chapter 1). As they became major vehicles of civic activism in democratizing South Korea, they were distinguished from other volunteer organizations in civil society by (1) financial and political independence from the government, (2) activism for institutional and social change, and (3) grassroots participation. The three civic organizations (PSPD, the two DFS branches, and FOA) adhered to these moral codes to varying degrees over time, depending on the scope and method of their activism and their political context. Oriented toward institutional reforms and broad social change through monitoring political and economic powers, PSPD has emphasized its independence from the state but inevitably paid secondary attention to grassroots participation. Although able to maintain its financial independence, its political independence from the government has become complicated: they worked closely with the government, and its former officers and staff activists entered institutionalized politics. Simultaneously, its ideological commitment to grassroots participation has motivated PSPD to practice ongoing critical self-reflection and make adjustments in its civic identity and activism. Dealing with a wide range of women's issues in specific local contexts, the two DFS branches (NE Branch and GY Branch) have combined the provision of urgent services for local residents with broader social change from a feminist perspective. Because both of the DFS branches made steady use of project-based government funding to manage their auxiliary facilities or public facilities outsourced by the local governments, they did not officially highlight their financial independence from the government. Nevertheless, they have maintained political independence to pursue their own feminist activism, but their growing reliance on local government financing has subjected them to varying degrees of bureaucratic control and placed a strain on their time and human resources being available for other activities. Parallel to PSPD's ideological commitment to grassroots participation, DFS branches' underlying feminist civic identity has motivated them to engage in ongoing critical self-reflection regarding their activism. Addressing various issues concerning foreign migrants from empowering migrants to educating Koreans about them, FOA has a combined focus on institutional change and the provision of urgent services for migrants. Unlike DFS local branches, it chose not to pursue project-based government funding and to work within its limited resources from membership fees and volunteer support. Although financial scarcity created hardships for its activism, which at times threatened its existence, financial independence spared FOA from being controlled by the government bureaucracy. Instead of running programs or facilities outsourced by local governments, for example, it relied on local members and supporters and reached out to other civic organizations to build coalitions for institutional reforms and broad social change. Its small size and the single focus on migrant issues contributed to its survival without government funding.

THE PEOPLE'S SOLIDARITY FOR PARTICIPATORY DEMOCRACY: HYBRID OF PROFESSIONAL ADVOCACY AND MEMBERS' PARTICIPATION

Founded in 1994 by a few hundred lawyers, professors, religious leaders, and former activists, PSPD became a leading citizens' organization in South Korea.[3] As one of the major civic organizations, it has introduced and popularized a new repertoire of activism and represented the new activism in a South Korean context, which has been characterized by professional advocacy for institutional reforms at a national level. Organizationally, its headquarters are located in downtown Seoul with a multitude of auxiliary centers, committees, and teams. It has allowed a few provincial branches, but they have been exceptions rather than the norm.[4] In other words, it is different from a traditional membership organization with multiple local chapters or branches that are run by the members themselves.

PROFILES OF THREE CITIZENS' ORGANIZATIONS

This organizational form is similar to the type of professional advocacy organizations without members that had grown rapidly in the United States since the 1970s (see chapter 1), but professional activism of its full-time staff has been combined with the importance of lay members for ideological and practical reasons. In 2020, it had approximately fifty full-time paid staff who were responsible for its daily work, and more than 150 officers were responsible for making important decisions about its vision, identity, and activities. There were about 14,500 dues-paying members. As its name indicated, ordinary people's participation has been central to its view of a democratic society and civic activism. Practically, membership fees have been the primary source of its income. This is in contrast to its counterparts in the United States and the European Union, which have received sizable grants from various foundations and governments. In the absence of such grants, PSPD has relied on membership dues to maintain its financial independence from the state. As a result, PSPD has become a hybrid organization, using professional advocacy but relying on the participation of lay members. As a distinct aspect of its civic identity, this hybrid nature has generated an underlying tension between the practices of professional advocacy and the ideal of grassroots participation.[5]

Financial and Political Independence from the Government

Financial independence from the government would be a normative ideal of any civic organization, especially if its activism focuses on monitoring the state's power. This moral code gained particular intensity in South Korea given the history of authoritarian control over volunteer organizations and its lingering legacy even after democratization. PSPD constructed and has retained its civic identity by maintaining complete financial independence from the state. It has not received project-based government funding, which was established in 1998. This independence is difficult to sustain, but it has been touted as a hallmark of PSPD's civic identity and therefore a fundamental source of its moral authority. Its financial independence is clearly and repeatedly emphasized in its major and minor publications, as well as on its website.[6] Regular membership fees have been the primary source of its income, accounting for 70 to 75 percent of its revenue in a given year. The remaining income has been drawn from donations and annual fund-raising events.[7] During its early years in the 1990s, however, the organization struggled to survive and experimented with various types of "revenue-generating projects," ranging from book publication parties/sales and art performances to an auction of goods owned by celebrities. Its financial situation has improved significantly since 2000, when its membership reached the threshold of 10,000 for the first time. Although fluctuating over time, membership has stabilized above this threshold, enabling PSPD to live up to the ideal of financial independence from the state.[8]

Self-defined as a vigilant sentinel monitoring the workings of the state, PSPD has tried to maintain its political independence from the government even when it was supportive of progressive civic organizations. In the aftermath of the Asian financial crisis (1997–98), the Kim Dae-jung government launched the Council for the Second National Construction in 1998. Municipal and provincial governments followed the lead by establishing branches. Meantime many NGOs joined a "national movement" (*kungminundong*) to "save the country" and collaborated with the national and local councils. Echoing the history of colonial struggle, the national movement relied on local and national drives to collect personal jewelry and other possessions to raise funds. Although the movement was considered legitimate and even necessary during the national crisis, PSPD maintained its distance from it because such movements commonly ended up being led by the government and mass media, co-opting ordinary citizens' initiatives and voluntary activities.[9] During Roh Moo-hyun's government, which was also supportive of progressive citizens' organizations, PSPD maintained critical distance from it in terms of global military and trade issues. PSPD opposed South Korean involvement in the Iraq war, leading the first antiwar movement in the country. It also opposed the South Korea-U.S. Free Trade Agreement (KORUS FTA) signed by the Roh administration.[10]

However, this critical distance coexisted with PSPD's increasing cooperation with the progressive government. As a result, its relationship with the government became rather complicated. Generally, such cooperation concerned social welfare issues, including national health care, national pension, and minimum living wages (see chapter 4). The government worked with PSPD because it offered useful ideas and analysis for developing and reforming policy and law. In the absence of properly functioning political parties with continuity, which is considered a norm in older democracies, PSPD played the role of a quasi-political party in this regard.[11] Beginning with the Roh Moo-hyun government, officers of PSPD were invited to join various government committees, and several PSPD officers were appointed to government positions.[12] In addition, civic activism to democratize electoral politics galvanized a growing number of former PSPD officers and staff activists to run for elected offices in the central and local governments and in legislative bodies.[13] Consequently, the boundary between PSPD and the progressive government and ruling party became relatively fluid. PSPD clarified that those officers who were elected to the National Assembly ran as individual professionals in law and other academic fields and not as representatives of PSPD. Nonetheless, concern about tainting its moral authority based on political independence from the government was sufficient for PSPD to strengthen its guidelines on its officers' political activities.[14] Since 2002, it has applied a code of ethics to regulate the political activities of its officers and staff activists. According to its Articles of Association, its officers have to resign if they join a political party, run for elected offices, or are appointed to public offices (Article 41). Its officers and staff members cannot participate in election campaigns for a specific political party and candidate by offering endorsements or canvassing activities.[15]

Prior to the growing entry of former PSPD officers and staff activists into institutionalized politics, the 2000 General Election Campaign led by PSPD stirred up conservative social groups (see chapter 1), and these groups consolidated in the mid-2000s. This national campaign was a refreshing effort to shake up institutionalized politics by weeding out corrupt and incompetent politicians. In the polarizing political context, the conservative groups criticized PSPD for violating "political neutrality" and accused it of becoming "the red guard of the political power" and a "power bloc above law."[16] Although this type of portrayal was an ideological exaggeration, such external criticism facilitated internal reflection on PSPD's relationship with the government in particular and with institutionalized politics in general. In the context of political polarization, the controversy over the political neutrality of citizens' organizations became a national concern. In January 2003, the Korea NGO Studies Association held a public discussion on "How do we see the political participation of citizens' movements?" As the controversy over the political neutrality of citizens' organizations became more heated that year, PSPD took internal actions. In March it engaged in an external meeting with other civic organizations on the same issue for citizens' organizations in general; in April, PSPD held a lengthy meeting of its officers and all staff activists to reflect on and evaluate its changing position as a political power. Through serious deliberation of competing positions, PSPD concluded it would keep its political neutrality as it defined its meanings in accordance with its civic identity. The underlying principle was that each citizens' organization should be able to determine the level of its own political involvement. It defined political neutrality as distinct from the aims of a political party whose objective was to gain control of the state but not as political indifference or a simple absence of involvement in politics, which was the view highlighted in conservative criticism.[17] Political independence, which the discourse of civil society promoted as a moral code, captures PSPD's view more accurately than the idea of political neutrality.

In the context of the polarization of national and local politics between conservative and progressive camps, the relationship between the government and PSPD alternated between a balance of cooperation and critical distance during the time the progressive government was in power and alienation during the time the conservative government was in power. The conflict between PSPD and the conservative government became sharper regarding military and security issues, topics that have seen the least democratization in the workings of the state's power.[18] Cooperative interactions with the progressive government have complicated PSPD's political independence, but hostile separation ironically affirmed it. This complex situation raises important questions regarding how to define and practice political independence from the government and how to negotiate the boundary between political powers and civic organizations.

Activism for Institutional and Social Change

Using its civic identity as a sentinel that monitors state powers and economic powers, the PSPD has tried to reform the government, the judiciary, the legislature, and major business corporations by championing clean and effective operations free of corruption and incompetence. Thanks to a very broad scope of activism, PSPD has dealt with diverse issues, ranging from national elections and social welfare for all citizens to the problems surrounding credit card abuse and college tuition. I focus on a few examples here that highlight the organization's hybrid civic identity and its major repertoire of activism. It has pursued activism to bring about legal and policy changes toward democratization with broader national ramifications

PROFILES OF THREE CITIZENS' ORGANIZATIONS

FIGURE 2.4. PSPD staff activists in front of the National Assembly Building (*simusik; ritual of beginning work for a new year*), 2023; placards read "unbreakable power of citizens." *Source:* Provided by PSPD

(see figure 2.4). In addition, in line with its ideological commitment to grassroots participation, it has also addressed mundane issues that speak directly to the daily experiences of citizens. Its repertoire of activism includes press releases, lawsuits, research and publications, and public discussions, as well as street campaigns, signature drives, marches, and protest performances (figure 2.5). Regarding its primary focus on institutional change, I describe its activism to promote and protect the political and civil rights of all Koreans. With regard to its secondary focus on grassroots participation, I describe its activism to solve common problems affecting ordinary citizens in their daily lives.

The reform of electoral politics has been a major and enduring issue for PSPD because of its centrality to procedural democracy in terms of grassroots participation. It joined force with other citizens' organizations to improve the basic conditions for citizens' participation in election campaigns.[19] PSPD's reform efforts focused on the restrictive nature of election laws in South Korea that reflected its authoritarian legacy. Specifically, the Election Law prohibited political expressions by individuals and civic organizations, including support for or recommendation of specific candidates,

PROFILES OF THREE CITIZENS' ORGANIZATIONS

FIGURE 2.5. Single-person fasting protests to support enactment of the Anti-Discrimination Law, 2022; placard reads "Let's struggle to achieve a spring of equality." *Source*: Provided by PSPD

soliciting support for them, and publicity for specific candidates during an election campaign period of 180 days. Its initial reform effort was in response to the criminalization of a handful of citizens for violating the law (Article 93) during the 1996 general parliamentary election. Without reform, this law would continue to criminalize a large number of computer users who expressed their personal opinion about candidates on the internet. In 1998, there were already more than three million internet users in South Korea.[20] Activism to eliminate this restrictive election law continued throughout the 2000s and 2010s using lawsuits, protests, press releases, signature collection campaigns, and public discussions.

Building on the election law reform movement, PSPD led a novel effort to weed out corrupt and incompetent candidates during the 2000 general election. In collaboration with the Environmental Movement United and the Women's Associations United, it formed the Citizens' Solidarity for the General Election and conducted public polls and received overwhelmingly supportive responses for this work. Encouraged by the results, PSPD expanded the movement from Seoul to the entire country. The immediate goal was to eliminate corrupt and incompetent candidates, but the movement also aimed to eliminate an article of the Election Law that prohibited NGOs' involvement in election campaigns.[21] The current law prohibited citizens' organizations from supporting specific candidates during the campaign period.[22] In contrast, labor unions were allowed to support candidates, which was seen as a violation of equity.[23] The impact of the new coalition movement was phenomenal. It resulted in elimination of fifty-nine candidates from the final list of eighty-six corrupt candidates and generated enthusiastic public approval for effectively shaking up politics as usual.[24] This approval resulted in a dramatic upsurge in PSPD membership from approximately 6,100 in 1999 to more than 10,000 in 2000. By 2004, its participation in electoral politics expanded to include active support for specific "citizen candidates" as well as the dissemination of information about problematic candidates.[25] In 2007, PSPD continued its activism to reform the Election Law, which still unduly restricted voters' expression of ideas and participation in campaigns, and formed the 100 Voters' Committee to examine policies proposed by presidential candidates. In 2012, the coalition of civic organizations achieved a limited reform of the Election Law, which allowed for political expressions via the internet.[26] This struggle will continue until the freedom of political expression regarding a political party or a candidate is fully protected for citizens' organizations.[27]

Activism to reform the use of Seoul Plaza showed PSPD's civic engagement despite a shifting political context. Roughly 13,000 square meters in size and located in the heart of the downtown, the plaza was created in 2004 as a component of the project to commemorate the sixtieth anniversary (2005) of the Korean Liberation from Japanese colonial rule. It was intended to be both a recreational and a civic space for individual citizens and organizations. During the entire summer of 2008, the plaza was turned into a sea of candle lights by citizens protesting against the importation of U.S. beef suspected of mad cow disease. Alarmed by the unexpected size and duration of the public protests, the conservative Lee Myung-bak government cordoned off the plaza by erecting walls around it. In 2009, when former President Roh committed suicide in the middle of a politicized investigation of his family members by his conservative successor, the public arranged his altar near the plaza, but the government again closed off the plaza by deploying riot police buses around it. In the face of these recurring authoritarian responses, PSPD began a movement to replace the approval system required to use Seoul Plaza with a reporting system. It collected signatures from the public and collaborated with progressive media. It drafted a bill to reform the plaza article (*jorye*), but it was discarded by the National Assembly, which was controlled by the conservative ruling party. The conservative political forces in the national and Seoul governments and assemblies continued for a few years, but the 2011 election of Park Won-soon, a former leader of PSPD, to the office of mayor of Seoul led to reopening the plaza. Along with this change, the approval system was replaced by the reporting system.[28]

Since 1997, PSPD has carried out activism to "restore small rights" to balance its primary focus on state power with attention to common problems that ordinary people deal with in their daily lives. This category of activism began with listening to ordinary citizens and identifying their common problems. PSPD assisted citizens with legal consultations and other necessary supports. Recipients of this type of assistance became volunteer activists, albeit temporarily, and helped expand the movement. As the movement gained momentum, its initial focus on individual rights broadened to reforming institutional mechanisms. A good example of this development was activism concerning mobile phones, which had rapidly become a necessity for ordinary Koreans. In 2001, there were twenty-seven million mobile phone users, more than half of the entire population. Initially, PSPD began a "movement to reduce mobile phone charges" (1998–2000). The number of mobile phone users grew explosively in the late 1990s, and Korean consumers were paying far higher fees than their counterparts in other industrialized countries. PSPD contested the rationality of higher service fees that the public generally overlooked. By collecting over a million signatures and filing a lawsuit against Korea Telecommunications (KT), PSPD was able to get the fees reduced. About a decade later, PSPD revisited the issue to address a broader issue of transparent information about mobile phone service charges; it filed a public interest lawsuit against the Broadcasting and Telecommunication Committee and ultimately won the case.[29]

Grassroots Participation

As a professional civic organization, PSPD has tried to maximize the impact of its activism through advocacy at the national level. But its primary focus on institutional changes through legal and policy reforms generated a structural barrier for active participation of its lay members and other ordinary citizens who cannot access or use such cultural capital. The structure

PROFILES OF THREE CITIZENS' ORGANIZATIONS

of professional advocacy requires full-time attention and technical expertise at a certain level, but ordinary people have to work for living and do not have such expertise and experience. Professional advocacy was beneficial to the functioning of the state in the absence of policy-generating political parties, but this orientation constrained PSPD's limited resources for reaching out to lay members and facilitating their substantial participation in its activities. Consequently, for a majority of lay members participation has meant the regular payment of membership fees, but only a minority (less than 5 percent) of them have been actively and regularly involved through volunteer services as officers of executive committees, supporters for staff members, and volunteer activists for specific projects. About 10 percent joined its educational events.[30] Occasionally, lay participation became larger during special campaigns and protest marches, and there have been voluntary gatherings of lay members for socializing over common hobbies such as singing, running, hiking, traveling, and photography. Although these small gatherings have been facilitated by the "Members' Gathering" (MG), a formal organizational component, they are a feature of traditional membership organizations that have been incorporated into the professional advocacy organization: that is, building fellowship rather than grassroots civic activism for institutional changes (figure 2.6).[31]

FIGURE 2.6. Members' camp, 2019; the placard reads "The March 1 protest meets today's candlelight protest." *Source*: Provided by PSPD

This level of grassroots participation is not unusual for a large professional advocacy organization in a society privatized by neoliberal globalization. However, as discussed in chapter 1, the ideological significance of broad active grassroots participation has been a strong element of the civic identity of PSPD (as well as of other leading South Korean civic organizations). The perceived discrepancy between the reality and the ideal has generated both internal and external criticism, which can be summarized as a "citizens' movement without citizens." Initially emerging in the late 1990s in the discourse of civil society, the criticism was commonly used by conservative opponents to undermine PSPD's moral authority. PSPD's critical self-reflection on this problem became more pronounced after the 2004 general election, which led to a sizable decrease and stagnation in its membership base.[32] During my research, I encountered individual officers, staff members, and lay members who considered this critique "unfair" and "unrealistic." Yet the prevailing view was that PSPD should increase its efforts to attract lay members and facilitate their active participation in its activism.[33]

Responding to the majority view on the problem of a "citizens' movement without citizens," PSPD has made substantial and symbolic efforts to facilitate active participation of its members.[34] It has increased the participation of lay members in decision-making and in running the organization by including them in the ranks of officers/executive committee members. These lay officers included heads of the Members' Gatherings and members representing diverse age, sex, and regional groups who were recommended by the General Meeting Preparation Committee and then selected through lottery. In 2014, ninety-five of 114 officers came from the lay membership, comprising 83.3 percent of its officers. In its early years in the mid-1990s, there were no lay members among the officers, but their numbers grew throughout the 2000s, especially in the 2010s.[35] On the symbolic front, prior to its twentieth anniversary in 2014, PSPD carried out an extensive renovation project—the "citizens' playground project"—remodeling its own building and creating public space that would be inviting and available for public uses. Constructed in 2007, this five-story building was primarily the workspace for its full-time staff members with a café on the first floor. PSPD converted the office space on the second floor into an open auditorium with movable walls and expanded the café and connected it to the auditorium. It also converted the basement into an auxiliary auditorium with walls that can be used for exhibitions. By offering substantial space and facilities for diverse activities and participation by its members and the

PROFILES OF THREE CITIZENS' ORGANIZATIONS

general public, PSPD intended to affirm its civic identity as an organization for members and potential members based on their active involvement.[36]

TWO DFS LOCAL BRANCHES IN THE GREATER SEOUL AREA: BALANCING FEMINIST IDENTITY AND GRASSROOTS ACTIVISM

Founded in 1987, DFS became a leading women's organization that has pursued feminist social change through institutional reforms and members' participation. In light of the persistent gender hierarchy in South Korea, civic activism oriented toward "gender equality" is important to diversify civil society.[37] Similar to PSPD, the founding members of DFS (about 200) were largely from the educated middle class and were composed of professors, former activists, religious leaders, and writers. To popularize its feminist movement through grassroots participation, in contrast to PSPD, it built local branches in the greater Seoul area and in major provincial cities in the 1990s and 2000s. As a result, it has maintained a dual structure of a headquarters and multiple local branches. Between 1989 and 2013, it also operated a nonprofit food cooperative (co-op) as the vehicle to reach out to local women, most of whom were not familiar with feminism or civic activism (figure 2.7). Its co-op stores were developed in the headquarters and in three

FIGURE 2.7. Food co-op general meeting, 2005 *Source*: Provided by NE Branch

local branches in the greater Seoul area but not in the provincial cities. The number of co-op–only members dominated its membership bases for both headquarters and the branches. In 2010, as a result of the expansion of co-op members, the total membership of DFS approximated 30,000. When the food co-op was separated, membership was drastically reduced to a few thousand for the headquarters and a few to several hundred for the two active branches chosen for this book.[38] The headquarters is excluded from this study because it resembles PSPD in terms of its hybrid civic identity at a smaller scale. In contrast, the local branches have been run by lay members who became officers, staff, and other volunteers/participants for various local and at times national activities. NE was the first local branch, and it began in 1992; the GY Branch began in 1996. Although these branches adhered to the main goals and activities of the headquarters, they developed growing autonomy when addressing local issues they found compelling and worthy.[39]

Financial and Political Independence from the Government

As local bodies of the feminist civic organization, the NE Branch and the GY Branch have promoted "gender equality" (*seongpyeongdeung*) and "women's human rights" (*yeoseong ingwo*n) as fundamental principles of democratic society. They cherish the ideal of financial independence from the government for their autonomy and sustainability, but they have not emphasized this in public presentations because they have relied on various forms of government funding for their activism. To be clear, like other progressive civic organizations in South Korea, the two local branches relied on their membership fees as the primary source of income. Over time, however, their reliance on membership fees decreased as government funding grew, especially for the NE Branch. This difference between the two local branches stemmed from their difference in terms of local sociopolitical context. During the 2000s, when the food co-op was integrated into these branches, the membership fees covered between 50 and 60 percent of their annual budgets, and the rest was covered by fund-raising activities, donations, and small-scale project-based funding from the government. In terms of fund-raising and donations, the NE and GY branches are women's organizations and have faced many more challenges than PSPD and other larger gender-mixed organizations. This reflects a deeper structural problem of women as a social minority who own significantly less wealth and earn less employment income than men. In addition, a majority of members in the two branches are housewives who are not employed outside of the home or involved in paid employment. Hence officers, staff activists, and other active volunteers spent arduous energy and time organizing effective fund-raising events, ranging from a one-day restaurant and tea house to sales of products their members have crafted (figure 2.8).[40]

Throughout the 2000s, the financial situations of the local branches improved significantly as their food co-op stores multiplied, attracting a large number of women as co-op members.[41] It was a period when recurring problems of processed food in general and factory-produced meat in particular sensitized the South Korean public about food safety and the connection between an industrialized diet and illness.[42] In the early 2000s, when marketing a "well-being" trend spread like wildfire to capitalize on shifting public sentiments about food and diet, a new market for organic and environmentally friendly foods expanded.[43] In this context, DFS co-op stores grew rapidly. The co-op began as an informal network with a minimum of five members who regularly ordered agricultural produce directly from farmers. In 2000, both the NE and GY branches had only one co-op

FIGURE 2.8. Pop-up restaurant for fund-raising, 2018 *Source*: Provided by GY Branch

FIGURE 2.9. Food co-op members meeting with a woman farmer/producer, 2006 *Source*: Provided by NE Branch

store each. By 2011 both branches had opened four stores each.[44] As discussed in chapter 5, the financial improvement made possible by the larger membership enabled local branches to experiment with certain ideals of co-ops against the backdrop of neoliberal capitalism (figure 2.9). Yet the dominance of co-op membership also posed a challenge to DFS's feminist civic identity, generating a recurring concern about its goal of feminist social change beyond providing healthy and trendy food for urban consumers.

When the food co-op separated from the local branches, the membership bases and revenue contracted considerably for the branches. Both branches have tried to increase their membership throughout the 2010s without noticeable success. During this decade, GY Branch membership fluctuated from more than 500 and NE Branch from less than 400. Subsequently, government funding became more critical to activism efforts by these local branches. During the 2000s, when membership fees were the largest source of revenue and government funding was relatively small, public funding was already significant for social welfare programs that the local branches launched and maintained.[45] Public funding in the form of project-based grants enabled them to pay staff and to pay other basic expenses for their auxiliary centers and programs. Their financial dependence on public funding grew, especially for projects that provided social services to the broader public of local residents rather than only to their members. The expansion of their social services became possible in the aftermath of the two major financial crises, reflecting the growing power of neoliberal governance, when national and local governments poured funding into civic organizations to support social welfare programs.[46] As a majority of South Koreans were negatively affected by the crises, provision of urgent welfare services became a major policy issue shaping national and local elections and civic activism. By 2017, GY Branch's budget grew to one billion won (USD $1 million) and almost half of its revenue came from government funding.[47] Financial reliance on the government became more noticeable as the NE Branch steadily increased its cooperation with the Seoul metropolitan government after the 2011 election of a new mayor. From 2014 to 2016, the NE Branch showed a rapid increase in government funding of its total revenue from 3.9 percent (2014) to 37.1 percent (2015), and then 58 percent (2016). In contrast, its revenue from membership fees and donations proportionally decreased.[48]

The local branches' growing financial dependence on public funding has complicated their political independence from the government, which has been important to the civic identity of DFS as a progressive feminist organization. Independence became particularly significant against the historical backdrop of many women's organizations that had been controlled by authoritarian regimes and were reduced to being their policy arms.[49] The two local branches have managed to maintain political independence to an extent; they continued to monitor local governments and local legislative bodies from the feminist perspective to promote gender equality and women's human rights. They have also used public funding to pursue their own programs and activities that serve their local communities. Yet, as was true for PSPD, increasing cooperation with local governments has generated internal debates and reflections on the meaning of political independence in connection with their feminist civic identity and activism. As discussed in chapter 5, the democratic appropriation of neoliberal governance that was developing under progressive administrations played a significant role. First, their cooperation with local governments was embedded in the institutionalization of "women's policy" (*yeoseongjeongchaek*) during the progressive governments under Kim Dae-jung and Roh Moo-hyun. Under the rubric of the women's policy, national and local governments collaborated with progressive women's organizations to promote gender equality by enacting and reforming laws and implementing policies.[50] After establishment of the Ministry of Women and Family in 1998 (which later became the Ministry of Gender Equality and Family), there were increasing opportunities for the two local branches to work with local governments on social welfare issues (for example, childcare, health care, and education, as well as counseling and shelter for survivors of domestic violence and sexual violence).[51] Second, in the context of the neoliberal transformation of Korean society, this collaboration took a specific form of outsourcing public facilities and services to NGOs. Chapter 5 discusses how this pattern of partnership subjected the local branches to government bureaucracies and led to internal discussions about their feminist civic identity and activism.

Similar to PSPD, the local branches developed hostile relationships with conservative governments under Lee Myung-bak and then Park Geun-hye. Overall, the government restricted public funding opportunities for progressive citizens' organizations and retreated from policies promoting gender equality and social welfare serving the general citizenry.[52] In particular, the Lee administration excluded DFS branches and other progressive civic organizations from project-based government funding after they participated in a series of 2008 candlelight protests against the import of U.S. beef suspected of mad cow disease. The central and local governments blacklisted these civic organizations and screened them out when they applied for project-based government funding. However, as discussed previously, the Seoul metropolitan government controlled by progressive politicians also generated political opportunities for the NE Branch. This illustrates the growing significance of political affinity between government and civic organizations and further complicates the meaning and practices of political independence for the two DFS branches in relation to local governments.

Activism for Institutional and Social Change

The NE and GY branches have gained more autonomy to pursue local issues important to them over time, but they have also coordinated with the headquarters to maintain the integrity of DFS's feminist activism and identity. The common issues that have brought them together include (1) gender equality in families, workplaces, politics, and mass media representation; (2) women's bodies and health, which revolved around reproduction, sexual harassment, and violence, as well as care work; and (3) the food co-op and environmental issues. Because housewives are an absolute majority of their members, the local branches tend to focus on gender equality in families rather than in workplaces.[53] To change the institution of the family, the local branches joined larger national movements to reform the Family Law and to establish gender-sensitive family policy. To promote gender equality in politics, they have monitored local governments and local assemblies. This monitoring of local political powers began in the early 2000s and became a steady portion of their activism repertoire under the "analyses of government budget and policy from a gender-sensitive lens."[54] To change institutional politics, the NE and GY branches participated in local electoral politics to increase women's representation in local assemblies. In the context of the national civic movement to shake up national electoral politics, the branches identified their "women candidates" and supported them for election.[55] Officers, staff activists, and active lay members immersed themselves in local politics and were energized by the victories of their candidates.[56] Recognizing the mass media as a powerful institution that shapes public perceptions of gender, the branches have monitored media representation for violations or undermining of gender equality and women's human rights. Results of this monitoring were disseminated through press releases and via the internet with demands for changes and campaigns for public education.[57]

The repertoire of activism for institutional change has coexisted with the provision of urgent social services for local residents. Differences between the two branches in this regard are noteworthy. Although both have paid attention to feminist issues such as sexual violence, domestic violence, and childcare, they differed in how they delivered social services for these common problems (figure 2.10). The GY Branch relied on their own modest auxiliary centers, which were established in the 2000s for counseling, shelter, and childcare, whereas the NE Branch delivered similar social services through public facilities outsourced to it by the Seoul metropolitan government. As discussed in chapter 5, the branch carried out public-private partnership projects competently, and as a result their contracts were extended

FIGURE 2.10. Campaign against sexual violence, 2019 *Source*: Provided by GY Branch

and the duration of their initial projects were renewed. These projects ended up spanning the entire decade of the 2010s.

Activism concerning the nonprofit food co-op and environmental issues have been the most popular and resulted in attracting local women to the NE and GY branches and thus also expanding their membership bases. Due to their quotidian nature, these issues were commonly perceived as not political or less political than other activism issues and did not make housewives uncomfortable. In comparison, local women perceived active participation in electoral politics by supporting a specific candidate too political, especially if the women were conservative.[58] Because of this common sensitivity to political engagement, although the co-op was integral to DFS, co-op membership ("co-op members") was distinguished from DFS membership ("full members") in terms of membership fees and expectations of their involvement in civic activism beyond purchasing healthy food. This ambiguous but formal distinction between the two types of memberships reflected the underlying tension between the popularization

PROFILES OF THREE CITIZENS' ORGANIZATIONS

of feminist activism and the integrity of feminist civic identity and activism. DFS is a feminist organization that relied on the nonprofit co-op for popularization of its activism, but a majority of co-op members were largely interested in the consumption of healthy and trendy food but not necessarily interested in feminist social change.

Both branches used co-op stores as sites for drawing in local women and reaching out to them in the mundane context of buying and selling food, sharing information about food, or food-tasting events. Active co-op members working in the stores recruited potential members and encouraged new members to get involved in other activities beyond food consumption. Co-op members occasionally organized a group trip to meet farmers who produced grains, fruits and vegetables, and fish and meat. The active members also connected co-op activism to school lunches for local children (see chapter 5). They organized activities to promote environmentally friendly food to be used for children's school lunches. Environmental activism for both branches commonly took the form of protests and campaigns against the construction of a tunnel, a golf course, and other structures that damaged the health and integrity of their local residential and natural surroundings. It also took the form of recycling and reuse of old goods in local flea markets.[59]

Grassroots Participation

The moral code of grassroots participation has been particularly important to the civic identity of the two local branches, which were created precisely for that purpose. As is true for PSPD, the local branches have witnessed an enduring gap between the ideal of active broad grassroots participation and the reality of everyday practices in their branches. Unlike PSPD, the gap does not stem from the structure of a professional advocacy organization focusing on national issues. Rather, it has stemmed from their pursuit of feminist civic activism, which challenges naturalized norms about gender, family, and individualistic solutions to problems through commodity consumption. I address this further in chapter 5. Here I discuss shared efforts by the local branches to promote grassroots participation.

First, they have provided their members with educational events to learn about feminism, social issues, and current affairs. The processes of education and interactions with other members have been oriented toward

FIGURE 2.11. Feminist sex education (menstruation), in a middle school, 2006 *Source:* Provided by NE Branch

affirmation of women's bodies and individual selves (figure 2.11). The branches have also encouraged and invited lay members to join various project committees that carried out local, or at times national, activism to promote gender equality and women's human rights in families, workplaces, politics, and the mass media. In the case of the GY Branch with a few auxiliary centers, members participated in the day-to-day running of its counseling center and shelter for survivors of sexual and domestic violence and the after-school childcare center.

Second, following a model from the headquarters, both branches have used "small group gatherings" to facilitate lay members' own initiatives. Lay members have organized and run small group gatherings to pursue activities of their own choosing; popular activities have included feminist book reading and discussion, feminist film screening and discussion, learning an easy musical instrument and performing together, learning traditional Korean dance and music, and making monthly snacks for local schoolchildren. Generally composed of several to a

PROFILES OF THREE CITIZENS' ORGANIZATIONS

FIGURE 2.12. Traditional farmers' music group, 2008 *Source*: Provided by NE Branch

dozen members, these gatherings took place one to four times a month and were used to foster a sense of fellowship and solidarity. Some gatherings lasted more than a decade, as was the case for a traditional farmers' music group, a feminism study group, and a snack-making group (figure 2.12). There have also been unique small group gatherings reflecting the specific local contexts of these branches. The GY Branch witnessed the development of a small group gathering of women who were single parents and family providers and a gathering of male members who studied feminism together.[60]

Third, active members participated in various capacities in running the nonprofit food co-op and its stores. Some volunteered to work as part-time sales persons in co-op stores, and others became deeply involved in managing the co-op as board members and officers. Other members served on a committee to take care of food items to be procured and distributed. Unlike other civic activism, co-op activism required business skills and know-how to be sustainable in a growing competitive market for organic and environmentally friendly food in urban Korea. Those members involved in co-op management had to learn basic business skills and experienced both challenge and meaningful personal growth.[61]

The diverse avenues for grassroots participation discussed here highlight fundamental differences between PSPD and the DFS local branches. The local nature of these branches facilitated gradual participation of their lay members in various capacities. Lay members were invited and encouraged to participate in committees established to carry out their activism. As some of them developed interests in more involvement through personal connections and satisfaction from nondomestic activities, they became volunteer staff or half-time or full-time paid staff if funding was available. Leaders of the branches commonly grew into the position through gradual processes of involvement accompanied by encouragement and cooperation. Hence there is a significant dimension of personal growth from housewife to activist. Resonating the classic feminist motto that the "personal is political," such personal change embodied the convergence of the personal transformation and civic activism for social change. However, the local branches have coped with the problem of a small number of active lay members volunteering for various project committees and local activism organized by the branches. After the separation of the food co-op, the NE Branch members fluctuated at around 360 members during the 2010s.[62] The GY Branch maintained a larger membership base of around 500.[63] There has been some stagnation in their membership bases along with the aging of active members without a significant influx of new members. This underlying problem has generated internal reflection and discussion.

FOA: A SMALL ORGANIZATION WORKING FOR FOREIGN MIGRANTS

Founded in 2002, the Friends of Asia (FOA) is a small local organization that has pursued institutional change and public education, as well as the provision of urgent social services for foreign migrants who came to Korea to work, marry, or study.[64] This focus on a single issue is different from the wide range of social, political, and economic issues PSPD and DFS local branches address. FOA's attention to legal and policy changes beyond the provision of social services distinguishes it from other volunteer associations working for foreign migrants in the tradition of charitable activities directed to the vulnerable or the less fortunate. As the number of foreign migrants in South Korea increased in the late 1980s, multiple organizations sprang up to deal with the issue in the traditional model of a charity, but FOA approached the issue as a citizens' organization in the framework of equal human rights and institutional change. This organization is also different from other comparable ones in terms of its attention to educating native Koreans about migrants' human rights, histories, and cultures. In 2020, it had roughly 150 dues-paying individual members and a local Christian church as an organizational supporter. Although it is small, FOA managed to open tiny auxiliary facilities such as a "research center" and a "multicultural library" in the 2000s.[65]

Financial and Political Independence from the Government

The moral code of independence from the government has been important to FOA's civic identity. Like PSPD, it has managed to keep its financial independence by relying on membership fees (*hoebi*) and donations (*huwongeum*). This was possible because it has relied entirely on volunteer labor even for activist staff, who facilitated members of various committees established for specific projects. Like PSPD and local DFS branches, its officers, advisors, and a director also volunteered their labor. A small local organization, during its early years FOA relied extensively on personal sacrifice and donations. The founder used her personal inheritance to start the organization, and she received long-term support from a scholar who donated his book sales royalties. As the initial source of funding became depleted, FOA had internal discussions regarding whether it would seek the project-based government funding available for civic organizations. With popularization of foreign migrant issues under the government's trendy policy of "multiculturalism" in the late 2000s, there were growing opportunities to receive government funding and other resources to be tapped. In particular, reflecting the spread of neoliberal governance, the government of Gyeonggi Province, where a large number of foreign migrants were employed by small businesses, promoted "multicultural" events and programs in partnership with local NGOs.[66]

However, FOA decided not to pursue government funding because it had observed serious problems with government policy and the handling of foreign migrants. The change of political leadership from progressive to conservative in national and local governments made this option even less desirable despite FOA's lack of a secure source of funding. The conservative government under Lee Myung-bak excluded progressive civic organizations from funding opportunities after the national protest against importing U.S. beef, a further reminded to FOA of the negative consequences of public funding. Its homepage has highlighted that "The FOA is run by citizens' voluntary support money without money from the government or big corporations." To sustain members' financial support, FOA practiced transparent accounting by making their expense reports publicly available on the website for easy access and reading.[67]

Financial independence has been critical to FOA's political independence from the government. Many NGOs dealing with foreign migrant issues worked with local governments and managed programs outsourced by the authorities, but FOA carried out investigative research on dire situations of undocumented migrant workers and published reports critical of government policy that demanded policy and legal change. A good example of this type of activism can be seen in its responses to the tragic deaths of migrants detained in Yeosu Foreigners Protection Center during an accidental fire in February 2007. Although the detention facility was located in the southernmost tip of the country far away from FOA, it organized a public discussion in association with other local civic organizations and took part in relay protests against the detention of undocumented migrants who were categorized as "illegal." Whenever possible, FOA investigated hazardous and exploitative working conditions of foreign migrants employed by small local businesses and joined other civic organizations protesting against inhumane policies or marching for policy changes to advocate for migrants' human rights. Its critical distance from the central and local governments would have been difficult to sustain if FOA collaborated with local governments, which paid far more attention to entertaining cultural events featuring ethnic food, clothes, and art performances. Although FOA organized such cultural events (on a much smaller scale) for its own members, migrants, and local residents, they were in the context of developing human connections and mutual understanding of differences and similarities rather than being a spectacle to be staged and consumed.

PROFILES OF THREE CITIZENS' ORGANIZATIONS

Activism for Institutional and Social Change

Although a small organization with very limited resources, FOA carried out an array of innovative activism efforts for broader social change beyond providing urgent services for foreign migrants. For broader social change, FOA's tiny auxiliary research center conducted a series of investigations to identify urgent problems commonly faced by migrants that required policy changes. Its volunteer activists educated themselves and local residents about migrants' human rights to change societal attitudes toward this growing social minority. In particular, it made efforts to educate the local youth to influence the future generation's attitude toward foreign migrants. FOA activists visited local schools to teach students about migrants' dire living and working conditions and their human rights violations and tried to inculcate cosmopolitan neighborliness in local students. To complement these lectures, it tried to facilitate personal interactions between native South Koreans and migrants to enhance mutual understanding of cultural differences and similarities. These interactions usually took the form of summer camps and cultural or sporting events, and they commonly included conviviality over eating, singing, bicycling, and talking and gesturing (for communication through the language barrier). At times volunteer activists conducted street campaigns to promote public awareness of migrants' human rights issues and to collect signatures for institutional change.

Similar to DFS local branches, FOA combined its activism for institutional change with the provision of urgent social services for migrants because of their vulnerable political, social, and economic conditions. Its social services began with a Korean language class and expanded to basic medical and legal services and fund-raising for a migrants' shelter. Because these social services were voluntarily provided by its members, the details are discussed under grassroots participation.

Grassroots Participation

The moral code of grassroots participation has been applied to foreign migrants as potential or actual members. In contrast to other organizations specializing in migrants' issues that treated foreign migrants as marginalized victims, FOA tried to envision them as potential agents of their own empowerment and social change. Because migrant workers were tied up with paid employment and had vulnerable legal status, activities promoting their grassroots participation tended to focus on the marriage migrants who became wives of Korean men. Although many of these women also wanted to work outside the home to gain personal autonomy and to remit money to their natal families, many of them became housewives who gave birth to children and took care of parents-in-law at home. FOA experimented with training marriage migrants to work as staff activists, lecturers of their own national histories to be delivered at local schools, and interns working for other co-ethnic migrants. FOA organized a small writing group for them to share their fictional and nonfictional stories and to publish them for internal uses and public dissemination (figure 2.13). As laudable as these innovative efforts were, there was a significant gap between the ideal of migrants as active agents and the reality of their structural barriers, including legal, economic, linguistic, and other cultural ones. There was uneven access to and capacity to use cultural/symbolic capital between volunteer activists and foreign migrants. These barriers generated an enduring hierarchy between native Koreans and foreign migrants that could not be easily overcome but which volunteer activists and participants tried to mitigate during their interactions.

The moral code of grassroots participation was applied to South Korean members as well. As observed in PSPD and the DFS branches, grassroots participation had two major dimensions: regular payment of monthly membership fees to sustain the financial and therefore political independence of the civic organization and voluntary involvement in various FOA activities or taking initiatives in creating and running a project. It recognized volunteer activists as "someone who shares their limited time for other people's human rights." Active members worked as youth volunteers, Korean-language instructors, multicultural library managers, and members of various committees for specific projects (figure 2.14). In contrast to this relatively uplifting activism, FOA members have also participated in regularly visiting foreign migrants who are detained in the "Foreigners' Protection Center" (*oegugin bohoso*) in Hwasong City. Most of these detainees were arrested simply because they did not have documents that the Immigration Office required. This activism is called "*majung*" (receiving a guest) to counteract the inhumane treatment of detainees in the euphemistically

FIGURE 2.13. Multicultural library in the FOA office, circa 2015 *Source*: Provided by FOA

PROFILES OF THREE CITIZENS' ORGANIZATIONS

FIGURE 2.14. Celebration of FOA's anniversary, 2022 *Source*: Provided by FOA

named detention facility, which highlights the darkest aspect of foreign migrant issues in South Korea. During their biweekly visits, FOA members tried to convey useful information to detained migrants who were waiting to be deported against their will and to nurture human connection with them.[68] Majung activism shockingly sensitized volunteer activists to the harsh reality of foreign migrants in South Korea.

CONCLUSION

The detailed profiles of PSPD, the NE and GY branches of DFS, and FOA have been thematically discussed to show their shared civic identity as progressive citizens' organizations as well as their differences regarding each organization's specific civic identity and activism. Their shared civic identity is based on their adherence to the moral codes of independence from the government, activism for institutional and social change, and an ideological emphasis on grassroots participation. However, they vary significantly in terms of the degree to which they practice these moral codes and how they do so in any given period as well as over time, depending on the scope and method of their activism and the social and political context confronting each organization. Focusing on institutional reforms and broad social change through monitoring the major political and economic powers on a wide range of national issues, PSPD has emphasized its independence from the government but paid secondary attention to grassroots participation. Although it has been able to maintain financial independence from the government by relying on its relatively large membership and donations, PSPD's political independence became complicated as its cooperation with progressive governments grew and its former officers and activist staff entered institutional politics. Meanwhile its ideological commitment to grassroots participation has motivated the organization to conduct ongoing critical self-reflection and to make adjustments in its civic identity and activism.

Dealing with a wide range of women's issues in specific local contexts, the two DFS branches have tried to balance broad institutional change with the provision of useful or urgent services for their members and local residents. Although more conducive to grassroots participation, their activism for social service provisions was developed in the context of an increasing partnership with local governments à la neoliberal governance. As their dependence on government funding grew in proportion to the reduction of their membership bases, especially after the separation of the food co-op from DFS, they struggle to maintain civic autonomy. Their local identities were intended to popularize feminist activism, but their overarching feminist civic identity has been in tension with these goals in specific local contexts. These two complications have generated opportunities for internal reflection on their feminist civic identities and activism.

Addressing various issues concerning foreign migrants, from their empowerment to the education of Koreans about them, FOA has also tried to balance institutional change with the provision of urgent services for migrants. Unlike DFS local branches, it chose not to receive government funding and to work with its limited resources from membership fees, donations, and other forms of volunteer support. Although financial scarcity created hardship for its activism and threatened sustainable operation, it spared FOA from being controlled by government bureaucracy. Instead of running programs or facilities outsourced by local governments, for example, it reached out to other civic organizations for solidarity movements for institutional reforms and broad social change. Its small size and the single focus on migrant issues contributed to its survival without government funding. In-depth examinations of these three organizations and their civic activism follow, specifically how each has negotiated with neoliberalism as it has dealt with problems generated or aggravated by neoliberalism as a dominant mode of ruling, characterized by the logic of the market and neoliberal governance.

Chapter Three

NEGOTIATING WITH THE MARKET IN NEOLIBERAL SOUTH KOREA

> Courage to borrow money becomes a weapon to make money. When I am working, I am a laborer but when money is working, I am an investor. We all have a right to be rich.
>
> —K BANK COMMERCIAL[1]

> Both aspects may ultimately be traced back to one and the same effect of money, namely to grant separation and mutual independence to those elements that originally existed as a living unity. On the one hand, disintegration concerns individual personalities and thereby makes possible the convergence of similar interests—however divergent and irreconcilable—in a collective form. On the other hand, this disintegration also affects the communities and makes internal and external communalization difficult for the now sharply differentiated individuals.
>
> —GEORG SIMMEL, *THE PHILOSOPHY OF MONEY*, 379

The K Bank commercial poignantly captures how individuals are exhorted to become investors and get rich while distancing themselves from working like laborers in neoliberal South Korea. It comes from a series of advertising campaigns—"We all have a right to get rich" (*Wurineun modu bujaga doel gwolliga itta*)—that K Bank in South Korea launched in May of 2022 targeting the "MZ generation." The campaign title was produced in consultation with its MZ-generation employees in the bank to appeal to actual and potential customers in their twenties. The ad campaign became very popular and attracted more than 5.7 million viewers on YouTube by early July of 2022. It represented young adults as proactive customers who see finance as an active tool for becoming rich and having fun accumulating money. This celebration of money as a means to realize the "right to get rich" underscores the rise of the financial market as the mechanism of accumulation in neoliberal capitalism.

The market as an economic institution has a very long history, but it was not until late in the twentieth century that the market was zealously promoted as the model for organizing politics and society beyond economic activities. This "market fundamentalism" has transformed the world through an unflinching belief in the doctrine of the "free market," in which transnational capital flows out and is the source of prosperity and freedom that has restructured all areas of human lives, including education, health care, childcare, and religion.[2] As a result, the logic of the market as an essential component of neoliberalism has reshaped civic activism. Peter Dauvergne and Genevieve Lebaron highlight this ongoing transformation as "the corporatization of activism" and document that major activist organizations in the world have come to operate like business corporations.[3] This finding is based on their study of transnational NGOs originating in the West such as Amnesty International, World Wildlife Fund (WWF), Greenpeace, and Oxfam. Furthermore, in the United States an entire corporate subindustry has developed to supply "grassroots participation" in the form of lobbying.[4] These scholars are deeply concerned about the negative consequences of the market model for activism that undermine its capacity to question the status quo and imagine an alternative to it.

In this chapter critical studies of the relationship between the market and civic activism are examined by looking at how and to what extent four citizens' organizations (PSPD, the GY and NE branches, and FOA) in South Korea have been affected by the market's ascendance and negotiated with it. As neoliberalism, particularly neoliberal governance, has blurred the boundaries between the state, the market, and civil society around the world through practices of partnership, the discourse on "business corporations' social contribution activities" (*gieobui sahoegongheon hwaldong*) has emerged and spread in South Korea in the twenty-first century. This discourse was accompanied by growing practices among major corporations of donating their resources in the name of social contributions, establishing a section in charge of "social contribution programs," and incorporating volunteer services into the evaluation of their employees' performance.[5] To the public's surprise, the Federation of Korean Industries (*Jeon-gyeong-nyeon*) organized a high-profile international seminar in 2005 titled "Responses of Korean Industries to Corporate Social Responsibility" to promote business management of social responsibility.[6] This ongoing change has generated the so-called governance of business corporations and NGOs, which has replaced public services and programs.

Against this backdrop, first I examine the extent to which the social contribution activities of business corporations are relevant to the four citizens' organizations. Second, to document how these organizations have negotiated with the market, I discuss three practices of social relations that are alternatives to the market and are used by PSPD, the two DFS branches, and FOA, respectively: (1) the "gift economy" based on donations, (2) the nonprofit feminist food cooperative, and (3) the "prefigurative" practices of building solidarity with migrants. Finally, I examine deeper ways in which the market mechanism has shaped the workings of these organizations. Using archival and in-depth interview data, I discuss the adoption of three market techniques that are used by these organizations to varying degrees: (1) membership fees as the primary indicator of commitment, (2) a growing need for "marketing" activism to potential and current members and supporters, and (3) reenvisioning civic activism as "fun, enjoyable, and sustainable" activities.

The comparative analysis of the four organizations shows that the corporatization of activism as a global trend does not uniformly affect all types of NGOs. There is an elective affinity between the global trend and a large advocacy organization such as PSPD, which has professionalized its routine operations for efficiency. Smaller local organizations are far less inclined to adopt branding or marketing techniques for practical and ideological reasons. More important, all of the four citizens' organizations have adopted basic market techniques to sustain activism and simultaneously resist individualizing and dehumanizing tendencies by developing communal social relations as integral aspects of their civic identities in opposition to the logic of ruthless competition, privatization, and profit maximization. Although the gift economy and prefigurative practices continue to exist, the food co-op discontinued as the main tool of feminist grassroots social change when it was separated from the feminist civic organization due to the powerful global force of the market. These complexities deepen our understanding of the evolving relationship between civic activism and the market beyond the thesis of the corporatization of activism. Crucial to this deeper understanding is the full recognition of civic activism as symbolic action imbued with moral meanings. Their negotiations with the market are accompanied by interpretations of these practices in connection with civic identities and the moral code of citizens' organizations.

BUSINESS CORPORATIONS' "SOCIAL CONTRIBUTION ACTIVITIES": HOW RELEVANT TO THE FOUR CITIZENS' ORGANIZATIONS?

The social contribution activities of business corporations (or "corporate social responsibility") have modified the relationship between the market and civil society organizations in South Korea, but their influences are not uniform across different types of organizations. In the four progressive citizens' organizations on which I focus, social contribution activities have been indirectly or marginally relevant. None of the four citizens' organizations I examine here receive direct donations from major corporations. This results from mutual distrust and caution. Given their largely critical positions on big business, major corporations have not been interested in supporting them, and the citizens' organizations have maintained their moral authority and independence by distancing themselves from business donations.[7] As discussed in chapter 1, the ideological polarization of politics between conservative and progressive camps sensitized the four citizens' organizations to the negative public perception that citizens' organizations were "getting money from the government and business corporations." In particular, PSPD, a leading civic organization, has been exposed to a smear campaign by the conservative mass media criticizing its fund-raising event.[8]

However, there are indirect uses for business corporations' donations. For PSPD, its indirect link to such donations is made in the context of working in cooperation with other civic organizations for coalition projects. Recognizing dire financial conditions for many civic organizations, PSPD established a principle that it would join coalition projects involving an organization funded by a business corporation as long as the organization did not clearly violate fundamental values of PSPD.[9] For GY and NE branches of DFS, a feminist organization, the indirect link to business donations happens when they receive project-based funding from the Women's Foundation. Established in December 1999 by the coalition of 124 women's organizations, the foundation is the first public interest foundation in South Korea.[10] One of its main objectives includes financial support for women's movements.[11] The Women's Foundation collected the "women's fund" through business donations and various fund-raising campaigns. Similarly, FOA, a smaller local organization that supports foreign migrants, received indirect corporate funding from public interest foundations, including the Beautiful Foundation and the Human Rights Foundation.[12]

In the past, FOA had received a direct donation of a small sum from a bank under its social contribution program. Mr. Kang, a volunteer/staff activist, conveyed his observation about corporate contributions:

> **KANG:** In the beginning of the previous administration [referring to Roh Moo-hyun's] it [corporate contribution] was growing but lately it has decreased a lot. *Corporations are keen on figuring out orientation of the government.* They can be tax-audited if they support many citizens' organizations critical of the government. But a real difficulty for us is that business firms are entities for selling things to make money. So they don't contribute without conditions. They also tend to package things big and showy. It is stressful to deal with such difference. We talk about a small event but they like to make it big. So we rarely receive a corporate contribution except a bank which donated 100,000 won [about USD $90.00] each month. But it will end in a short while.
>
> **MOON:** How did that relationship begin?
>
> **KANG:** The company approached us first. It turned out that *its founder had some personal experience of studying abroad and working as a laborer.* He was interested in supporting foreign migrants.[13]

After the bank's contribution ended, FOA has maintained the principle of financial independence from both the government and big business corporations and has relied on voluntary financial support from individuals.[14] His comments draw our attention to how business firms' donations can be influenced by a government's political orientation even after its power over big business has been significantly reduced in the process of neoliberal globalization. This enduring power of the government is corroborated by other activists.[15] His comments also applied during the 2008 global financial crisis, which negatively impacted business firms. FOA's experience with business corporations' social contribution activities highlight major political and economic factors affecting the trend.

Regarding the incorporation of volunteer service into evaluations of employees' performance, such encouragement or requirements have generated little consequence for the four citizens' organizations. Studies of volunteer services in South Korea indicate that volunteers largely choose social service or charity organizations—that is, an older category of civil society organizations—rather than the citizens' organizations oriented to social change and movements.[16] In sum, although the social contribution activities of business corporations opened opportunities for business and civic organizations to form partnerships to pursue public interests, the uneven power relations between big corporations and civil society organizations often led to neoliberal co-optation. The corporate power to shape other civil society organizations directly has sensitized progressive organizations on how to pragmatically use corporate resources while protecting their civic identities.

In the social contribution section established within big business corporations, a global trend has developed around the joint marketing and sales of branded goods. These practices show how the idea of corporate social responsibility has been inflected in reality by powerful business practices rather than transforming corporations into socially responsible organizations. South Korea has been exposed to this global trend. As early as 1998, Yeong-hui Yang, Secretary of Global Care in South Korea, suggested that NGOs adopt sales of goods during their fund-raising campaigns instead of asking for donations from business corporations. In response to voices of concern about such commercialization, he elaborated that this would be acceptable if NGOs choose "wholesome products" from "wholesome business corporations."[17] There was also a voice promoting professionalization of fund-raising beyond the one-time event to sell goods, which was not very reliable.[18] These views coincided with the global spread of ethical consumption or political consumption as a form of activism.[19] This development highlighted the centrality of commodified consumption in our lives in the twenty-first century. Consumption has become a quasi-political symbolic activity that expresses our identity and status aspirations beyond the practical activity of satisfying basic needs.

Yet the practice of joint marketing and sales of branded goods has not been adopted by the four citizens' organizations analyzed here. They have regularly or irregularly used fund-raising activities involving sales of goods for profit to supplement membership fees under the rubric of "profit-earning project" (*suiksaeop*).[20] As discussed in chapter 2, PSPD outgrew this practice as its membership and donations increased and managed to cover its basic operational costs, whereas the local branches of DFS have regularly used this practice to supplement their lack of membership fees.[21] These branches have largely sold what their members have crafted and services that they could provide. Examples commonly included food, beverages, household goods, and personal goods. Occasionally, the branches were able to organize special entertainment shows or performances for fund-raising. As a smaller local organization, FOA used a profit-earning project to raise additional funds to establish a shelter, but it has not used it in recent years due to a shortage of personnel and its growing reliance on online communication. Although these fund-raising activities adopt a market practice, the level of commodification has been minimal especially in comparison with transnational NGOs actively working with big business corporations to brand their images and sell branded goods as a regular way of raising funds.[22] Now I turn to how the four citizens organizations converged and diverged in negotiating with the market.

PRACTICING ALTERNATIVE SOCIAL RELATIONS TO THE MARKET

In this section I discuss different ways in which citizens' organizations can distance themselves from the fragmenting and dehumanizing consequences of the market. They have practiced social relations alternative to the logic of competition and profit maximization. Each organization developed its own practice, depending on its organizational features and civic identity. PSPD established donations of goods and services as a core mechanism of its gift economy. The DFS branches established nonprofit feminist food co-op stores to carve out space for developing social relations alternative to the market in capitalist society. FOA established prefigurative practices of cultivating solidarity between its Korean members and foreign migrants.

Donations, Gift Economy, and Building a Sense of Community

Members of PSPD have donated office supplies, furniture, equipment, and food items for use by their staff activists and volunteer activists. Other organizations have used donated goods occasionally, but PSPD established donations as a routine mechanism to secure material resources necessary for its smooth working. Gwan-su, a staff activist, explained the details of this practice:

We don't get an approval for buying supplies and other things unless we asked for donations from our members. We use *Participatory Society* [house organ published monthly and also available online] bulletin. It is well established that we buy goods only when there is no donation. There are a lot of donations. During this summer, for example, we carried out a street campaign to collect signatures to pass a [Seoul] Plaza Act [discussed in chapter 2], and we needed a lot of bottled water. So we asked for a water donation and received a lot. We also needed A4 papers; we had to make 80,000 copies of a signature collection form and that was a lot. Many members employed in companies were more than willing to make copies [in their offices] and bring them to us.[23]

The flow of donations to support specific projects generates and strengthens the sense of community by building and maintaining solidarity around common activities and common goals. It enables lay members to make a useful and valuable contribution to the organization and at the same time enables the organization to publicize its activities to its lay members. Because of these enabling effects, PSPD calls the act of donating resource "giving wings to fly" (nalgaereul darajuda).

Around major holidays, small gifts in kind are donated as symbolic recognition of the staff's hard work by members. In particular, older members who are merchants or business owners send food and decorative items to convey their appreciation of staff activists. Reflecting a traditional cultural practice of the precapitalist era, these gifts serve to foster noncapitalist social relations in the civic organization. Donations and gift-giving together in this context resonate with studies of the gift economy by anthropologists and sociologists; the gift economy *prioritizes* use value and symbolic values over profit (exchange value) and thereby fosters a sense of community.[24]

In comparison with commercial transactions, gift-giving and donations generate feelings of gratitude and obligation for reciprocity in the future, especially when it satisfies a recipient's need, and thereby increases the sense of solidarity. The practices of a gift economy contribute to the preservation of human relations that cannot be reduced to commercial transactions. They are particularly significant when South Korean society has been rapidly transformed by the individualizing force of neoliberalism. The critical observation of unmooring and weakening social bonds under globalizing capitalism has existed since the nineteenth century.[25] In the twenty-first century, transnational and neoliberal capitalism has intensified the unmooring dissolution of our collective existence. When consumption of commodities can satisfy one's needs and desires with increasing convenience and speed, we easily forget our interdependence with other members of society.[26] This simultaneously separating/freeing and isolating consequence of commodity consumption contrasts practices of gift-giving as economic and social activities that have coexisted with commodity exchanges. Although not entirely free from existing inequalities in society, gift-giving and donations enhance emotional and social ties among individuals through the ethic of reciprocity in the context of enduring interactions.[27] In neoliberal South Korea that celebrates individual choice and freedom through "buying power" and "credit" (which is a debt to be paid with interests), they promote a sense of solidarity with the organization and its members.

This attention to the presence of a gift economy does not mean that it should be a defining feature of all citizens' organizations in South Korea. Rather, it identifies a specific way in which a civic organization negotiates with the market as an essential mechanism of neoliberalism. In the case of PSPD, its gift economy has served both pragmatic and symbolic functions for its maintenance. This example highlights how the old practice of gift-giving is used to preserve an alternative to market relations, whereas the innovative use of "crowdfunding" to raise resources for public projects and civic activism is a new way of appropriating market practices for civic activism. For example, in partnership with Naver, a major internet search engine company in South Korea, the aforementioned Beautiful Foundation established Happy Bean, an online platform for crowdfunding in 2005, and has raised funds for civic projects.[28] Following this model, various organizations and individuals have used "political or civic" crowdfunding. These diverse responses to the market illustrate the extent to which the market model is simultaneously resisted and adopted by civic activists and their supporters.

Feminist Nonprofit Food Cooperative (from mid-1990s to 2013): Experimenting with Noncapitalist Social Relations

The GY Branch and NE Branch of DFS opened their first co-op stores in 1997 and 2000, respectively, as a major vehicle to reach out to local women.[29] These co-op stores multiplied during the 2000s, reaching four each for both local branches by 2011. The stores existed as integral components of the branches until 2012 and 2013, when the co-op was finally separated from DFS and became a separate entity that joined a collective of other food co-ops. Through various practices, the co-op stores became sites where social relations alternative to the capitalist market were envisioned and experienced. The growth of co-op membership and stores cultivated a potential to turn commodified food consumption into civic activism for social change. Foremost, in the context of transnational consumer capitalism, the co-op redefined food as "materials for living" (*saenghwaljae*) rather than as commercial goods (*sangpum*) or commodities to be sold and bought for profit. This redefinition stressed the utility of food rather than its exchange value. It also reclaimed the social dimension of eating beyond being merely a personal and private activity. Unfortunately, these stores closed as a result of the powerful market force that proliferated a multitude of competitors selling organic or environmentally friendly food as commodities. Nevertheless, the co-op stores made a valuable contribution to shifting the public's perception of food, environment, and well-being.

Active co-op members practiced alternative social relations in procuring and consuming the materials for living. In 2004, when the South Korea-U.S. Free Trade Agreement (KORUS FTA) negotiations began (see chapter 4), they called mundane food items such as rice, soybean products, and dairy products "materials for living that change the world." In doing so, it resisted the logic of the WTO regime, which has undermined food sovereignty and safety in the name of free trade and intellectual property rights. It launched special educational campaigns for both adults and children, including how to cultivate organic rice and how to make tofu with locally grown soybeans that were not genetically modified (GM) as an element of a healthy-eating education.[30] In particular, rice consumption became a symbol of supporting local farmers as the FTA and the WTO regime seriously undermined their livelihood. The co-op carried out a campaign for living with co-op rice for one year and promoted various products made from local rice, including breads, noodles, and liquor. The promotion of organic rice to protect local farmers continued in 2005.[31] Soybeans are the main ingredient for making traditional Korean fermented products, soy sauce (*ganjang*) and soy paste (*doenjang*), and popular items like tofu and soy milk. These food items came under assault by the massive import of GM soybeans, which were aggressively marketed by multinational food companies and imported to Korea.[32] Korean consumers encountered the massive import of dairy products from cows fed with GM corns and soybeans.[33] Active co-op members met with organic dairy farmers and organized events to cook and taste dishes made with this meat.[34] These activities were oriented toward the underlying goal of building alternative social interactions and relationships between producers and co-op members to transform local communities through participation and cooperation.[35]

Affirming its feminist identity, co-op members made efforts to find women farmers as their suppliers. They also recognized wives of farming families by using their names along with their husbands' when they listed producers of co-op goods. These practices were intended to reverse the invisibility of women as agricultural producers who are commonly hidden as unpaid family workers. This was particularly significant given that organic farming required far more intensive manual labor to avoid the use of chemical pesticides and fertilizers. Starting in 2003, co-op members visited women farmers in their regular field trips to production sites to build solidarity and social connections.[36] Co-op members demanded changes of product names when the names reflected sexism in the larger society. For example, a ham product containing natural honey was named "man's morning" (*namjaui achim*), connoting honey as a substance that increases virility. Co-op members discussed this issue and decided to ask its producer to change the name, which was accepted by the producer. At times they even asked for modification of a company's name. There was a dried pollock company in the Yeonggwang area by the name of "*Yeonggwang miss gulbi*," connoting a beauty pageant objectifying women's bodies. The company renamed itself "new age gulbi."[37] Given the relatively small scale of the DFS co-op, this type of constructive response is unlikely to happen in mainstream capitalist markets. It reflects social relations formed around shared values beyond business transactions.

Building collaborative social relations with producers became transnational in the context of increasing globalization of food production, circulation, and consumption. In 2006, responding to member demands, the co-op included imported food products that could not be produced locally, such as coffee and sugar. In these cases, it embraced the practice of using "fair trade" goods.[38] By 2009, it sold coffee from Columbia directly purchased from local producers, Mascobado sugar (produced by an indigenous brown sugar manufacturing method) from the Philippines, olive oil from

Palestine, and chocolate from Columbia produced without child labor and directly imported from its producers. Although global fair trade was far from a perfect solution for commodified human relations generated by transnational consumer capitalism, in the absence of a better alternative, the co-op accepted the practice of buying and selling these fair trade products.[39]

The co-op's growth increased financial resources for active members to develop new programs and projects and strengthen existing ones with the goal of turning co-op members into full members or at least raising their consciousness beyond merely purchasing safe and healthy food for their own families. These efforts ranged from "a day to meet co-op members," "co-op informational meetings," and regular co-op committee meetings to organizing field trips to farming sites and meeting with local producers. Through these activities, some housewives became volunteer activists and then members of local co-op boards. In fact, a majority of the co-op leaders were housewives, who had little previous experience of participation in social movement organizations and local politics. This positive transformation conveys the brightest picture of civic efficacy cultivated in the context of the co-op movement. This group of women was a numerical minority, but their transformation illuminates the extent to which an alternative space like the co-op can work in a capitalist society. The proximity of co-op stores to their residences increased interactions with other members, staff, and officers and helped build enduring social relations.

However, a persistent gap remained between active co-op members and a majority of co-op members, who were not interested in going beyond purchasing "environmentally friendly" (*chinhwangyeong*) or "organic" (*yuginong*) food for their family members. Their lack of willingness to become actively involved beyond food consumption need not be reduced to thoughtless indifference or a failure to exercise their civic efficacy. This majority attitude reflects the dominant subjectivity normalized by the neoliberal society; women were encouraged to see themselves as individual consumers who can satisfy their own needs and solve their problems by buying commodified goods and services. They were also encouraged to see themselves as human capital whose values must be maximized through investment in themselves. Because money is central to ensuring their personal choices and sense of the self, many people were supremely interested in making money rather than engaging in other types of activities, including civic participation and community building.

The supreme need to make money eroded the co-op's potential to expand social relations that are alternative to the market in neoliberal South Korea. The accelerating mobility of transnational capital affected co-op members of the GY and NE branches, who were largely middle-class housewives. In the aftermath of the 2008 global financial crisis, they were forced to look for paid employment to compensate for decreasing household income vis-à-vis rising costs of living and particularly the cost of children's education. As discussed in chapter 5, in-depth interviews with DFS lay members and staff showed that a majority of members in local branches were attracted to programs and projects that gave them opportunities to acquire licenses or certificates useful for employment as paid counselors and lecturers; mirroring its feminist orientation, these programs and projects dealt with sex education for schoolchildren, sexual violence prevention, and family counseling. The keen interest in obtaining certificates also echoed a larger trend in Korean society shaped by neoliberalism, namely, practices of investing in the privatized self and branding it for material gains: the individual learns to accumulate credentials and sell herself to the highest bidder. During fieldwork in 2009, staff members and officers conveyed the increasing difficulty of finding housewives available for volunteer activities in the co-op because many of them were busy taking classes that would help them find paid employment to support their children's education, which had become fiercely competitive.

Meanwhile, the acceleration of neoliberal capitalism through FTAs and the WTO regime deteriorated food safety and thereby contributed to the popularization of organic or environmentally friendly food. The growing popularity of such food among Korean consumers expanded their commercial market in the 2000s and 2010s. In 2021, supermarkets and grocery stores of various sizes commonly sold such food in urban Korea. The rapid proliferation of commercial stores seriously weakened the viability of the DFS co-op. Without reaching and maintaining a large scale and professionalization in distribution, it could not survive. Its unique identity as a feminist social movement organization became an even more constraining condition in the fiercely competitive market for healthy safe food. In 2009 and 2010, the co-op renamed itself the "happiness-focus food co-op" and reestablished its identity to cope with growing financial difficulty and sustainability. Some co-op stores had to close and were absorbed into other stores.[40] At the general meeting in the spring of 2012, DFS decided to separate the co-op from the parent organization. The co-op stores under the headquarters became independent of the DFS, and other branch co-ops followed suit.[41]

In contrast to the enduring gift economy integrated into the work of the PSPD, the food co-op ceased to exist as an integral component of DFS branches because it had to compete directly with the market. The co-op presented a potential to alter the nature of mundane practices of buying and selling food, and it reminded us of the daunting challenge of doing so in the neoliberal market. This valuable experiment provides lessons for us to consider in the future.

Prefigurative Practices of Cultivating Solidarity Across Power Differences

As a smaller local organization promoting solidarity between Koreans and foreign migrants, FOA has resisted social relations with the market by pursuing friendships based on equality and mutual understanding. Given the profound structural inequality between native Koreans and foreign migrants, such friendships are an aspirational goal rather than a given reality (see chapter 6). Drawing on studies of social movements in the United States, I adopt the term *prefigurative* to describe FOA's practices of pursuing equality and solidarity.[42] FOA is a small local organization without many resources, and it has focused on quality and substance rather than on expanding its size and visibility through government or business funding. It maintains a small database for volunteers and communicates with them about its civic identity. In-a, a volunteer in her mid-twenties who taught Korean language to migrants for five months, conveys her understanding of the civic identity:

> In fact, this is not a center for Korean language education but a center for foreign migrants' welfare. *Ultimately, I am not just teaching them, but am becoming their friends.* I've been learning this. So when I come for the class, we also talk about our lives, like a wedding and a weekend. Sometimes we eat a meal together. We talk a lot about our routine activities. This can help them adjust to their lives in Korea.[43]

She volunteered as a Korean teacher while she prepared for a test to become a secondary school teacher. Most of her students were women who married Korean men, and this is why In-a mentioned a wedding. Their common gender identity and proximity in age facilitated interactions for developing friendships rather than a relationship solely between teacher and student.

Teaching a Korean language class can lead to involvement in a protest because, as In-a explained, volunteer teaching is a practice to cultivate equal friendship and solidarity with foreign migrants. Hye-jeong, another volunteer in her thirties who had been teaching the Korean language for three years, describes her gradual change:

> *Here we're not just teaching Korean language* and at times we join a protest if a situation demands. . . . Initially, I came here to teach the language and was not interested in it [joining a protest] at all. Then, one day, there was no class and I was in Seoul because I live there. There was a protest gathering in Seoul but it was difficult for people here to join; it's rather far away. I was asked to join if possible. So accidentally I was dragged into it. I felt a bit scared and strange because I've never done that before. I might get into an accident or even get arrested. I worried what if these things that I saw only in TV news really happen to me. So I was a bit scared. But when I saw foreign migrants there, I understood why they were there, like their spirit of struggle. They went to the front [of the protest site] and talked about their experiences, both positive and negative. There was also a group performing singing and dancing.⁴⁴

Hye-jeong had been a government employee but changed her job and was a commercial cram school teacher at the time of this interview. She had not been politicized prior to her interactions with foreign migrants, but her repeated exposure to their lives of hardship and struggle moved her to occasionally participate in protest gatherings in solidarity with them.

Prefigurative practices of cultivating solidarity with foreign migrants can be transformative for some FOA members. After serving as a volunteer Korean language teacher for almost three years, Hong-seok, an executive of a small company, retired early and became more fully involved in his activism. Because he was a forty-nine-year-old father and husband, many people around him were startled by his unusual decision. Most of them could not understand why he would give up a secure well-paying job, especially in this era of widespread employment insecurity. He explains his difficult decision in terms of his own search for a meaningful life outside the market mechanism:

> The Korean language class was my only participation in a citizens' organization. I was interested in such involvement but I haven't actually done so until then. I think I got great satisfaction. I received much more than I gave. In the near future whatever I do, I think I need to carry out activities for developing solidarity rather than just for giving like charity....
>
> I had roughly thirty fellows who studied Korean language with me. Five or six among them were really bright and ambitious. They were interested in passing the Korean Language Proficiency Test. Like TOFEL or TOEIC, when you get a high score, the Korean test can enhance your chance to enter a good firm or a good university. In fact, it is highly unlikely for foreign migrants who came here with work permits to get a chance to be hired by a good company. But the test can work as a significant plus when these fellows seek for employment in their own countries. It is not easy at all to come and study on Sunday after working so hard for six days. In order to obtain the Class 4 in the test, one needs to study full time at least for a year because it is very difficult. But they were so motivated and I was studying with them not only Sunday, but also some week nights after our work. I was rather exhausted, but I couldn't forget the passion in their eyes. Going through that experience, I was thinking that energy I gained from working with them had sustained me during my week days. That's why I feel that I received more than what I gave.[45]

The prefigurative practices of building solidarity with foreign migrants as equal friends requires varying degrees of change and even transformation on the part of native Korean members. This change and transformation became possible through recurring personal interactions with foreign migrants and by gaining awareness of their situations. As a locally based organization, FOA has provided a valuable space for its active members to cultivate human relations outside of the market. I now turn to the discussion of how the four organizations' negotiations with the market have led to the adoption of common market techniques to pursue activism and maintain their civic identities using differentiating strategies.

ADOPTING ESTABLISHED MARKET TECHNIQUES TO SUSTAIN ACTIVISM

The market mechanism converts everything into a commodity to be sold for profit and promotes commodity consumption as a personal choice and empowerment. The assumption is that individuals are equally free to engage in such commercial exchange relations. Founded and operating in the current era of neoliberal globalization, the four citizens' organizations studied (PSPD, GY and NE branches of the DFS, and FOA) are inevitably shaped by the market mechanism that mediates almost everything through money. Although they are nonprofit organizations pursuing social change, they have been compelled to adopt the following market techniques to sustain their organizations and activism to varying degrees: (1) membership fees as the primary means of commitment, (2) a growing need to "market" their activism to potential and current members and supporters, and (3) reenvisioning activism as fun and enjoyable, and therefore sustainable activities.

Membership Fees: The Primary Means of Support

For all four organizations, the institution of membership fees indicates the dictate of a market technique in expressing membership commitment. Preceding the current era of neoliberal globalization, membership fees had become more significant than ever before. Although payment of fees is neither the only responsibility for members nor the only marker of membership, it has become the fundamental condition for it. Members can perform volunteer services and donate goods, but these are considered additional to the payment of fees. Dues-paying members are different from temporary volunteers who provide useful services for various programs run by these organizations.[46] For all of them, actual membership begins with the payment of fees and ends with stopping to do so. Computer and smartphone technologies have enhanced the ability of these organizations to monitor payment of membership fees.[47] For PSPD and DFS branches, members who pay regularly are commonly counted as "real numbers" (*silsu*), and those who have not done so for some time are called "imaginary numbers" (*heosu*). Hence each organization regularly or irregularly "cleans up" its membership base by removing those imaginary members for the necessary calculation of their revenues and budgets.

Variations in how each organization carries out the task of cleaning up depend on the availability of its resources. PSPD, with relatively more resources than the other organizations, has a few staff activists who regularly reach out to members who have fallen behind on their payment. The activists encourage them to resume their payment, and they remove them if they decide to withdraw their membership. The activists regularly remove a sizable minority of members who become inactive in their payment and unresponsive to their outreach. Because the removal of inactive members has offset the growth of new members and stagnated membership as a whole, PSPD introduced a category of "bracketed members" (*boryuhoewon*) for those who would need more time to decide on their membership status.[48] GY Branch and NE Branch also try to clean up their membership bases by removing inactive members, but their lack of personnel limits their ability to reach out to inactive members.[49] In 2019, NE Branch was able to make a monthly list of members who did not pay membership fees but could not follow up with each one of them as planned.[50] Being a smaller local organization, FOA had dealt with this matter informally and ambiguously. As it has become more reliant on internet communication with its members over time, it regularly thanks members for their financial support and promises transparent accounting. It has distinguished "members" (*hoewon*), who make regular financial contributions, from supporters (*huwonja*), who irregularly contributed donations and other services. In sum, the payment of fees as the fundamental marker of membership and the primary means of support for the organizations reflects how profoundly the market mechanism dictates the work of civic activism.

However, precisely because money is used to sustain nonprofit organizations and their civic activism, members of the four organizations commonly interpreted the payment of fees emphatically as an extension of their capacity and form of participation. For a majority of lay members who juggle with paid employment, family responsibilities, and other personal commitments, regular payment of the fees serves to extend their constrained capacity. Ui-pyo, a forty-two-year-old school teacher who had been a PSPD member for fourteen years, explains:

UI-PYO: I'm very much interested in human rights organizations, Dasan Human Rights Center and Human Rights Education Center. I also support organizations related to sexual minorities. I am a school teacher. So I am also interested in parents' organizations.
MOON: What does it mean for you to support citizens' organizations financially?
UI-PYO: With all those organizations I support, I have developed some sort of relationships. *I am interested in their activities but I cannot be directly involved in them all. Instead, I support them with a small amount.* I am not just paying money but interested in what they are doing. So I regularly read monthly newsletters.[51]

A common view emerging from the four citizens' organizations is that a financial contribution only is passive participation but it is a serious commitment. It is passive in comparison with traditional face-to-face involvements in campaigns, fund-raising, protests, and other activities concerning the running of an organization. Song-hui, a mother of two sons in her late forties, describes her gradual change from a passive to an active member of the NE Branch over time:

After getting married, I had to juggle between family and work. I couldn't get involved in social organizations. So *I just paid membership fees and received newsletters*. I worked for an IT company for about twenty years and quit five years ago. My children entered junior high schools, and I had to pay more attention to them. I was also exhausted from the work. For a year I was still just a member, but I was encouraged to join a steering committee. Then I got involved in various Small Group activities.[52]

The payment of membership fees is a serious commitment because most members have to pay each month from their limited financial resources. Especially in the era of repeated financial crises and widespread employment insecurity, the monthly payment can deter individuals from joining a civic organization. I ask Young-nim, a single woman in her mid-forties and a member of the NE Branch for two and half years, whether she tried to recruit new members among her friends and acquaintances:

Generally, people have a sort of negative response to membership fees. So I am cautious about approaching them. Because they don't think that they have to pay when they don't get direct benefits from it. . . . In fact, I was like that, fairly self-absorbed and not interested in larger social issues that were not directly related to me.[53]

The meaning of money as an extension of capacity of an individual who has to carry out multiple functions and responsibilities resonates with theoretical insights on money in modern society as articulated by Karl Marx and Georg Simmel.[54] Approaching the topic of money from different angles, both Marx and Simmel converged on its enabling function for individuals who were separated from their traditional social networks based on families, kin groups, and neighbors as crucial mechanisms of access to resources. The enabling effect of possessing money and using it to buy and consume what one can choose has made money extremely appealing to numerous individuals. *It is in this sense that the market mechanism was not just colonizing civic activism but being adopted for its utility by individuals and civic organizations as a precondition for sustaining civic activism.*

The meaning of membership fees as an extension of individual capacity also reveals a shift in its meaning over time. In-depth interviews with multiple individuals over a decade in the four citizens' organizations show a broad change in terms of their common understanding of civic activism from a sense of obligation or duty to an individual interest in and choice for what is personally worthy and meaningful. The old meaning of financially supporting a citizens' organization highlights a recurring sense of being indebted to their friends, acquaintances, or even strangers who sacrificed themselves to work for social and political change and their wish to do their own share when they became able to do so. The sense of indebtedness implies either a concrete personal connection to individual activists or an emotional or ideological connection to the era of democratization movements during which an interviewee came of an age and matured. Migyeong, a woman in her late forties who left student activism and became a small business owner to support her family after marrying and having children, describes her motivation for supporting PSPD.

> I gave up my privilege as a daughter of an affluent family and became a student activist. I couldn't imagine my present life back then. I was living in a

shabby house [with other political activists]. We're so poor. One morning a senior fellow died from carbon monoxide poisoning. It was so senseless that he ended his life like that. He was very bright. It was too much to bear. I felt regret and frustration. It seems that I *feel indebted* in my mind and I become a supporter and helper of activists. There are a lot of people like this around me. While there are former student activists who capitalize on their past to get ahead, there are also people like me who *carry a burden* in their mind.[55]

She belongs to an age cohort commonly known as the 586 generation (born in the 1960s, attended college in the 1980s, and reached in their fifties during the 2010s) whose lives were profoundly shaped by student movements for democratization. Although there are individual variations among members of this cohort, its subset tends to develop a lingering sense of being indebted. This contributed to their support for civic activism or becoming staff activists of citizens' organizations. At the same time, some former political activists of this generation have become the current Establishment in South Korea, joining political, economic, and cultural elites.

A relatively new meaning of the membership fee as an extension of individual capacity highlights the pursuit of individual interests and their search for meaningful things to do. There is a striking absence of the expression "being indebted" in this recent interpretation for financially supporting a citizens' organization. Instead, there are recurring references to doing what an individual is interested in. Jun-hui, a member of FOA for seven years, describes her own involvement story this way:

> I've *been interested in foreign migrants* for some time. Their situations were terrible. Now things are a bit better for them, but fundamental conditions have not changed. The media still report migrants issues from a perspective of charity, and I can't believe all these. Korean people have been wronged and suffered a lot, haven't we? How can our society treat migrants like that after having gone through much hardship ourselves? I was studying political science in a graduate school, but *it was not fun*. So I took a leave of absence and was *looking for something interesting to do*. I ran into the FOA and was suggested for an internship. I worked as an intern for six months, and I managed various activities like a staff activist. Then I quit the internship and took a teacher's employment test. Since I began my teaching job, I've been just paying the membership fees.[56]

Paid employment enables Jun-hui to spend her money to do what is interesting and meaningful to her, but simultaneously it constrains her from becoming more involved as she did during her unpaid internship. This dynamic of paid work and lack of time and energy for other activities, including civic activism, contributes to the spread of advocacy organizations like PSPD in which the members' main contribution is to pay their dues. This resonates with Simmel's theoretical insight that money-based urban society produces and promotes associations or organizations that allow for fleeting or low-intensity involvement.[57] This underlying transformation of civic activism from direct face-to-face participation to fleeting engagement and low-intensity involvement poses both a challenge and an opportunity for civic organizations pursuing activism. I return to this issue in the conclusion of this book.

A Growing Need to "Market" Their Organizations to Potential and Current Members and Supporters

Operating in the era of neoliberalism, the four citizens' organizations have been exposed to a growing trend to market themselves to potential and current members and supporters. As discussed previously, in the noncommercial interpretations of membership fees, these organizations usually do not interpret the recruitment of new members and supporters as well as maintaining current members and supporters in the language of marketing. Yet the broader social and cultural context of neoliberal South Korea dominated by the market turns the recruitment and maintenance into selling social movement issues by publicizing them as being worthy of members' monetary contribution. Two related factors are at work here: (1) stagnation or even a decrease of membership size, and (2) a growing competition for attention and money from the public as consumers and citizens. There is a significant difference between PSPD and the three smaller local organizations in terms of their acceptance of or susceptibility to marketing as a technique of organizational management.

As discussed in chapter 2, the four citizens' organizations have experienced stagnation or decreases in membership in the context of economic insecurity and the precarity of life that have become pervasive and intensified by neoliberal globalization. This common problem has forced them to consider specific diagnoses and remedies. Although there are differences in their diagnoses and remedies, common remedies include more active or effective promotion of their activism and identification of members' interests and concerns. These basic rational remedies to increase their members inevitably involve dealing with the growing competition for attention and money from the public as Korean society has become more and more market dominated. Consequently, civic activism has become only one of multiple leisure activities that can be pursued during nonworking hours; a plethora of leisure and entertainment options attract attention and money from the public as consumers. Moreover, there are numerous civic organizations pursuing diverse issues. To become visible and recognizable, the four citizens' organizations are exposed, to varying degrees, to a trend to professionalize their publicity and communication and adopt marketing techniques. In conveying how PSPD has modified its programs for lay members over time, Yeong-sik, a staff activist in charge of members' activities, explains:

> In 2009 we reopened our "citizens' education" and it's been running quite well.... In the past, just like other [citizens'] organizations, we used this program to publicize our activities and achievement. But now we pay attention to mutual learning and communication with members beyond the one-way transmission of information. So we offer what people need, as well as what we need to educate. In the past, we naturally dealt with political and social issues but after the reopening, we developed classes on arts, humanities, and even self-exploration.[58]

This diversification reflects a larger social context into which both commercial and public venues for adult education have explosively expanded since enactment of the Lifetime Education Act and Ordinance in 1999.[59] This legal change coincided with the gradual spread of a five-day workweek and more leisure time. These social changes led to the proliferation of commercial Culture Centers offering classes on arts, humanities, health and fitness, and self-exploration and discovery. Many local governments also joined the trend by opening or expanding their local Culture Centers as an integral component of public welfare facilities. The neoliberal transformation of South Korea has synergized with the old popular interest in education and cultivation as an enduring status symbol. Encouraged to see themselves as human capital whose values need to be maximized through investment in themselves in various forms, a large number of individuals has taken advantage of these opportunities. Consequently, progressive citizens' organizations that have offered adult education classes for their current or potential members have been compelled to compete with commercial and public facilities.

However, the four citizens' organizations are not equally equipped with the necessary resources for such an upgrade and professionalization. As a large advocacy organization, PSPD is more equipped than the other three organizations and hence more susceptible to the allure of marketing techniques than its smaller local counterparts. To retain its members, PSPD has emphasized how to cultivate an enduring sense of belonging among members by communicating with them. Over time it has developed various techniques to mitigate the impersonal nature of its large membership. It established and has modified the practices of welcoming new members with orientation kits and thanking continuing members with anniversary gifts for their lasting commitment. Since the early 2010s, it has updated its publicity and communication by expanding its online presence in Facebook, Twitter (now X), Kakao Talk, and podcasts.[60] In the context of publicizing its activism to potential members and supporters, as well as maintaining existing ones, PSPD began to use the language of marketing and discuss how to promote and protect its "brand."[61] In recent years, it has repeatedly mentioned the necessity of using marketing professionals for more effective publicity.[62] This is a significant change from several years ago when publicity was not seen in the language of branding and professional marketing. When I interviewed Gi-yeong, a staff activist in his thirties who began as a volunteer activist, he shared this observation of publicity efforts in 2009:

> This year we did publicity campaigns, like Flower of Sharing campaign, several times with *Hangyoreh Newspaper*. It's an annual event to announce "please support the PSPD and become a member." But as the team leader [referring to his colleague being interviewed together with him] pointed out, we gain a sizable increase of our membership through the success of our projects and positive recognition from it, rather than publicity campaigns. It doesn't mean that we don't make direct publicity efforts. We have a Communication Team that is planning to collaborate with other newspapers to carry out such campaigns.[63]

The emphasis on substance rather than marketing of image is distinguishable from the naturalized use of the term *brand*. It remains to be seen if PSPD's interest in efficiency and professionalization will lead to the corporatization documented by Dauvergne and Lebaron. Studies of French transnational NGOs show that professionalization does not automatically mean business corporatization, the dominant trend in the United States, or being subject to the government's control.[64] Here again the meaning of civic identity that the four citizens' organizations maintain and promote is critical to a specific outcome.

As local organizations with fewer resources and far fewer members, both DFS branches and FOA have been less susceptible to the allure of marketing techniques. As feminist organizations aspiring to support and empower local women, GY Branch and NE Branch approached the problem of stagnant or decreasing membership not through marketing techniques but through their substantial engagement with existing members and identification of diverse interests and concerns of local women. Yet the paucity of resources, especially staff and volunteer activists, has prevented them from pursuing this solution for years. Their few staff activists are already overworked carrying out multiple projects financed by public funds, and they cannot pay sufficient attention to existing members.[65] As a smaller local organization, FOA has increasingly relied on internet communication with its current members and potential members who visit its website. It has largely avoided the pressure of marketing in accordance with its civic identity, which pursues social movement and social change by questioning the status quo.[66]

Reenvisioning Civic Activism as "Fun, Enjoyable, and Thereby Sustainable" Activities

The most profound influence of the market dominance on civic activism can be identified in reenvisioning activism as fun and enjoyable activities in order to be sustainable. The shifting perception and attitudes emerged in direct response to the 2008 explosion of spontaneous massive candlelight protests against the import of U.S. beef suspected of having mad cow disease (see chapter 4).[67] Not organized by any established citizens' organizations, the protests began with a few junior high school students who were deeply worried about unsafe food and expanded swiftly through social media. Most participants in these offline protests, which took place from May to July of 2008, were citizens without any previous involvement in activism or social movements. Outside the influence of established citizens' organizations, grassroots citizens of various age and all walks of life were motivated by their shared concern about food safety and shared demand for proper government handling of the matter. In the process of their collective interactions, these participants turned their protests into occasions for festive and fun activities.[68] In response to the spontaneous mass protests, major citizens' organizations including PSPD joined them in support of grassroots citizens. This development profoundly shook citizens' organizations in terms of their movement's culture, which was characterized by rather rigid rituals and a somber spirit.

Historically, consumer capitalism played an active role in promoting fun, enjoyment, and play as legitimate sources of motivation against a sense of duty or obligation inculcated by religious and other traditions. This cultural shift has replaced the spirit of seriousness and formality in various political and social areas, including civic activism. As this logic of the market is adopted, I argue that the meaning of fun, enjoyment, and play have been reinterpreted by members of citizens' organizations. The spirit of fun, enjoyment, and play has been an integral attribute of being human, but multiple layers of intricate social mechanisms had suppressed and regulated this for various reasons. As major social theorists have analyzed from different angles, consumer culture has reversed the practices of asceticism and antimaterialism in many traditional cultures around the world, including major world religions. By aggressively spreading instant gratification and "repressive desublimation" (à la Marcuse) among growing masses of people for convenient and ubiquitous commodity consumption, consumer culture has replaced the ascetic discipline and somber spirit for hard work to produce and a duty to maintain a collectivity, which founded the industrial capitalist world. The prevailing ethos of consumer culture has been characterized by fun, pleasure or enjoyment, and play, coupled with the messages of liberation or empowerment tied to personal choice, expression, and self-improvement.[69] By validating and popularizing fun, enjoyment, and play, consumer capitalism has anointed them as the desirable and legitimate source of motivation and even as the goal. Their escalating importance as a source of self-motivation and goals in our time reveals the decline of the spirit of seriousness and formality in various areas of public and private lives in modern and postmodern societies.[70] Consequently, we are living in a world in which not only rest and leisure activities but also learning, working, healing, eating, and praying should be fun, playful, and enjoyable. Now civic activism in South Korea has joined the band wagon!

The theoretical and empirical studies of commercial culture and consumerism document both positive and negative consequences for individuals and society. The positive affirmation of commercial culture highlights its individualizing and democratizing tendency. As Simmel argued, money as the medium of exchange in the capitalist economy is profoundly individualizing in that it frees individuals from family, kinship, and community as sources of security and satisfaction for their needs and desires.[71] Regardless of ascriptive social status, commercial culture can turn everyone with money or credit into a consumer who is supposed to gain equal access to buying and selling in a marketplace. In particular, commercial culture in urban areas has liberated women and the young from traditional patriarchal controls in their communities and families.[72] This equalizing tendency to undermine traditional hierarchy has allowed individuals to make their own choices in various matters of life. The increasing significance of individual choice goes beyond the mundane activities of buying and selling goods and services. Even religion has been profoundly reshaped by the forces of commercialization. Major world religions, including Buddhism, Christianity, and Islam, have adopted the commercial paradigm and have been transformed into a matter of lifestyle choices for individuals. As religious authorities decline, individuals can mix and match their own religious beliefs and practices from the marketplace of diverse religions. For its survival and relevance, organized religion competes to recruit lay members by using an array of commercial and marketing techniques.[73] Although there are long histories of coexistence and symbiosis between markets and places of worship in many societies, this contemporary commercialization is qualitatively distinct in the transformation of religion into individual consumer choice with "minimalistic" loyalty and commitment.[74]

Given the stagnation or decrease of grassroots participation in the four citizens' organizations (and beyond) for a decade or two, reenvisioning activism as fun and enjoyable activities would be compelling for its sustainability. To my question about how civic organizations like PSPD can improve its sustainability, Gi-yeong replied:

We lack personnel very much to communicate with members online and offline. We cannot attend to a large number of our members. *These days people need to enjoy their activities.* We've been encouraging our members to join offline activities if they agree with us. This is certainly important, but we are not doing well in terms of facilitating our members to do what they desire to do. We don't decide and just tell them what to do, but we work with them to find out what they want to do. We certainly need to fight for urgent matters, but we also need to study together and reflect on basic values like progress, justice, etc.[75]

His words recognize that lay members will enjoy their involvement in activism if they can pursue what they want to do, and he suggests that staff activists need to work with them by talking, thinking, and studying together. This type of fun and enjoyment is evidently different from those of commodity consumption. In the context of the civic organization, sources of fun and enjoyment are redefined. This positive appropriation continued over time. Reflecting on his work as a full-time activist, Yeong-sik commented:

As I mentioned earlier, the point [about activism] is sustainability. So we can produce good results. Endurance and sustainability will enhance our knowhow and capacity. We [he and his colleagues] talk a lot about how we can work *with fun and laughter*. In the past social movement was coupled with dedication and sacrifice. This has changed a whole lot, and now we look for what is *enjoyable and sustainable*.[76]

His view resonates with annual evaluations of lecture programs offered under "akademi neutinamu" [academy zelkova tree]. The programs were considered to be one-way inculcation without dynamic interactions and dialogues with participants. It also resonates with the recurring emphasis on making PSPD activities and accomplishments easy for the public as well as its members to accesss and understand.[77] Reenvisioning civic activism as fun and enjoyable activities is closely connected to PSPD's ongoing modification of its civic identity. To make civic activism fun and enjoyable, the civic organization needs to shake up its old culture of formality and hierarchy, which still separates professional activists from lay members or volunteer activists, and facilitate what motivates them to get involved for social change.

GY Branch and NE Branch of DFS have been dealing with the same challenge of how to make activism fun and enjoyable in order to be sustainable. The annual review of the NE Branch captures the common underlying challenge in the language of a paradigm shift in how to make feminist activism relevant and appealing to ordinary citizens.

> Activism is possible only through moving people emotionally. In the past, the typical movement method was to identify gender issues, monitor, resist, and criticize problems for change. Indignation energized activism. . . . Now *this method seems to be neither appealing nor interesting to people.* We need to understand how local women feel about their daily lives to identify issues compelling to them. We need to address concrete problems in their daily routine that burden and trouble their lives. To do so, first of all, I suggest that we *begin with what people like and enjoy*; programs and activities that are *rather light and interesting.*[78]

The somber spirit to identify and solve problems of gender inequality, which was fueled by indignation for injustice, does not motivate ordinary people troubled by various problems any more. The feminist civic organization needs to figure out what motivates them, and a sensible way to do so in the neoliberal society is to begin with what people find enjoyable and fun. Although this suggested shift is not a panacea for declining interest in civic activism and has its own shortcomings, the recognition of fun and enjoyment as legitimate and desirable sources of motivation ironically reflects the logic of consumer capitalism that percolates through the local branches.[79]

For FOA, a smaller local organization that was established much later than PSPD and the DFS branches, the centrality of personal interest and enjoyment to members' support for and participation in it has been present from the beginning. Like Jun-hui, many others I interviewed conveyed a common theme of personal interest and enjoyment as motivations for getting involved in the organization. For various reasons, they developed an interest in foreign migrant issues and shared FOA's emphasis on building solidarity with them as equal human beings and friends. Its small size makes communication and maintenance of the basic values more manageable. Although members have different reasons for their interest in migrant issues, it is personal interest and a sense of meaningful enjoyment that sustained their support and participation in FOA's activities. Those who worked as volunteer teachers of the Korean language for foreign migrants found their work "interesting" and "enjoyable." They enjoyed their interactions with migrants and developed meaningful human relationships through the medium of teaching the Korean language.

Now a challenge for citizens' organizations in reenvisioning civic activism would be how to reclaim what constitutes fun and enjoyment in the face of a powerful commercial culture that has historically anointed them as a dominant source of motivation. As Gi-yeong articulated, fun and enjoyment can be redefined as thinking, studying, and acting together to figure out how to understand our own lives and hopefully to solve our problems. Many active members of DFS branches found their activism "interesting" and "enjoyable" because it provided them with opportunities for reviving and developing their nondomestic skills and expanding their interactions with other people until their involvement became overburdened due to the lack of personnel. They also enjoyed the fellowship and camaraderie of like-minded people not only in face-to-face interactions but also when they do not meet and interact personally. Active members of FOA enjoyed their personal interactions with foreign migrants and cultivated human relationships with them. At the same time, what feels like fun and is enjoyable to most people in consumer capitalist society is already structured or "overdetermined," and fewer and fewer people seem to find activism for social change fun and enjoyable. Most human beings would enjoy activities and experiences that are affirming, beautiful, and caring without excessive stress, which stems from rigid hierarchy and competition. Such activities and experiences would include artistic, healing, intellectual, sporting, and other respectful interactions with other human beings. The citizens' organizations need to infuse these activities into reinterpreting and practicing activism as fun and enjoyment.

CONSTRAINED BY THE MARKET: CHALLENGE OF SUSTAINING AND REPRODUCING PAID ACTIVISTS

Civic activism pursued by the four citizens' organizations ultimately relies on full-time or part-time staff activists who carry out their routine operations from day to day. Officers as volunteer professional advisors and lay members as supporters and volunteer activists are important, but staff activists are indispensable to their organized and sustained form of activism.

NEGOTIATING WITH THE MARKET IN NEOLIBERAL SOUTH KOREA

As discussed in chapters 4 through 6, the transformation of Korean society has led to the stagnation or decrease of lay memberships in the four civic organizations. As the major source of financing, membership fees are directly connected to the sustainability of staff activists and thereby their generational reproduction as well. In combination with overwork, inadequate pay generally resulted in frequent job turnover for a majority of staff activists. The inadequate pay was insufficient to raise children and support a family. This was a major reason for full-time staff turnover, especially among male staff, whose gender role expectation still included being a primary family provider.[80] As the market has grown ever more dominant, inadequate pay has also led to a common difficulty in recruiting a younger generation of activists.[81] The total number of applicants for staff activist positions decreased in major citizens' organizations, and those who would apply called to inquire about salary. This younger generation of staff view themselves as employees rather than as activists.[82] Even in 2006, a survey of two hundred full-time activists of citizens' organizations showed that the majority of them were satisfied with their work as activists, but the younger they were the more they were interested in changing their career. Their alternative career options included academia (26 percent), self-employment (16 percent), government or university research centers (14 percent), and others including a return to farming (17.5 percent); only 3.5 percent listed a political career.[83]

The common problems of sustaining staff activists and their generational reproduction affected the four citizens' organizations somewhat differently.[84] PSPD, a leading organization with relatively more resources, raised salary and improved other working conditions for its full-time staff activists.[85] As a leading citizens' organization, it attracted graduates of "prestigious" universities in South Korea. Although many of the PSPD staff found their work meaningful and fulfilling, they had to cope with financial difficulties especially if they had a family to support. Some of them had spouses who earned secure incomes, and others stayed on in their activist positions for a few years until their personal lives required that they find a sufficient source of income.[86] Gwan-su, a staff-activist for seven years, shared his own experience:

> When I was single, I wasn't thinking about salary because it was fine for covering my own expenses. After getting married, I encountered a different situation. Anyhow recently, wages have decreased for many people in

our country, but our salary remained the same. As a result, our salary level increased relatively. There are numerous people unemployed, especially among the young. So among those who apply to the PSPD, there are so many people with extremely high education. This is a trend these days. Even entry-level white-collar salarymen are highly educated with MA degrees and other credentials. So staff activists cannot draw their moral authority from sacrificing despite their high educational qualifications. Instead, I think we need to be paid adequately in comparison with a standard of decent living in our society. Moral authority alone would no longer work to sustain staff activists.

[To pay staff activists adequately] we need more members, and more revenue enables us to hire more staff members. I've been thinking about this matter for some time. The whole boundary of NGOs should expand as a field. So some of us here change jobs after a while and can come back. If the PSPD is the only one around, we have to go into another field and cannot come back. I am not sure if I can call it industry, but this kind of service field should expand and *become recognized as a regular industry*. Then there can be positive competition and improvement of services and the salary can improve.[87]

What is noteworthy about his thoughtful comments is that the political economy of maintaining and reproducing staff activists dictates the adoption of the market logic as a rational way to run the organization. Although this is not identical with the commercial corporatization through branded marketing and sales of branded goods, the more basic mechanism of the market exerts a powerful pressure to professionalize activism. In fact, the market logic accepted by Kwan-soo was echoed by a lay member who used to be a former activist. Mi-gyeong, a middle-aged businesswoman, spoke about activism as a job:

Relatively speaking, the PSPD has more young staff members. This means that it is getting by OK. It has more resources, more supporters, and therefore it can afford to select high-quality activists. It seems that everything is ruled by the logic of capital. I'd like to ask this. You guys talk about general will but *strictly speaking activism is your job. If so, you need to produce a result, and that's what the market dictates*. If you work this much, there has to be results of that work. We human beings want to see concrete results. I support them but cruelly supporters have to ask them what they have produced.[88]

Most of the members I interviewed tended to stress how they were impressed by the hard-working staff activists, but Mi-gyeong's voice, especially as a businesswoman, revealed the increasing influence on civic activism of the market logic of rationally calculating input and output.

The ascendance of the market as a core mechanism of neoliberalism was accompanied by the political and cultural shift in society. The first generation of activists in the citizens' organizations usually hailed from college student activism and related social connections and therefore accepted financial disadvantage as an integral aspect of pursuing their meaningful work. But this group was replaced by a younger generation who viewed professional activism as a paid employment and career. Student activism as an enduring aspect of campus culture rapidly declined as neoliberalism restructured higher education in Korean society. As PSPD expanded and became better known to the public, it hired a younger generation of full-time staff through open public recruitment, and this new group consider themselves professional "employees" rather than dedicated "activists."[89] Young-so, a seasoned staff activist made this observation:

> **YEONG-SO:** When you look at our staff activists, we have more younger ones than before. They have not experienced students' movement, and they have a different perspective.
> **MOON:** Do they consider activism as a job?
> **YEONG-SO:** Oftentimes so. I don't think that is negative but natural. In the past staff activists joined the PSPD to pursue institutional reforms and agonized greatly about them. Now, younger activists join us after seeing our campaigns and projects because those activities resonate with their own interests. Put it specifically, they are more interested in social welfare or labor issues rather than social movement. This type of fellows makes up a majority among staff activists who join us now.[90]

For DFS's GY and NE branches, the problems of sustainability and generational reproduction of staff activists were more precarious, especially after separation of the food co-op and the subsequent reduction in their membership. They managed the financial difficulty by seeking public funds from local governments and public interest foundations, but these external funds ironically undermined their ability to strengthen their membership base.[91] Although ideologically maintaining their identities as local social movement organizations promoting grassroots women's participation and empowerment, in practice they functioned as social welfare service providers. The executive offices of the GY and NE branches relied on full-time or part-time activists, but frequent turnovers generated instability and weakened their ability to communicate with members. During the decade of the conservative government and the financial crisis, reproducing leadership for the local branches became more difficult. Election of the progressive mayor of Seoul Metropolitan also had an unintended consequence that further weakening activities of local citizens' organizations because he attracted local activists into government-sponsored projects and activities.[92] In responding to my question about major obstacles to sustainability of the local branches of DFS, Won-jin, a staff activist in her thirties who worked in both local branches and the headquarters, offered this opinion.

> First of all, monthly pay [of staff activists] is quite low even though it is over the minimum wage. It has to increase to an adequate level. But in fact, this cannot be done because we have a limited source of financial support. A majority of our members are women, and they cannot make large financial contributions. . . . Another problem is relative deprivation among younger activists. Unlike the older generation who were influenced by student movement culture, they view their activist work as employment. They compare their working conditions with those of their friends and acquaintances working in big corporations. If you do so, it would be hard to continue, but I also have a different view. Of course, the monthly pay needs to be raised, but I also think that *our generation grew up under the capitalist system and became so dependent on material things. It'd be very important to realize such dependency.* I live as an activist and money is not sufficient, but I can manage. It's not like activists are living miserably. Of course, if you have a child and family to support, you cannot work as an activist. That is really sad and deplorable.[93]

Her comments highlight a generational shift in terms of perception and attitude, along with the practical problem of pay insufficient to support a family. Coupled with widespread employment insecurity, the dominance of the market turned human activities, including civic activism, into commodified labor. Only those who can resist this dominant value through critical reflection can endure in their work as paid activists. Yet these activists should be supported by a spouse or partner with a stable source of income or be single without any dependents.

FOA managed the problems of sustaining and reproducing staff activists by relying on volunteer activists and limiting its activities to what its resources allowed them to do. Although this was not an ideal situation, it sustained its commitment to the integrity of its civic identity. It gradually evolved into a more internet-based citizens' organization in which its staff activist coordinated programs for its members as volunteer activists. Although this staff activist was committed, the heavy reliance on one or two individuals did not secure its long-term viability. Similarly, there was the underlying problem of its stability and generational reproduction, which stemmed from the small membership base and its primary reliance on limited membership fees.

CONCLUSION

In this chapter I examined how and to what extent the four civic organizations have negotiated with the market as a dominant force in neoliberal South Korea in pursuing their activism and maintaining their civic identities. Ongoing interactions between these organizations and the market reveal a complex relationship. The comparative discussion of these civic organizations illustrates diverging as well as converging patterns in these relationships. To begin with common patterns, in response to the global spread of "social contribution activities" of business corporations, all of them have kept a distance from this trend by choice and by default. On the one hand, they adhered to their moral code and civic identity as organizations that pursue democratizing social change; therefore, they were cautious about direct monetary engagement with business corporations. On the other hand, in the context of conservative governments and recurring financial crises, business corporations did not reach out to them as social movement organizations. At the same time, all of the organizations have adopted the ubiquitous market practice of monetary payment as the fundamental marker of membership and commitment. At a deeper level, all of these organizations have been influenced by consumerism that is aggressively promoted by the neoliberal market and market constraints on the maintenance and reproduction of their staff activists.

The first influence is reflected in the recurring discussion of making civic activism fun and enjoyable. This shifting view allows us to see the power of commercial culture that has anointed fun and enjoyment as legitimate and even desirable sources of motivation and the gradual acceptance of this public sentiment by the citizens' organizations and their activists. Although activists reinterpret the content of fun and enjoyment away from commercial culture, they have adopted this rhetorical symbol to remain relevant and relatable to the public. The second influence is reflected in the common challenge of paying adequate salaries to full-time activists.

For diverging patterns, the four civic organizations show a varying degree in the acceptance of marketing to deal with the growing pressure to publicize their activities and increase their membership size as the source of finance. In terms of marketing technique and professionalization, a larger organization like PSPD that focuses on national issues and influence has been more prone to professionalization, albeit not necessarily in the manner of commercialization observed by global NGOs. But PSPD is more susceptible to the language of professional marketing in reaching out to potential members and publicizing their civic identity and activities. For both DFS local branches and FOA, the allure of marketing techniques and professionalization are far less appealing for both ideological and practical reasons. In terms of resisting the neoliberal market by developing social relations that are alternatives to the logic of profit, deregulation, and privatization, each organization developed its own unique practice with varying degrees of success. PSPD established donations of goods as a routine process for obtaining necessary resources. As an important aspect of its gift economy, this practice serves both practical and symbolic functions; it brings its members and staff activists together in their cooperation and enhances their understanding of interdependence and feelings of gratitude, thereby contributing to a sense of solidarity and community. The GY and NE branches of DFS experimented with organic food co-ops as a space for cultivating and expanding noncommercial and communitarian relationships around food consumption. FOA has encouraged prefigurative practices by its members to cultivate solidarity with foreign migrants as fellow human beings and friends. Unfortunately, the co-op's experiment came to an end precisely because it had to compete with commercial businesses in the expanding market for organic and environmentally friendly food.

At the same time, this challenge highlights the need to develop a strategy and tactics to engage with market forces in pursuing civic activism. The food co-op, as an integral component of the feminist organization and as a vehicle to reach out to local women, contributed to the growing public awareness about food safety and environmental issues.

In the next chapter, I examine how these organizations negotiated with neoliberal governance.

Chapter Four

NEOLIBERAL GOVERNANCE I

Collaborative Law and Policymaking and Undermining Grassroots Participation

> Governance is not identical with or exclusive to neoliberalism; it was not part of the neoliberal imaginary set out by Milton Friedman or F. A. Hayek and had little place in neoliberal transformations in Latin America or South Asia in the 1970s and 1980s. However, as it matured and converged with neoliberalism, governance has become neoliberalism's primary administrative form, the political modality through which it creates environments, structures, constraints and incentives, and hence conducts subjects.
>
> —WENDY BROWN, *UNDOING THE DEMOS*, 122

> "Partnership and new governance" were the founding slogans of the NGO-Government Cooperation Forum. Back then [2003], members of the forum who were senior officers of the central government were unfamiliar with the term, governance. But now [2014] it is accepted as a common-sense word by even ordinary people, as well as government officials, activists of citizens' organizations, those related to business, and researchers.
>
> —HYEONG-YONG YI, "THE STATE, DESIGNED WITH GOVERNANCE," 388

Introduced to South Korea in the context of neoliberal globalization, governance has evolved to become a new paradigm of organizing the state–society relationship in the name of promoting democracy in the twenty-first century.[1] Translated in Korean as collaborative ruling, which refers to the collaboration among diverse social actors to solve a problem, governance generally conveys positive connotations in tune with competence and democracy. Few people can argue against the ideas of collaboration and partnership as few people can do so against kindness, love, or happiness. Precisely because of the commonsense understanding of these words, political organizations and actors mobilize them as a rhetorical tool to "frame" their identities and practices appealingly and thereby obfuscate reality or even mislead their actual and potential supporters. As discussed in the introduction, I use governance as a key concept to capture the altering and altered relationships among the state, business, NGOs, and individuals. Neoliberal governance refers to "governing that is networked, integrated, cooperative, partnered, disseminated, and at least partly self-organized" under the rubric of "business model and business metrics."[2]

Recognizing that civic activism is neither a panacea nor a moral paragon, in this chapter I examine how neoliberal governance enables and constrains the civic activism pursued by the People's Solidarity for Participatory Democracy (PSPD) in the twenty-first century. In the aftermath of two global financial crises (1997 and 2008), neoliberalism as a hegemonic political rationality has transformed South Korean society, including the relations between the state and society. In the name of "liberalizing" and "globalizing" the economy, politics, and society, the Korean state, regardless of the political orientation of the ruling party, has promoted deregulation and privatization in terms of collecting and distributing crucial resources. As a result, economic inequality has skyrocketed, and a majority of people in South Korea have been exposed to intensifying widespread employment insecurity and precarity of life in general.[3] In coping with these major problems, neoliberal governance brought together the government and citizens' organizations and thereby simultaneously enabled the pursuit of democratization by citizens' organizations and undermined it.

The salient examples of activism discussed here include a series of movements to promote universal social welfare for all citizens; reform big business unhinged by deregulation in an effort to democratize the economy, protect small business owners and ordinary citizens as financial consumers; and to stop the Free Trade Agreements between South Korea and the United States (KORUS FTA). These examples together show the extent to which neoliberal governance enabled PSPD activism by creating political opportunities for cooperation and partnership between the state and leading citizens' organizations and the extent to which neoliberal governance constrained such activism by imposing the rules of neoliberal order and closing the boundary of negotiation in partnership. In taking advantage of political opportunities, PSPD reinterpreted neoliberal governance by insisting on the notion of public interests, which neoliberal governance undermines through business practices of privatization, deregulation, and wealth accumulation. Although pursued by different paths, PSPD's civic activism focused on legal and policy changes at the national level. In the absence of stable progressive political parties that carry out research and devise policies, PSPD prioritized its role as a quasi-political party and functioned primarily as a sentinel for the political and economic powers and secondarily as a protector of the vulnerable through legal and policy changes. This role of a quasi-political party has been somewhat modified by the presence of a progressive party since the 2000s; cooperation with this party became an option. This repertoire of activism generated enduring and recurring tension with its civic identity based on the moral code of grassroots participation.

The organizational feature of PSPD as an advocacy group run by full-time staff activists necessitates a comparison with advocacy NGOs elsewhere that are also professionalized in the context of neoliberal globalization. Critical studies of such NGOs argue that they are not so much a vehicle of democratization that promotes equality, participation, and civility, which the liberal perspective on civil society idealizes or romanticizes as "corporatization," "co-optation," or "neoliberal pacification" of social movements and activism.[4] Here specific sociopolitical and historical contexts matter a great deal, and we need to recognize significant local variations in advocacy NGOs without overgeneralizing them. Rather than presuming their fixed nature, NGOs needs to "be understood as being fluid and protean, composed of a diverse spectrum of non-state organizations capable of both challenging and extending the influence of neoliberalism."[5] Against the hegemonic rise of neoliberalism, citizens' organizations in South Korea have forged their moral codes and struggled to adhere to them to maintain their civic identity. Local specificity and contingency explain precisely why we need to pay attention to how PSPD activism is related to neoliberal governance in South Korea.

MONITORING POLITICAL AND ECONOMIC POWERS AND PROTECTING ORDINARY CITIZENS

To examine how PSPD negotiated with neoliberal governance in pursuing its activism, I discuss the following four movements: (1) movements to expand social welfare for all citizens, (2) movements to reform big business (chaebol: economic conglomerates fostered by the developmental state in the past), (3) movements to protect small business owners and ordinary citizens as financial consumers, and (4) movements to stop the KORUS FTA. According to PSPD's own accounts, these movements represented its major activism efforts and were formative for its civic identity and growth.[6] These movements together established and maintained its civic identity as a monitor of the major economic and political powers and protector/supporter of ordinary citizens and the marginalized in society. When the state and society were undergoing neoliberal restructuring, PSPD carried out these movements to solve widespread problems of economic insecurity and precarity of life. Lasting for different time spans with varying degrees of success, these movements show the ways in which PSPD and its members understood their activism and dealt with the organization's civic identity in response to internal and external criticism of its activism and their efforts to make their activism more participatory. As previously noted, there was an underlying tension between PSPD's identity as a professional advocacy organization and its ideological commitment to grassroots participation in its activism. It often mobilized the horizontal network of social movement organizations to take advantage of political openings for partnership with the government in making and reforming law and policy. However, this enabling condition also led to the production and reproduction of the internal structure of hierarchy between lay members and professional staff activists in terms of cultural/symbolic capital. The analysis of PSPD activism shows that neoliberal governance allowed for such activism as long as it did not challenge its core logic of privatization, deregulation, and capital accumulation.

Movements to Establish Social Welfare for All Citizens

Developing in the decades of neoliberal globalization, PSPD's activism to establish social welfare for all citizens was formative for its civic identity. Its first task-oriented committee was the Social Welfare Special Committee, and its first task aimed at instituting a "national minimum living standard for all Koreans." A series of universal social welfare activism efforts carried out by PSPD focused on ensuring minimum standards for income, health care, education, housing, employment, and the provision of specific care or support services. This line of activism gained special urgency in the aftermath of the IMF crisis when unemployment, homelessness, suicide, and family dissolution became widespread. These activism efforts also questioned the dominant view of welfare as "benevolent charity" for the needy by the state and promoted welfare as "all citizens' right that the state is responsible for."[7] Between June of 1998 and September of 1999, PSPD played a leading role in the coalition movement to legislate a new social welfare law, later named the National Basic Living Protection Law.[8] In solidarity with a wide range of organizations representing labor, religion, the poor, and women, PSPD joined force with the Kim Dae-jung government, which was sympathetic to progressive civic activism. PSPD organized public policy hearings, drafted bills, and collaborated with major political parties for support. The law was enacted in 1999 and has been in effect since October 1, 2000. When the conservative Park Geun-hye government (2013–2017) attempted to undo this law, PSPD resisted this and successfully organized a coalition movement.[9] In recent years, it has tried to expand actual beneficiaries of the protection law by revising it.[10]

The legal and policy activism for universal welfare was the turf of PSPD officers and full-time staff activists. The core actors of this movement were lawyers and professors specializing in social welfare issues, and they were supported by dedicated staff and volunteer activists. Because of their professional expertise (cultural capital), the progressive government invited these lawyers and scholars to join various committees working on social welfare. Interactions between these activist professionals and the government were not always symbiotic and smooth because the former advocated for universal welfare for all citizens, roughly on the model of the welfare state in Western Europe in the 1950s and 1960s. But Kim Dae-jung's government was pressured to work within the neoliberal paradigm particularly with regard to flexible labor, essentially a euphemism for capital's right to fire labor at its will. These professionals dealt with their disagreement and power imbalance with the government by relying on a broad coalition of diverse social movement organizations that included labor, women, religion, the disabled, and teachers because they were not narrowly tied to any specific social groups working for their own welfare but were promoting welfare as a public interest for all citizens.[11]

Another source of significant conflict was between PSPD activists and the democratizing state's administrative and legislative bureaucracies with their vested interests and inertia. As serious discussion of a social welfare bill began in 1999, various government departments and offices clashed with the Budget Planning Office over funding for new welfare programs. The Ministry of Labor and the Ministry of Social Welfare continued to disagree on budgetary matters tied to legislation in the bill until President Kim

Dae-jung publicly announced his decision to establish the National Basic Living Protection Law. Legislators in the National Assembly who dealt with the welfare bill showed a lack of understanding and urgency in passing the bill. PSPD activists, in coalition with the diverse citizens' organizations, persuaded both major political parties represented in the National Assembly and put pressure on them. Leaders of the coalition of citizens' organizations also persuaded the Hannara Party, the conservative opposition party, in face-to-face meetings and brought together two pivotal legislators from the ruling party and the opposition party to pass the bill.[12]

This welfare activism confirmed and maintained PSPD's civic identity as a professional advocacy organization, but it did not go well with its ideological commitment to grassroots participation in its activism. To complement this professional advocacy activism, PSPD carried out a series of campaigns for living with a monthly minimum expense in shanty towns. After securing consent from residents of select shanty towns, it reached out to volunteers to participate in the experiment in 2004, 2007, and 2010. College students, legislators, and some celebrities, mostly non-PSPD members, joined staff activists to live in shanty towns and raised public awareness and pushed the government to raise the minimum living expense.[13] This activism developed into a movement to establish a "living wage" as opposed to a "minimum wage" in the 2010s.[14]

Although urgent and necessary for a large number of Koreans struggling to make a living, as well as substantive democratization of Korean society, the movements to establish social welfare for all citizens were structurally constrained by neoliberal governance. Despite PSPD's activism to turn social welfare into a universal right for all citizens, the Kim Dae-jung government—the first Korean government to pursue social welfare and social insurance as its core policy issue and work with citizens' organizations—established a social welfare system that became "regressive and selective." Essentially paired with secure employment, the system provided social protection for illness, unemployment, and aging for the middle strata of employees who are white-collar professionals or blue-collar workers of chaebol corporations.[15] The social welfare system overlooked the rapidly growing masses of people whose employment became insecure through the expansion of "flexible" labor practices, which has been a core aspect of neoliberal restructuring of the economy.[16] The system also overlooked the self-employed who were owners of small family businesses, which became impoverished by the further expansion of big businesses into their commercial interests. This economic group has rapidly grown as a result of the flexible labor regime that has undermined employment security, and their impoverishment has stemmed from the deregulation of big businesses.

PSPD (and cooperating citizens' organizations) intended to establish the National Basic Living Protection system as a modern public assistance program universally available to all citizens, but the government tied the system to secure employment, when paradoxically these working conditions had been rapidly eroded as a result of the neoliberal restructuring of the economy. Regardless of the political orientation of the ruling party, for the first two decades of the twenty-first century, the government adhered to traditional conditions such as the presence or absence of a family provider or supporter in determining eligibility of an individual recipient for basic living protection. Consequently, the incomplete expansion of the public social welfare system has aggravated inequality rather than mitigated it, and it has deepened the schism among three groups of Koreans: those who enjoy both public social welfare and private resources due to their secure employment; those who can access public social welfare but do not own private resources due to their fluctuating employment; and those who can access neither and rely on limited public aid due to their unemployment or underemployment.[17]

Movements to Reform Big Business Deregulated

A well-known component of this category of activism was a "small shareholders movement" that mobilized the obscure economic position of small shareholders to make big business accountable. Conventionally, citizens used their economic position as workers/producers and consumers to mobilize an organized labor movement and consumer movement. However, as the South Korean economy became more financialized and large corporations became increasingly preoccupied with generating short-term profits to satisfy their shareholders, PSPD recognized the potential for civic activism by small shareholders who, at least in theory, could come together to form a group large enough to exert some pressure on big business. PSPD symbolically used the small shareholders' rights to make big business accountable for their corrupt and undemocratic practices. The symbolic and performative nature of this movement does not reduce its significance in influencing PSPD's activism to reform big business. Rather, the characterization recognizes that the movement was initiated again by lawyers and scholars who had expertise on the workings of the capitalist economy as opposed to grassroots members of specific socioeconomic groups struggling for their economic interests.[18]

The small shareholders movement was formative in the establishment and consolidation of PSPD's civic identity as a sentinel to monitor the state and big business. The movement emerged in response to neoliberal globalization (in particular, financialization of the economy) and continued over a decade from the late 1990s to the late 2000s. Essentially, in association with neoliberal governance, this movement shows how the transformation of economic and political power in the twenty-first century generates the possibility of a new form of activism. In the context of democratization, in April of 1996, the Kim Young-sam government announced a "new big business policy" (*sindaegieop jeongchaek*) to reform the economic conglomerates' ways. But this reform for transparent and clean business practices was soon dislodged by the Asian financial crisis, which was caused in South Korea by big businesses' excessive loans to fund rapid expansions into unrelated fields. Following the dictates of the IMF rescue package, the government deregulated the economic conglomerates to provide the engine of national economic recovery and growth and shifted the IMF loss caused by businesses to the multitude of citizens, increasing financial support and tax benefits for big business.[19]

Innovatively tapping the position of small shareholders for civic activism, PSPD began its movement by joining the 1997 shareholders' general meeting of Jeil Bank, which provided Hanbo Steel with a series of massive loans; the steel company precipitated the 1997 Asian financial crisis in South Korea by opening the floodgate of failed loans given to major economic conglomerates. PSPD filed a lawsuit against the bank for its undemocratic decision-making during the shareholders' general meeting and won the case. Building on this victory, PSPD investigated the Samsung Group's succession from father to son and demanded accountability for the illegal transfer of wealth from the company to the owner's son, Jae-yong Lee. Samsung Electronics issued a large number of debentures to Mr. Lee to enable him to purchase a large number of its expensive blue-chip stocks at an artificially low price. PSPD mobilized a multitude of Samsung small shareholders to file a lawsuit against the economic powerhouse and pressed for reform and disclosure of crucial information to shareholders. It took twelve years, from 1997 to 2009, for the small shareholders and PSPD to win the case. In the meantime, similarly utilizing small shareholders' rights, PSPD expanded the movement to other major economic conglomerates, including Hyundae, Daewoo, LG, and SK in the aftermath of the IMF crisis. These major big businesses committed illegal or irregular practices of prioritizing the accumulation of private wealth in owners' families at the expense of the corporations' growth. To take advantage of the public sentiment for "Conglomerate Reform" and to promote grassroots participation, PSPD launched a "campaign to own ten shares of the major big corporations" throughout the late 1990s. As the advocate and representative of these small shareholders, PSPD participated in annual shareholders' meetings to challenge dubious and undemocratic corporate practices and filed lawsuits against powerful trustees.[20]

As the activism to reform big business through legislation and policy targeted the economic core of the neoliberal order, activist professionals and staff activists of PSPD had to deal with fiercely powerful resistance from business and the government. As a leading activist professional recollected, the core PSPD activists had experienced continuous tension and conflict against economic conglomerates and small and medium businesses and banks working for big business, as well as government organizations. In particular, they encountered numerous slanders and obstructionist maneuvers by big business and its supporters. These tactics were emotionally draining because most of the core activists had family members, relatives, or friends who were working for those business and government organizations, and they had to alienate themselves from their family members, relatives, and friends to pursue the reform movement.[21] In pushing their economic reform bills in the face of strong opposition, these activists organized numerous press releases on their positions, held public hearings and discussion meetings, pursued online signature-collection campaigns, and organized street protests to pressure the Ministry of Finance and the Ministry of Law into action. They also actively lobbied individual lawmakers and policy officers of the major political parties. Despite their heroic efforts, in the aftermath of the 1997 Asian financial crisis, the government and major political parties agreed to most of the demands for further deregulation made by big business; subsequently, PSPD's activism to reform big business and stop the attempt to increase economic inequality often failed.[22]

The small shareholders movement tied to broader economic reform was enabled by neoliberalism, which has promoted financialization of the economy. It recast the minor participants in the financialized economy as a source of civic activism that could promote economic democratization as opposed to individuals merely interested in making short-term profit through stock investment. The movement also symbolically reversed the fragmentation and isolation of individuals whose relations to other human beings were literally reduced to the "cash nexus" in neoliberal South Korea with extensive financialization. In mobilizing financial actors, PSPD insisted on the public nature of a business corporation, especially big business, and its collective responsibility, articulating an alternative view to rectify the neoliberal view of the corporation as a privileged entity that stood above societal and governmental regulations.

Nevertheless, at its core the movement was symbolic and performative as much as it was serious and strenuous. Activist professionals and staff activists had mobilized small shareholders rather than these shareholders voluntarily organizing as a socioeconomic group to promoted their own material interests. Also, the small shareholders movement stayed within the boundaries of financial capitalism and middle-class activism. In the rapidly polarizing economy between the rich and the poor, a vast majority of Koreans could not afford to own stocks. It was largely the middle class with secure employment who could invest in stocks and securities to increase their private wealth. More important, the mentality and practices of stock investment has shown that the focus is on short-term profit through quick selling and buying. The movement could not reverse the devastating trend of the "flexible labor" regime that has undermined and destroyed the livelihood of millions of people.

Movements to Protect Small Business Owners and Ordinary Citizens as Financial Consumers

PSPD complemented its civic activism of monitoring major political and economic powers and holding them accountable by developing a series of movements to protect grassroots citizens who dealt with mundane problems in their daily lives. Pursued under the rubric of "a movement to find small rights," these activism efforts were intended to "soften" and "popularize" the serious and professional image of PSPD activism among the public.²³ In the context of neoliberal economic restructuring, it focused on two social groups: small business owners and financial consumers. For small business owners, PSPD identified store rent as a core condition for their economic survival when competing with Korean and other transnational big businesses. This economic group was especially affected by the IMF crisis and the subsequent deregulation of the economy because they were self-employed and largely without resources other than their own labor and unpaid family labor. The civic organization carried out activism efforts to enact a law to protect small business owners by collaborating with them as well as with progressive lawmakers and other civic organizations. PSPD organized a series of public hearings and discussions, drafted a bill, and pressured legislators to adopt the bill and enact it; PSPD also monitored the process of lawmaking in the National Assembly in the early 2000s. After arduous and persistent efforts, the National Assembly passed the Commercial Building Rent Protection Law in December of 2001, and it has been in effect since the beginning of 2003. The passage of the rent protection law and its revision benefited at least four million small, self-employed business renters.

However, the problem of exploitative rents being charged to small business owners resurfaced in 2013, and PSPD resumed its movement to reform the law and was able to accomplish a modicum of success. Although mitigated by this activism, the problem of small business owners' debts has been persistent in neoliberal South Korea and was further aggravated by the Covid-19 pandemic. In the summer of 2022, PSPD put pressure on the government, political parties, and the financial industry to address massive debts of small business owners, which approached USD $1 trillion (roughly *ilcheonjo* won in Korean).²⁴ The underlying structural problem stems from the deregulation of loan markets and their interest rates, which led to the explosion of predatory lenders who have taken advantage of desperate small business owners. In comparison with the use of a liberal law promoting the rights of small shareholders in a capitalist economy, this activism highlighted the limits of the liberal view in contract law, which assumes that the parties involved are equals, and the idealized role of the state as an arbiter to balance the unequal power between the parties.²⁵

Another dire problem faced by small business owners was aggressive competition from big businesses in the retail sector, especially regarding groceries and other common household goods. The problem was a direct result of the deregulation of distribution and retail markets and opening them to transnational supermarkets and convenience chain stores. Implemented initially by the Kim Young-sam government as a policy of globalization, deregulation opened a floodgate for big businesses to enter and dominate the retail markets and destroyed small self-employed local businesses. Roh Moo-hyun's government, which was progressive in the Korean political context, completed the process of deregulation by abolishing the protection of small and medium businesses in certain retail sectors designated to be suitable for them.[26] Consequently, in 2007 alone, 848,000 small self-employed businesses were closed, and in 2008, roughly 800,000 similar businesses were closed; these small business owners joined the newly impoverished.[27] In response, PSPD collaborated with affected small business owners and other civic organizations to support their economic survival through legal reform, which revolved around the revival of rational regulation of big businesses.

Neoliberal restructuring of the economy has been accompanied by its financialization. In a financialized economy, ordinary people as consumers are not merely buying goods and services but are also borrowing money to bolster their necessary and aspirational consumption. The key tool of this financialization targeting consumers has been credit cards. The use of credit cards among South Koreans has grown explosively since the 1990s. In 1999, fewer than 40,000 credit cards were issued, and the total amount of credit card usage was roughly 90 zillion won (USD $90 billion). By 2002, approximately 100 million credit cards were issued, and the total amount of credit card usage soared to roughly 443 zillion won (USD $443 billion) in 2001. The volatile growth of credit card use was a direct result of the deregulation of the financial market. In the aftermath of the Asian financial crisis, the Kim Dae-jung government viewed consumption bolstered by credit cards as a major way to revive the national economy. With mounting problems caused by the deregulated issuance and use of credit cards, the government further removed a cap on credit card cash advance services. Credit card companies raked profits from excessively high interest rates and high service fees. Consequently, credit card debt became a dire socioeconomic problem. In the early 2000s, news media reported numerous incidents of murder, suicide, and armed bank robbery linked to mounting credit card debts. In 2003, the problem of credit card debt was turned into a "big crisis" as the number of insolvent credit card debtors reached three million, which represented approximately 10 percent of the entire economically active population in South Korea. Observing the problem of exploding credit card debt, PSPD began a civic campaign to stop indiscriminate issuance and use of credit cards and move toward rational regulation of credit card practices. It began with research into the problem and then issued press releases and employed online and offline gatherings, signature collections, and a hotline to support affected consumers and to achieve the goals of legal reform and public education.[28]

A related problem affecting a large number of people as financial consumers was the proliferation of high interest rates caused by the deregulation of formal and informal loan markets in the aftermath of the Asian financial crisis. Following the IMF structural adjustment, Kim Dae-jung's government virtually eliminated a 25 percent cap on the interest rate in the formal loan market and guaranteed an excessively high interest rate of 66 percent in the informal loan market in the name of reversing its underground operation. As a result, a large number of borrowers became insolvent debtors, went bankrupt, and even became victims of violent private loan sharks.[29] Since 1999, in collaboration with other civic organizations and progressive lawmakers, PSPD activism sought to mitigate and solve the problem through legal reform that could restore proper regulation of financial markets.[30] It accomplished partial success in achieving this goal. In 2013, the ratio of household debt to disposable household income in South Korea was 163.8 percent, far higher than the 135 percent in the United States, which was hit severely by the 2008 financial crisis.[31]

Deregulation of banking destructively affected relatively affluent middle-class people who could save and invest with local or regional banks. Categorized as the secondary financial sector, this type of bank was initially established to cater to ordinary citizens, small shop owners, and small and medium businesses, all of whom were marginalized in the primary financial sector servicing big businesses and big investors. However, as the boundary between savings banks and investment banks became blurred in the process of deregulation and financialization of the economy, savings banks were allowed to issue astronomical investment loans.[32] This became possible after a cap on the line of credit was eliminated in 2005. When investment loans turned out to be insolvent, the immense losses were transferred to a multitude of individual savers and investors. A prime example of these recurring problems was the 2011 Savings Bank crisis caused by astronomical real estate loans. PSPD tried to remedy the problem by investigating the government's failure to regulate banks, pursuing legal reform, and working with financial consumers victimized by it.[33]

Like the preceding examples of PSPD activism, the movements to protect the vulnerable or marginalized in the neoliberal economy were enabled by the political opening generated by neoliberal governance but structurally constrained by the neoliberal logic of deregulation, privatization, and accelerated accumulation of capital. As a result, PSPD continued to make almost Sisyphean efforts to deal with the recurring problems of increasing debts among small business owners and financial consumers.[34] In doing so, it has relied on its established repertoire of activism: legal and policy reforms pursued by activist professionals, dedicated staff activists, and volunteer activists with support from a coalition of other citizens' organizations and social movement organizations. To the extent that debts have functioned as a main mechanism to siphon wealth from the masses of citizens into the few superrich in neoliberal society, PSPD activism to democratize the financialized economy through the aforementioned ways has been constrained.

Movements to Stop the South Korea–U.S. Free Trade Agreement (KORUS FTA)

Since the North America Free Trade Agreement (NAFTA) was signed by Canada, Mexico, and the United States in 1993, the FTA has functioned as a core mechanism to establish and spread the neoliberal global order.[35] The KORUS FTA came into being through highly contentious politics that stretched over six years from the beginning of the FTA negotiation in early 2006 to its taking effect in 2012. In the name of free trade, the KORUS FTA required thorough "opening of markets" with an emphasis on the service industry, investment, and intellectual property rights, as well as agriculture through deregulation and privatization. Ironically, it was the Roh Moo-hyun administration that presented it as an inevitable and beneficial tool for economic growth that would expand exports and strengthen the competitiveness of Korean businesses. However, in practice, the FTA primarily benefited a handful of export-oriented big businesses at the expense of a large number of small and medium businesses that became further reduced to subcontractors exploited by big businesses. More important, it undermined national sovereignty in terms of the legislative and judicial power to devise and implement public policies.[36]

It is noteworthy that contrary to the rhetorical appeal of the term "free," the entire process of KORUS FTA negotiations and ratification were anything but free and democratic for a majority of Korean citizens whose lives would be profoundly and negatively affected by it. There were neither public hearings organized by the government nor public deliberations in the National Assembly (NA). Not only were ordinary citizens ignored but the NA was also ignored. Powerful trade bureaucrats, who were ardent supporters of neoliberal economy, refused to disclose the FTA drafts or the results of negotiations and refused to report to the NA. The government, regardless of political orientations of the ruling party, imposed its decisions without transparency and accountability. In November of 2011, the Lee Myung-bak government forcefully passed the FTA ratification bill in the NA without the participation of the Democratic Party, the major opposition party.[37]

Soon after the government announced its plan to negotiate the FTA, in March of 2006 citizens' organizations formed the Pan-National Movement Headquarters (PNMH) to stop the FTA. PSPD joined the PNMH and participated in a series of large street protests during 2006 and 2007. At the same time, utilizing its extensive experience conducting legal and policy studies, PSPD investigated the specific content of the FTA and the controversies and confusions it generated. Based on this study, it tried to inform the general public through a press conference as well as on its website and through publications. It also worked with the NA, which had the institutional power to ratify international treaties like the FTA. Designated as the organization in charge of collaborating with the NA within PNMH, PSPD organized a NA Members Workshop on the FTA and managed the NA Members Group to Study the FTA, which became the NA Members Emergency Meeting to Oppose the Rough-and-Ready Signing of the FTA. It also monitored the NA activities concerning the FTA and discovered not only that the FTA bill was never sent to the NA but also that both South Korea and the United States agreed not to open the bill to the public for three years.[38]

In April of 2008, when the Lee Myung-bak government accepted the demand to ease the conditions for U.S. beef imports (as an element of the FTA), the movements to stop the KORUS FTA encountered a series of massive candlelight protests across the country concerning beef imports. The easing of the conditions included approval of beef imports made from cows that were older than thirty months. This change became highly controversial because the global outbreak of mad cow disease in the recent past affected mostly cows older than thirty months, and in response many countries in the world restricted the import of beef made from cows to younger than thirty months. This unexpected explosion of grassroots activism energized many citizens' organizations, and they formed a coalition to support spontaneous candlelight protests (the National Countermeasure Meeting to deal with the Danger of Mad Cow Disease). The ad-hoc coalition rapidly grew to include more than 1,800 groups and organizations across the country. For the first time in its history of activism, PSPD and other citizens' organizations followed the lead of spontaneous individuals and small groups, who were mobilized by the heightened fear regarding food safety and anger at the government.[39] This experience further sensitized citizens' organizations like PSPD to reflect critically on its professionalized and organized method of activism.

To their satisfaction, spontaneous candlelight protests, which lasted more than one hundred days and were supported by the coalition, were able to reverse U.S. beef imports and pressured the two governments to renegotiate. Despite their peaceful, orderly, and festive manners, the enduring massive protests triggered the Lee Myung-bak government's violent suppression of citizens' organizations and individuals. Deploying the police force, the government arrested PSPD staff members and subjected the organization to seizure and search for the first time in its history. The government and the police filed damage compensation lawsuits (of several hundred thousand U.S. dollars) against PSPD and the National Countermeasure Meeting, as well as their major activists. In addition, conservative citizens' organizations encouraged local merchants to file similar compensation lawsuits against participants of the candlelight protests. For years, PSPD lawyers defended these individuals and organizations.[40]

What deserves our attention in this example of PSPD activism for the analysis of the contradictory relationship between democracy and neoliberalism is the striking contrast between the neoliberal rhetoric of freedom and democracy and the underlying presence of the repressive state apparatus. Although neoliberal governance enabled democratizing activism by generating political openings for cooperation between PSPD and the state (e.g., the government and the National Assembly), the state's tolerance for its activism fluctuated, depending on the perception of how a particular issue was critical to maintaining and fortifying the neoliberal order. The centrality of the KORUS FTA to establishing and expanding the neoliberal order made PSPD activism against it more threatening than other issues. This example shows how repressive and centralized power coexist with the decentralized mode of neoliberal governance that relies on the freedom and responsibility of individuals and organizations to join in partnership with the state; as long as activism does not threaten core interests of the state and its major actors, neoliberalism enables democratization; but when such activism transgresses, the coercive power resurfaces.

POLITICS OF CIVIC IDENTITY: MEANINGS OF "GRASSROOTS PARTICIPATION"

The activism discussed previously illuminates how PSPD tried to complement its professional advocacy with grassroots participation in solving or mitigating serious problems caused or aggravated by neoliberal globalization. It also enables us to look into the pragmatic division of labor between the full-time staff as professional activists and lay members as volunteer activists and how the hierarchy between them determined access to and use of cultural/symbolic capital in articulating claims and demands and disseminating them. The content of this division of labor is important to PSPD's hybrid civic identity because it turns the moral code of grassroots participation into concrete practices by imbuing specificity into the normative ideal. The meanings and expectations of grassroots participation were neither uniform nor static in PSPD, a large organization that has been joined by diverse individuals and situated in shifting sociopolitical contexts. At least three different meanings of grassroots participation are embedded in the division of labor between staff activists and lay members over time. The first meaning highlights the interactive cooperation between staff and volunteers in carrying out specific projects beyond simple clerical assistance. The second meaning stresses members' enduring support for the staff through payment of membership dues and their occasional participation in PSPD events. The third meaning deemphasizes grassroots participation as being secondary to PSPD in favor of more professionalization.

The first meaning of grassroots participation is found among lay members who see themselves as active agents of social change and who joined PSPD to get involved in meaningful activities. Although a numerical minority in PSPD history, this type of active member was more visible in its earlier years than in later years when it became a larger organization with national recognition and influence. These members expected to learn new information and increase their understanding and skills through working closely with staff activists. They also contributed their own skills and expertise to specific projects. They desired substantial participation beyond performing simple chores to assist the staff. They were rather disappointed at "Members' Gatherings," which consisted mostly of hobby groups, and the lack of members' gatherings oriented toward grassroots activism facilitated by the staff. This was the source of the recurring criticism of "citizens' movements without citizens." Tae-seong, who joined PSPD in early 2000 as a college student and was employed elsewhere when I interviewed him, was directly involved in the project to legislate the Commercial Building Rent Protection Law. He said his role as a volunteer activist in this project was his "most satisfying and happiest" experience in the organization. Although the law was a "watered-down version" of what PSPD had promoted, he cherished it as "one of the earliest legislative achievements in its history" that "everyone involved in the project was excited about."

However, Tae-seong's narrative of civic activism also revealed enabling and constraining factors for active and meaningful grassroots participation that posed a challenge to PSPD's hybrid identity:

> I think it [his substantial participation] was possible because I was a college student. I was also given an interesting and meaningful task. As frequently said, most volunteer activists have performed only simple tasks because of the structure. I feel that this is something that the PSPD has to strike a balance. When I joined first, there wasn't much to do other than cleaning and organizing a storage. . . . I couldn't think I was participating and I was agonizing over it. Then An-jin brother [referring to a staff activist] came and asked me to join his project because I studied law. When we [referring to lay members] are given meaningful tasks, I saw, most of us can *endure* at least six months. With simple tasks, people don't come. They can't last a week because they wonder if they became members to do that kind of chore.[41]

During his active participation, he encountered many members who were troubled by simple volunteer activities given to them and tried to help them understand the structural constraints. He aptly summarized what he had repeated with disappointed members:

> It'd be hard to find activities you find satisfying and desirable here unless you can make a continuous time commitment. Because these people [referring to staff activists] have to continue their projects until they achieve their goals. Their work requires various concerns; first security, second capacity to carry out tasks, third professionalism. Hence they cannot just assign important tasks to anyone willing to volunteer. Volunteers without experience and knowledge can delay or even derail a project. That's why simple chores were assigned.

His observation captures the enduring structure of PSPD activism, which is run by full-time activists oriented toward legal and policy change, and the inevitable hierarchy between them and lay members as volunteer activists. Ideologically committed to grassroots participation, PSPD elevated lay members to "volunteer activists" (*jawonhwaldongga*), distinct from the more common term "volunteer service provider" (*jawonbongsaja*). Having experienced a gap between the ideal of volunteer activist and daily practices of volunteers, Tae-seong hoped that PSPD could strike a balance between the practical goal of completing its projects on time and facilitating members' meaningful participation in civic activism.

Whereas Tae-seong pointed out the challenge of "striking a balance," Ho-sang, a high school graduate who became a seasoned manager in a construction business and joined PSPD in 1999, described a different experience. Ho-sang was actively involved in a project and collaborated with staff activists and other members.

> At first, we [referring to active members] began with monitoring the expenses spent by our Ward Chief, but we don't know the issue at all. So staff activists prepared materials for us to learn the issue and its context. They explained the Information Disclosure Act that allowed us to monitor the public budget and encouraged us to do it for ourselves. We were working on the ground and moving on foot. When we encountered some obstacles, they offered suggestions. We went to a Ward Hall and talked to an official in the General Affairs Section. We came back to the staff and shared problems

we had with him, and the staff advised us to avoid any political discussion with him and stay focused. Sometimes we discussed what to do and how to do it until midnight and one o'clock in the morning, and the staff facilitated us until the end.[42]

Ho-sang cherished the sense of solidarity and fellowship from working closely with other volunteer activists and staff activists. Each project took roughly a year or longer to complete, so sustained interactions and collaboration generated a strong sense of solidarity and fellowship. He observed a shift in PSPD culture during the mid-2000s that was marked by the waning attention to members with enthusiasm for active participation. He believed that this change made many active members who joined PSPD in its earlier years leave the organization. The large context of this comment was a significant decline in its membership in early and mid-2000s after its dramatic increase in 2000 and 2001.[43] From the perspective of active members like Ho-sang, PSPD would need a few staff activists fully in charge of facilitating members' activism. Ho-sang commented that the growing number of staff activists in the 2000s was not accompanied by the creation of such staff activists.

> Back then, in early 1999, there were about 2,000 members, but there were more people who came to meetings [referring to project-related business meetings] than now. There was a shortage of meeting rooms, and we had to reschedule our meetings to get a room. Now we can get a meeting room easily; we call today to get a room tomorrow. . . . Back then there were fewer staff activists, perhaps a fifth of the current size. I cannot understand that the PSPD still doesn't have a staff activist focusing on members' activism. It means that this is not a priority, and members like us are neglected. This is a common opinion among active members.[44]

Although Ho-sang's recollection was not accurate on specific numbers, it was right about the priority of PSPD in its ongoing development as a professional advocacy organization.[45] During its formative years (1994–2001) when its membership grew rapidly, there was more fluidity in its civic identity and more energy to experiment with personal and intense interactions between lay members and its staff. Once it became a large organization with national recognition, PSPD had to maintain the status quo by managing and adding centers, committees, and task-oriented teams run by full-time staff. It aptly prioritized its competence to accomplish specific legal and policy outcomes and thereby sustained itself as a respected civic organization; but it rarely prioritized actively facilitating lay members to practice the ideal of volunteer activists.[46] Given its limited resources in general and the moral code of financial independence from the government as the foundation of its moral authority and popular appeal in particular, it would be difficult to hire a few new staff activists exclusively focusing on facilitating lay members' volunteer activism. It could not ask the existing staff to take on more responsibilities because they were already overworked.[47]

The first meaning of grassroots participation, as substantial and enduring engagement, reveals two competing views on Bourdieu's rule of professional monopoly in political action as a symbolic action. Tae-seong's view affirms the rule as being inevitable for the pragmatic and effective workings of PSPD, whereas Ho-sang's view contests the rule by emphasizing the importance of ongoing education and facilitation of lay members' capacity to develop and use their cultural/symbolic capital. The outcome of PSPD's move toward more professional advocacy rather than toward the cultivation of lay members' cultural/symbolic capital affirms the following rule: as long as lay members have rhetorical skills and other professional expertise, they can participate substantially, but the organization is reluctant to dispense its limited resources to continuously cultivate lay members' cultural/symbolic capital. This reality shows that the normative ideal of equality in democracy is always inflected by hierarchy in terms of symbolic/cultural capital.

The specific organizational dynamic of PSPD as a professional social movement organization leads us to the second meaning of grassroots participation, which has been common and dominant. Many lay members and staff activists share a pragmatic understanding of grassroots participation, which essentially means assistance for the staff activists who carry out full-time activism to improve society. This common view accepts the division of labor between the staff as professional activists and lay members who have their own full-time jobs elsewhere and have family responsibilities. It also reflects their commonsense attitude that an organized group will be more effective than isolated individuals in solving or addressing social problems. In contrast to the normative ideal of grassroots participation, which PSPD connoted by adopting the new term *volunteer activist*, diverse lay members

I interviewed over time did not see themselves as playing active and substantial roles. The moral code of grassroots participation is a source of legitimacy and moral authority for the civic organization rather than what a majority of lay members expect their civic roles to be in society structured by differentiation, professionalization, and commercialization. The following observation by a staff activist, who moved between full-time activism and full-time employment in publishing, captures this common understanding.

> Those who come to us are quite satisfied by supporting us to do our job better. They think of participation not so much as taking part in decision-making and insisting on their own ideas as supporting us. They joined the PSPD because they shared our views and orientation. Well, in fact, it is us who need their active participation. Last year during the candlelight protests [referring to a series of popular protests against the import of U.S. beef suspected of mad cow disease in 2008] and this year there have been increasing gatherings, campaigns, and protests. We become dissatisfied with their supportive roles. So we keep texting them about when and where these gatherings are happening. When we go out to the street, the number of people matters a great deal to get attention and have an impact.[48]

The pragmatic view of grassroots participation is common among lay members who joined meetings, attended events, or performed volunteer activities. In comparison with a majority of members who paid membership dues only, they are relatively active participants in the organization. Yet they distinguished themselves from full-time staff activists and explained their participation as supporting the organization. An active member who kept his membership for ten years conveys this idea:

> I heard that, "citizens' organizations without citizens." . . . It's criticism voiced by the conservative media. I am participating as a member and citizen as much as I can. I attend a steering committee meeting if I can make time, a good lecture, or a campaign. I have some photographic skills. So I did some volunteer activities.[49]

After discussing the difficulty of changing society through civic activism despite democratization, another relatively active member, a substitute teacher (*giganje gyosa*), commented:

> They [referring to the staff activists] are fighting without giving up on behalf of us. I feel thankful. These days, most people are struggling and worn out. When I encounter daily news, I am quite worried, but staff activists here give me positive energy. They must be exhausted from so much work, but they are doing something important. I feel vicarious satisfaction from supporting them.[50]

The delegation of civic activism to staff activists and limited participation among lay members has been the reality of grassroots participation in PSPD. Only a minority of members participate in volunteer activities to support the staff or are responsible for specific projects.[51] This structure would be fine with many other professional advocacy organizations elsewhere, but in South Korea it has generated recurring debates internally and externally. This is the power of the moral codes that have shaped citizens' organizations as a vehicle for civic activism. The underlying gap between the ideal and the reality of grassroots participation has provided critical self-reflection for PSPD, but a minority of lay members stressed more rigorous professionalization for PSPD's activism.

According to this view, as society has become more technical and knowledge-based, civic activism also needs to be more specialized and professionalized for effective outcomes.[52] A lay member, who majored in physics in college and is married to a staff activist, conveys this view:

> Generally, I agree with them [views of PSPD], but sometimes not quite. For example, nuclear power plant issues. Many [citizens' organizations] advocate its abolition without data. . . . I have talked to activists many times whenever there are occasions for informal chats, but it seems that I cannot persuade them. I want to discuss the issues with actual data rather than ideological commitment, but there are few who can do so. Perhaps it's better to talk to the Green Party.[53]

A lay member and former activist in other organizations who became a small business owner to support her family after marriage voices the need for professionalization more explicitly:

> I think the PSPD is the best among citizens' organizations. It has kept its core well. It became quite successful. Nevertheless, it has its clear limitations. I have a love and hate relationship. . . . Because it has covered so

many issues in so many fields, oftentimes multiple people [staff activists] cover professional fields without necessary expertise. I feel frustrated when I see that during the candlelight protests [referring to 2008 protests against importing U.S. beef] and Seweolho protests [referring to the 2014 sinking of the ferry Seweol].[54]

Although PSPD accepts professionalism as an indicator of the high quality of its staff activists, this minority view poses tension with its ideological commitment to active broad grassroots participation. Not only does this view affirm the rule of professional monopoly in political action as symbolic action, but it also resonates powerfully with the underlying dynamic of associational lives in South Korean society as an urban and money-based one. Georg Simmel's theoretical insights are useful here. In *The Philosophy of Money*, he argues that in such a society associational lives of individuals undergo a significant transformation; there is a profound shift from extensive personal interactions for fellowship to specific goal-oriented interactions with less extensive personal involvement.[55] Given the goal of PSPD, broad long-term social change through institutional reforms, it would be effective to professionalize its staff activists not only in terms of their full-time activism but also in terms of their professional knowledge of the subject areas with which they deal. At the same time, this rational goal orientation overlooks a deeper meaning of civic activism as a democratic practice; as the code of grassroots participation highlights, it is also about the messy processes of involving ordinary citizens and encouraging them to take active or even leading roles in improving their own lives and society.

It is important to distinguish the practice of individual capacity promoted by democratizing activism that PSPD pursued from the neoliberal practice of individual capacity. Although both tend to converge rhetorically on keywords such as freedom and responsibility, the former is predicated on equality with other members of a group, community, or society whereas the latter is predicated on the privatized accumulation of capital. Democratic individual capacity seeks self-determination in a society where one lives with other members, whereas neoliberal individual agency seeks choices in marketplaces by selling and buying commodities. As the examples of PSPD activism show, the rhetorical convergence or proximity allowed PSPD to appropriate neoliberal governance by reinterpreting it as democratic governance; this appropriation is tolerated as long as its activism does not seriously threaten the core logic and practices of neoliberalism.

Nevertheless, PSPD does not transcend its own social and political context; it is significantly influenced by both the allure and the pressure of professionalization and economic thinking. Professionalization of activism is intimately paired with the heightened emphasis on achieving a specific goal and producing a specific result in a short term, which reflects the ever-growing power of economic metrics that revolve around the doctrine of "efficiency" that neoliberalism as a political rationality has intensified. Although professionalization of activism for an advocacy organization like PSPD is necessary to a certain degree for its proper functioning and sustained existence, it has to be balanced by substantial and enduring grassroots participation. Otherwise, professionalized activism can easily turn into neoliberal governance.

The tension between the normative ideal and the daily practice of grassroots participation remains unresolved, but the persistent problem of grassroots participation has become a more pronounced concern as its membership is aging and stagnant. To be certain, this problem shows PSPD's capacity for critical self-reflection and does not diminish its leading position as a competent and successful advocacy organization. Observed in the slow influx of new members, especially from the younger generation, the growing concern stems from various external and internal factors/changes. I argue that these factors/changes are directly and indirectly linked to the neoliberal transformation of Korean society. Those who were in their twenties and thirties in the 2010s came of age in the aftermath of the two major financial crises in 1997 and 2008. Throughout their lifetime they were extensively exposed to and inculcated with the neoliberal logic of privatization, investment in the self as human capital, and the accelerated accumulation of wealth, which shapes their personal attitudes and behaviors. Culturally, neoliberalism became hegemonic in Korean society through its appealing rhetoric of self-motivation and self-improvement, which celebrated a sense of individual capacity and empowerment.[56] As a result, the younger generation has become less inclined to join civic activism, which promotes collective and cooperative solutions for common problems. Both staff activists and lay members are aware of how ongoing intensification of employment insecurity and fierce competition has negatively impacted the younger generation. A staff activist who worked in PSPD for seven years and was in charge of citizens' participation teams observed this trend:

> The most painful thing is that suicide is the number one cause of death among those who are in their teens and twenties. We're trying to pay attention to youth issues. They have almost no voice because they are cornered and there are few places for them to do so. We're making a division focusing on youth issues. So we can support them to organize themselves and advocate for themselves. . . . College students have changed so much. Unlike the old days, they are excessively focused on their grades and consider their friends as competitors. These days professors and TAs [teaching assistants] rarely supervise exams because students report about other students who cheat. They are severely locked up by competition. Cram schools are now mandatory rather than optional.[57]

A college student, who took a leave due to her tuition burden and joined a PSPD internship program, conveys her ongoing realization of the problem of neoliberal thinking and practices during the program:

> What is echoing in me a lot is we've been taught to compete, survive, and to solve problems on our own using our ability rather than doing something together. Because we're raised that way, we are more inclined to try to overcome problems for ourselves without blaming society or other people even when we cannot do so and feel self-disdain. So when we young people gather, we always joke that you're trash and I am more trash than you. We coined *"naregi"* (a new slang word that abbreviates I am more trash).[58]

The prospect of civic activism for older-generation Koreans has also been negatively affected by the neoliberal transformation of society, which has profoundly undermined employment security in at least two ways. First, in the face of shrinking secure jobs and intensifying competition for them, men and women have spent more time finding jobs and keeping them. When they cannot find good jobs, they have to work longer hours or work multiple jobs to eke out a living.[59] Consequently, even if one is interested in civic activism for social change, it has become more difficult to pursue it. Second, PSPD's activism to deal with the negative impacts of neoliberal globalization has been very important and almost heroic in the face of these obstacles, but it has only mitigated the negative impacts. Neoliberal globalization as a macro force of social change has been too powerful to stop in the short run; even the developmental state in South Korea, which dictated the economic conglomerates, reorganized itself as a neoliberal actor that bolsters their transnational operations. Both liberal and conservative governments in South Korea for the past two decades accepted neoliberal globalization.[60] As a result, a majority of ordinary people have felt that the legislation of social welfare laws and laws to protect victims of deregulated financial capitalism have not translated into concrete improvement in their own lives. These two factors together have contributed to growing skepticism about civic activism and the stagnation of PSPD membership.

At the same time, spontaneous activism outside citizens' organizations has intermittently erupted using mobile communication technology. Reflecting on this development, a staff activist articulated his observation of significant cultural change in activism and society.

> There has been a sea change among our members and citizens outside in terms of their enthusiasm for participation. In the past, they were rather passive, but now they are quite active. They are not merely cheering us up, but also directly involved and make their own voices heard. Due to the internet, especially smartphones, the distinction between staff activists and lay members became blurred. In the past we were leading them in a way in terms of information and organizing, but now [there is] not much difference. We all access information almost simultaneously. In the past, people came to know certain situations and developments after we had discussion meetings and press releases, but now people can find out what they want to know through the internet. They can sort out information they encounter. In my memory, the 2008 candlelight protests against mad cow disease were decisive. Since then the whole atmosphere of a public protest changed very much. I was a greenhorn back then but was given the task of taking care of the candlelight protests countermeasure meetings. I was dispatched to the site and was extremely surprised. In the past a protest gathering was organized in advance with a beginning and an end. A majority of participants were members sent by labor unions and citizens' organizations. Now 90 percent of participants are ordinary citizens and volunteered to join. To them a preorganized schedule does not mean much. In the past a protest gathering began with People's

Ritual, major hosts' talks, a political speech, and a couple of free speeches at the end. Then [during the 2008 protests] there were numerous free speeches by participants without any organizing. People were lined up for their turns.[61]

Young-seo's extensive comments highlight how technological change is dissolving the rule of professional monopoly in activism, reducing the division of labor between staff activists and lay members and thereby the underlying hierarchy between the two groups. This democratization, along with the festive informal protest culture, undermines the professionalization of activism and bodes positively for its development. Nevertheless, as studies of internet-based activism reveal, spontaneous individualized activism has its own limitations that stem from the lack of organization and continuity.[62]

CONCLUSION

By focusing on four salient examples of PSPD activism, I have explained how and to what extent its democratizing activism is enabled and constrained by neoliberal governance. The examples show the extent to which the large advocacy organization, prioritizing legal and policy reform, takes advantage of political openings generated by neoliberal governance to work with the state in dealing with daunting problems caused or aggravated by the neoliberal transformation of South Korean society. Attention to the details of PSPD activism helps us comprehend both its accomplishments and limitations beyond one-dimensional accounts of neoliberal corporatization or pacification of a professional social movement organization. Its sustained focus on monitoring the powerful and protecting and supporting the vulnerable has demonstrated substantial and at times heroic accomplishments in mitigating daunting problems. At the same time, close analysis of its activism reveals that PSPD is allowed to appropriate neoliberal governance into democratic action as long as it does not threaten the core logic of neoliberalism.

Its extensive cooperation with the state to establish a universal social welfare system produced significant improvements in social welfare for Koreans but developed into a regressive and selective system because it could not challenge the flexible labor regime, a core component of the neoliberal global order. Its movement to monitor big business highlighted a social meaning of corporation alternatives to the neoliberal version and produced a significant symbolic curb on big business in the absence of government regulation. Yet it was not able to partner with the state for this activism, which targeted big business (anointed as the engine of economic growth and recovery), and the movement remained within the boundaries of financial capitalism and middle-class activism. PSPD cooperated with the state to protect small business owners and ordinary citizens as financial consumers and was able to provide these vulnerable social groups with urgent support, but its movements were constrained by the core component of the neoliberal global order. PSPD worked with the National Assembly to stop KORUS FTA, but these efforts were fiercely rejected by the state because they challenged the core mechanism of the neoliberal global order.

PSPD's advocacy model of activism based on professional staff has generated a thorny problem of hierarchy between staff activists and lay members in the Korean context. I discussed how PSPD has dealt with this difficult problem in neoliberal South Korea to gain a deeper understanding of the convergence and differentiation between democratizing activism and neoliberal governance.

In chapter 5, I focus on two local branches of a leading feminist organization that have moved away from the advocacy model and the hierarchical division between staff activists and lay members. By recasting lay members as major activists, these branches have tried to adhere to the moral code of grassroots participation in their activism efforts to solve or mitigate problems affecting the lives of women. Their activism also enables us to identify an additional pattern in how democratizing activism is enabled and constrained by neoliberal governance.

Chapter Five

NEOLIBERAL GOVERNANCE II

Grassroots Participation Through Private-Public Partnership and Undermining Civic Autonomy

> Hope of women's movements lies in the masses of grassroots women, who represent 80 percent of the entire body of women and are changing the world. A minority of activists have to communicate with these ordinary women and support them to empower themselves as groups. . . . Additionally, for the future of women's movements in this Neoliberal era, it is necessary for the movements to establish Women's NGO Schools to train activists with professionalism who can participate in policy decision-making as a partner in governance.
>
> —FROM *A TWENTY-FIVE-YEAR HISTORY OF KOREAN CIVIL SOCIETY MOVEMENTS*[1]

Narrating the history of women's movements to reform policy for a quarter of a century, this feminist scholar highlights the two important challenging issues PSPD has dealt with: grassroots participation and training activists with professionalism in neoliberal South Korea. These issues were present during the 2010 local elections, when "environment-friendly free lunch" (*chinhwangyeong musang geupsik*) for schoolchildren became a controversial national issue. It divided the South Korean electorate between universal social welfare and limited welfare for the needy. Progressives and their allies framed free lunch as a universal entitlement for all children regardless of their parents' socioeconomic status, but conservatives and their allies framed it as an assistance limited to the needy. In the aftermath of the 2008 global financial crisis, however, feeding schoolchildren good free food gained growing appeal for a broad spectrum of voters. When various NGOs came together to form a coalition to advocate the free lunch as an element of universal welfare, the two local branches of Democratic Friends Society, GY and NE, joined local governments in promoting the progressive view of free school lunches. In particular, Goyang City established an Environment-Friendly School Lunch Provision Center in 2011. In partnership with municipal authorities, the GY Branch food cooperative (co-op) participated in running the Civil and Government Collaborative

Management Council, the highest decision-making body in the lunch provision center.[2]

This vignette on private-public partnerships is an example of the popularized model of neoliberal governance "that is networked, integrated, cooperative, partnered, disseminated, and at least partly self-organized" under the rubric of "business model and business metrics."[3] Further developing the outsourcing of public services, this practice has been actively promoted with the rhetoric of democratization and efficiency à la the language of finance. As discussed in the introduction and chapter 1, this positive view of neoliberal governance is particularly visible in studies of public administration and mainstream political science in South Korea and elsewhere. In contrast, critical studies of governance aptly highlight that under the rhetoric of privatization and partnership to solve problems or achieve common goals, practices of neoliberal governance have often replaced public programs and services that use full-time regular government employees with commercial ones that rely on temporary and irregular workers, or worse, unpaid volunteers. In Japan, where civil society has been dominated by service-oriented local organizations rather than national advocacy organizations, the private-public partnership has reduced civil society organizations to an expedient tool of neoliberal governance.[4] This critical insight, however, is rather one-dimensional; it overlooks certain enabling conditions the neoliberal partnership generated for or contributed to democratizing activism. Attention to this neglect does not have to overlook a series of destructive consequences of neoliberal transformation of a society in reality, but it is intended to deepen the analysis of the relationship between democracy and neoliberalism. In South Korea where civil society shows a motley combination of advocacy organizations and service-oriented ones (see chapter 1), local organizations relying on their lay members' activism are primarily concerned with the provision of necessary social services. In this chapter I delve into how civic activism pursued by local organizations is simultaneously enabled and constrained by neoliberal governance.

As local feminist civic organizations, the GY and NE branches of the Democratic Friends Society (DFS) have functioned primarily as providers of urgent social services for local women and residents and secondarily as supporters of national issues in collaboration with DFS headquarters and other organizations. In the aftermath of the 1997 and 2008 economic crises, government funding became central to their activism because membership bases stagnated or were even eroded. It is through government funding in the form of project-based grants and outsourcing under private-public partnerships that neoliberal governance enabled lay women's activism. These methods of public funding for social services and programs reduced local feminist organizations to a tool of neoliberal governance, but it enabled local women to become "volunteer activists" (*jawonhwaldongga*). Nevertheless, the unequal partnership of these branches with local governments generated tension between grassroots activism and their civic identity based on the moral codes of independence and institutional change.

Two Local Branches (GY Branch and NE Branch) of DFS: Improving Women's Work and Health

To examine how neoliberal governance has both enabled and undermined activism of GY Branch and NE Branch, I focus on the following examples of their activism efforts: (1) a project to run a local childcare center to "socialize" women's privatized care work, (2) projects to build women's "health networks" and "local health ecosystems," (3) projects to improve women's (insecure) employment, and (4) projects to socialize women's food work for children. Pursued as major projects by the local branches, these activism efforts were instrumental in establishing and maintaining their feminist civic identity. The issues of childcare, health, employment, and food for children became major welfare issues at a national level by the end of the first decade of the twenty-first century as South Korea was rapidly restructured by neoliberal globalization. In contrast to PSPD, which remained financially independent of the government, the two DFS branches carried out most of their activism with partial or full funding from local governments. Yet these branches infused their feminist perspective into the publicly funded projects with varying degrees of success. They tried to reclaim the communal or social nature of women's privatized labor in childcare and food work. They tried to restore a social dimension to privatized problems of women's employment and the health of women and local residents. These examples of activism together illuminate significant roles that local branches played in promoting social welfare for local women and other residents and protecting the vulnerable through the provision of necessary social services. The local branches grappled with their feminist civic identity as they encountered two complications: (1) activism tied to government-funded projects served a larger number of local residents with urgent services but at the expense of the long-term goal of societal transformation, and (2) the dominance of such activism marginalized autonomous activities among local members outside government funding and thereby undermined their participation.

Project to Socialize Childcare Beyond Women's Privatized Care Work

Turning childcare from women's privatized labor into a social welfare service needs to be discussed in the context of broader demographic and political change in South Korea. In response to the rapid decline of childbirth and persistently low birth rates since the turn of the twenty-first century, the government began to pay attention to the care of babies, children, and the elderly. In 2004, it reformed the Infants and Toddlers Care Act to expand the categories of public childcare services, and in 2005 it enacted the Low Birth and Aging Society Basic Law to cope with the problem of the aging society. But neoliberal governance shaped the specific mechanism through which the government chose to deliver childcare as public services. Beginning with the Roh Moo-hyun government, it has privatized public childcare by funding commercial and noncommercial facilities and issuing vouchers to individual citizens in need. The most common method of funding these facilities involved the generation of low-paying and temporary jobs for childcare workers, who were predominantly women.[5] In particular, the government funded the Unlimited Carework Project, which led to the swift multiplication of public and commercial childcare facilities.[6]

The GY Branch's activism on childcare revolved around *Kkumteuri* (Dream Sprouter), its afterschool childcare center.[7] As an "auxiliary" to the branch, the center was a major vehicle to carry out feminist activism that addressed local needs.[8] It opened in 2007 to take care of schoolchildren whose parents were unable to attend to them because of their paid employment.[9] As a modest facility accommodating one to two dozen children, its smooth operation relied partly on government funding but more heavily on various types of volunteer activists and supporters contributing labor, money, or other resources. The center identified local children in dire need and enrolled them for adequate care by its teachers (whose wages were paid by government funding) and volunteer activists. It provided local schoolchildren with academic tutoring, life mentoring and counseling, food, cultural activities, and social interactions with peers and adults.[10] It combined the emphasis on schoolwork with other necessary behavioral training (for example, instruction to reduce aggressive behaviors and bullying) through counseling, play, and cultural activities.[11] To the GY Branch's dismay, however, the center was closed in 2019 due to a confluence of factors that highlight the complicating effect of neoliberal governance on civic activism.[12]

The scope of cooperation involved in running Dream Sprouter crossed the formal boundaries among civil society, the market, and the government. In 2009, the after-school childcare center joined the Goyang City Local Childcare Centers United as a founding member and shared management know-how and other resources with participating childcare centers. It also reached out to diverse local organizations, ranging from government agencies and businesses to civil society organizations, and developed a local network linking various businesses, public facilities, and private volunteering.[13] Internally, Dream Sprouter formed a Management Advisory Committee composed of volunteer activists, local residents, parents of the centers' children, and municipal assembly members, and this committee discussed the center's current issues and programs. It used the local network of schools, businesses, and social organizations to identify children in need.[14]

The after-school childcare center established and affirmed the moral code of grassroots participation at multiple levels. To provide children with stable personalized care, it relied on volunteer activists who interacted with the children and their parents for a wholistic approach to childcare. Volunteers and supporters included GY Branch members and other local residents, including college students who volunteered as mentors to individual children.[15] Facilitating their participation through ongoing communication and mutual trust, Dream Sprouter continued to focus on strengthening stable relationships among children, their parents, teachers, volunteer activists, supporters, and the management advisory committee. It also promoted children's participation in its programs for their own positive experience of personal change and empowerment.[16]

In 2015, however, Dream Sprouter's head reported growing problems of decreasing enrollment, reduced funding, and overwork among staff and volunteer activists.[17] The number of children enrolled directly affected the amount of government funding received and the stability of the center's budget, and problems followed in domino fashion. The decline in the number of children was both demographic and socioeconomic. Demographically, South Korea has recorded one of the lowest birth rates in the world since the early 2000s, which significantly reduced the total number of schoolchildren, especially in primary schools.[18] Economically, children of lower-class families moved frequently due to escalating economic insecurity, particularly housing and job insecurity, in the aftermath of the 2008 financial crisis. Socially, there was a steady growth in both commercial and public childcare facilities during the 2010s as the central government and society at large considered the persistent low birth rate a major national problem with far-reaching economic, political, and social ramifications and, thus, offered incentives to families to have children. Subsequently, primary schools established childcare programs on their premises to take care of children after regular school hours. To capitalize on this trend, commercial childcare facilities multiplied in the form of kids' cafés, libraries, and cram schools. A cultural and economic divide developed as affluent families sent their children to commercial cram schools with better facilities for academic drills and poorer families kept their children in the after-school childcare programs provided by their schools. This distinction generated a social stigma toward public or noncommercial facilities, which led to the avoidance of Dream Sprouter if both parents worked for a living and needed after-school childcare. Only those children who could not afford to go anywhere else came to Dream Sprouter, and they did not stay enrolled for long. As a result, the center became like a "bus stop" en route to the desired cram schools. Finally, the GY Branch had to close the center.[19]

Projects to Build Women's Health Network and Local Health Ecosystem

In comparison with GY Branch's activism involving Dream Sprouter, the NE Branch's activism on health issues involved extensive collaboration with the local government at a much larger scale. The NE Branch began the women's health network project in 2012 when it was selected by the Seoul metropolitan government to run it.[20] The project was the first case of outsourcing that experimented with neoliberal governance to promote local women's health by bringing the government, civil society, and the market together and facilitating grassroots participation. Under the leadership of Seoul's new mayor, Park Won-soon (October 2011–July 2020), the metropolitan government tried to develop a democratizing model of governance that was to serve as an example to be used by other local governments. As a showcase, the women's health network project had a tight time frame of seven months but was generally well funded. Similar to the GY Branch's efforts with Dream Sprouter but on a larger scale, the NE Branch built and managed a network of citizens' organizations, occupational organizations, traditional membership organizations, public welfare agencies, and commercial health care businesses. In contrast to Dream Sprouter, however, the daily running of the women's health network project relied entirely on full-time or professional staff members paid with government funding.

Although initiated by the metropolitan government, the women's health network project allowed the NE Branch to infuse its feminist perspective into various stages of its development. The branch organized workshops for brainstorming ideas, trained "women's health leaders," and constructed a women's health café as an integral element of building its online infrastructure.[21] During later stages, it hosted an annual women's health festival for wider publicity and participation and distributed calendars and diary notebooks to local women.[22] The training of women's health leaders was particularly significant for its feminist activism because these leaders became local activists who carried out women's health programs in their localities from "a gender perspective," which paid attention to a broader social context of gender relations.[23] This reconceptualization of women's health in practice was neither smooth nor easy; there was a significant gap between the branch's feminist expectations of the women's health project and those of the general public and other participating organizations, which tended to narrowly focus on immediate health issues and medical problems.[24] In the absence of an established convention of equal partnership between the government and women's civic organizations, the NE Branch promoted its view by tapping the political opportunity structure created by the new leadership in the metropolitan government that was looking for an innovative model to build its legacy. Gradually, the old hierarchical mode of interaction between the government and civic organizations began to change.[25]

The women's health leaders identified their local projects based on the specific needs of local residents their organizations served. There were seven bottom-up grassroots projects, including adolescent's sexuality and the health of diverse groups of adult women focused on lower-income female family providers, employed women, housewives, civic activists, professional postpartum assistants, women farmers, and consumers of a food co-op.

These projects recognized the diversity and differences among women and how the feminist perspective reenvisioned women's health beyond the conventional understanding of it narrowly as the absence of illness or mere physical health. The program for lower-income female family providers approached their health from a mind-body connection and was based on their "social opportunities for becoming masters of their own lives." The program for employed women focused on self-defense skills and developing the basic physical capacity to defend oneself in workplaces. The program for housewives used clothes-making as a process of healing through rediscovering the joy of manual labor while also talking together about their own lives and a need to develop a new fashion that could enhance women's health. The program for postpartum assistants paid attention to the high stress and chronic fatigue of women who worked as paid care workers for other women who delivered their babies. This program also resonated with the activism for women's insecure employment because it became a prevalent type of women's employment characterized by unstable and exploitative working conditions.[26]

The women's health network project continued for three years (2012–2014) with modifications in its annual thematic focus, building on the local organizational network, online and offline infrastructure, and know-how from its first year. In particular, the NE Branch provided women's health leaders with advanced training to enhance their capacity to infuse its holistic feminist perspective into women's health issues.[27] During those years, the NE Branch managed to develop more or less equal partnerships with local government agencies based on trust and cooperation. Through hard work, the health project became an "exemplary case of positive partnership between the government and civil society." Hence the NE Branch decided to continue the women's health project after its three-year term ended regardless of the government's continued partnership and funding. Impressed by the branch's accomplishments, the metropolitan government extended the project for three more years.[28]

During the second term (2015–2017), the women's health network project was expanded into the "local health ecosystem project." This expansion reflected an ongoing effort by the metropolitan government under the progressive mayoralty to establish "universal social welfare" through a ground-up process. This process started with individual towns and wards; good health was considered an essential element in building a universal social welfare system.²⁹ However, the good plan was seriously undermined by the resurfacing of the old way of working of local governmental bureaucracy, which contained multiple agencies and actors with vested interests in maintaining or strengthening their own organizational interests and power. The Dobong Ward Healthcare Center (*bogeonso*) represented the local bureaucracy, whereas the NE Branch represented local civil society organizations.³⁰ Collaboration between the two encountered two major problems. First, there were two different sections within the health-care center responsible for the new health ecosystem project and the old management of local health, respectively, which made smooth coordination difficult. Necessary communication was lacking between the health-care center staff (for example, between the "village nurse" and "social welfare workers") and the grassroots health leaders trained by the NE Branch. Second, after the showcase period, government funding became inadequate to support the expanding project of a local health ecosystem. A board meeting in November 2016 showed the unraveling of the project marked by overwork and understaffing, especially in the Ward Healthcare Center.

> The health-care center is overburdened with its established tasks. The health network project should be transferred to another section. Seoul City made the decision and the health-care center followed and it [the center] does not have its own will. If we say that we cannot do [the project], the center cannot.... We currently have two full-time staff activists, but we really need more personnel. Wouldn't it be working well if the city guarantees salary of additional activists even if they are part-time?³¹

The two problems stemmed from the underlying power difference and inequality between government and the feminist civic organization in the local context. After promoting and practicing neoliberal governance as a showcase for liberalization and democratization, the local government bureaucracy reverted to its authoritarian mannerism in handling citizens' organizations given its historical and cultural legacy.³² This dynamic reproduced the entrenched attitude of dominance and control toward citizens' organizations and ordinary citizens. In response, the NE Branch made the local health leaders working in the health-care center to improve the chance for grassroots voices to be heard.³³ Its efforts to deal with the conflict did not prevail, and the project ended at the end of the second term.

Projects to Improve Women's (Insecure) Employment

In the aftermath of the major financial crises in 1997 and 2008, women's insecure employment became one of the major welfare issues for DFS as a feminist organization. Acutely reflecting a major consequence of the neoliberal restructuring of the South Korean economy since the 1990s, marked by the "flexible labor" regime, the issue of insecure employment has impacted women far more extensively than men. In 2019, women represented 63.5 percent of all part-time workers in South Korea; this part-time employment accounted for 20.8 percent of all women's employment but only for 8.9 percent of all men's employment.[34] The entirety of insecure employment, including full-time but temporary employment and other convoluted forms of employment, would be much larger than the scale of part-time employment. Gender disparity is evident even when both men and women service workers are being paid below the minimum wage (10,000 won per hour): 10 percent of male service workers earned below the minimum wage compared to 25 percent of their female counterparts.[35] The problem of women's insecure employment was not an isolated labor issue but a social issue with immediate and far-reaching consequences for the individual, her family, and society as a whole. Recognizing its gravity, DFS headquarters turned it into a major national issue, and local branches would cooperate on and be dedicated to this for a long time. Initially, activism to improve women's insecure employment was supported by the Ebert Foundation Fund from Germany at DFS headquarters, but the GY and NE branches tapped into various local resources to pursue their own paths of activism.

The GY Branch collaborated with DFS headquarters in carrying out this activism. It focused on restaurant workers, study-practice paper tutors, and cleaners because these service jobs represented the three most common sources of employment for women who have been segregated in the secondary labor market. The secondary labor market is composed of small businesses that hired fewer than five employees as day laborers under highly exploitative and dangerous working conditions.[36] Throughout 2013, the branch newsletters featured women and paid work because it became the single most urgent issue for women, many of whom had not been in the paid labor market due to caring for their own children and other family responsibilities but who needed to return to the labor market. Housewives had to find paid work because their husbands' incomes were reduced or they lost their jobs altogether.[37] Pursuing both policy change and cultural change to destigmatize the "menial" service jobs, GY Branch members participated in various phases of this project over several years; they planned and prepared for research to investigate actual situations of restaurant workers and organized street campaigns to publicize their findings and influence the public's perception of restaurant workers. The investigative research involved talking to women workers directly and distributing a "human-rights manual for restaurant workers" to empower them.[38] The branch also contributed to drafting policy bills, organizing public discussions, and distributing research findings to policymakers. Along with this type of policy-oriented effort, the local branch pursued symbolic change to destigmatize the restaurant worker by coining a respectful term (*charimsa*) to identify them as an occupational group.[39]

The GY Branch also identified a culturally peculiar source of insecure employment available predominantly to women, but it could not achieve the same level of success because this job was performed in isolation and categorized as "self-employment." The peculiar employment was "study-practice paper tutors" (*hakseupji gyosa*). This job highlighted the confluence of a few major social changes shaped by neoliberal globalization in South Korea. As secure employment disappeared and the competition for it was intensified, families with schoolchildren invested more in their children's education to improve their academic record and thereby their competitiveness in the labor market. The following comments by a GY member poignantly capture the common attitude and routine practices among numerous Korean families and individuals:

> As wages decrease and employment becomes unstable, the society becomes unstable. As consumption is reduced and the gap between the rich and the poor increases, social problems are growing even more than before, affecting healthcare, social welfare, education, and housing. Hence, everyone is preoccupied with accumulating personal credentials. In order to cope with ever-shrinking job opportunities, we invest everything we have in our children's [education] and endlessly devote ourselves to preparing for classes and tests to get certificates.[40]

Study-practice papers refers to papers containing academic test questions, and they are subscribed to by schoolchildren to hone their skills for successfully taking the examinations. "Tutors" distribute these papers by visiting individual households and teaching individual students at home. This service is less expensive than a traditional private tutor or a commercial cram school and therefore more affordable to a larger number of families. Like piece work employees, these study-practice paper tutors are paid by the number of papers they sell and are not given any other basic benefits or legal protections. Due to its labor-intensive nature and vulnerable working conditions, it has been a profoundly feminized area of employment; but ironically they were categorized as "self-employed" and therefore "business owners."[41]

The GY Branch expanded its project to other common areas of women's insecure employment, including retail sales in big supermarket chains, department stores, and outlet stores. Recognizing that "these women workers are treated less [well] than the goods that they sell and remain invisible," the branch members monitored major retail chain stores in their city to identify problems in working conditions and to increase the human rights of women workers in retail sales. They carried out local campaigns, public discussions based on their research on workplaces, and suggested municipal ordinances for policy reforms.[42] In 2017, the GY Branch continued the project for women's insecure employment by focusing on irregular workers employed in the public sector. Despite its popular image as a decent form of employment due to the stability associated with public employment, the branch survey of women workers revealed their underlying insecurity and inequality in public employment. Financed by the Gyeonggi Province Gender Equality Fund, the GY Branch also carried out research on women's employment issues, ranging from the lack of employment opportunities, especially for the young and women with children, to exploitative working conditions for women workers.[43]

To pay attention to its own members, the GY Branch also facilitated a Small Group meeting named "One Fence (hanultari)," among its members, who were single mothers and family providers. The group began for their mutual assistance and developed into a "community-based employment cooperative" to realize women's economic self-reliance. They were given various educational programs during this development, including workshops along with ongoing interactions for mutual support.[44] The GY Branch facilitated these members to identify a viable co-op business for them to run.[45]

In contrast to GY Branch's activism to improve women's insecure employment, the NE Branch pursued large-scale projects by accepting the charge to run the Dobong Ward Women's Center from 2012 onward.[46] The center was initially created as a multipurpose public facility promoting local women's welfare, but the branch strengthened its occupational training programs and created women's employment projects under its leadership. As a result, the women's center functioned as a core mechanism for offering a range of useful services to improve women's employment.[47] This transformation of the women's center was further facilitated by the creation of the Women's New Job Center in 2014 as a component of the women's center.[48] The NE Branch developed a comprehensive infrastructure to improve women's employment in its locality. To support women as employees and small business owners, it provided them with individual and group counseling and consultation services. It also created and ran the New Job Women's Internship, which was designed especially for women who had been out of the job market for a long time. To continue its support for women's employment through various stages, the branch facilitated the formation of small groups for networking and mentoring among women as students of occupational training classes, new employees, and the newly self-employed. It ran regular monitoring programs for new employees to avoid job turnovers and offered stable support for them to adjust to their new workplaces. It also ran monitoring programs for employers to improve women's working conditions.[49]

Thanks to its successful operation of the women's center, the NE Branch was able to renew the outsourced management of the center twice in row and continued its projects for women's insecure employment until 2021.[50] This civic activism effort (discussed in detail in the section on the politics of civic identity) reveals the ambivalent consequences of neoliberal governance that outsourced public services on local feminist activism. On a positive note, even though the center (including its existing employees) was "entrusted" (outsourced) to the NE Branch and was funded entirely by the central and local governments, its women's employment projects enabled the local branch to pursue its own feminist activism to a significant degree.[51] For example, instead of merely supplying elderly care workers in the rapidly aging society, the branch opened a Support Center for Elderly Care Workers in 2018.[52] As the center's leading manager, the branch could infuse its feminist perspective into planning and running programs, as well as into the training of its staff members who were paid by the government. Instead of reproducing narrowly focused vocational classes commonly offered by government agencies, the branch approached women's (insecure) employment projects from a broad perspective of "women's empowerment through diverse education."[53] It made conscious efforts to alter the framework of managing the women's center from its feminist perspective.

Projects to Socialize Women's Food Work for Children

Dream Sprouter, the auxiliary childcare center at GY Branch, was a site of local grassroots activism funded partly by the government, but the NE Branch's activism for children's welfare took two forms without government funding: a coalition movement tied to the National Network for School Meals (*hakkyogeupsikjeonguknetwok*) and lay members' Small Group activities. The National Network was a coalition of diverse civil society organizations that promoted free quality school meals for all children.[54] In 2008 (preceding the development in GY Branch briefly mentioned at the beginning of this chapter), the NE Branch joined a northeastern Seoul chapter to realize "environment-friendly and free school meals" for all children. The issue appeared initially in the area as early as 2003 after local residents collected 12,000 signatures in support of an ordinance for free school meals, but its Ward Assembly rejected the initiative. The movement regained momentum as the Seoul Municipal Assembly enacted the ordinance in March 2009, but there was uneven progress in following this legal change at the level of individual wards. To pressure its local assembly, which had been lagging in enacting the ordinance, NE Branch members participated in a series of semi-monthly business meetings, street campaigns, signature collections, protests, and press releases until the ordinance was finally enacted in 2011.[55]

One of multiple press releases issued by the northeastern Seoul chapter during its cooperation for free school meals interpreted the School Meals Ordinance the Seoul Assembly passed as follows:

> Environment-friendly free school meals are a way to realize children's universal welfare. As No-hyeon Kwak, the Superintendent of Seoul, mentioned a while ago, there are no rich children and poor children. There are only rich parents and poor parents. Hence a free school meal is a child's welfare right,

not a parent's right. When welfare is not generally applied to all children, it becomes patronizing and stigmatizing. We hope that all children in this land grow up healthy and bright without the shadow of discrimination.[56]

This progressive view of free school meals tried to maximize the effect of the ordinance by stating that "the state and local governments must provide administrative and financial supports for good-quality school meals." In line with this view, the NE Branch carried out the project for a few years by getting involved in a range of activities. It conducted a survey of students in ten local high schools to assess the quality of school meals.[57]

Establishment of free school meals resulted from the combination of persistent cooperative civic activism in the context of significant political change that was epitomized by the election of the aforementioned Seoul mayor, who embraced the free school meals as a matter of universal welfare rights. It is important to situate the local grassroots activism for free and environmentally friendly school meals in the larger sociopolitical context. Throughout the 2000s, neoliberal globalization exacerbated economic insecurity and precarity of life for a majority of South Koreans, and the 2008 global financial crisis only added additional blows. In this context, free school meals became the first welfare issue that drew national publicity and influenced the outcomes of local and national elections by dividing the electorate into two opposing camps.[58] Although opponents approached it as a welfare service limited to the needy in the name of fiscal conservation, the electorate overwhelmingly supported the establishment of free school meals as children's universal welfare right.

Activism for free school meals was oriented toward institutional change, but a handful of NE Branch members formed a Small Group and carried out their food activism in the form of providing urgent services for local children. Named *sipsiilban* (every little bit helps), the Small Group was the oldest among several such groups in the branch. Its members offered monthly snacks to local schoolchildren who did not meet the criteria of "lower-income" families eligible for government aid. Group members identified children by surveying public "study rooms" and "after-school classes" in local schools. As a small operation, this food activism relied entirely on the members' voluntary work and its supporters' donations of various resources.[59] This activism focused on the urgent need of a handful of local children, and therefore its impact was fairly limited, but it affirmed the branch's civic identity as being tied to the moral codes of grassroots participation and independence from the government. It also provided group members and their supporters with a sense of making a difference through working together and expanding their privatized food work to a source of social welfare for local children.

THE POLITICS OF CIVIC IDENTITIES: MEANINGS OF "LOCAL FEMINIST ORGANIZATION"

The examples of activism discussed here allow us to examine how various ways of carrying out feminist activism in local contexts generated internal discussions about feminist civic identities and strategies. All three moral codes were related to the discussion of what it means to be a local feminist organization: grassroots participation, long-term social change, and independence from the government. In neoliberal South Korea, this discussion revolved around the relationships between the local DFS branches and local governments that became increasingly complex through neoliberal governance of networking, partnership, and cooperation as participation while activism among local residents had been stagnant or even in decline. These two factors, the proliferation of neoliberal governance and the stagnation and decline of local participation, are like two sides of the same coin. As financial and other forms of support from their members and other local residents stagnated or declined, the local branches had to seek government funding and partnership with local authorities to sustain and expand their activism. Relatedly, the local branches were also drawn to the significant increase in political and economic resources made available by neoliberal governance. I discuss specific ways in which local branches dealt with a gap between their complex reality and the ideal of local feminist organization in accordance with the moral codes of citizens' organizations.

Although the two local branches, like other progressive citizens' organizations, continued to cherish the normative ideal of grassroots participation, such autonomous and active participation by their members and other local residents had been declining for socioeconomic reasons. Aforementioned examples of Every Little Bit Helps (NE Branch) and One Fence (GY Branch) would approximate the ideal because they were initiated and run by lay members organizing themselves into the Small Groups, which are consciously devised as a vehicle for grassroots activism in DFS. On a positive note, these Small Groups provided urgent social services for local residents with a vision of social change promoted by DFS branches. But these Small Groups were struggling to survive rather than thriving to expand due to the lack of incoming new members. Similarly, the oldest Small Groups in both branches were in decline or ceased to exist as a result of decreasing participation. For example, the NE Branch had a Small Group for learning and performing traditional farmers' music; the group performed regularly in various events hosted by citizens' organizations. It was disbanded in 2016 after existing for eleven years because the number of participants decreased but new members did not join after old members retired. Many other commercial and public places had been developed where individuals could learn and practice farmers' music or other hobbies in better facilities.[60] As discussed in chapter 4, this development was shaped by the passage of the Lifetime Education Law (*pyeongsaeng-gyoyukbeop*), which led to the proliferation of public and commercial cultural centers. The impact of this development on Small Group activities resonates with the situation of Dream Sprouter, the childcare center that combined local initiatives for daily operation with government funding.[61] As neoliberal globalization generated economic insecurity and precarity of life in general, more and more people concentrated on paid employment: trying to keep it, preparing for it, and finding it. An activist staff in the NE Branch, who worked there for four years at the time of this interview, conveyed her observation of this significant change:

> **SUN-GYEONG:** We try to recruit our members through various events and activities. The most popular one is the class for training a youth sex education lecturer. A group of people who received the education last year go to local schools this year and teach sex education classes.
> **MOON:** Does the training class offer a certificate for the lecturer?
> **SUN-GYEONG:** Yes, everyone wants to earn some money, even a very small sum. Some people join our organization through the class. Others join because they are impressed by activists living diligently. I recruit local mothers through the monitoring of childcare centers. When we organize a Members' Meeting Day, we also carry out multiple lecture projects. But in comparison with efforts we make, there aren't many new people.[62]

As noted, neoliberal globalization has also brought social or cultural change in people's attitudes toward more privatization, fragmentation, and commodification. A head of GY Branch, who had been a DFS member for twenty years, shared her keen observation:

> They [referring to new members] come and go and are very narrowly interested in what they need but nothing else and what's going on elsewhere. More and more so. As a result, it is difficult to bring together members. For example, those who receive our training for professional counselor for sexual violence victims are generally interested in counseling and training. If thirty people come for the training course, about ten people join our organization but only one or two of them are interested in other issues. The rest focus only on their own needs and interests, nothing else. They are quite individualized. That is exactly what our society has become. For some time now, we don't do things together, are not interested in things around us, and don't pay attention to other peoples' lives. Everyone has become busy with making a living, focus on my child only, my house only. Our society taught people to survive for themselves, and this mentality has infiltrated everywhere. Organizations have become like that.[63]

The problem of a stagnant membership base compelled the local branches to reach out to local residents to try to reduce the gap between its long-term social change (in accordance with the feminist vision of a good society) and the urgent needs and interests of local residents. The difficulty is well captured by the following example. In 2014, the NE Branch facilitated a Small Group named Compassion and Healing (*gonggamgwa chiyu*) to address the common concern regarding child-rearing among its lay members. As local and autonomous activism, the small group made use of its senior members to share their own knowledge and experience and tried to enhance fellowship among participating members. Injecting its feminist perspective with communitarian ethos, the small group focused on building a mutual support network for mothers who would need healing from privatized childcare through sharing their experiences; this orientation was clearly distinguished from other locally based childcare groups that brought mothers together to raise their children "successfully." Yet the small group didn't last due to the lack of members' participation.[64] The exigency of raising "successful" children overshadowed the broader and deeper feminist concern with healing women as mothers and transforming social relations established around privatized child-rearing. Dealing with the enduring problem of stagnant or declining grassroots participation, an officer of the NE Branch, which developed a growing collaboration with the government, voiced the challenge poignantly:

> This is a year when we could not laugh away "solidarity equals the receipt of money." We feel lingering regret about being unable to achieve the initial goal of recruiting fifty new members, but we are still asking a question. How can we build a benevolent cycle of *making our members enjoy and be excited about volunteer participation in members' activities* or at least make them so proud of being our members because they hear good things about our activities and hence they feel proud of paying membership fees.[65]

Along with the ideal of enthusiastic and proud grassroots participation, her words highlight the sobering political economy of civic activism. Although it is an option to do away with government funding as PSPD and FOA have done, it may not be a viable option for many small or medium-sized organizations. The two local branches' partnership with local authorities discussed here led to unintended complications in their activism and thus also reflection on their feminist civic identities.

The continuum of partnership between the local branches and the local governments, ranging from project-based funding to an outsourced management of entire public facilities, allows us to look into how unequal power between government and local civic organizations tends to undermine the autonomy of the local organizations while they try to turn neoliberal governance into a political opening for substantive democratization. Dream Sprouter, the GY Branch's auxiliary childcare center, coped with the double jeopardy of a decrease in participation by volunteer activists and the undermining of its autonomy over time. In 2016, there was an internal discussion on whether or not the center should be closed.[66] The discussion was summarized like this.

> It is difficult to keep the center's unique color (based on its focus on human rights and feminism) while funded by the government for its operation. As a result of various changes over the past decade, we have lost the initial intention (*chosim*) and seem to run it out of habit. Moreover, *because it is free,*

parents tend to lose attention and interest. We experienced recurring dilemmas over how to strike a balance between values that DFS pursues and the complex reality of running the center.[67]

This summary sheds light on the complex reality of local grassroots civic activism partially funded by the government. The availability of government funding for childcare facilities initially benefited Dream Sprouter's operation, but the growing reliance on this funding subjected it to bureaucratic control by the local government. Government funding required that all childcare programs in the center to be evaluated in documentable fashion according to its rules, and this generated extra work for the two teachers who needed to focus on the children.[68] In addition, Dream Sprouter was not authorized to identify and choose its own children; selection took place elsewhere, and the children were sent to the center.[69] These practices flew against the GY Branch's expectation of the government as the provider of legal and physical infrastructure rather than as a micromanager of its daily operation. The GY Branch considered its community-based childcare center as a site where childcare was realized as a public service rather than just a private responsibility and where future citizens were raised with communal and democratic values. The branch also viewed the center as a specific way to support and empower local women who had to work for a living. These important moral values were overshadowed because Dream Sprouter had to follow the bureaucratic rules and control for continuity of funding.[70] Bureaucratic regulation is necessary for accountability when using public resources, but its rigid routinization in the form of micro-control of the daily workings of the center undermined its autonomy and experimental spirit in bringing local actors together to care for children.

Childcare activism pursued by Dream Sprouter suggests that neoliberal governance marked by partnership and cooperation between a civic organization and government can promote democratizing social change only if this partnership maintains autonomy for the local organization such as GY Branch. Then government funding works as an enabling condition. It is not accidental that the discourse of civil society in South Korea identified independence from the government as its moral code. However, government's recognition of the autonomy of a civic organization requires deeper and broader cultural change that internalizes democratic values of equality and self-determination beyond the appearance of partnership. The neoliberal emphasis on business metrics converges with bureaucratic monitoring of funding usage and undermines the autonomy of the local civic organization.

Even in the successful case of the Women's Health Project, the model of neoliberal governance led to growing control by the government bureaucracy and the unintended consequence of undermining the autonomy of NE Branch. Even under progressive new leadership, the government bureaucracy had its own established dynamic. The government project came with its own time frame and specific rules to follow. NE Branch was controlled by this set schedule and detailed guidelines; as a result, it not only was overworked but also could not spend enough time to deliberate with other participating organizations for broader and deeper issues beyond specific tasks and the narrow projects to be accomplished. Many "unnecessary administrative procedures" drained its energy and time to pay attention to important and broader aspects of the women's health network project. Essentially, the existing government bureaucracy and administrative procedures dictated the NE Branch's efforts, thereby negatively affecting its activism by reducing its autonomy in following its own course of action for better results.[71] This problem was further aggravated when the Local Health Ecosystem project followed the women's health network project. The July 2016 minutes of its monthly steering committee meeting conveyed this concern:

> We need to evaluate the [local health network] project continuously, but we agonize over what it means for us to continue. Among the four wards which have carried out the project, it is only our ward that has the same staff and agency as the last year's.... The healthcare center staff in charge also changed, and we needed the process of communicating with them and ironing out our differences. We feel heavy pressure. The project began as an integral aspect of the village welfare project, but its four major issues are working separately without coming together to enhance local residents' quality of life. It is agonizing trying to decide how to bring them together.[72]

These examples show largely negative consequences of government funding for the autonomy of a civic organization, but these effects are not necessarily automatic. They depend on the history and the culture that structures the relationship between the state and civil society organizations.[73] In Norway, the government has demanded more accountability and transparency by civic organizations in return for public funding but has left many other aspects of its relations with these organizations unregulated, which indicates substantial mutual trust based on their sense of interdependence rather than government's dominance over such organizations.[74] In contrast, the South Korean example shows government's dominance, which reflects lingering authoritarianism as the historical and cultural legacy. The funding requires applications, and their success entails reporting on funded projects, which increases bureaucratic management and leads to a need to hire more full-time staff in charge of these matters or diverting the time and energy of existing staff. Although government funding initially enables the resource-poor branches to accomplish some of their projects and goals, it generally undermines the energy and time their staff members have to focus on various issues critical to their local members.

Aware of the power differential between the government and itself, the NE Branch tried to balance its feminist activism with resources from the government by discussing the pros and cons of running the Women's New Job Center as an integral part of the Women's Center that was entrusted to it. The March 2014 steering committee meeting summarized the issues this way.

> **PROS:** The Women's New Job Center will draw necessary policy attention to women family providers, one of the most vulnerable but neglected social groups, and provide the NE branch with a chance to grow as an organization for masses of ordinary women. The focus on single mothers can also offer a productive starting point for other related projects that empower them and this is a worthy project for DFS. We can encourage women and care for them better than other organizations. If the project is to be implemented in our area, we should be doing the project with a feminist mindset.
> **CONS:** What can the branch gain from running the New Job Center? We're pursuing social movement and social change but it is highly likely that our involvement in the center will subject us to the control of the Ministry of Women and Family. Moreover, the kind of jobs that the center will create are mostly irregular jobs rather than secure regular jobs. Our involvement will overburden us and drain our energy.[75]

The pros and cons are equally valid and compelling; there is no easy resolution for how to maintain and modify feminist civic identity in connection with government authorities. An officer of the branch aptly asked, "What sort of volunteer gathering among our members can we do if we don't do this type of government-funded project?"[76] As discussed previously, the NE Branch decided to run the government project and tried to infuse its feminist perspective into it as much as possible.

Simultaneously, the successful management of the local Women's Center shifted the NE Branch's focus from its own members to the broader public of local residents. This ironic problem was noticed by an external inspector who evaluated its 2014 activities and performance.

> On the one hand, the branch excelled in carrying out a wide range of projects competently, and it is difficult to think that all these activities were done by this local organization. On the other hand, I wonder if the pursuit of those diverse projects generated positive synergy for each participant and planner involved. Additionally, if those projects have strengthened the identity of DFS and enhanced its individual members' capacity.... There was a problem of the lack of active participation among members of the Health Team. It would be necessary to examine how the project about women with illness could be connected to the project to prevent violence against women through improving social perception. In terms of the overall structure of activities, there was a separation between lay members clustered around Small Groups and activist staff focusing on all other projects. In the long run this can lead to a negative consequence of undermining the local base and therefore needs to be paid attention to.[77]

The report resonated with NE Branch officers and activists and contributed to ongoing efforts to figure out what it means to be a local feminist organization. The gap between lay members and activist staff running projects funded or outsourced by the government affirms the rule of professional monopoly in activism as political action. Even though these staff hailed from grassroots laity, they were transformed into professional activists working full-time or part-time with pay. Government funding further encroaches on the autonomy of civic organizations. It would be ideal if a local organization like the branch could attend to both its own members and the wider public of local residents. In the absence of enough resources, the question becomes either/or rather than both. This thorny question is linked to the underlying tension between broader long-term institutional change and addressing the urgent needs of its members or local residents. It is also linked to the tension between intellectual analysis and imagining an alternative society versus coping with urgent problems by providing necessary social services.

CONCLUSION

By focusing on four examples of activism pursued by two local branches of DFS, I examined how the popularized model of neoliberal governance, marked by partnership, cooperation, and networking between civic organizations and governments both enabled and constrained local feminist activism. The examples illustrate to what extent small to medium-sized local organizations relying on volunteer activists rather than professional activists benefit from public funding and outsourcing and are constrained by it. Paying attention to the details of these activism efforts highlights the complexities of the enabling and constraining conditions feminist organizations like GY Branch and NE Branch face.

Initially, government funding enabled GY Branch to maintain its childcare center, Dream Sprouter, as a feminist experiment to socialize childcare through networking and cooperation among diverse social groups, including business. Over time, however, the government's narrow focus on the head count of children cared for at the center constrained the branch from pursuing its own vision of socialized childcare. This primary concern with head counting reflected the economic metrics of neoliberalism, which turns almost everything into a matter of quantitative efficiency and financial calculation. In exchange for continued funding, especially when its volunteer activists and supporters dwindled, Dream Sprouter could not choose the local children it would take care of and instead had to accept a list of children given to them by government agencies involved in the partnership. In addition, the neoliberal transformation of the larger society negatively affected childcare activism. The number of local volunteer activists and supporters decreased in the face of escalating economic insecurity. Neoliberalism as a dominant political rationality has promoted the market as the desirable model of organizing human lives, and childcare has become an additional commodity to be purchased in a marketplace.

Because commercial childcare boasted better facilities than public ones and are culturally accepted as being more desirable, middle-class families did not develop interests in supporting public childcare facilities. Parents of such families would prefer paying for better facilities for their own children without paying for children of lower-class families. This lack of communal social thinking and practice among middle-class families reflected an individualized solution for childcare with money to purchase commodified services just as the government's narrow focus on budget and limited childcare services for lower-class families reflected neoliberal governance that has adopted business metrics for public services.

Outsourcing women's health and local health projects enabled NE Branch to experiment with its feminist view of health, which recognizes gender relations and other broader social contexts of individual health. For the first three years, the branch was allowed to develop programs and organizational infrastructures necessary for infusing and expanding this wholistic approach to health. It was promoted as a "showcase" of successful governance by the mayor of Seoul, who used to be a leader of PSPD and a veteran of citizens' movements. During this earlier period, a tight time frame and specific goals imposed by the government were constraints, but they were relatively manageable. For the next three years, however, NE Branch had to cope with more constraining conditions, which did not directly result from neoliberal governance but from bureaucratic inertia tied to vested interests and hierarchy. The division within the local government bureaucracy in charge of health issues and the resurgence of hierarchical thinking vis-à-vis civic organizations undermined NE Branch's energy and autonomy. Business metrics common to neoliberal governance was not a primary factor in this case for at least two reasons. First, in comparison with childcare issues, which had drawn national attention for more than a decade, the problems of an aging society and women's health and local health were new local issues; their novelty and limited scope have not yet mobilized extensive commercial and public interests in them. Second, outsourcing was intended to be a successful showcase of governance, and the emphasis was on the positive partnership rather than on budgetary regulations commonly leading to the micro-control of an organization being funded.

Due to its far-reaching scope and centrality to the neoliberal order, the issue of women's insecure employment mobilized both GY Branch and NE Branch, but they chose different paths in their activism. GY Branch pursued autonomous activities partially funded by the local government, and NE Branch pursued the outsourced activism of running a local Women's Center as its organizational hub. GY Branch cooperated with DFS headquarters to improve women's employment and utilized project-based government funding to implement its own programs without compromising its autonomy. Limited funding without excessive government control under the rubric of governance enabled local activism, but local participation in civic activism tends to dwindle in neoliberal society marked by economic insecurity in general and employment insecurity in particular. NE Branch has competently run the Women's Center with an array of auxiliary organizations and diverse programs to improve women's employment. On the one hand, this was a positive example of outsourcing that enabled local women's activism to address the urgent problem because the interests of NE Branch and the local government in improving women's employment converged. In particular, local women who became actively involved in the outsourced project grew as volunteer activists and became professional activists. On the other hand, a growing gap developed between this group of volunteer activists and local members of the NE Branch. Echoing the problem of PSPD discussed in chapter 4, which affirmed the rule of professional monopoly in political action, the success of local activists with the outsourced program led to the marginalization of local members and their autonomous activities.

In contrast to NE Branch's outsourced activism in health projects and women's employment projects, activism to socialize women's food work for children was pursued without government funding or outsourcing. To pursue policy change, NE Branch joined a coalition movement of various civic organizations under the rubric of the National Network for School Meals, and it appropriated the notion of neoliberal governance for autonomous cooperation among citizens' organizations (and some local businesses). To serve local children with meals, NE Branch relied on its local members' Small Group activities. The autonomous coalition movement was successful in achieving the goal of implementing free school meals as a universal welfare right for all children in the sociopolitical context in which growing number of voters supported the policy and elected government officials also supported it. In contrast, Small Group activism declined in neoliberal South Korea for Dream Sprouter and other activities of volunteer activists.

The diverse examples of activism discussed in this chapter negotiated with neoliberalism by engaging with neoliberal governance to varying degrees and were differently enabled and constrained by it. Is this variation significantly related to the nature of activism issues in terms of challenging and bolstering core values and mechanism of neoliberalism? All of the issues except women's insecure employment focus on caring human beings, especially marginalized social groups, but even women's employment involved taking care of women as vulnerable workers. Rather than directly challenging the core values and mechanism of neoliberalism, such as financialization of the economy (for accelerated accumulation of capital) and market fundamentalism, these activism efforts tended to repair damages done to marginalized social groups, including children, local women, and residents who are not wealthy and powerful. In chapter 6, I turn to an example of local activism that refused neoliberal governance.

Chapter Six

REFUSING NEOLIBERAL GOVERNANCE AND PURSUING PREFIGURATIVE ACTIVISM

When we cross borders, we become foreigners. If they don't have legal residency, they are not criminals. Just like us, they dream about happy lives, work, love, and raising their children. They are our neighbors. Even though their skin colors look different, they were born in Korea and their hometowns are in Korea, but they were labeled as illegal residents as soon as they were born. There are no illegal people but only the undocumented. When they work here, they are workers here.

—FROM A FOA BROCHURE; AUTHOR'S TRANSLATION

On August 19, we paid our eleventh visit to the Hwaseong Foreigners Protection Center (*oeguginbohoso*). Since the tenth visit last time, among the protected foreigners (*bohooegugin*) whom we had been meeting, one left [Korea], one was transferred to another institution, and one was out for a medical treatment. Then three new foreigners asked for meetings with us. As a result, we met the same total number of eleven foreigners. During our last visit, all protected foreigners had their chest X-rays taken [because one of inmates there tested positive for tuberculosis]; so we asked them about their test results and fortunately everyone was O.K. . . . To my frustration, from August 21 in-person visits to the protection center were entirely suspended again due to the rapid resurgence of COVID-19. The government heightened its quarantine system to the level Two. Our in-person visits became one of [the] rare occasions for consolation and hope for protected foreigners, who had been severely stressed by living detained, but even such a visit is not allowed. I feel very frustrated about the Ministry of Law that continued to catch people into the protection center. I don't understand what it is going to do. There are many people who cannot return to their countries even if they want to because airline routes have been closed. Migrants are capable of contributing to our society in many necessary areas. These days it is not easy to bring new migrants [due to the pandemic]. If so, why not making those migrants legal who have already adapted to our society without big problems and embrace them? In this period of COVID pandemic, we cannot solve problems with conventional thinking. We really need to shift how we think.[1]

This postscript is one of many written reflections on face-to-face visits to foreign migrants who are detained by the Korean government because they are categorized as "illegal." These visitors are dues-paying members of FOA or their supporters who voluntarily join biweekly visits to the center to meet detained migrants. Named *majung* [receiving a guest] by FOA, these meetings reveal the vulnerability of the migrants' structural position in the global economy. As uprooted outsiders, they are forced into "dangerous, difficult, and dirty work" (3-D work) that most native Korean citizens have avoided even though neoliberal globalization has replaced secure jobs with insecure ones. Foreign migrants fill the growing gap between the increasing demand for secure jobs and their decreasing supply, but their human rights are structurally violated to accelerate the accumulation of profits through exploitation of more vulnerable labor by more deregulated and mobile transnational capital. In comparison with PSPD and the two local branches of DFS discussed in earlier chapters, FOA has focused on this more visible consequence of neoliberal globalization—foreign migrants who look different from typical Koreans.

As South Korea moved from a country sending out its people as cheap laborers to one receiving foreign migrants, many civil society organizations were developed to deal with issues concerning migrant workers. A majority of these organizations focus on providing charitable services in accordance with the frame of assimilation (or what the government ironically named "multiculturalism"), but FOA has pursued a rather different path of activism. It has tried to create a social space in which native Koreans and foreign migrants interact and build solidarity as equal members of society beyond the provision of urgent services. As discussed in chapter 3, I call this orientation of FOA activism *prefigurative* to highlight its emphasis on solidarity based on equality, which does not yet exist but is considered in their vision in advance and experimented in practices whenever possible. In discussing prefigurative activism, I delve into how FOA activism efforts are enabled and constrained by neoliberal governance, in particular, and neoliberalism, in general, as the dominant mode of ruling through (1) Korean language classes, (2) cultural projects to educate Koreans about migrants and recognize their equal rights and full humanity, and (3) the majung, which refers to the biweekly visits to undocumented foreign migrants detained in the Hwaseong Foreigners Protection Center. These examples highlight how a small local organization managed to maintain and defend its civic identity by modifying and reinventing its repertoires of activism as the government policy on foreign migrants appropriated its practices and ideas through neoliberal governance using partnership and outsourcing to deliver new social services. In particular, the government's promotion of "multiculturalism" à la neoliberal governance modified FOA's activism over time as it endeavored to maintain its civic identity based on the codes of independence from the government, grassroots participation, and activism for broad social change.

BUILDING SOLIDARITY WITH FOREIGN MIGRANTS AS FELLOW MEMBERS OF KOREAN SOCIETY

Since its establishment in 2002, FOA activism has promoted human rights for migrants from other Asian countries and their equality with Koreans by offering urgent services and other necessary programs. As one of its oldest support programs for migrants, Korean language class has provided migrants with the ability to function in Korean society. Korean language proficiency can mitigate their structural vulnerability in workplaces and other social settings, enabling them to speak, comprehend information, and fight back. To balance this learning of Korean language by foreign migrants, FOA has pursued educating native Koreans about migrants' cultures and designed and implemented various programs and events. This underlying principle of reciprocity in learning about each other resonates with FOA's prefigurative activism, which emphasizes building solidarity based on the recognition of equality. As the government's appropriation of multiculturalism generated a proliferation of Korean language classes and other cultural programs and events, FOA shifted its primary activism from cultural programs to regular visits to the protection center to change the predicament of foreign migrants caught between expulsion and detention.

Clarification is necessary here to avoid confusion about FOA's refusal to accept neoliberal governance. Their refusal is expressed most visibly in a refusal of government funding, which is situated in the context of popular practices of neoliberal governance. The government's appropriation of multiculturalism has been translated into numerous projects carried out by outsourcing and funding in partnership with diverse types of NGOs. FOA has also maintained its critical distance from business metrics, which directs neoliberal governance.

Korean Language Class (*hangugeogyosil*)

Comparable to the GY Branch and NE Branch of DFS, as a local organization FOA combined its activism for institutional and long-term social change with the provision of necessary social services. This began with a Korean language class because language skills were essential for migrants to work and live in Korea. The language class has been offered by FOA since 2002; its size has fluctuated over time, but it has always relied on volunteer activists who were interested in performing social services in their locality.[2] Their backgrounds were diverse in age, gender, and occupation. Some volunteer teachers had a background in Korean language instruction, but many of them did not, and they learned how to teach through their own trial and errors and discussions with other volunteer teachers. In my in-depth interviews with a dozen of these teachers over time, I learned that teaching the Korean language has been one of the most interesting and enjoyable activities for them as FOA members or supporters. A high school senior who participated in FOA initially to earn an academic credit for his volunteer services to enhance his chance to study in the United States for his college degree, commented:

> There are several things that make me feel good and I enjoy. I have been teaching Korean language, and that makes lives of foreign migrants easy. So I feel a bit of pride in my small contribution to supporting their adjustment in Korea. It's also interesting to listen to life stories of migrants. Once I was teaching a Vietnamese woman in a one-to-one lesson because there weren't other students. She started to tell me how difficult it was for her to come to Korea; she had to pay money for a specific test and things like that. After hearing about her hardship, I wished she could earn a lot of money and send it back to her home.[3]

This student volunteer represents a popular trend among students of foreign language high schools where a majority of students go abroad for their college education in this era of neoliberal globalization. Students commonly pursue volunteer services through local or national NGOs because it can enrich their personal experience and thereby enhance their personal statements, which are an essential component of their college application packages.[4] This trend reveals an ironic twist of a common neoliberal practice unexpectedly enabling volunteer activism that actually or potentially changes an individual. Neoliberalism in South Korea and elsewhere has promoted educational and other investments in the individual self as human capital in preparation for intensifying competition in the labor market. Although volunteer service can easily be reduced to an "asset" to enhance an individual's market value or competitiveness, this outcome is neither automatic nor predetermined. As discussed in the next section, Jun-han, like many other volunteer teachers, was expanding his outlook and attitude as a result of his interaction with migrant workers. There is also a circuitous way in which foreign travel in the era of neoliberal globalization enabled volunteer activism of Korean language teaching among members and supporters of FOA. Among a dozen interviewees I met during my fieldwork in 2009 and 2015, a third of them had experienced multiple foreign travels or lived in foreign countries for several months to several years. This personal exposure to foreign cultures and societies contributed to their interest in teaching Korean to foreigners when they looked for opportunities for volunteer service.

The personal enjoyment and satisfaction of FOA members and supporters teaching Korean language needs to be understood in conjunction with the difficult circumstances facing foreign migrants who took these classes at FOA. Hye-jeong, a woman in her thirties who taught Korean language for three years at FOA, conveyed her observations of the harsh reality of her migrant students along with her aspiration to improve the quality of her class for them:

> I guess I'd like to develop a systematic approach. As you probably know, there are well-known Korean Language Academies at Korea University and Yonsei University. They offer one-to-two-year programs and when students complete them, they achieve significant improvement in their proficiency. We can't do that here because of difficult circumstances. Migrants (*ijumin*) work every day and they come to the class only one day a week on Sunday. I personally would like to use a step-by-step systematic method, but migrant workers we teach here deal with a very harsh reality. They cannot come [to a class] if they are avoiding the arrest of "illegal workers." They cannot come if they have to do [an] extra shift in their workplaces. I hope the whole situation improves; it'd be great if we have better textbooks. I'm hoping but the reality is very tough.[5]

Her observation reflected the following profile of migrant workers who came to the Korean language class: the majority were young, in their early to mid-twenties, and worked six days a week from 9:00 A.M. to 6:00 P.M. but commonly worked longer than twelve hours a day. Their workplaces were small factories located in remote rural areas that hired fewer than five employees. Public transportation was relatively limited, and on Sundays when they came to language classes public transportation was even less frequently available than on week days. As a result, they had to wait for a long time, and waiting became difficult to bear during the cold winter and the hot summer.[6]

Between these two polar examples—a teenager with no previous experience of teaching Korean language and an adult with significant experience and a desire for more systematic instruction—were numerous men and women who passed through the Korean language class as volunteer teachers and contributed to the improvement of Korean language skills for migrants. On a rolling basis, FOA paired a volunteer teacher with a few migrant students for Sunday classes and coordinated a regular meeting of volunteer teachers to discuss their teaching experience and maintain the quality of their classes. Despite its limited resources and constrained circumstances of migrant students, FOA tried to ensure good classes. Chihyeon, a FOA member for two years, explained a modified arrangement that volunteer teachers made.

> We changed the curriculum because students cannot come continuously. This applies to teachers as well. Even though a migrant student is enrolled for a year, he stops attending and comes back after three weeks or eight weeks. So it was difficult to make continuous improvement, and we decided that the same teacher will continue. . . . For example, I teach from lessons 1 to 5 and another teacher does lessons 6 to 10. If one of my students finished lesson 1 but was absent for three weeks and returned, he stays with me to learn lesson 2. If he has already finished lesson 5, he goes to the other teacher, to start from lesson 6 naturally.[7]

The division of labor among volunteer teachers shows their cooperative effort to deal with the uncertainty for both the students and themselves. The uncertainty in migrant students' lives is described by Hye-jeong, and the uncertainty in teachers' lives stemmed from the secondary nature of volunteer work in a capitalist society. As I observed during my research, a majority of volunteer activists had full-time paid jobs or were between jobs. Unlike members of PSPD and those of the two DFS branches, no FOA members and supporters were old enough to be retired. Because these teachers have to prioritize their full-time jobs, the division of labor made their teaching responsibilities more manageable.

A noteworthy change in the background of Korean language teachers over time is the emergence of those who specialize in teaching Korean as a foreign language. During my interviews with FOA members in 2009, I did not encounter a single person with this academic training, but in interviews in 2015 I encountered a few such individuals; all of them were women in their twenties. This change reflected the rapid growth of international marriages between Asian or other foreign women and Korean men and the children of these couples who attend primary and secondary schools. The government has paid ostensible attention to these families under the rhetoric of "multicultural family policy" (*damunhwa gajok jeongchaek*).[8] Reflecting the steady growth of multicultural students, teachers' colleges established programs specializing in Korean language instruction. In neoliberal Korea, where secure employment has been rapidly evaporating, school teaching has become a highly coveted job, and competition for teaching jobs has become fierce.[9] Some young adults who need to invest in themselves to increase their competitiveness in the teaching job market have specialized their teaching areas and find a niche in Korean language instruction. They came to FOA to gain experience teaching Korean as a foreign language before their full-time employment or in pursuit of meaningful volunteer services using their skill after their employment, or both.

The shift in the background of volunteer teachers over time reveals an intricate structure and the unintended consequences of neoliberalism in Korean society in terms of paid employment and volunteer work/activism. Neoliberalism, which has promoted investment in the individual self through formal and informal education in preparation for increasingly insecure employment, allowed for the emergence of professionally trained Korean language teachers and inadvertently facilitated their involvement in volunteer work. In-a, a woman in her late twenties who received her MA degree in Korean language education, had taught migrants for five months when I met her and interviewed her in the summer of 2015. As a way to gain teaching experience, especially during the initial stage of her career, she came to FOA and volunteered for Korean language teaching. However, she expanded her instrumental thinking about teaching the language and changed her attitude about it in the process of interacting with specific migrants as fellow human beings. As discussed in the next section, Chun-han, a high school senior we met earlier, went through a similar change over time. This group of volunteer teachers consists of a minority of individuals who came to perform volunteer work to strengthen their position in the neoliberal labor market, but their instrumental thinking went through significant change over time in the face of human suffering. This is a twist in what I observed in the study of the two local branches of DFS in the previous chapter where employment insecurity generated by neoliberal restructuring of the economy has undermined people's interest in volunteer work. They feel less secure financially and less motivated to pursue volunteer activism because they are pressured to focus on preparation for paid employment.

A majority of individuals, however, invest in themselves differently, and those who have some economic security invest in themselves to enhance their health and appearance. This broad trend is captured by Sam-sook's observation when I ask if she had talked about her involvement in FOA and had ever encouraged her acquaintances and friends to join:

> When I chat with them about how I spend my weekend, I talk about my teaching from 2 to 4 on Sunday afternoon. I suggest that they come if they're interested because it's enjoyable. They show interest but few actually come.

I then asked her, why do you think that is the case?

> Well, mothers in my neighborhood and vicinities lead very busy lives. They spend their leisure time exercising for health and fitness; you name it, yoga, golf, squash, all kinds of sports. They also go out together for lunch. So reasonably good restaurants are generally crowded with housewives during daytime. They feel secure from doing things in groups and avoid anxiety about uncertain lives. And those who really struggle to making a living have to work (*arbait*) outside the home.[10]

The Korean language class was intended to improve migrants' language skills, but it also functioned as a way to build meaningful human relationships between Korean teachers and foreign migrants. Chi-hyeon conveys the underlying social dimension of the language class as well as his enjoyment:

I prefer teaching the introductory level because a new fellow who can't speak Korean at all can make a more visible improvement than a fellow who takes the intermediate-level class. You can see clearly the difference between no speaking and no listening and some speaking and some listening, but you cannot see much difference between some speaking and some listening and a bit more speaking and listening. I feel really good to see this kind of noticeable improvement among beginners. I also like being the first teacher that they [migrants] meet when they come to FOA. Sometimes I struggle [with] how to communicate with fellows who cannot speak Korean, but by trial and error we came to understand each other and laugh together and continue. I really like the feeling of a connection being developed.[11]

There were also very sad memories of migrant students who returned to their countries after their labor contracts expired or those who were expelled or killed. Hye-jeong reminisced over a few "friends" she became attached to through her Korean language class:

There were more friends who returned [to their countries] after their time here [in Korea] expired. Intermittently they are coming back in my memory. There was a student who was really sincere. He moved to another region and then came back to this area to work. I didn't hear from him for some time and later heard that he died from an explosion in a factory. I remember him more than other friends because he was so sincere. I won't be able to forget. Recently, a friend returned to Vietnam and could not be contacted. I developed a lot of feeling of attachment (*jeong*) to her. Perhaps her phone number has changed. It is rather hard to be separated.[12]

During its first decade, when Korean language classes had multiplied under the government's multicultural policy and programs, FOA linked its language class to other socializing events, including summer camps, end-of-year parties, hiking or mountain climbing, and sporting events, to build meaningful human relationships. I observed a sporting event in the fall of 2009 that was co-organized by FOA and a local chapter of the Democratic Labor Union. Modeled after a popular sporting event (*undonghoe*) organized by schools and workplaces, the event featured a soccer game competition among two teams composed of migrant students, FOA members and supporters, and union members. Soccer was played by men, and a tug of war was played by both men and women. These events were accompanied by sharing a meal, beverage, and snacks, which generated conviviality and fellowship.[13]

FOA also used the Korean language class as a medium to enrich the lives of migrant workers beyond obtaining the pragmatic skill. It paid attention to the one-dimensional image of migrants among the public as a source of cheap and expandable labor; the exigency of working and earning money also influence migrants themselves to see themselves as such. To recognize their full humanity, FOA periodically published Korean writing collections produced by migrant students. These writings ranged from short essays and short stories to Korean translations of children's stories from the home countries of migrant students. The sporting events were dominated by male migrant workers, but these activities of literary expression were dominated by female "marriage migrants" who married Korean men.[14] The significance of Korean language class to recognize migrant workers' full humanity through literary and playful activities was organically connected to various projects to educate Koreans about migrants' cultures.

Projects to Educate Koreans About Migrants' Cultures: Popularization and Appropriation

This category of activism was central to FOA's civic identity as a citizens' organization focusing on migrant issues until the government began to promote its own version of "multiculturalism" and appropriated it. The emphasis on educating Koreans about foreign migrants' cultures reflected FOA's prefigurative and ideal vision of them as equal members of Korean society whose cultural differences ought to be recognized by Koreans and taught to them rather than being erased or suppressed under the de facto framework of assimilation. By learning about the culture and history of migrants, the founder of FOA noted that Koreans could overcome their ignorance of migrants and prejudice against them as merely miserable strangers from poor countries and therefore the objects of charitable services at best.

FOA's cultural approach was rather uncommon in the early to mid-2000s. A majority of civil society organizations working for migrants paid attention to the immediate problems of unpaid wages and work-related injuries, which were quite common and serious. Without neglecting these urgent issues, FOA aspired to move beyond the narrow economic focus and prefiguratively envision Korean society as a place where native Koreans and foreign migrants would live together as equal members. Tapping into its local identity, FOA reached out to migrant workers and encouraged them to join it to deal with their common problems; and it reached out to local Korean residents, especially schoolchildren, to educate them about the new members of Korean society. It organized various cultural events at mostly small scales, which could lead to personal interactions between local residents and migrant workers over sharing food, music, dance, and playing sports and games together. Migrants themselves took part in these events and introduced their own cultural practices and history and expressed their equal humanity. In autonomous and local contexts, these participatory events allowed migrant workers to move away from their stereotypical image as foreigners who came to Korea solely to make money and highlighted their full humanity. These cultural events were complemented by lectures and workshops on migrants' human rights offered to local residents and in experiential classes for local schoolchildren. FOA's founder described the significance of the cultural education this way:

> It was deeply satisfying to see local children playing with migrant workers and spending time together and enjoying each other's cultures. These children would not behave like many adult Koreans, who look down upon them just because they came from poor countries. I was able to observe their [children's] change. For example, when I talk to the kids who came to an experiential class, "kids, this time uncle so and so [*ajeossi so and so*] is going to be kicked out," or "uncle so and so is going to get married," their responses became much more personal and connected. The kids wanted to see these uncles again and missed them. I saw the making of a new public space of living peacefully and respectfully together. This was the most satisfying thing to me; we are creating such space together.[15]

Ironically, during the "participation government" (*chamyeojeongbu*) of Roh Moo-hyun, FOA's cultural approach was appropriated by the government's increasing promotion of multiculturalism.[16] In 2008, the Multicultural Family Support Act was passed under the succeeding conservative government. In the name of supporting civil society organizations and social minorities, the legal change accelerated the proliferation of public funding for local welfare centers, which led to the multiplication of projects concerning foreign migrants. In the popularization of neoliberal governance, this development played out in the form of outsourcing public facilities and services to local civil society organizations. Such private organizations were drawn to carrying out government-sponsored projects or managing public facilities in the model of the NE Branch's outsourced activism. As multiculturalism became trendy because it highlighted a bright and pleasant facet of foreign migrant issues, local governments themselves hosted cultural events on a large scale. The FOA founder summarizes this transformation as follow:

> It's not only local organizations which received funding, but also the government has begun to do so. Seoul City hosted a [multicultural] festival. This type of project gets several 10-million won [several tens of thousands of U.S. dollars] and there was even a cultural event that received 100 million won [USD $100,000]. It's like a one-time Sunday festival, mobilizing migrant workers for food and cultural experience. As this type of event got repeated, the migrants were used again and again, and they came to feel bad. . . . In our own town there are currently eight or nine organizations that carry out migrant-related projects funded by the [local] government.[17]

Neoliberal governance, which was actively adopted by the government in promoting its multicultural policy, hollowed out the significance of cultural education to which FOA adhered. The massive influx of government resources into local organizations (both public and private) popularized various repertoires of activism initiated by small organizations like FOA. In addition to cultural events and Korean language classes, recycle and reuse shops became standard features offered by Residents' Welfare Centers and Multicultural Family Support Centers (public organizations) and various religious and secular organizations (private). The Roh government also established the Workers' Support Center, which was larger than the welfare center in terms of budget and the size of facilities, and replicated it across various cities. These workers' centers copied programs and events about migrant workers. As a result, there were numerous replications of similar programs and activities concerning foreign migrants and the initial meaning of the cultural approach FOA aspired to promote was often lost.[18] The appropriation and co-optation of culturally oriented activism by neoliberal governance prompted FOA to develop different repertoires of activism. Instead of organizing its own cultural events, it has cooperated with other progressive organizations to host and support a human right arts festival. At the same time, it shifted its focus to what most other organizations dealing with migrant issues have neglected. Now we turn to such activism.

Majung Activism: Regular Visits to Detained Migrants

Majung activism began in 2016 in response to the persistent problem of detaining undocumented migrants at Foreigners' Protection Centers prior to their expulsion to their countries of origin. It is not an exclusively FOA activism but a coalition project that has involved other groups and organizations. Majung is a Korean word for receiving visitors with welcoming hospitality; such visitors can be friends, relatives, or strangers, but they have been culturally expected to be treated with care and respect. Using the Korean word, FOA has heightened the stark contrast between its vision of how foreigners ought to be treated and the reality of treating them like prisoners. This naming reflects FOA's prefigurative activism—detained migrants are envisioned as welcomed visitors despite the reality. Among a few such detention centers in South Korea, FOA chose the Hwaseong Foreigners Protection Center, whose location is relatively close to its office. Regular visits were temporarily suspended during the Covid-19 pandemic (from August to October of 2020) but have lasted for several years. This activism still continues among other social groups and individuals FOA had worked with for it, but FOA itself recently discontinued its involvement.[19] The detention of migrants reveals the hidden underbelly of neoliberal globalization, which has selectively deregulated and accelerated the mobility of capital but has further confined the mobility of human beings as expendable labor. The practice of detention became an integral aspect of the mechanism of processing foreign migrants in South Korea; the country has not accepted them as permanent residents or naturalized citizens but made active use of them as a source of exploitable labor.

FOA organized biweekly visits among its members and supporters in a group usually on Wednesdays to meet with individual detainees ("protected foreigners") and organized weekend visits on Saturdays ("majung day") to accommodate those who could not participate during weekdays. These majung visits have been carried out to support individual detainees personally and to publicize their collective ordeal and improve their situations in South Korea.[20] A weekday visit lasts a whole day, and majung activists meet detained migrants during a morning session and an afternoon session. Saturday visits are allowed only in the morning, which limits the number of migrants a majung group can meet. Each meeting is allowed for approximately ten to twenty minutes and rarely longer than half an hour, during which majung activists listen to detained migrants to learn about their urgent needs and problems, and activists convey useful information and news from their families outside. Urgent necessities for migrants included international phone cards, underwear, and books. Corresponding to detention centers in the United States and elsewhere, detained migrants in South Korea were categorized as "illegal" because their work visas had expired or they did not possess documents required by the Korean government. They have been confined like prisoners without a definite date of release. Some of detainees have been there more than four years, and others have been there for several months.[21] Most majung visitors deplored the constrained and unhealthy living conditions of these detainees and were energized to improve the situation.[22] Hyeon-ok, a mother and human rights foundation official, described her shocking experience as follows:

> There is a foreigners protection center in Hwaseong, Gyeonggi Province. It is run by the Republic of Korean state. I am curious how foreigners are protected.
>
> The exterior is not unfamiliar. It feels like a prison located in a remote rural area. I grew up in a place with a prison and remember occasionally passing by it. Today I went through the same procedure as what I did when I visited my daughter, who was recently put into a police jail for violating the Public Assembly and Protest Law. I filled out an application form, dropped off my mobile phone and purse, and according to a schedule, I was able to meet foreigner Mr. N. We could see each other's faces through a clear plastic barrier. We used telephone receivers to greet each other and talk. . . . Their lives are those of detention rather than of protection. In the name of human rights and protection, they are being violated.
>
> I also met migrants from Kenya and Nigeria, a totally different cultural sphere from Korea. I don't know details of why they came to this unfamiliar country. Nor do I know how they lived in their own countries. A sure thing that I do know is that they are same human beings as we are.[23]

Despite and because of the abject conditions of unfreedom, majung activists try to build human relations and solidarity with detained migrants by meeting the same individuals until they leave Korea or are released. Sook-ja, a volunteer activist, poignantly and poetically articulates the hardship of migrants her group has been visiting, intertwined with her lurking sense of disorientation.

> Driving for an hour and forty minutes, we arrived at the Protection Center. Applying for face-to-face meetings, we went to a room for conversations. Exchanging eye greetings, we asked how we were doing, *from the inside to the outside* and *from outside to inside*. Talking in Korean as much as possible through telephone receivers, we occasionally shared laughter.
>
> A wait for two weeks became condensed into these twenty to thirty minutes. Stories of five people whom we have met four times, including this morning and afternoon. A wife who just delivered a baby, a date of returning to a home country, and his unpaid wages. Whereabouts of money he saved in Korea and his eye surgery after being injured in a dormitory, and his loss of vision and industrial accident insurance.
>
> And then this person, an Uzbek who was one of fifty-five foreigners under protection at the Yeosu Protection Center, when a fatal fire accident broke out on February 11, 2007, which became a corner of contemporary Korean history.[24] He was neither among seventeen injured nor expelled from Korea. He received neither compensation money nor alimony. He suggested that he and his coworkers in a room cover their mouths with wet towels and crawl to escape. Escaped from the accident site to a hospital, from the hospital to a workplace because he obtained "a chance to work again in this land."
>
> His first encounter with the protection center was Yeosu and the second one was Hwaseong. During the face-to-face meetings, I felt vertiginous as if I just got back from a time travel. They gazed at *"the outside" from the inside* of the Protection Center and told us *"the inside" of this society*. Returning to Daewha-dong, for a moment I felt *confused if here is "inside" or "outside."* Source of this confusion was this, unfreedom.[25]

Her reflection on the experience of majung visits illuminates how the usual hierarchy between native Koreans and foreign migrants, as who are free outside the detention center and who are unfree inside it, respectively, turns into a sort of solidarity through the disorienting convergence of the inside and the outside. As "free" Koreans outside the center, her group could not freely visit the detained migrants inside and had to wait two weeks to see and talk briefly with the migrants. After learning about the personal tribulations shared by the migrants, her group could not do much more than just listen. Although harkening could relieve the suffering of the affected, the magnitude of their unresolved problems was daunting, especially the story of a Uzbek, and it made her wonder if she was free after all. Similarly, she also saw the contradiction of "free" society that imposed unfreedom on fellow human beings simply because they came from somewhere else and did not have official documents.

The emphasis on solidarity predicated on equality between migrants and native Koreans is also implicitly applied to the relationship between lay members and director/staff activists. Majung activism minimizes a hierarchical distinction between staff activists and volunteer activists, and the separation between FOA members and nonmembers who are called supporters. Naming all participants as majung activists, this practice reduces the rule of professional monopoly in political actions as symbolic actions. As interactions and communications among FOA members are increasingly being conducted online, diffused and simultaneous access to information has facilitated the organization of majung activism. As long as the commitment to equality and self-determination of foreign migrants is present, FOA will use various resources, including computer technology, to develop new ways of activism that sustain and further develop its civic identity, which revolves around becoming friends with foreign migrants.

MEANINGS OF BEING A "MOVEMENT ORGANIZATION" AND BECOMING "FRIENDS WITH FOREIGN MIGRANTS"

Responding to the government's appropriation at a massive scale of its repertoire of activism, FOA leadership modified the focus of their activism in light of the moral codes of citizens' organizations. It underwent a series of internal discussions about its activism and identity, especially in the face of waning resources. It decided to cut back on cultural events and social services that were replicated elsewhere and instead to focus on investigative research into the conditions of foreign migrants and archive its findings, as well as on the promotion of members' participation in its own local projects to support migrant workers. The founder established the Asia Education and Culture Studies Center and headed this research center.[26] In accordance with the code of independence from the government, FOA decided not to pursue government funding to run government-sponsored projects or facilities. Experiencing the workings of both progressive and conservative governments sensitized FOA to how government resources could co-opt civic activism and how the government withheld resources at will. FOA learned that it would be difficult to maintain its identity as a movement organization pursuing social change if it was controlled by government funding and its bureaucracy. Ms. Jang explained this complex process:

> I think we'll be ruined if an organization like us holds onto them [government-sponsored projects or facilities] because we'll have heartburns if we want to do a movement but we are stuck with bureaucratic procedure. People around us kept encouraging us to join, but I as a founder and head said let's not do it because that was not our goal. Let's recommend it to other suitable people. One of the Workers' Support Centers was entrusted to Catholic nuns and another was to Buddhist monks. These support centers carried out many projects we did in the past. In addition to Buddhism and Catholicism, Protestantism, Won-Buddhism, and Anglicanism are also involved in running migrant projects within local welfare centers.[27]

The expansive involvement of religious organizations in running migrant support centers speaks volumes about the power of neoliberal governance used by the government as a component of democratization of Korean society through participation, partnership, and cooperation. It reveals the extent to which volunteer activism is framed by neoliberal governance. Yet organizations like FOA also show how the dominance of neoliberal governance is actively resisted. Observing a common ambition to expand a local organization and its influence through government funding and outsourcing, a volunteer staff activist elaborated on guarding against rapid growth and the judicious use of government's resources.

> We want to go independently. Of course, financial issues are important, but if there are more staff activists than what we need for our projects, it will negatively affect grassroots participation. . . . Such growth should be natural from substantial growth of our own projects, leading to the broadening

of citizens' common understanding. Among many such citizens, some may become full-time or professional activists.... Even if we have natural growth of staff activists, we're more interested in facilitating activists overseas and migrant activists here. For continuity and integrity of our core projects, we need to be independent of the government as much as possible. I don't think we can accept a government funding up to a certain percent. Yes, there was an exception. This year, for example, we received less than 1 million won from Paju City to organize a summer camp program for workers because someone introduced us to the funding opportunity. But that was a temporary event, not our core project. For a temporary event, we can make use of available funds, but for a core project, we need to be independent.[28]

By modifying its activism and adhering to its core values, FOA was able to reaffirm its civic identity against the shifting political and social context. Its core value continues to be creating and maintaining social space for building solidarity between native Koreans and foreign migrants. Reflective of this ongoing effort, a new lay member described her experience of joining FOA.

I received an invitation to "daytime party" at the FOA and came to meet migrants. I felt both anticipation and worry about what if the meeting turns out to be awkward. But it was an unnecessary misgiving because they approached me more actively than I did, with their hearts open. There were senior migrants who have lived in Korea for a long time and spoke fluent Korean, junior ones who have been here only a few months, and (Korean) others who serve and support. It was space for all of us naturally mingling together. We shared dishes from different cultures and played games together and in the process they were no more "strangers" and the group became "us."[29]

Jun-han, a high school senior, conveyed an evolving sense of solidarity in the process of teaching the Korean language class.

At first, it was really fascinating to see foreigners who could speak our language comfortably and who were chatting and laughing in our language. Then, my initial curiosity and fascination was followed by an understanding that I could connect to them through playing together and exchanging our cultures; these interactions are befitting to the age of globalization. I also learned more about the problems of migrant workers and joined their protest in front of the Seoul Station. We were demanding an end to the violent treatment of migrant workers.[30]

Majung activism affirmed FOA's civic identity as an organization promoting the human rights of migrants, but it highlighted a difficult question of how to bridge the daunting gap between its prefigurative vision of migrants as equal members of Korean society and the hierarchical reality that they faced as outsiders. Its activism for broad social change was articulated by its lay members and leaders. Recollecting a photo of migrant brides and their children with Korean husbands, an anonymous member wrote this:

> This is a picture from our picnic at Lake Park. It's an old picture; the children have grown big now and this tells me how much time has flown away. There are children who live with their moms and those who don't. Each mother who left has her own story. I wish that our efforts can improve their lives but that's not necessarily the case. This teaches me what we can do is not helping others but living together with them. The relationship between helper and the helped reveals hierarchy in society. Hence, when people talk about us as the helper, I feel frustrated.[31]

The aspiration for building solidarity with marginalized migrants through mundane interactions resonates with FOA's answer to the question of how to reduce the hierarchy between foreign migrants and native Koreans. The following anecdote shows how its members paid attention to their behavior to treat migrants as equal friends who deserve hospitable care and respect.

> I am trying to approach migrants without the tinted lens of charity and feeling sorry for them. I share this with the FOA. The fact of the matter is that we are not in a situation of meeting as equals because of their circumstances, but we do our best. Mr. Kang [referring to a volunteer staff activist] makes a lot of efforts to treat them as our "equal friends." For example, when we took a camping trip together, he brought food for us by purchasing good quality and organic food for migrants. *I was rather shocked. Most of us would buy cheaper food to save money, and Mr. Kang himself does not buy expensive food at home.* But he did so to express his care and respect for them.[32]

A few years later, its new leader articulated what being a movement organization and being friends to migrants means. By emphasizing a need to move from sympathy to solidarity, he communicated the enduring civic identity of FOA.

> Sympathy for those who are suffering is a good starting point, but it is not good to lock them under the gaze of sympathy. We need to build solidarity with those who are suffering beyond sympathy because such sympathy is based on the strict separation between those who dispense it and its recipients. Sympathy givers are those who have a bit more and do not suffer or suffer less. The givers will feel offended if the recipients do not feel grateful and claim their rights. *Sympathy is sustainable only when its recipients stay in miserable conditions.* In contrast, s*olidarity with those who were suffering begins with identification with them*; the understanding that I am helping them not because I am better than them but because I recognize that they are the same human beings like myself who are entitled to rights I enjoy.[33]

The politics of FOA's civic identity shows how a small local organization can manage to maintain and defend its identity by adhering to its core values and modifying its activism in the face of its appropriation by the government. Its small size and local nature facilitated this reorientation by allowing for the continuity in leadership and membership in terms of its underlying values and the goals of its activism. Its small size also facilitated reorientation in an unexpected way: unlike the NE Branch, it was not considered a sizable local organization that the government was interested in; therefore, it was relatively easy to refuse to go along with the trendy neoliberal governance of partnering with and working for the government. Being a small organization, FOA has to deal with the underlying problem of a lack of resources and how to mitigate this difficulty through volunteer activism by its members.

CONCLUSION

In this chapter I analyzed the complex ways in which neoliberalism enabled and constrained the prefigurative activism FOA has pursued. Although it refused to adopt neoliberal governance to sustain the core of its activism and thereby its civic identity, neoliberalism as a dominant political rationality continued to shape its activism. By supporting foreign migrants, whose structural position in South Korea was shaped by neoliberal globalization, FOA established and maintained its civic identity as a social movement organization and promoted migrants' human rights in its locality and educated native Koreans about their cultures as well as their precarious situations. In response to the government's appropriation of its repertoire of activism under the "multiculturalism" policy, FOA maintained and defended its civic identity by modifying the focus of its activism and redirecting it while maintaining its core values based on the prefigurative vision of migrants as equal members of society. This adjustment was facilitated by being a small local organization, which allowed for continuity in leadership and membership in terms of their values and orientations. Instead of expanding its activism through partnership with the government, it chose to maintain its financial independence from the government and relied on limited resources from its members and supporters. While dealing with the persistent difficulty of scarce resources, FOA was able to stay away from bureaucratic control by the government. At the same time, it continued to combine the long-term goal of achieving equality between native Koreans and foreign migrants with the provision of urgent social services for migrants unequal to Koreans.

In circuitous ways, neoliberalism enabled individual activism in FOA in the Korean language class. In neoliberal Korean society, where employment insecurity is pervasive, individuals learn to invest in themselves as human capital to be valorized and thereby become more competitive in the labor market. Some foreign language high school students are drawn to volunteer their service at FOA to strengthen their college applications overseas with impressive or unusual résumés. Similarly, some college or graduate students major in teaching Korean language as a foreign language as a niche for the growing population of "Korasian" children of international marriages between Korean men and Asian women. To gain teaching experience, use their skill for meaningful activities, or both, these young teaching professionals come to FOA for volunteer service. Although many of these volunteers are initially motivated by pragmatic considerations, they can evolve through their personal interactions with migrant students as specific persons. As these volunteer teachers learn more about the unjust and harsh reality of migrants' lives, they develop a grounded understanding of the prefigurative activism of building solidarity with migrants across hierarchy and difference.

Neoliberal globalization has also contributed to volunteer services in FOA in a circuitous way by popularizing foreign travels as opportunities to enjoy and invest in oneself. Young people as students have traveled abroad for study and leisure, but adults have traveled abroad for work, on the job training, and leisure. The popularization of foreign travels, when such travel lead to long-term stays, enables some Koreans to become interested in foreign migrants in South Korea.

As a small local organization focusing on the single issue of foreign migrants, FOA has minimized the hierarchy between professional staff activists and lay members and thereby mitigated the rule of professional monopoly in activism. To compensate for their small size, the distinction between members and supporters is minimized, and nonmembers are welcomed to participate in volunteer activities. FOA has a director/leader and a staff activist working part-time, but they have focused on facilitating and working with volunteer activists and supporters. In contrast to PSPD and the two local branches of DFS, FOA's pursuit of activism emphasizes working together, which can be observed in majung activism. The contradictory relationship between democracy and neoliberalism as seen through FOA activism can be summarized thusly. FOA rejected neoliberal governance in the form of partnership and working with the local government, which appropriated FOA's cultural and educational projects as the means to recognize the full humanity of migrants and their equality with native Koreans. This appropriation also compelled FOA to modify its repertoire of activism and pursue majung activism, which reveals the dark side of migrant issues that cultural events commonly obscure. At a micro level of individual members and supporters, neoliberalism in circuitous ways enabled the activism of young volunteer teachers of the Korean language class.

CONCLUSION

Reflecting on the Intertwining of Democracy and Neoliberalism

> Democracy is neither a form of government that enables oligarchies to rule in the name of the people, nor is it a form of society that governs the power of commodities. It is the action that constantly wrests that monopoly of public life from oligarchic governments, and the omnipotence over lives from the power of wealth. It is the power that, today more than ever, has to struggle against the confusion of these powers, rolled into one and the same law of domination. . . . This can provoke fear, and so hatred, among those who are used to exercising the magisterium of thought. But among those who know how to share with anybody and everybody the equal power of intelligence, it can conversely inspire courage, and hence joy.
>
> —JACQUES RANCIÈRE, *HATRED OF DEMOCRACY*, 96, 97

> Liberalism and liberal democracy are not neutral and innocent legacies and institutions that have been attacked by neoliberalism and capitalism but played an active role in the rise to dominance of neoliberal governmentality.
>
> —ALEN TOPLIŠEK, *LIBERAL DEMOCRACY IN CRISIS*, 205

In this book I have examined how three different citizens' organizations in South Korea negotiated with neoliberalism in the processes of pursuing activism to deal with problems caused or aggravated by the neoliberal transformation of society. I focused on the market and governance as the main mechanisms of neoliberalism, a dominant mode of ruling in the twenty-first century. Although sharing the moral codes of civic activism to varying degrees (see chapter 2), these organizations showed differences from one another in terms of primary goals, repertoire of activism, and size. These organizational features shaped how they interacted with the market and neoliberal governance in their pursuit of democratizing activism. An in-depth analysis of their activism during the past two decades revealed the complex intertwining of democracy and neoliberalism, which is marked by a contradictory relationship between the two modes of ruling. The market and neoliberal governance simultaneously facilitated or

CONCLUSION

enabled civic activism pursued by these organizations and constrained or undermined it. The intertwining of democracy and neoliberalism in South Korea (and other non-Western societies) suggests that democracy is not one-dimensionally undermined by neoliberalism, as many theoretical and normative critiques highlighted or implied; social groups fighting for democratization also appropriated the market and neoliberal governance as tools for their civic activism. The presence of social groups and their capacity to build and maintain solidarity with a wide range of other social groups to form a political majority was a crucial factor in the evolution of the relationship between democracy and neoliberalism. Here I summarize the findings of this study and explain how the market and neoliberal governance facilitated/enables and constrained/undermines democratizing civic activism as three different organizations accepted and resisted various aspects of neoliberalism. Then I discuss the enduring and recurring tension between professionalized activism and grassroots participation as a central challenge for democratizing civic activism in the twenty-first century. Expanding on this internal dynamic of civic activism, I explain how neoliberalism contained democratizing civic activism by allowing democratization that did not challenge its core values and practices. The presence of this boundary reveals the continuity between neoliberalism and liberal democracy as a product/brand globally promoted by the West, especially the United States. Only by cultivating solidarity and becoming a political majority can civic activism challenge this boundary and weaken the hegemonic power of the political and economic elites.

HOW DID THE MARKET SIMULTANEOUSLY FACILITATE AND CONSTRAIN DEMOCRATIZING CIVIC ACTIVISM?

As the market became a hegemonic model organizing human activities beyond the economy, its specific tools and ethos have influenced civic activism pursued by the three different citizens' organizations I studied. On the one hand, in the common practice of membership fees as the primary indicator of commitment, money facilitated the expansion of their activism by making members' participation convenient and low-intensity. For busy urbanites working to make a living and performing family responsibilities, paying monthly membership dues and reading newsletters or monthly publications were more manageable than other active engagement. On the other hand, the prominence of monetary membership in the citizens' organizations turned civic activism that members supported into what would be akin to one of many commodified services consumers could purchase in the marketplace. This ironic twist took place against the backdrop of resistance by the citizens' organizations to certain logical parameters of the market, including privatization, fragmentation, and the accumulation of profit. PSPD, a professionalized, nationwide, large organization, encountered growing pressure to make use of a marketing technique to maintain current members and to reach out to potential members. Less professionalized, local, smaller organizations, such as the two DFS branches and FOA, encountered much less pressure due to the combination of a lower degree of professionalization and the more personal nature of interactions with their members in local contexts.

The ambivalent effect of money (as the medium of market relations) on civic activism resonates with Georg Simmel's theoretical insight in *The Philosophy of Money*; he argues that a money-based society transforms the very nature of associational life and activities by making them more widespread among a wide range of disparate individuals who would not come together without the equalizing mediation of money, but it simultaneously makes their involvement or participation of low intensity. The rapid growth of PSPD's members in the late 1990s and early 2000s coincided with the further professionalization of this advocacy organization, subsequently marginalizing volunteer activists who were interested in deep and intense involvement (see chapter 4). The nonprofit food co-op experimentation of the GY and NW branches of DFS illustrated the simultaneous processes of widening membership while lessening their participation. Both branches enjoyed the expansion of their membership base through the food co-op, which was consciously established as a vehicle to reach out to local women who were familiar with neither feminism nor activism for social change. A majority of these co-op members purchased organic or environmentally friendly food, but they did not become interested in deeper or more intense involvement in local activism. This bifurcation was well reflected in the formal dichotomy of membership categories adopted by DFS (branches as well as the headquarters). By using the categories of "full members" and "co-op only members," the feminist organization accepted its members' choice in terms of how much they were willing to pay for membership and how deeply they could get involved in the organization. The GY and NE branches hoped that the initial exposure to co-op activities would encourage many co-op only members to become full members, but a combination of factors prevented this from happening (see chapter 5). A majority of FOA's members also showed low-intensity involvement, and participation by those who became active was commonly motivated by personal interests in career development or fun and enjoyment.

Fun and enjoyment as a legitimate source of motivation for civic activism and other activities reflected a market ethos, which was shaped by human actions and interactions mediated by money (see chapter 3). As Karl Marx and other theorists have noted, money is not only equalizing but also secularizing or disenchanting because it removes the hierarchical and symbolic meaning from human interactions. The cold calculation of money dissolves everything solid into air and profanes everything sacred. The deeper moral, religious, and philosophical meanings that provided motivation were replaced by access to immediate and individual sources of fun and enjoyment if not by the naked desire for wealth and power. Although citizens' organizations could disseminate their own views of the specific content of what constitutes fun and enjoyment to attract potential members and keep current members, they were pressured to compete with the mainstream view of fun and enjoyment shaped by commercial culture. For example, in offering educational lectures and hobby classes, PSPD and DFS local branches were literally competing with commercial cultural centers that attracted consumers with better facilities and a wider range of choices.

The ambivalent effect of money on civic activism, simultaneously expanding the membership base of citizens' organizations but reducing members' participation, deepens our understanding of how the market affected civic activism. As a major mechanism of neoliberal ruling, the market democratized civic activism, illuminating specific details beyond the broad theoretical and normative analysis. In *The Theory of Communicative Action*, Jürgen Habermas argued that "the lifeworld" was colonized by the market logic of profit and the state logic of power (the "systems"). The progressive citizens' organizations in South Korea resisted the profit logic while pursuing democratization. Simultaneously, these organizations appropriated market techniques to strengthen their activism and thereby weakened the level of engagement in civic activism.

CONCLUSION

HOW DID NEOLIBERAL GOVERNANCE SIMULTANEOUSLY ENABLE AND UNDERMINE DEMOCRATIZING CIVIC ACTIVISM?

The idea and practices of governance in the form of partnership and cooperation with nonstate actors generated a political opening for citizens' organizations to work with the central and local governments, especially when they were controlled by progressive political groups. PSPD participated in developing, implementing, and reforming policy, and its focus on national policy required professional expertise and experience. As Pierre Bourdieu argued, this model of activism made cultural and symbolic capital salient, and thereby strengthened the monopoly of professionals in civic activism as political action broadly defined. The two DFS local branches participated in the implementation of local government's programs and built and maintained their own programs with partial funding from local governments. This outsourcing and funding support reflected neoliberal governance, but it was simultaneously appropriated by the citizens' organizations to pursue their own democratizing activism and constrained their activism. In constraining civic activism, neoliberal governance combined the partnership with traditional mechanisms of bureaucratic control and dominance, which was not neoliberal per se, but the neoliberal restructuring of the labor market contributed to the constraint by generating employment insecurity and pressuring people to focus on paid employment, thereby preventing them from becoming interested in civic activism. FOA, a smaller local organization with a single issue focus on foreign migrants, refused to use neoliberal governance, but its activism was influenced by the neoliberal transformation of society.

PSPD has maintained its identity as a large professional advocacy organization that focuses on legal and policy changes at the national level. With these organizational features, it functions as a sentinel, analyzing the changing political and economic powers and acting as a protector/supporter of the marginalized as the neoliberal transformation of Korean society intensified economic insecurity and the precarity of life. Maintaining its financial independence from the government and focusing on institutional change, its activism was carried out primarily by its full-time staff activists, supported by lay members as well as by officers who are professional experts in law and other fields. In pursuing its civic roles, PSPD took advantage of political openings created by neoliberal governance under the

CONCLUSION

progressive government and actively collaborated with it to achieve legal and policy reforms concerning social welfare and economic security. Its activism efforts produced varying degrees of success, depending on the nature of the issues. Their professional mode of advocacy activism institutionalized the division of labor between staff activists and lay members and generated recurring tension with its moral code of grassroots participation. This division of labor in activism highlighted PSPD's participation in policymaking and legal reforms as a partner of the state, which was democratizing, and it was accompanied by the relative marginalization of its lay members. Neoliberal governance facilitated democratizing participation of PSPD as a professional civic organization, but the rule of the professional monopoly in a political field marginalized lay members as occasional assistants and limited contributions of membership fees. The initial presence of more engaged and symmetrical interactions between lay members as volunteer activists and staff activists declined over time and was replaced by the clear division of labor between them as its membership grew significantly (see chapter 4). Major examples of its activism show the extent to which PSPD tried to complement its professionalized activism with grassroots participation and how the significance of this moral code to its civic identity led to the internal discussion among its members and staff activists of the meaning of grassroots participation.

The GY Branch and the NE Branch of the women's organization (DFS) established their identity as local feminist organizations by supporting local women in developing their civic capacity as volunteer activists. In this process, they provided useful services for their members and pursued policy changes in cooperation with their headquarters and other local organizations. In contrast to PSPD, these branches relied on a small number of committed volunteer activists who organically grew from their position of lay members. Utilizing these organizational features, the local branches functioned as a vehicle to tap into women's potential to become agents of democratic and feminist social change. While practicing this moral code of grassroots participation, they struggled to achieve financial independence, especially after their membership base decreased as a result of the separation of the food co-op from the branches (and headquarters) in the context of neoliberal economic restructuring. Even prior to this separation, both branches took advantage of project-based government funding for civil society organizations, which became institutionalized as a feature of political democratization in the late 1990s. In the face of growing financial insecurity, both local branches took an active part in making good use of project-based government funding to pursue their feminist activism.

After the separation of the food co-op, the two local branches diverged in their method of activism. The NE Branch was able to expand its activism by running public programs and facilities entrusted to it by the municipal government of Seoul, which was controlled by progressive leadership during the 2010s. This growing cooperation with the government, in the model of neoliberal governance of outsourcing public services, enabled them to provide local residents with necessary social services, and at times it enabled their own members to participate in civic activism. However, it led to the unintended consequence of their subjection to bureaucratic control. In the case of GY Branch, which did not engage in running outsourced public services, its own local projects became more dependent on government funding as membership fees shrank, and this dependency also produced a similar problem on a smaller scale. Moreover, the GY Branch witnessed its partnership with municipal governments grow in a reverse relationship to their members' autonomous activism. Specifically, activism in the form of Small Groups activities became stagnant and even declined. Both the direct management of outsourced public services (NE Branch) and the growing financial reliance on the government for local service programs (GY Branch) led to a growing gap between organic activists who became full-time or part-time activists and lay members who were left behind with shrinking resources (see chapter 5). This confirms the rule of the monopoly of professional activists even in the case of medium-sized local organizations that emphasized grassroots participation in local contexts. Comparable to PSPD, the local branches were enabled to pursue their activism by neoliberal governance, but in the process of neoliberal economic restructuring, which undermined their membership base through widespread employment insecurity, this funding became dominant and led to growing bureaucratic control that undermined their autonomous activities. This complex dynamic of funding and bureaucratic control in the middle of expanding market logic and increasing employment insecurity raised a deeper question about how to bridge the gap between the feminist goal of empowering women as a group and women's individualized interests and aspirations shaped by the neoliberal transformation of society. These two related developments resulted in internal discussions linked to

CONCLUSION

the moral codes of grassroots participation and activism for social change versus the provision of urgent social services and thereby the meaning of their identities as local feminist organizations.

FOA has managed to maintain its civic identity as a small local organization dedicated to the promotion of foreign migrants' human rights and the education of native Koreans about their precarious situation. While providing urgent services for foreign migrants, which ranged from Korean language classes to legal and medical services, FOA pursued their long-term goal of building solidarity with migrants as equal members of Korean society. At times FOA cooperated with other local and national organizations to achieve policy change beyond its locality. Like the GY and NE branches, it relied on its members and supporters as volunteer activists; but unlike these branches, it decided not to use political openings generated by neoliberal governance for partnership with local authorities. This decision allowed FOA to avoid the common dynamic of a monopoly of professional activists by blurring the division of labor between volunteer activists and staff activists. As discussed in chapter 6, this decision resulted from the consideration of various factors among FOA core activists/leaders; it boiled down to the combination of their core values and identity as a social movement organization and its structural position as a small local organization in the crowded field of multiple organizations working on migrant issues. Responding to the rise of the government's "multiculturalism" policy, which appropriated FOA's repertoire of activism, FOA modified and redirected its method of activism and kept its autonomous civic identity. This adjustment was facilitated by being a small local organization with continuity in leadership and membership in terms of their values and orientations. Instead of expanding its activism through partnership with the government in the form of project-based funding or outsourcing, FOA chose to maintain its financial independence from the government and relied on limited resources from its members and supporters. Although dealing with the persistent difficulty of scarce resources, FOA was able to stay away from increasing bureaucratic control by the government. At the same time, it continued to grapple with the long-term goal of achieving equality between native Koreans and foreign migrants and provided urgent social services for migrants who structurally remain unequal to Koreans.

FOA's refusal to engage with neoliberal governance provides us with an uncommon but valuable mode of negotiating with neoliberalism. As a small local organization led by volunteer activists focusing on the single issue of foreign migrants, its limited resources and activities allowed it to maintain limited visibility and status, thereby sustaining an autonomous civic space in accordance with its primary goal. As discussed in chapter 6, the goal was to cultivate solidarity between its Korean members and foreign migrants prefiguratively as equal members of Korean society. The emphasis on equality between foreign migrants and native Koreans was also applied to the equality between lay members and de facto staff activists/volunteer activists. At its core, FOA was concerned with the qualitative transformation of society, which could not be measured by the quantitative metrics of efficiency à la the model of accounting (which neoliberalism popularized across higher education, civil society, medicine, and other areas beyond the economy). FOA's experience suggests that a multitude of small local organizations working alone or together in coalition whenever necessary can promote democracy.

Despite its refusal of neoliberal governance, FOA's activism was sometimes shaped circuitously by the neoliberal transformation both positively and negatively. On the one hand, neoliberalism facilitated its activism in the following ways. First, in dealing with increasing employment insecurity caused by the neoliberal restructuring of the economy, many individuals in South Korea embraced the neoliberal view of the self as (human) capital whose value should be enhanced through "investment." As higher education became a major investment in the self to enhance the individual's value in the labor market, some young men and women became interested in volunteering to teach the Korean language to foreign migrants because this experience could strengthen their résumé for college application or offer a chance to practice their teaching skills prior to their paid employment as Korean teachers. This initial exposure to FOA activism evolved into long-term involvement when volunteers became exposed to FOA values and became aware of the situation of foreign migrants. Second, with the explosive growth of foreign travel in the era of neoliberal globalization, increasing numbers of Koreans traveled for leisure, education, and work. The personal experience of foreign travel, especially long-term stays, sensitized some individuals to the issues of foreign migrants in South Korea. These individuals came to FAO to meet and interact with foreign migrants, and in the process of getting involved some of them embraced FOA's values and developed a sense of solidarity with the migrants over time.

CONCLUSION

On the other hand, neoliberalism constrained FOA's activism in the following way. As observed in the two DFS branches, FOA's membership base became stagnant and declined as employment insecurity escalated and more individuals spent their time and attention keeping their jobs, looking for jobs, and working multiple jobs to make a living. The membership decline led to a serious problem of chronic financial instability because membership fees were the primary source of financing for FOA, and this was tied to its identity as a civic organization independent from the government financially as well as politically.

PROFESSIONALIZED ACTIVISM, GRASSROOTS PARTICIPATION, AND NEOLIBERALISM

The case studies of the citizens' organizations in South Korea illustrate how the rule of the monopoly of professionals in political actions and interactions works in civic activism. This rule of monopoly persists unless individuals and organizations pursuing civic activism pay conscious attention to the hierarchy among various groups of activists and lay members and guard against it. The democratizing participation in institutionalized (national) politics and the democratizing partnership with local governments, which involved professional staff activists (PSPD) and full-time or part-time volunteer activists who evolved into professional activists (DFS branches), were accompanied by the marginalization of lay members. This recurring dynamic reminds us that individuals and groups involved in democratizing activism are not a homogeneous group but are hierarchically differentiated by various social factors, particularly in terms of their access to and use of cultural capital, which is critical to the effectiveness of their political actions and interactions. This dynamic suggests that democratization benefits the most privileged in a given society first or more often than other social groups; although it is a positive and desirable process of social change, democratization takes place in a specific social context in which power inequality and differentiation still operate. The structure of existing power dynamics marginalizes lay members (of PSPD and the NE and GY branches) in the process of democratization, and thereby reveals the complicated reality of democratizing civic activism.

However, this recurring dynamic does not mean that a civic organization should altogether do away with professionalization and the management of outsourced public services. We do need different types of civic organizations performing different but necessary tasks. In the specific context of South Korea where political parties have not adequately carried out the function of developing and reforming policy and law, civic organizations like PSPD have been necessary and even indispensable. In the context of South Korea where feminist women's organizations do not have diverse sources of funding, as in the NE and GY branches, it is necessary for them to take advantage of government funding and partnerships to infuse feminist values into the bureaucratic routine and widen the scope of their activism. Simultaneously, small local organizations such as FOA need to pursue disengagement with neoliberal governance and adhere to activism that is limited in terms of its scope but that sustains their core values, and they need to cooperate with other local and national civic organizations. The recurring dynamic of the rule of the monopoly of professionals in political actions sensitizes us to how to reduce the intrenched hierarchy in terms of the access to cultural capital (and other forms of capital) among individuals and social groups involved in democratizing civic activism. Without being balanced by equally focused engagement with grassroots members, such activism soon drifts away from its grassroots base and develops the monopoly of professional activists in political fields.

To be clear, professionalization is not a unique feature of neoliberalism; as Max Weber theorized, it is a distinct feature and a broad tendency of modern society characterized by "rationalization," intellectualization, or disenchantment. It reflects the rise and spread of instrumental rationality to identify narrow specific goals and the most efficient means to achieve these goals using focused and specialized knowledge and experience. Although the consideration of efficiency is necessary because resources indispensable for human lives are commonly limited, the exclusive focus on efficiency delegitimizes a wide range of other alternative values as being unworthy or undesirable. Efficiency became a prioritized value in modern society where scientific knowledge enabled us to maximize our control of the physical environment and industrial capitalism accelerated the production of material goods and services and thereby the accumulation of wealth. Its economic orientation makes the value of efficiency a core component of neoliberalism, which is a mode of ruling that expands the economic metric to almost everything in human life. This continuity or affinity between modern instrumental rationality and neoliberalism explains why this mode of ruling incorporates professionalization.

CONCLUSION

Applied to civic activism, professionalization promotes efficiency and credibility among the general public as well as among activists themselves. Yet an exclusive focus on efficiency is not primarily oriented toward the promotion of democratic values and practices such as equality among individuals and self-determination. Although professionalization can make civic activism effective in achieving specific goals, Jacques Rancière argues that professionalization promotes meritocracy rather than democracy. Hence a civic organization with a strong professional orientation needs to be vigilant about reaching out to grassroots citizens and communicating with them. As my interviews with staff activists of PSPD who specialized in managing lay members documented in chapters 3 and 4, they tended to accept the professionalization and specialization of activism as something that strengthened their civic organization. Some of them even consider civic activism in the form of professional advocacy as a type of "public service industry." This highlights the extent to which the business model has shaped the minds of professional activists who consciously fought against the negative impacts of neoliberal economic restructuring. It also reveals a legitimate desire for a modicum of financial security for professional activists whose salaries have been grossly inadequate, especially if they have families to support. Staff activists and volunteer activists at the two local branches of DFS also perceived the professionalization of activism as something positive and desirable because it meant building capacity for local women and gaining respect for their experience and knowledge (see chapter 5). Somewhat differently, volunteer activists at FOA were conscious of the distance professionalization could generate between staff activists and lay members, but they saw professionalization as necessary for investigating problems and finding solutions (see chapter 6).

The marginalization of lay members raises two issues. First, democracy, defined as a mode of ruling that promotes and practices equality among all citizens including a numerical majority of ordinary people without special merit, would face serious challenges in any contemporary society in which professionalization, expertise, and information are central to its functioning. Professionalization must be balanced by grassroots participation in various aspects of political, economic, and cultural affairs for self-determination and democracy to survive. In a neoliberal society where efficiency, commonly measured by financial accountability, is highly prioritized, democracy as such would be stigmatized as a daydream because the equality of human beings as fellow citizens cannot be measured by the economic metric of efficiency. Democracy is a value, and its practices do not generate the rapid accumulation of wealth and power. As Jacques Rancière points out, democracy has to wrestle against this pervasive and dominant tendency in contemporary societies. Second, if interpreted as a reflection of the marginalization of ordinary people as a majority in politics, the marginalization of lay members would measure the extent to which neoliberalism had become hegemonic and the extent to which ordinary people feel exhausted from overwork and feel despair to do anything to change their situation. The combination of hegemony, exhaustion, and despair would be undermined when more and more ordinary people encounter and experience alternative values and practices to neoliberalism in communities of solidarity to deal with their problems. Expanding the discussion of how democratizing civic activism internally generated hierarchy between professionalized activists and lay members, the following section explains how neoliberalism externally constrained democratizing civic activism.

DEMOCRATIZING CIVIC ACTIVISM CONTAINED BY NEOLIBERALISM: THE CONTINUITY OF LIBERAL DEMOCRACY AND NEOLIBERALISM

The case studies of the citizens' organizations revealed that their activism was repeatedly circumscribed by the boundary of neoliberalism as a dominant mode of ruling. That is, they were able to pursue democratizing activism as long as it did not undermine the core values and practices of neoliberalism, including casualization of labor (maximization of labor's vulnerability), deregulation of big business (maximization of capital's mobility and wealth accumulation), and privatization. PSPD's activism to promote universal social welfare for all citizens achieved a significant improvement in the basic livelihood for vulnerable citizens, but it could not curb the development of universal welfare into a regressive system that protected those who already had secure employment more than those who suffered from insecure employment or no employment at all. In the face of fierce resistance from big business, PSPD could not fully accomplish its goal of regulating economic power so it was responsible for problems it produced against ordinary citizens as small business owners and financial consumers. In its struggle against the KORUS FTA, PSPD had to cope with the combined forces of government and big business to the point of alienating the government that had been supportive of progressive citizens' organizations. The two local branches of DFS were allowed to pursue their democratizing activism as long as their activism did not directly challenge the core values and practices of neoliberalism. The GY Branch was able to carry out local programs to run a childcare center and feed local children regularly because feminized childcare and food work did not pose a direct threat to neoliberal core values and practices. The NE Branch was able to pursue feminist activism to provide various social services for the health of local residents and the employment of local women within the neoliberal framework. In its effort to strengthen women's insecure employment, NE Branch activists experienced conflict between being a provider of urgent employment services and being a civic organization working for institutional and structural change. It experienced a similar conflict in pursuing its local health ecosystem project. FOA's activism showed the peril of persistent economic instability as a result of its refusal to engage with neoliberal governance. This is an indirect but powerful way to control a civic organization in a neoliberal capitalist society.

The recurring pattern of containing and constraining civic activism by neoliberalism illuminates the centrality of existing power politics among different social groups in society to the contradictory intertwining of democracy and neoliberalism. As the case studies demonstrate, civic groups pushing for democratization can appropriate tools of the market and neoliberal governance to pursue their activism. Yet without forming a political majority with a wide range of ordinary citizens against the economic and political elites, civic organizations cannot undermine neoliberalism, and their activism will be contained within its boundary. This means that liberal or "bare" democracy is not simply undermined by neoliberalism through vulnerable labor, privatization of public services, and the deregulation of big businesses, but also that these changes resulted from the absence or weakness of social groups actively fighting for democratization and resisting the undermining of democracy. This absence or weakness reflects the hegemony of neoliberalism in the Gramscian sense as well as the exhaustion and despair among lower-class citizens.

To understand the hegemony of the neoliberal order, albeit contested but surprisingly resilient, we need to recognize how liberal democracy has been promoted as a product/brand since the end of World War II and the beginning of the Cold War. Although liberal democracy was identified

CONCLUSION

with the "free market" economy and civil and political rights, it marginalized social and economic rights to benefit from social and economic development. This marginalization points to the continuity between liberal democracy and neoliberalism. During the rivalry between the capitalist West and the communist East, the United States, as "the leader of the Free World," developed the welfare state and established "democratic capitalism" to prove the superiority of capitalism over communism.[1] Several European countries incorporated socialism into their politics and economies extensively and permanently, but socialist democracy was not actively promoted during the Cold War in the rest of the world. After the fall of communism, the United States was the only superpower aggressively promoting a "new world order" (read as neoliberal order) along with liberal democracy. The neoliberal recycling of liberal democracy was coupled with the removal of institutional arrangements for the welfare state that curbed the destructive consequences of capitalism for vulnerable social groups and the overall fabric of society. Seen from a critical angle of the "instrumentalization" of liberal democracy during the Cold War, liberal democracy globally promoted as a product/brand in the aftermath of the Cold War has been undermined by the reduction of democracy to the free market economy and individuals' civil and political rights at the expense of social and economic rights.[2] Clearly, the civil and political rights of individual citizens are necessary and important but are not sufficient conditions for democracy. By equating equality with equal votes, which has become a ritualized practice in many plutocratic societies, and equating freedom or self-determination with the freedom to choose commodities in marketplaces, which has neglected the social and economic rights of individuals as equal citizens, liberal democracy easily lends itself to neoliberalism.[3] What is urgently needed in our time is not so much blaming neoliberalism for the weakening of democracy but learning how to change the hearts and minds of ordinary citizens to join forces to form a political majority against the political and economic elites who have benefited enormously from neoliberalism.

NOTES

INTRODUCTION

1. Throughout this book, pseudonyms are used to protect identities of interviewees. All interviews quoted are translated by the author unless otherwise noted.
2. The majority of irregular workers are most likely to be those under 20 years of age, those over 60 years of age, and women with children. A majority of the young have been college students working part-time in service sectors that pay minimum wages or lower. See Hagen Koo, "Rising Inequality and Shifting Class Boundaries in South Korea in the Neo-Liberal Era," *Journal of Contemporary Asia* 51, no. 1 (2021): 1–19, http://doi.org/10.1080/00472336.2019.1663242.
3. It is important to remember that neoliberal globalization was actively promoted by the West as a core component of the New World Order that the United States promoted in replacing the Cold War superpower rivalry. See Quinn Slobodian, *Globalists: The End of Empire and the Birth of Neoliberalism* (Cambridge, MA: Harvard University Press, 2020), for a broader intellectual history of how neoliberalism was globalized from its initial identity as an economic and political theory developed in central Europe during the mid-twentieth century.
4. Samuel S. Kim, ed., *Korea's Globalization* (Cambridge: Cambridge University Press, 2000).
5. Similar to the "shock doctrine" to which many other Third World countries were subjected, the rescue package was dictated by the global trinity of economic institutions: the International Monetary Fund (IMF), the World Bank (WB), and the World Trade Organization (WTO). See Richard Peet, *Unholy Trinity: The IMF, World Bank, and WTO* (London: Zed, 2009); and Naomi Klein, *The Shock Doctrine: The Rise of Disaster Capitalism* (New York: Picador, 2007).

INTRODUCTION

6. Pierre Dardot and Christian Laval, *Never-Ending Nightmare: The Neoliberal Assault on Democracy*, trans. Gregory Elliott (London: Verso, 2019); Wendy Brown, *Undoing the Demos: Neoliberalism's Stealth Revolution* (Brooklyn, NY: Zone, 2015); Pierre Dardot and Christian Laval, *The New Way of the World: On Neo-Liberal Society*, trans. Gregory Elliott (London: Verso, 2013); Masoud Kamali, *Neoliberal Securitization and Symbolic Violence: Silencing Political, Academic, and Societal Resistance* (Cham, Switzerland: Palgrave Macmillan, 2021); Ilkka Kärrylä, *Democracy and the Economy in Finland and Sweden Since 1960: A Nordic Perspective on Neoliberalism* (Cham, Switzerland: Palgrave Macmillan, 2021); Nicholas Copeland, *The Democracy Development Machine: Neoliberalism, Radical Pessimism, and Authoritarian Populism in Mayan Guatemala* (Ithaca, NY: Cornell University Press, 2019); Aurora Donzelli, *Methods of Desire, Language, Morality, and Affect in Neoliberal Indonesia* (Honolulu: University of Hawai'i Press, 2019); P. J. Boock, *Norwegian Social Democracy: From Revolution to Consumerism in the Norwegian Welfare State* (Lexington, KY: Independently published, 2018); Ritanjan Das, *Neoliberalism and the Transforming Left in India: A Contradictory Manifesto* (New York: Routledge, 2018); Wumaier Yilamu, *Neoliberalism and Post-Soviet Transition: Kazakhstan and Uzbekistan* (Cham, Switzerland: Palgrave Macmillan, 2018); Eva Cherniavsky, *Neocitizenship: Political Culture After Democracy* (New York: New York University Press, 2017); David Lea, *Neoliberalism, the Security State, and the Quantification of Reality* (Lanham, MD: Lexington, 2017); Emel Akçali, ed., *Neoliberal Governmentality and the Future of the State in the Middle East and North Africa* (New York: Palgrave Macmillan, 2016); Juan Pablo Ferrero, *Democracy Against Neoliberalism in Argentina and Brazil* (London: Palgrave Macmillan, 2016); Analiese Richard, *The Unsettled Sector: NGOs and the Cultivation of Democratic Citizenship in Rural Mexico* (Stanford, CA: Stanford University Press, 2016); and Peter Kingstone, *The Political Economy of Latin America: Reflections on Neoliberalism and Development After the Commodity Boom* (New York: Routledge, 2011).
7. Elisabeth S. Clemens and Doug Guthrie, "Introduction: Politics and Partnerships," in *Politics and Partnerships: The Role of Voluntary Associations in America's Political Past and Present*, ed. Elisabeth S. Clemens and Doug Guthrie (Chicago: University of Chicago Press, 2011), 10 (emphasis in original).
8. Tessa Morris-Suzuki, *Japan's Living Politics: Grassroots Action and the Crisis of Democracy* (Cambridge: Cambridge University Press, 2020). See also notes 46 and 47.
9. Jasper Ayelazuno, *Neoliberal Globalization and Resistance from Below: Why the Subalterns Resist in Bolivia and Not in Ghana* (London: Routledge, 2019); Ali Aslam, *Ordinary Democracy: Sovereignty and Citizenship Beyond the Neoliberal Impasse* (New York: Oxford University Press, 2017); Donatella Della Porta, Francis O'Connor, Martin Portos, and Anna Subirats Ribas, *Social Movements and Referendums from Below: Direct Democracy in the Neoliberal Crisis* (Bristol, UK: Policy, 2017); and William E. Connolly, *The Fragility of Things: Self-Organizing Processes, Neoliberal Fantasies, and Democratic Activism* (Durham, NC: Duke University Press, 2013).
10. Marcus Board, *Invisible Weapons: Infiltrating Resistance and Defeating Movements* (New York: Oxford University Press, 2022); Palma Carvajal and Juan Francisco, *Advocacy NGOs and the Neoliberal Pacification of the Demands of the Street* (London: Palgrave Macmillan, 2021); Aldo Madariaga, *Neoliberal Resilience: Lessons in Democracy and Development from Latin America and Eastern Europe* (Princeton, NJ: Princeton

INTRODUCTION

University Press, 2020); Copeland, *The Democracy Development Machine*; Damien Cahill and Martijn Konings, *Neoliberalism* (Cambridge, UK: Polity, 2017); and Colin Crouch, *The Strange Non-Death of Neoliberalism* (Cambridge, UK: Polity, 2011).

11. Gabriel Rockhill, *Counter-History of the Present: Untimely Interrogations Into Globalization, Technology, Democracy* (Durham, NC: Duke University Press, 2017), chap. 3.
12. Jacques Rancière, *Hatred of Democracy* (2005; repr. New York: Verso, 2014), chap. 2.
13. Sheldon Wolin, *Democracy Incorporated: Managed Democracy and the Specter of Inverted Totalitarianism* (Princeton, NJ: Princeton University Press, 2010), 60.
14. William Blum, *America's Deadliest Export: Democracy and the Truth about US Foreign Policy and Everything Else* (London: Zed, 2013); and Noam Chomsky, *Deterring Democracy* (New York: Hill and Wang, 1991).
15. Rockhill, *Counter-History of the Present*, 87–88, 16.
16. Kathleen M. Blee, *Democracy in the Making: How Activists Groups Form* (New York: Oxford University Press, 2012), 3
17. Kathleen Belew, *Bring the War Home: The White Power Movement and Paramilitary America* (Cambridge, MA: Harvard University Press, 2018); Alexandra Minna Stern, *Eugenic Nation: Faults and Frontiers of Better Breeding in Modern America* (Berkeley: University of California Press, 2016); Nansook Hong, *In the Shadow of the Moons: My Life in the Reverend Sun Myung Moon's Family*, written with Boston Globe reporter Eileen McNamara (New York: Little, Brown, 1998); and Stuart A. Wright, ed., *Armageddon in Waco: Critical Perspectives on the Branch Davidian Conflict* (Chicago: University of Chicago Press, 1995).
18. Michael L. Gross, *Ethics and Activism: The Theory and Practice of Political Morality* (Cambridge: Cambridge University Press, 1997).
19. Jan Liu, *Shifting Dynamics of Contention in the Digital Age: Mobile Communication and Politics in China* (New York: Oxford University Press, 2020); Rita Stephan and Mounira M. Charrad, eds., *Women Rising: In and Beyond the Arab Spring* (New York: New York University Press, 2020); Marco Giugni and Maria T. Grasso, *Street Citizens: Protest Politics and Social Movement Activism in the Age of Globalization* (Cambridge: Cambridge University Press, 2019); Jessica K. Taft, *The Kids Are in Charge: Activism and Power in Peru's Movement of Working Children* (New York: New York University Press, 2019); Richard Youngs, *Civic Activism Unleashed: New Hope or False Dawn for Democracy?* (New York: Oxford University Press, 2019); David Chiavacci and Julia Obinger, eds., *Social Movements and Political Activism in Contemporary Japan: Re-Emerging from Invisibility* (New York: Routledge, 2018); Sonia Alvarez, Jeffrey Rubin, Millie Thayer, Gianpaolo Baiochhi, and Agustin Lao-Montes, eds., *Beyond Civil Society: Activism, Participation, and Protest in Latin America* (Durham, NC: Duke University Press, 2017); Susanne Brandtstadter and Hans Steinmuller, eds., *Popular Politics and the Quest for Justice in Contemporary China* (New York: Routledge, 2017); Della Porta, O'Connor, Portos, and Ribas, *Social Movements and Referendums from Below*; Paolo Gerbaudo, *The Mask and the Flag: Populism, Citizenism, and Global Protest* (New York: Oxford University Press, 2017); Ran Wei, ed., *Mobile Media, Political Participation, and Civic Activism in Asia: Private Chat to Public Communications* (New York: Springer, 2016); and Peter Dahlgren, "Civic Identity and Net Activism: The Frame of Radical Democracy," in *Radical Democracy and the Internet: Interrogating Theory and Practice*, ed. Lincoln Dahlbert and Eugenia Siapera (London: Palgrave Macmillan, 2007), 55–72.

INTRODUCTION

20. Cigdem Cidam, *In the Street: Democratic Action, Theatricality, and Political Friendship* (New York: Oxford University Press, 2021); and Florence Passy and Gan-Andrea Monsch, *Contentious Minds: How Talk and Ties Sustain Activism* (New York: Oxford University Press, 2020).
21. Brian Caterino and Phillip Hansen, *Critical Theory, Democracy, and the Challenge of Neoliberalism* (Toronto, Canada: University of Toronto Press, 2019); Aslam, *Ordinary Democracy*; and Bryn Jones and Mike O'Donnell, eds., *Alternative to Neoliberalism: Towards Equality and Democracy* (Bristol, UK: Polity, 2017).
22. Brian K. Grodsky, *Social Movements and the New State: The Fate of Pro-Democracy Organizations When Democracy Is Won* (Stanford, CA: Stanford University Press, 2012); and Gi-wook Shin and Paul Y. Chang, eds., *South Korean Social Movements: From Democracy to Civil Society* (London: Routledge, 2011).
23. James M. Jasper, "Cultural Approaches in the Sociology of Social Movements," in *Handbook of Social Movements Across Disciplines*, ed. Bert Klandermans and Conny Roggeband (Cham, Switzerland: Springer, 2010), 59–109; Jeffrey C. Alexander, *The Civil Sphere* (New York: Oxford University Press, 2006); James M. Jasper, *The Art of Moral Protest: Culture, Biography, and Creativity in Social Movements* (Chicago: University of Chicago Press, 1997); and Hank Johnston and Bert Klandermans, eds., *Social Movements and Culture* (Minneapolis: University of Minnesota Press, 1995).
24. Charles Tilly, "From Interactions to Outcomes in Social Movements," in *How Social Movements Matter*, ed. Marco Giugni, Doug McAdam, and Charles Tilly (Minneapolis: University of Minnesota Press, 1999), 253–70.
25. Specifically, Pierre Bourdieu writes, "The homology of position between intellectuals and industrial workers is a source of an ambiguous alliance, in which cultural producers, the dominated among the dominant, supply to the dominated, by a sort of embezzlement of accumulated cultural capital, the means of constituting objectively their vision of the world and the representation of their interests in an explicit theory and in institutionalized instruments of representation." See Pierre Bourdieu, "Part III: Symbolic Power and the Political Field," in *Language and Symbolic Power*, ed. John B. Thompson, trans. Gino Raymond and Matthew Adamson (Cambridge, MA: Harvard University Press, 1991), 162–251, at 245.
26. See Weber's discussion of status group versus social class. Max Weber, "Class, Status and Party," in *From Max Weber: Essays in Sociology*, trans. and ed. H. H. Gerth and C. Wright Mills (1948; repr. Boston: Routledge & Kegan Paul, 1974), 180–95.
27. Bourdieu, "Part III: Symbolic Power and the Political Field," 229.
28. Bourdieu, 230–31.
29. Bourdieu, 192, 193.
30. Bourdieu, 172, 173.
31. Bourdieu, 181.
32. Bourdieu, 194.
33. Bourdieu, 188.
34. Bourdieu, 190.
35. In their theory of neoliberalism as a political rationality, both Wendy Brown and Pierre Dardot and Christian Laval distinguished it from Foucault's concept of "governmentality," but they draw extensively on Foucault. See Thomas Lemke, *Foucault's Analysis of Modern Governmentality: A Critique of Political Reason*, trans. Erik Butler (London: Verso, 2019); and Michel Foucault, *The Birth of Biopolitics: Lectures at the Collège de France, 1978–1979*, ed. Michel Senellat (New York: Palgrave Macmillan, 2008).

INTRODUCTION

36. Nelson D. Schwartz, *The Velvet Rope Economy: How Inequality Became Big Business* (New York: Anchor, 2021); Hong-sik Yoon, *Hanguk bokjigukkaui giwongwa gwejeok 3: Sinjayujuuiwa bokjigukka, 1980-nyeonbuteo 2016-nyeong*kkaji [The origin and trajectory of the South Korean welfare state. Vol 3. Neoliberalism and the welfare state—from 1980s to 2016] (Seoul: Sahoepyeongnon Academy, 2019); Noam Chomsky, Peter Hutchison, and Jared P. Scott, *Requiem for the American Dream: The 10 Principles of Concentration of Wealth & Power* (New York: Seven Stories, 2017); Peter Ranis, *Co-ops Confront Capitalism: Challenging the Neo-Liberal Economy* (London: Zed, 2016); Thomas Piketty, *Capital in the Twenty-First Century* (Cambridge, MA: Harvard University Press, 2014); Anders Aslund, *How Capitalism Was Built: The Transformation of Central and Eastern Europe, Russia, and Caucasus, and Central Asia* (Cambridge: Cambridge University Press, 2013); Crouch, *The Strange Non-Death of Neoliberalism*; and Jane L. Collins and Victoria Mayer, *Both Hands Tied: Welfare Reform and the Race to the Bottom in the Low-Wage Labor Market* (Chicago: University of Chicago Press, 2010).
37. Peter Dauvergne and Genevieve Lebaron, *Protest Inc.: The Corporatization of Activism* (Cambridge, UK: Polity, 2014); Edward T. Walker, *Grassroots for Hire: Public Affairs Consultants in American Democracy* (Cambridge: Cambridge University Press, 2014); and Akihiro Ogawa, *The Failure of Civil Society: The Third Sector and the State in Contemporary Japan* (Albany: State University of New York Press, 2009).
38. Michael Thompson, *Twilight of the Self: The Decline of the Individual in Late Capitalism* (Stanford, CA: Stanford University Press, 2022); Namhee Lee, *Memory Construction and the Politics of Time in Neoliberal South Korea* (Durham, NC: Duke University Press, 2022); Cherniavsky, *Neocitizenship*; Brown, *Undoing the Demos*; and Dardot and Laval, *The New Way of the World*.
39. Zygmunt Bauman, *Liquid Modernity* (Cambridge: Polity, 2000).
40. In the fields of public administration and civil society studies in South Korea, governance as a concept and practice has been represented as the democratization of governing, in contrast to the traditional concept of government. See Seong-su Ju, *Hanguksiminsahoesa: minjuhwagi 1987–2017* [A history of Korean civil society] (Seoul: Hakmin, 2017); and Sang-pil Park, "A Framework for Assessing the State Governance," *Journal of NGO Studies* 9, no. 2 (2014): 1–24.
41. For South Korea, see Min-jae Yoon, *Minjuhwa ihu hanguksahoewa sinjayujuui: daetongnyeong rideosipkwa tongchiseong* [Korean society after democratization and neoliberalism: presidential leadership and governmentality] (Seoul: Oreum, 2017).
42. Brown, *Undoing the Demos*, 22.
43. Dardot and Laval, *Never-Ending Nightmare*, 101, 118.
44. The financialization of the Korean economy in the aftermath of the Asian financial crisis had a pervasive cultural impact on ordinary people's attitudes toward making quick money through investment. This cultural change was amply reflected by the explosion of self-help books on investment and making big money quickly. The publication in early 2000 of *Buja appa gananhan appa: bujadeuri deulyojuneun 'don'gwa 'tuja'ui bimil*, which was a translation of Robert T. Kiyosaki's *Rich Dad Poor Dad: What the Rich Teach Their Kids About Money That the Poor and Middle Class Do Not* (1997), marked a rapid spread of cultural fever for investment as a new way for everyone to make big money quickly, not just for the rich with extra money to invest. The cultural fever also prompted a Korean publisher to republish an older book, *The Science of Getting Rich*, which was originally published by Wallace D. Wattles in

1910; the Korean translation was entitled *Dangshindo bujaga doel gwolliga itta* (You have a right to be rich, 2004). For critical studies of this cultural and social change, see Hyunmee Kim et al., eds., *Chinmiran jeok: Sinjayujuuineun eotteoke ilsangi doeeonna* [An intimate enemy: How did neoliberalism become our routine lives] (Seoul: Ihu, 2010); and Tae-seok Jeong, "Gieobui siminsahoe jibae: Siminsahoeui gieopsahoehwa" [Business corporations' rule of civil society: corporatization of civil society] *Miraegongbang* 5 (2008): 141–64.
45. Bauman, *Liquid Modernity*, 186.
46. Dardot and Laval, *Never-Ending Nightmare*; Caterino and Hansen, *Critical Theory, Democracy, and the Challenge of Neoliberalism*; Bonnie Honig, *Public Things: Democracy in Disrepair* (New York: Fordham University Press, 2017); Wolfgang Streeck, *The Delayed Crisis of Democratic Capitalism*, 2nd ed., trans. Patrick Camiller and David Fernbach (London: Verso, 2017); Brown, *Undoing the Demos*; and Dardot and Laval, *The New Way of the World*.
47. Jonathan Hopkin, *Anti-system Politics: The Crisis of Market Liberalism in Rich Democracies* (New York: Oxford University Press, 2020); Henry A. Giroux, *Terror of Neoliberalism: Authoritarianism and the Eclipse of Democracy* (New York: Routledge, 2018); Bons Vormann and Christian Lammert, *Democracy in Crisis: The Neoliberal Roots of Popular Unrest* (Philadelphia: University of Pennsylvania Press, 2017); and Lisa Duggan, *The Twilight of Equality?: Neoliberalism, Cultural Politics, and the Attack on Democracy* (Boston: Beacon, 2003).
48. For exceptional works, see Kyong-Min Son, *The Eclipse of the Demos: The Cold War and the Crisis of Democracy Before Neoliberalism* (Lawrence: University Press of Kansas, 2020); and Alen Toplišek, *Liberal Democracy in Crisis: Rethinking Resistance Under Neoliberal Governmentality* (London: Palgrave MacMillan, 2019).
49. Donzelli, *Methods of Desire*; Das, *Neoliberalism and the Transforming Left in India*; Alfredo Saad-Filho and Lecio Morais, *Brazil: Neoliberalism Versus Democracy* (London: Pluto, 2018); Yilamu, *Neoliberalism and Post-Soviet Transition*; Akçali, *Neoliberal Governmentality and the Future of the State in the Middle East and North Africa*; Ferrero, *Democracy Against Neoliberalism in Argentina and Brazil*; and Kingstone, *The Political Economy of Latin America*.
50. Madariaga, *Neoliberal Resilience*.
51. See Copeland, *The Democracy Development Machine*; and Richard, *The Unsettled Sector*.
52. For studies of the democratic expansion of human rights and civil and political rights in South Korea and Japan, see Celeste L. Arrington, *Accidental Activists: Victim Movements and Government Accountability in Japan and South Korea* (Ithaca, NY: Cornell University Press, 2016); and Mary Alice Haddad, *Building Democracy in Japan* (Cambridge: Cambridge University Press, 2012).
53. Copeland, *The Democracy Development Machine*; Cherian George, "Neoliberal 'Good Governance' in Lieu of Rights: Lee Kuan Yew's Singapore Experiment," in *Speech and Society in Turbulent Times: Freedom of Expression in Comparative Perspectives* (Cambridge: Cambridge University Press, 2018), 114–30; Hyug Baeg Im, "Authoritarian Developmentalism, Democratic Neoliberalism, and Economic Growth in Korea: Economic Growth in Different Policy Regimes," in *Growth, Crisis, Democracy* (London: Routledge, 2017), 196–221; and Richard, *The Unsettled Sector*.

1. THE DEVELOPMENT OF "CITIZENS' ORGANIZATIONS" IN SOUTH KOREA

54. Son, *The Eclipse of the Demos*.
55. Myeong-rae Jo, "Hanguk simiundongui wichiwa seonggyeok byeonhwa: gukka-siminsahoe gwangyereul jungsimeuro" [Changes in the position and nature of citizens' movements in Korea: Focusing on the state-civil society relation], in *Hanguk siminsahoeundong 25neyonsa* [A twenty-five-year history of civil society movements in Korea] (Seoul: Citizens Movements Information Center, 2014), 27–39.

1. THE DEVELOPMENT OF "CITIZENS' ORGANIZATIONS" IN SOUTH KOREA

1. Hye-jeong Gang, "UN-NGO hyeomnyeoknonui gandamhoe seongwhang" [Wild success of the meeting to discuss cooperation between UN and NGO] *NGO Times*, October 5, 1998, 9.
2. Dae-yeop Jo, *Hangugui siminundong* [Citizens' movements in South Korea] (Seoul: Nanam, 1999); Chul-hee Jeong, *Hanguksiminsahoeui gwejeok: 1970-nyeondae ihu siminsahoeui donghak* [The trajectory of civil society in South Korea: The dynamics of civil society since the 1970s] (Seoul: Areuche, 2003); and Dong-choon Kim, "Growth and Crisis of the Korean Citizens' Movement," *Korea Journal* 46, no. 2 (2006): 99–128.
3. For studies of the emergence of the "citizens' movement" from the democratization movement against a military dictatorship, see Namhee Lee, "From *minjung* to *simin*: The Discursive Shift in Korean Social Movements," in *South Korean Social Movements: From Democracy to Civil Society*, ed. Gi-Wook Shin and Paul Y. Chang, 41–57 (New York: Routledge, 2011); and Sun-Chul Kim, *Democratization and Social Movements in South Korea: Defiant Institutionalization* (New York: Routledge, 2016), chap. 2. Lee's study highlights the bifurcation of the citizens' movement and the people's movement, which was organized for and later by workers, farmer, and urban poor, whereas Kim's study highlights the continuous and recurring coalition between these two movements following the transition to procedural democracy.
4. Sun-mi Kim, "Siminundong wigi damrongwa baljeon bangan: Siminsahoe jihyeongbyeonhwawa gwallyeonhayeo" [The discourse of citizens' movements in crisis and a suggestion for a solution: Concerning the changing context of civil society], *Damnon201* 10, no. 3 (2008): 143–73; and Kim, "Growth and Crisis of the Korean Citizens' Movement."
5. Richard Youngs, *Civic Activism Unleashed: New Hope or False Dawn for Democracy?* (New York: Oxford University Press, 2019), chap. 5. Even among development NGOs, there are qualitative differences, depending on organizations and the level of analysis. A study of French development aid NGOs in the 2000s documents how such NGOs resisted the French state that promoted their technical professionalization to turn them into de facto government agencies. Instead, these French NGOs pursued their own professionalization in terms of private fund-raising and responded to the demands of their donor public and grassroots supporters. See Gordon D. Cumming, "French NGOs in the Global Era: Professionalization 'Without Borders'?" *Voluntas* 19 (2008): 372–94.
6. This self-description was printed in the inaugural issue of the Newspaper. See *NGO Times*, May 29, 1993.

1. THE DEVELOPMENT OF "CITIZENS' ORGANIZATIONS" IN SOUTH KOREA

7. In September 2006, the *NGO Times* began to publish sexual harassment cases committed by its president. To the public's disappointment, however, he did not handle the problem transparently. Instead, he used his position to obstruct justice, and subsequently the newspaper company was disbanded. To deal with this problem and its aftermath, concerned citizens' organizations formed a Common Countermeasure Committee. See Cheol-wu Yi, "<Siminuisinmum> satae haegyeol wihan gongdongdaechaekwi baljok" [The establishment of a Common Countermeasure Committee to resolve the situation of the NGO Times] *Saramilbo*, January 11, 2007.
8. Nicholas Copeland, *The Democracy Development Machine: Neoliberalism, Radical Pessimism, and Authoritarian Populism in Mayan Guatemala* (Ithaca, NY: Cornell University Press, 2019).
9. Richard Peet, *Unholy Trinity: The IMF, World Bank, and WTO* (London: Zed, 2009).
10. Zygmunt Bauman, *Liquid Modernity* (Cambridge: Polity, 2000).
11. Kyong-Min Son, *The Eclipse of the Demos: The Cold War and the Crisis of Democracy Before Neoliberalism*. Lawrence: University Press of Kansas, 2020.
12. David Lewis, "Nongovernmental Organizations, Definition and History," in *International Encyclopaedia of Civil Society*, ed. Helmut K. Anheiner and Stephan Toepler (New York: Springer, 2009), 1–10 at 5.
13. Hye-jeong Gang, "'Bijeongbugigu' gugjesahoeui sae juingong" ["NGO" a new protagonist of the international society], *NGO Times*, October 5, 1998, 8.
14. Comparatively speaking, the Korean term for nongovernmental, *mingan*, is similar to the Chinese term, *minjian*, because of their loose usage in contrast to the state, the official, or the government. See Liang Zhiping, "Rethinking Civil Society in China: An Interpretative Approach," in *The Politics of Affective Relations: East Asia and Beyond*, ed. Hahm Chaihark and Daniel A. Bell, 169–99 (Lanham, MD: Lexington, 2004).
15. Akihiro Ogawa, *The Failure of Civil Society: The Third Sector and the State in Contemporary Japan* (Albany: State University of New York Press, 2009); and Lewis, "Nongovernmental Organizations, Definition and History."
16. Robert D. Putman, *Bowling Alone* (New York: Simon & Schuster, 2000); Debra C. Minkoff, "The Emergence of Hybrid Organizational Forms: Combining Identity-Based Service Provision and Political Action," *Nonprofit and Voluntary Sector Quarterly* 31, no. 3 (2002): 377–401; and Theda Skocpol, *Diminished Democracy* (Norman: University of Oklahoma Press, 2003).
17. See Edward T. Walker, John D. McCarthy, and Frank Baumgartner, "Replacing Members with Managers? Mutualism Among Membership and Nonmembership Advocacy Organizations in the United States," *American Journal of Sociology* 177, no. 5 (2011): 1284–1337. The authors examined the common argument that such advocacy organizations without members replaced traditional membership organizations in the United States by conducting a quantitative analysis of empirical data drawn from the *Encyclopaedia of Organizations* from the late 1960s to the late 1990s. By highlighting mutualism rather than competition between membership and nonmembership in the organizations focusing on human rights, peace, and women, they argued that the two types of organizations collaborated rather than competed to replace each other.
18. Hui-yeon Cho, "14jang Siminundongui segaji saeroun gwaje [Three new challenges to the citizens' movements], in *Chamyeowa yeondaero yeon minjujuuiui sae jipyeong*

1. THE DEVELOPMENT OF "CITIZENS' ORGANIZATIONS" IN SOUTH KOREA

[New horizon for democracy that opens through participation and solidarity], ed. Seong-tae Hong (Seoul: Areuche, 2004), 336.
19. Seungsook Moon, "Overcome by Globalization: The Rise of a Women's Policy in South Korea," in *Korea's Globalization*, ed. Samuel S. Kim (Cambridge: Cambridge University Press, 2000), 126–27, 129. The WTO was formed as a result of the Uruguay Round that the United States began in 1986 under the auspices of the General Agreement on Tariffs and Trade (GATT) to hammer out a set of rules for world trade that was marked by "freedom" of investment and trade in all industrial sectors and the protection of intellectual property rights. Composed of 117 voting members with the power to enforce GATT provisions, the WTO, like the United Nations, has independent jurisdiction to oversee trade in agriculture, manufacturing, services, investment, and the production of intellectual property. The WTO regime generated the impetus for opening domestic markets in banking, insurance, and telecommunications, in which First World countries have unequivocal advantages over Third World countries.
20. Hong-sik Yoon, *Hanguk bokjigukgaui giwongwa gwejeok 3: Sinjayujuuiwa bokjigukka, 1980-nyeonbuteo 2016-nyeonggaji* [The origin and trajectory of the South Korean welfare state. Vol 3. Neoliberalism and the welfare state—from 1980s to 2016] (Seoul: Sahoepyongnon Academy, 2019); and Min-jae Yoon, *Minjuhwa ihu hanguksahoewa sinjayujuui: daetongnyeong rideosipkwa tongchiseong* [Korean society after democratization and neoliberalism: Presidential leadership and governmentality] (Seoul: Oreum, 2017).
21. This was initially a self-referential term used by those who questioned and challenged conservative forces that had ruled South Korean society. It has commonly been used to refer to those left of center in the South Korean sociopolitical context.
22. Initially, these two movements represented two distinct strands of activism in terms of goal, tactics, and ideology; but the changing relationship between the state and society in the context of democratization marginalized militant and radical approaches of the people's movement, and the citizens' movement came to represent the civil society. See Lee, "From *minjung* to *simin*: The Discursive Shift in Korean Social Movements."
23. Kim, *Democratization and Social Movements in South Korea*, chap. 2.
24. Kwang-yeong Shin, Don-mun Jo, and Eun Cho, *Hanguksahoeui gyegeumnonjeok ihae* [Understanding the Korean society through the theory of social class] (Paju: Hanulacademi, 2003).
25. No author, "Daehan YMCA yeonmaeng 'minjugaehyeok siminundong' symposium" [Korean YMCA Federation "citizens' movement for democratic reform" symposium], *NGO Times*, July 10, 1993, 9.
26. After autonomous local rule was revived in 1994 as an integral aspect of democratization, civil society discourse used a new term "citizen candidates" (*siminhubo*) to refer to candidates supported by various civil society organizations for municipal assemblies. In the 1998 local elections, such organizations included not only social movement–oriented citizens' organizations (for example, Environmental Movement United, Women's Associations United, and Citizens United for a Walkable City) but also occupational groups such as the Central Association of Agricultural Business Owners, National Farmers' Association, and Trade Unions (Byeong-gi Kim, "Siminjeongchisidae 'araerobuteo gaehyeok' sidong" [An era of citizens' politics and a

1. THE DEVELOPMENT OF "CITIZENS' ORGANIZATIONS" IN SOUTH KOREA

beginning of reform from below] *NGO Times*, June 15, 1998, 2–3). This usage suggests the expansion of the boundaries of citizens as agents of social change in connection with their involvement in activism rather than as a type of organization. Members of these traditional occupational associations are citizens who belong to the civil society when they actively participate in local elections as candidates.

27. No author, "Korean YMCA Federation 'citizens' movement for democratic reform' symposium," *NGO Times*, July 10, 1993, 9; No author, "Simindanche yeondaeneun sidaejeok yocheong" [Solidarity among citizens' organizations is a historical demand], January 29, 1994, 5.

28. Jang-jip Choi, *Minjuhwa ihuui minjujuui: Hanguk minjujuuiui bosujeok giwongwa wigi* [Democracy after democratization: Conservative origin and the crisis of Korean Democracy] (Seoul: Humanitaseu, 2002), 183. Along with anticommunism, which has been a persistent state ideology in South Korea, this liberal ideal of neutral public interests delegitimized people's movements organized by farmers, workers, and the urban poor who demanded economic redistribution and justice.

29. Hyo-mi Pak, "Gyeongjaengnyeok bilmi gajin iikdaebyeon gyeonggyereul" [Monitoring the interest advocacy justified by competitiveness], *NGO Times*, January 1, 1994, 6–7. No author, "Simindanche jungangjipjung beoseonal ddae" [It is time for citizens' organizations to move away from centralization.], *NGO Times*, May 21, 1994, 7.

30. Hye-jeong Gang, "Siminjajil nopyeoya minjusaheo doenda" [To become a democratic society citizens' qualities must be enhanced.] *NGO Times*, December 21, 1998, 6.

31. Yeong-hwan Bae, "Anpulineun gaehyeok siminundong hwalseonghwaro irwora" [Unaccomplished reform to be achieved through the activation of citizens' movement], *NGO Times*, June 1, 1998, 21.

32. No author, "Solidarity among citizens' organizations is a historical demand," *NGO Times*, January 29, 1994, 5.

33. Major examples of such included the Movement for Right Living, the New Village Movement, the Freedom Alliance, and the Veterans' Association. Even after the end of military rule in 1987, the New Village Movement Association, a major administered mass organization (AMO), received a large amount of funding from the state. From 1990 to 1994, it received 20 billion won (USD $20 million) for its annual budget, and under Kim Young-sam's government, which promised to reduce such funding, it received approximately 10 billion won (Hye-jeong Gang, "'Saemaeulundong' hwangyeongundong beorindadeoni?" [The "New Village Movement" pursued as an environmental movement?], *NGO Times*, June 22, 1998, 14).

34. Seungsook Moon, *Militarized Modernity and Gendered Citizenship in South Korea* (Durham, NC: Duke University Press, 2005), chap. 1.

35. Jong-seong Yu, "Jeonggigukhoe gaehyeokipbeop gwaje <2> minganhwaldong jayulseong bojang" [Regular National Assembly legislative reform issues <2> the protection of autonomy of NGO activities] *NGO Times*, September 11, 1993, 5.

36. Dae-seok Yang, "Saengsaege geuchin gwanbyeondanche jiwongeum saggam" [A nominal decrease of support money for pro-government organizations] *NGO Times*, November 20, 1993, 5.

37. Hyo-mi Pak, "Monitoring the interest advocacy justified by competitiveness," *NGO Times*, January 1, 1994, 6–7.

38. Byeong-jik Cha, *Sageoneuro boneun siminundongsa: Hyeondaesaui muljulgireul bakkun hanguksiminundong 20 jangmyeon* [A history of citizens' movements seen

1. THE DEVELOPMENT OF "CITIZENS' ORGANIZATIONS" IN SOUTH KOREA

through events: 20 scenes from citizens' movements that changed major streams of contemporary history in South Korea] (Seoul: Changjakgwabipyeong, 2014), 255.

39. Yeong-il Jeong, "NGO hagi himdeun nara, Hanguk" [Korea, a country difficult to run NGOs], *NGO Times*, April 17, 2006, 8.

40. Jeong, "NGO hagi himdeun nara, Hanguk."

41. According to the 2015 Social Survey Report conducted by the Statistics Bureau, individual donations in terms of money and goods decreased from 34.6 percent in 2013 to 29.9 percent in 2015, and the main reason for not donating was the lack of economic means: 60.9 percent in 2013 and 63.5 percent in 2015. This increase in the lack of economic means suggests that the growing economic precarity among a majority of Koreans has negatively affected donations for citizens' organizations in neoliberal South Korea. See Chang-won Yun, "Sahoe gongdongchewa sangsaenggwangye, geurigo saengmyeongnanum" [Social community, symbiotic relations, and sharing of life], in *Korean Civil Society Yearbook* (Seoul: Citizens Movement Information Center, 2017), 347–358 at 349.

42. The Economic Planning Board, a powerful government agency for economic development, articulated a need to change the form of government funding from handing out money to cover expenses to funding specific projects promoting public interests (Editor, "Simindanche hwalseonghwaneun seonjinguk jinip didimdol" [The activation of citizens' organizations is an important stepping stone leading to an advanced country], *NGO Times*, June 4, 1994, 15–16). Between 1994 and 1997 there was some limited government funding for NGOs. Since 1994, the central government annually granted funding for "projects practicing democratic community consciousness" carried out by NGOs and NPOs. These organizations applied for and received awards through open competition, but the funding amount per individual organization was not substantial, ranging between 10,000 and 70,000 won (USD $10 and $70). Since 1997, the Seoul metropolitan government similarly funded NGOs working for social, environmental, and transportation issues under the rubric of citizens' participation in municipal politics (Jeong-eun Seo, "Nuganuga simindanche domna?" [Who helps citizens' organizations?], *NGO Times*, June 22, 1998).

43. Modeled after established practices in Japan and the United States, this law included a postage discount of 25 percent for nonprofit organizations. See Robert Pekkanan, *Japan's Dual Civil Society: Members Without Advocates* (Stanford, CA: Stanford University Press, 2006); and Theda Skocpol, "Advocates Without Members: The Recent Transformation of American Civic Life," in *Civic Engagement in American Democracy*, ed. Theda Skocpol and Morris P. Fiorina (Washington, DC: Brookings Institution Press, 1999), 461–509. However, the law was accompanied by convoluted conditions for receiving the benefit. In practice, these conditions have often prevented citizens' organizations from taking advantage of the benefit (Yeong-il Yi, "Biyeongridanche upyeonyogeum harin keunuchegungman jeogyonghaejwo bulpyeon" [Inconvenience of the postage discount for non-profit organizations applied to only big post offices], *Hangyoreh Newspaper*, December 30, 2003). The rather mysterious conditions included (1) the head of a post office should be a government employee of class 5 or higher, and (2) a post office should be one of the "offices with mail concentration" (*upyeonjipjungguk*).

44. Jeong-eun Seo, "Jeongbu, 'jungnipjeok gigu' tonghae mingandanche jiwon neulyeoya" [The government must increase its support for NGOs through "neutral instruments."], *NGO Times*, July 20, 1998, 19.

1. THE DEVELOPMENT OF "CITIZENS' ORGANIZATIONS" IN SOUTH KOREA

45. Jo Saglie and Karl Henrik Sivesind, "Civil Society Institutions or Semi-Public Agencies: State Regulation of Parties and Voluntary Organizations in Norway," *Journal of Civil Society* 14, no. 4 (2018): 292–310; Johan Hvenmark and Filip Wijkström, "The Popular Movement Marinade: The Dominant Civil Society Framework in Sweden," in SSE/EFI Working Paper Series in Business Administration 2004:18, Stockholm School of Economics; Pekkanan, *Japan's Dual Civil Society*; and Skocpol, "Advocates Without Members."
46. Jeong-eun Seo, "The government must increase its support for NGOs through 'neutral instruments,'" *NGO Times* July 20, 1998, 19.
47. No author, "Bipanseryeok tanap bumerangdeol geot" [The repression of critical voices will become boomerang], *NGO Press*, May 11, 2009.
48. See Hye-su Jo, "MB jeongbu, bosu seonghyang danchee bojogeum pakpak mireojueotta" [MB government, actively funded organizations with conservative orientations], *Sisajeoneol* 1184 (June 26, 2012): 42–45; Hye-su Jo, "Bojogeum mikkiro simindanche gildeurina?" [Do you tame citizens' organizations with the bait of funding?], *Sisajeoneol* 1184 (June 26, 2012): 48; and Cheol Baek, "Gwanbyeondanche subaegeok hyeolse eonjekkaji julgeongayo" [Until when do you grant to pro-government organizations millions of bloody tax money?], *Weekly Kyonghyang* 1134 (July 14, 2015): 25–27.
49. See Yong-seung Jo, "'Gwollyeokgamsi' naesewotteon chamyoyeondae museoun gwollyeok geu jachero 'baljeon'" [The PSPD vocal about "monitoring the power" has 'developed' into the power itself], *Hanguknondan* (January 2011): 74–81, for a representative example of a conservative accusation that uses polarizing ideological code words.
50. Yeong-il Jeong, "Siminundong jiwon sahoejeok habui sigeup" [Social consensus on supporting citizens' movement is urgent], *NGO Times*, April 17, 2006, 9.
51. A case illustrating this problem was the Right Living Movement (RLM) during the 1998 general election. Founded by Roh Tae-woo's regime to check the New Village Movement Association and promote its election campaigns, the RLM declined during Kim Young-sam's civilian rule. But after a local election loss in 1994, Kim's ruling party resorted to the old tactic of using government-sponsored organizations for election campaigns and revived the RLM. In 1998, it had roughly 4,000 branches nationwide with over 100,000 members. These branches used some 190 rooms in local government buildings for free (Hye-jeong Gang, "Basalhyeop, 'bareun minganundong' beoliryeona?" [The Right Living Movement Council, would it pursue a "right NGO movement?"], *NGO Times*, June 15, 1998, 14).
52. They also worked to restore the autonomy of existing voluntary associations. For example, cooperatives in the agriculture, fishery, and livestock industries had long been closely controlled by the government. The leading organizations asked the government to legislate a uniform law to strengthen cooperative movements (Jong-seong Yu, "Jeonggigukhoe gaehyeokimbeop gwaje <1> chonggwal" [Regular National Assembly legislative reform issues <1> Summary], *NGO Times*, September 4, 1993, 5; Jong-seong Yu, "Regular National Assembly legislative reform issues <2> the protection of autonomy of NGO activities," *NGO Times*, September 11, 1993, 5; No author, "Korean YMCA Federation 'citizens' movement for democratic reform' symposium," *NGO Times*, July 10, 1993, 9).
53. In 1999, Kim Dae-jung's government upgraded and expanded a Blue House office in charge of dealing with "civil affairs" (*minjeong*) and assigned an officer exclusively

1. THE DEVELOPMENT OF "CITIZENS' ORGANIZATIONS" IN SOUTH KOREA

in charge of managing "civil society public opinion." Roh Moo-hyun's government went a step further and established a "civil society chief office" (*siminsahoesuseoksil*). See Cha, "Looking for a Tilted Balance," 22.
54. Yoon, *Hanguk bokjigukgaui giwongwa gwejeok*, 250–52.
55. Hye-jeong Gang, "Jeonguk simindanche gaehyeok chokgu hamseong" [A battle cry to urge citizens' organizations' reform nationwide], *NGO Times*, December 7, 1998, 12.
56. Byeong-gi Kim, "'Araerobuteo gaehyeok' wieseo kkeullyeogo?" ["Reform from below" pulling up from above?], *NGO Times*, December 14, 1998, 12.
57. Yong-in Jeong, "A Quarter Century of Citizens' Movements with Glory and Opprobrium: Can Its Heyday Be Returned?," *Weekly Kyeonghyang* 1136 (July 28, 2015): 33.
58. As this issue became politicized by conservative forces, which were threatened by the rise of progressive citizens' organizations, the Korean NGO Studies Association organized a public discussion titled "How to View the Political Participation of Citizens' Movements?" in the Press Center on January 28, 2003.
59. As a political outsider with a background as a human rights lawyer defending democracy activists under the military rule, Roh was elected through an internet-based grassroots movement initiated mostly by a younger generation. Besieged by the conservative political social establishment, he was impeached (for the first time in South Korean history) by the National Assembly, which was controlled by the conservative opposition party. To support the embattled president, his grassroots supporters organized a series of massive candlelight protests via the internet network and played an instrumental role in saving him from impeachment.
60. Editor, "NGO heobeu 'hamkkehaneunsiminhaengdong'" [An NGO hub "Doing-it-together Citizens Action"], *NGO Times*, January 9, 2006, 8.
61. Lewis, "Nongovernmental Organizations, Definition and History."
62. For example, this inclusive view is articulated by an officer of the National Policy Research Center (*Narajeongchaek yeonguhoe*), No author, "Korean YMCA Federation 'citizens' movement for democratic reform' symposium," *NGO Times*, July 10, 1993, 9.
63. Here the *2006 Korean NGO Directory* reverts to the common usage of NGOs as being interchangeable with civil society organizations.
64. In light of the discourse of civil society that initially identified civil society with progressive citizens' organizations, "civil society organizations" here refers to civic organizations focusing on legal and policy reform for broad long-term social change.
65. Editor, "Tujaengundong anin 'hapchi' paereodaimeul" [Not militant struggle but the paradigm of "governance"], *NGO Times*, February 20, 2006, 7.
66. Ibid.
67. Dong-bon Seol, "Siminsahoe gwangaekipjang andwae" [Civil society, not in the position of audience], *NGO Press*, August 10, 2009, 5.
68. Seung-man Kim, "'Goedam' gyosire 'chamgyoyuk' jeonhareo bojikhamnida" [We return to our work to practice "authentic education" in classroom of "spooky stories"], *NGO Times*, July 27, 1998, p. 21. In contrast, some government-sponsored organizations modified their relationship with the government and their main issues. In the 1990s, for example, the New Village Movement Association, one of the major government-sponsored organizations founded by Park Chung-hee in the early 1970s, replaced its leader with a more professional administrator (without ties to a ruling party and the government), adopted environmental issues, and has provided its

1. THE DEVELOPMENT OF "CITIZENS' ORGANIZATIONS" IN SOUTH KOREA

members with welfare services rather than mobilizing them for election campaigns of a ruling party. Hye-jeong Gang, "New Village Movement" pursued as an environmental movement? *NGO Times*, June 22, 1998, 14.
69. The local Christian churches paid attention early on to the perils of migrant foreign workers, whose numbers had been growing steadily since the late 1980s. When the Council for Dealing with Foreign Workers' Human Rights was formed in the mid-1990s, Reverend Myong-jin In was serving as the chair. Since 1992, his Protestant church had provided foreign workers with Sunday services in English, Korean-language classes, and health care, including counseling service (Jung-yang Son, "Inteobyu: In Myeong-jin moksa" [Interview: Reverend Myeong-jin In], *NGO Times*, January 15, 1994, 11).
70. Hye-jeong Gang, "YMCA, jibang bungwonhwa apjang" [YMCA, leading the localization and decentralization], *NGO Times*, April 6, 1998, 18–19. Following the Paris Standard adopted in 1855 by the General Assembly to found the World YMCA Federation, the YMCA in Korea also adopted a "strong social consciousness" in its mission statement. Building on this tradition, it explains its social-change orientation as a "church outside a church" and an "open church," based on a broad interpretation of "Christian-ness"; that is, everything has Christian-ness, and its contents change and evolve over time.
71. See the Heungsadan homepage at http://www.yka.or.kr/html/introduce/introduce .asp (accessed September 11, 2020).
72. Jeong-eun Seo, "Saenghwalhyeopdongjohapundong 'naeunsam' ilgunda" [Living Cooperative Movement cultivates a "better life"], *NGO Times*, May 11, 1998, 18–19.
73. No author, "It is a time for citizens' organizations to move away from centralization," *NGO Times*, May 21, 1994, 7.
74. Yeong-hwan Bae, "Siminsahoee deo gipsugi ppuri naeryeora" [Root deeper into the civil society], *NGO Times*, June 1, 1998, 6.
75. No author, "Jinbojinyeong tongsinnetwokeuro mukkeo seunda" [The progressive camp gathers its forces through communication network], *NGO Times*, May 11, 1998, 27.
76. In 1998 there was no formal law concerning volunteer activities despite an attempt to pass the Volunteer Service Promotion Law in 1994. It was not until 2005 that the Volunteer Service Activities Basic Law was passed to guide volunteer service by individuals and organizations. See Yun, "Sahoe gongdongchewa sangsaenggwangye, geurigo saengmyeongnanum," 350.
77. Hye-gyeong Kim, "Jawonbongsa hwalseonghwaga siminsahoe saljjiunda" [The activation of volunteer services enriches civil society], *NGO Times*, July 20, 1998, 24.
78. Kim, "Jawonbongsa hwalseonghwaga siminsahoe saljjiunda."
79. The growing influence of the leading citizens' organizations in the mid-1990s generated a public consensus on citizens' organizations as the central force for social change in democratizing Korea. According to a national survey of 700 employed adults in their twenties and thirties, conducted in 1994, the respondents chose citizens' movement organizations most frequently (82.8 percent in multiple replies) as the major force of societal reform, followed by the People's Movement (23.2 percent). The 700 respondents also indicated that citizens' organizations (50.4 percent) and the press and news media (41.6 percent) were institutions that would deal with societal corruption most fairly (No author, "20-30dae jikjangin 'sahoeuisik' seolmun"

1. THE DEVELOPMENT OF "CITIZENS' ORGANIZATIONS" IN SOUTH KOREA

[A survey of "social consciousness" among the employed in their 20s and 30s], *NGO Times*, March 5, 1994, 7). The East Asia Institute, in collaboration with *Jungang Daily*, had conducted "survey of public trust and influence of power organizations" since 2005. Its 2013 survey showed the steady decline of public trust and influence among major citizens' organizations between 2005 and 2013. On a scale of 0 to 10 (most trustworthy and influential), the group of major citizens' organizations marked 4.63 in 2005 and 3.9 in 2013 on public trust. See Won-taek Gang, Hyeon-u Yi, and Won-chil Jeong, "Yeoronbeuriping 136ho: 2013 pawojojik silloeyeonghyangneok josaui juyogyeolgwa" [Public opinion briefing no. 136: major findings of the survey of public trust and influence of power organizations], August 22, 2013, https://www.eai.or.kr/new/ko/pub/view.asp?intSeq=13445.

80. Editor, "An NGO hub 'Doing-it-together Citizens Action,'" *NGO Times*, January 9, 2006, 8–9; Ha 2015.
81. Jae-hwan Yi, "Siminundong 'jeonhwangiron' jeollyakhwadu" [The "theory of transformative period" for citizens' movement leads its strategic discourse.], *NGO Times*, March 6, 2006, 1. Guk-jin Gang, "Jinbojeongdanggwa siminundong son jabeumyeon sahoejinbo nakgwan" [Optimistic about societal progress when a progressive political party holds hands with citizens' movement], *NGO Times*, March 6, 2006, 7.
82. Yeong-il Jeong, "NGO yanggeukhwa . . . areumdaun donghaeng kkaejilla" [The polarization of NGOs . . . likely to break beautiful cooperation], *NGO Times*, April 10, 2006.
83. Jae-hwan Yi, "'Siminhwaldongjiwoncenteo' jaedan myeongching seonho" [Citizens' Activities Support Center prefers the category of "foundation," *NGO Times*, April 24, 2006, 2.
84. Gwan-yeong Oh, "Jibangseongeo apdun siminsahoeui mosaek" [Civil society's groping before local elections], *NGO Press*, August 3, 2009, 10.
85. No author, "Inteobyu: Pak Won-sun huimangjejakso sangimisa" [Interview: Park Won Soon, Executive Director of the Hope-making Center], *NGO Press*, June 15, 2009, 3.
86. Su-mi Eun cited by Guk-jin Gang, "Siminundongdo jojikjindan keonseolting badaya" [Citizens' movement also needs to get an organizational consulting], *NGO Times*, May 29, 2006, 6.
87. Charles Tilly writes, "a social movement . . . consists of *a sustained challenge to power holders in the name of a population living under the jurisdiction of power holders by means of repeated public displays of that population's worthiness, unity, numbers, and commitment*" (emphasis in original). See Charles Tilly, "From Interactions to Outcomes in Social Movements," in *How Social Movements Matter*, ed. Marco Giugni, Doug McAdam, and Charles Tilly (Minneapolis: University of Minnesota Press, 1999), 253–70, at 257.
88. Seok-gyu Go, "18, 19 segi Seourui waljjawa sangeopmunhwa: Siminsahoeui ppuriwa kwallyeonhayeo" [Waljja and commercial culture in Seoul during the eighteenth and nineteenth centuries: Concerning the root of civil society], *Seoul Studies* 13 (July 1999): 45–86.
89. Myeong-gwan Gang, *Joseonui duitgolmok punggyeong* [The landscape of back allies in Joseon] (Seoul: Pureunyeoksa, 2003), 151.
90. Myeong-gwan Gang, *Joseonhugi yeohangmunhak yeongu* [A study of yeohang literature in late Joseon Dynasty] (Seoul: Changjakkwabipyeong, 1997).

1. THE DEVELOPMENT OF "CITIZENS' ORGANIZATIONS" IN SOUTH KOREA

91. A gap between the neo-Confucian ideal of civility and its pragmatic translation into institutionalized practices tied to the reproduction of the hereditary status system sensitizes us to see how civility not only coexists with inequality but also serves as cultural capital to bolster it by contributing to a Gramscian hegemony of the status quo. This dynamic of civility as cultural capital is what Norbert Elias analyzes in his historical study of the "civilizing process" in Europe. Norbert Elias, *The Civilizing Process: The History of Manners and State Formation and Civilization*, translated by Edmund Jepbott (1939; repr. Oxford, UK: Blackwell, 1994). Eiko Ikegami explores a similar dynamic of civility and inequality in traditional Japanese society. See Eiko Ikegami, *Bonds of Civility: Aesthetic Networks and the Political Origins of Japanese Culture* (New York: Cambridge University Press, 2005). This comparative convergence suggests that civility oriented toward refinement and aesthetic appreciation can easily be channeled into a hegemonic source of distinction and the maintenance of inequality of social status among groups. To foster and maintain democratic solidarity, we need to develop different understandings and practices of civility. As the cross-cultural encounter with neo-Confucianism enabled the transformation of traditional Korean society, the cross-cultural encounter with imperialist powers from the West in the late nineteenth century allowed for the emergence of new notions and practices of civility.

2. PROFILES OF THREE CITIZENS' ORGANIZATIONS

1. This tree is widely known in Korea as a symbol of a traditional village and its gathering place. It was usually planted near a village pavilion because its branches spread widely and create protective shade under which villagers could gather to socialize. There are numerous very old Zelkova trees in South Korea, and some of them have been designated as "natural monuments" (*cheonyeonginyeommul*).
2. As a small country (the size of state of Indiana) with approximately 52 million people, population density in South Korea has been high. In particular, the density in Seoul proper with over 10 million residents has been extreme; there were 15,964 people per square kilometer in 2019. See Statista, https://www.statista.com/statistics/1112322/south-korea-population-density-by-province/#:~:text=The%20population%20density%20of%20Seoul,Seoul%20was%20around%209.64%20million (accessed January 14, 2021).
3. According to various studies, PSPD has played the leading role as a representative citizens' organization. A 2006 study of citizens' organizations shows that PSPD had been a major hub along with the Environmental Movements United, the Citizens' Coalition for Economic Justice, Citizens' Action Doing Together, and the YMCA; these organizations have occupied central positions in formal and informal networking with the state, mass media, and other organizations (Guk-jin Gang, "Daehanminguk siminundong 'heobeu'" [South Korean Citizens' movement's hub], *NGO Times*, January 2, 2006, 11).
4. One of the main reasons for PSPD's reluctance to create local branches was the possibility of abuses of its social capital and organizational resources by individuals and groups seeking their own political power bases. See Seungsook Moon, "The Interplay Between the State, the Market, and Culture in Shaping Civil Society: A Case

2. PROFILES OF THREE CITIZENS' ORGANIZATIONS

Study of the People's Solidarity for Participatory Democracy in South Korea," *Journal of Asian Studies* 69, no. 2 (2010): 479–505, at 488. This concern reflects the common occurrence of such abuse in both historical and current practices in Korean society, which are linked to authoritarian uses of various organizations to obtain and maintain political power.

5. This hybrid identity is a predictable organizational form as an outcome of pragmatically running a civic organization that often deals with the constraints of material and immaterial resources. In the post-1960s United States, hybrid civic organizations developed that combined identity-based service provision with advocacy in the context of the spread of new social movements. See Debra C. Minkoff, "The Emergence of Hybrid Organizational Forms: Combining Identity-Based Service Provision and Political Action," *Nonprofit and Voluntary Sector Quarterly* 31, no. 3 (2002): 377–401.

6. See People's Solidarity for Participatory Democracy, *Chamyeoyeondae 10nyeonui girok, 1994–2004: Sesangeul bakkuneun siminui him* [PSPD's record of the ten years, 1994–2004: Citizens' power that changed the world] (Seoul: PSPD, 2004). This work was published to celebrate PSPD's tenth anniversary. PSPD, *Chamyeoyeondae 20junyeon hwaldongbogoseo* [PSPD 20th anniversary activities report] (Seoul: PSPD, 2014). PSPD, *Chamyeoyeondae 2019 hwaldongbogoseo* [PSPD 2019 annual activities report] (Seoul: PSPD, 2020).

7. People's Solidarity for Participatory Democracy, PSPD 20th anniversary activities report, 2014, 59. Many PSPD officers have been influential professionals who have significant cultural and social capital. Compared with smaller and less influential citizens' organizations, this social and cultural capital has benefited PSPD's fundraising events.

8. Byeong-jik Cha, *Sageoneuro boneun siminundongsa: Hyeondaesaui muljulgireul bakkun hanguksiminundong 20 jangmyeon* [A history of citizens' movements seen through events: 20 scenes from citizens' movements that changed major streams of contemporary history in South Korea] (Seoul: Changjakkwabipyeong, 2014), 254.

9. Byeong-gi Kim, "'Araerobuteo gaehyeok' wieseo ggeullyeogo?" ["Reform from below" pulling up from above?], *NGO Times*, December 14, 1998, 12.

10. People's Solidarity for Participatory Democracy, Chamyeoyeondae 20nyeon hwaldong 100seon [100 selected activities from the twenty-year history of the PSPD], 2014, 382–88, 457–68.

11. Tae-seok Jeong, "Minjuhwa ihu hanguksahoeui byeonhwawa chamyeoyeondae" [Social change after democratization and the PSPD in South Korea], *Civil Society & NGO* 11, no. 2 (2013): 3–39.

12. According to the 2004 record of the Ministry of Administrative Autonomy, those who hailed from citizens' organizations in general participated in 19.6 percent of 249 government committees. In particular, 150 former and current officers of PSPD were appointed to 313 government positions. The State Human Rights Committee was headed by someone with a PSPD background from its first to the fourth head. In particular, conservative media highlighted "its transformation into a political power" by repeatedly citing a significant increase in PSPD officers who joined the government. During Kim Young-sam administration (1993–1998), only twenty-two positions were occupied by PSPD officers. The number grew to 113 positions during the Kim Dae-jung administration and 158 positions during the Roh

2. PROFILES OF THREE CITIZENS' ORGANIZATIONS

Moo-hyun administration. See Sang-jun Yi, "Chamyeoyeondae jeongbuui wiheomseong. Nomuhyeon jeongbuwa dejabu" [Danger of the PSPD government. Déjà vu with Roh Moo-hyun government], *Deilian*, April 10, 2018, https://dailian.co.kr/printPage2.html; Su-yeong Hong, "DJ-Nojeongbu banmyeongyosa 10nyeon <5> Gwolleoge muldeun simindanche" [DJ-Roh administrations reactionary 10 years <5> citizens' organizations colored by political power], *Dong-A Daily*, January 4, 2008, https://www.donga.com/news/View?gid=8529887&date=20080104; and Jaeyeon Jo, "Gwollyeok pyeonseunghamyeo jeongchidanche byeonjil . . . Moon jeongbuseon 'mansachamtong' yegikkaji" [Changing into a political organization by riding on the political power . . . even like a "free pass" in Moon's administration], *Munhwa Daily*, March 19, 2020, http://www.munhwa.com/news/news_print.html?no=2020031901031727328001.

13. Won-soon Park and Ki-sik Kim were among the most prominent examples of this change. Park was a human rights lawyer and founding member of PSPD and its first full-time leader from 1995 to 2001. In 2011, he was elected mayor of Seoul. While the national government was continuously controlled by the conservative party, Park was reelected in 2015 and governed the capitol city until June 2020 (when he apparently committed suicide after one of his employees filed a lawsuit for sexual harassment). Kim was also a founding member of PSPD and became a coleader (with Young-seon Pak) from 2002 to 2006, succeeding Park (People's Solidarity for Participatory Democracy, *Chamyeoyeondae 20nyeon baljachwi* [The PSPD's footsteps for 20 years], 2014, 128). Kim left the organization to pursue a political career and was elected to the National Assembly in 2012. During the Moon Jae-in administration, in 2018, he was appointed to the head of the Financial Supervisory Services, an integrated regulatory agency, but was forced to resign amidst a controversy.
14. People's Solidarity for Participatory Democracy, *Chamyeoyeondae 20nyeon jaryo* [The PSPD's resources for its 20 years], 2014, 162.
15. People's Solidarity for Participatory Democracy, *Chamyeoyeondae 20nyeon jaryo*, 2014, 58.
16. A culture war between the progressives and the conservatives began with an exchange of newspaper columns between Mun-yeol Yi, a renowned novelist articulating conservative views, and Jung-gwon Jin, a philosopher and public intellectual articulating progressive views. In February of 2000, in the midst of a national campaign to weed out corrupt politicians that was organized by a coalition of progressive civic organizations in preparation for the upcoming general election, Yi published a column titled "Reflecting on the Red Guard" in *Jungang Daily*. To summarize, without evidence, he compared the national campaign to the Red Guard of Mao Zedong during the Cultural Revolution in the People's Republic of China. In response, Jin wrote a column sarcastically titled "The Relationship Between Yi Mun-yeol and 'Mrs. Cow'?" This puzzling title reflected sarcasm based on a popular pornographic film trope of "Mrs. Cow," which referred to a woman with big breasts. To summarize, Jin criticized Yi's logical flaw in alluding to the relationship between the progressive government and the national campaign even after he himself acknowledged the lack of evidence. To gain popular appeal for his argument, instead of using academic language Jin pointed out that "Yi's logic is the same as the one used when someone states that Yi has a relationship with Mrs. Cow even though there is no evidence." See Byeong-jik Cha, "Looking for a Tilted Balance: Since 2000 the Political Neutrality Controversy," *Chamyeosahoe* 206 (January 2014): 21. For a recurring

2. PROFILES OF THREE CITIZENS' ORGANIZATIONS

controversy over "political neutrality" as put forth by conservative forces, see Right Society Citizens Meeting, "Toron: 'Gyowonui jeongchijeok jungnipseonge bichueo bon 'jeongyojoui jeongchitujaengeul malhada!" [Discussion: Speaking about the National Teachers' Union's political struggle in light of "school teachers' political neutrality"], proceedings of the meeting on April 7, 2016. Also see, Yong-seung Jo, "'Gwollyeokgamsi' naesewotteon chamyeoyeondae museoun gwollyeok geu jachero 'baljeon'" [The PSPD vocal about "monitoring the power" has "developed" into the power itself], *Hanguknondan* (January 2011): 74–81; and Seok-chun Yu and Hye-sook Wang, *Chamyeoyeondae bogoseo* [PSPD Report] (Seoul: Jayugieopwon, 2006).

17. Cha, "Looking for a Tilted Balance," 23, 24.
18. An illustrative example was the incident of the South Korean naval vessel *Cheonan* (1,300 ton). In March 2010, this vessel was mysteriously destroyed and sank, leaving forty-six of its 104 crew members missing. The military investigation team hastily concluded, without substantial evidence, that North Korea had torpedoed the vessel, which triggered public confusion and the suspicion of utilizing inveterate anticommunist and anti-North sentiments. To balance the incomplete official view for the Korean public and the world, PSPD explored a plan to disseminate its position statement based on available evidence. It collected signatures from the public and raised funds to produce an English letter to be sent to the UN Security Council, foreign embassies, and the foreign presses. After it delivered "the PSPD's Stance on the Naval Vessel *Cheonan* Sinking" to these global and foreign agencies in June, it became embroiled in a fierce ideological confrontation with conservative organizations. The National New Right United reported PSPD to the prosecutor for allegedly violating the National Security Law. In response, the progressive camp supported PSPD for raising necessary questions on the military and security issue that had serious ramifications for the entire Korean people and the world. See Cha, *Sageoneuro boneun siminundongsa*, 157–69. Such support resulted in gaining 1,800 new members (People's Solidarity for Participatory Democracy, *Chamyeoyeondae 20junyeon hwaldongbogoseo*, 2014, 17).
19. Hyung Chul Kim and Kyung Sun Hong, "Seongeoundongui jayuwa gongjikseongeobeop gaejeong bangan: simindancheui seongeobeop wibansaryereul jungsimeuro" [Freedom of election campaign and the revision of the public officials election law: Focusing on the cases of violation of the law by citizens' organizations], *Comparative Democracy Studies* 14, no. 2 (2018): 5–43.
20. Dong-pil Kim, "Hyeonhaeng seongeobeop 'pyohyeonui jayu' jeyak, jeongbominjujuui garomaga" [The current election law constrains "freedom of expression," obstructing information democracy], *NGO Times*, February 9, 1998, 29.
21. Cha, *Sageoneuro boneun siminundongsa*, 90–99.
22. Sang-hyeon Yi, "'Siminhubo' jeonggyejinchul jangbyeok noptta" ["Citizen candidates" faced with a high wall against their entry into the political world.], *NGO Times*, April 20, 1998, 2.
23. Yeong-hwan Bae, "Anpulineun gaehyeok siminundong hwalseonghwaro irwora" [Unaccomplished reform to be achieved through the activation of citizens' movement], *NGO Times*, June 1, 1998, 21.
24. People's Solidarity for Participatory Democracy, *Chamyeoyeondae 20junyeon hwaldongbogoseo*, 2014, 15.
25. Yeong-il Jeong, "Chongseonyeondaeeseo pulppuriyeondaekkaji" [From General Election solidarity to grassroots solidarity], *NGO Times*, May 15, 2006, 2.

2. PROFILES OF THREE CITIZENS' ORGANIZATIONS

26. People's Solidarity for Participatory Democracy, *Chamyeoyeondae 20nyeon hwaldong 100seon*, 2014, 148–51.
27. Hyung Chul Kim, "Simindancheui seongeochamyeohwaldong pyeonggawa hwalseonghwa bangan: 2016 chongseonsiminnetteuwokeureul jungsimeuro" [The evaluation of citizens' organizations' electoral participation movement: Focusing on the Citizens' Network for 2016 general election], *Election Studies* 8 (2018): 153–81.
28. Cha, *Sageoneuro boneun siminundongsa*, 147–56.
29. People's Solidarity for Participatory Democracy, *Chamyeoyeondae 20nyeon hwaldong 100seon*, 2014, 245.
30. People's Solidarity for Participatory Democracy, *Chamyeoyeondae 20junyeon hwaldongbogoseo*, 2014, 48, 49.
31. People's Solidarity for Participatory Democracy, *Chamyeoyeondae 20nyeon baljachwi* 2014, chap. 2.
32. People's Solidarity for Participatory Democracy, *Chamyeoyeondae 20junyeon hwaldongbogoseo*, 2014, 7.
33. Participatory Society Studies Center, "Jwadam: Chamyeoyeondae 20nyeon, dojeonkwa seongchal geurigo saeroun mosaek" [PSPD twenty years, challenge, reflection, and new exploration], a recording of the talk on June 10, 2014 (Seoul: PSPD). In fact, this view is shaped by progressive leaders of citizens' organizations and progressive political parties. For example, a writer of the Labor Party House Organ articulated the problem of equating civil society in Korea with citizens' organizations and stressed an urgency to rebuild civil society from the ground up in local communities. See Paeksun Choi, "Jinbojeok siminsahoeneun jonjaehaenneunga?" [Did progressive civil society exist?], *Miraeeseo on pyeonji* [A letter from the future], September 12, 2014: 53–56. The Labor Party House Organ, Seoul.
34. Yeong-seon Pak, "Chamyeoyeondae naebuuisagyeoljeonggujo yeongu" [A study of the internal decision-making structure of the PSPD], *Civil Society and NGO* 12, no. 1 (2014): 35–71.
35. People's Solidarity for Participatory Democracy, *Chamyeoyeondae 20nyeon baljachwi*, 2014, 123, 124.
36. Cha, *Sageoneuro boneun siminundongsa*, 268–72.
37. See Seungsook Moon, "Carving Out Space: Civil Society and the Women's Movement in South Korea," *Journal of Asian Studies* 61, no. 2 (May 2002): 473–500. Along with Japan, South Korea has the lowest level of gender equality among the OECD countries measured in terms of standard indicators, including women's representation in politics and the labor market and in leadership positions.
38. According to the annual General Meeting of the Headquarters, in 2007, the NE branch had 2,815 members, including 2,533 food co-op members, and the GY branch had 2,225 members, including 1,968 food co-op members (21st DFS General Meeting 2008, 23). In 2016, the NE branch had 349 members and the GY branch had 651 members (30th DFS General Meeting 2017, 102).
39. Close reading of the Headquarters' General Meetings minutes indicates that the relationships between headquarters and the branches have been evolving toward more equal and collaborative interactions for the internal democratization of the feminist civic organization. In the past, the headquarters took the initiative and directed major activities, but since the mid-2000s local branches have taken some initiatives for common projects, and there have been growing interactions among

2. PROFILES OF THREE CITIZENS' ORGANIZATIONS

branches and between branches and the headquarters for effective collaborative activism (DFS 2008, 2013, 2017, and 2019). This was confirmed in my interviews with leaders of the headquarters and the two local branches.

40. This information is based on in-depth interviews by the author and surveys of the proceedings of annual meetings of both branches. See GY Branch (2010 through 2020) and NE Branch (2011 through 2019).

41. In 2007, the NE branch had 2,533 "co-op only members" (saenghyeophoewon) and 282 "full members" (jeonghoewon), and the GY branch had 1,968 co-op-only members and 257 full members (DFS 2008, 23).

42. Since the 1990s, South Korean consumers have been exposed to local outbreaks of food contamination and global outbreaks of mad cow disease and avian flu, which threatened public health. By the 2000s, South Koreans had undergone a drastic shift in dietary practices, marked by the rising consumption of meat, refined carbohydrates, and unhealthy fats. This change led to the mounting problems of diet-related metabolic illness and obesity. See Seungsook Moon, "Buddhist Temple Food in South Korea: Interests and Agency in the Reinvention of Tradition in the Age of Globalization," *Korea Journal* 48, no. 4 (Winter 2008): 147–80.

43. Moon, "Buddhist Temple Food in South Korea."

44. Seungsook Moon, "Women's Food Work, Food Citizenship, & Transnational Consumer Capitalism: A Case Study of a Feminist Food Cooperatives in South Korea." *Food, Culture & Society*, 2021, https://doi.org/10.1080/15528014.2021.1892255.

45. In 2009, when it opened four auxiliary centers offering necessary social services, about a half of the GY branch revenue came from membership fees (23.2 percent), donations (17.4 percent), fund-raising events (3.7 percent), and other sources; almost 43 percent of GY branch revenue came from government funding to support its centers (GY Branch 2010, 160). Similarly, in 2010, before it was extensively involved in managing public programs and facilities, roughly 60 percent of NE branch revenue came from membership fees (43.8 percent), donations (14.8 percent), and fund-raising events (2.1 percent), with the remaining revenue coming from government funding (NE Branch 2011, 25).

46. This dynamic resonated with that of service-oriented civil society organizations in other countries. In the era of neoliberal globalization, many organizations have been reduced to outsourced stand-ins for retreating public services. See Akihiro Ogawa, *The Failure of Civil Society: The Third Sector and the State in Contemporary Japan* (Albany: State University of New York Press, 2009); and Nicole P. Marwell, "Privatizing the Welfare State: Nonprofit Community-Based Organizations as Political Actors," *American Sociological Review* 69, no. 2 (2004): 265–91.

47. GY Branch 2018, 211.

48. NE Branch 2017, 192. The percentage of membership fees reduced from 42.5 percent (2014) to 34.5 percent (2015), and then to 29.9 percent (2016); and donations reduced from 24 percent (2014) to 10.4 percent (2015), and then to 8.5 percent (2016).

49. Moon, "Carving Out Space."

50. See Seungsook Moon, "Overcome by Globalization: The Rise of a Women's Policy in South Korea," in *Korea's Globalization*, ed. Samuel S. Kim (Cambridge: Cambridge University Press, 2000), 126–46. It was in this context of institutionalizing women's policy that the first generation of leaders of DFS headquarters joined government committees and the National Assembly. Roughly after 2005, the next generation

2. PROFILES OF THREE CITIZENS' ORGANIZATIONS

leaders of the headquarters came from staff activists or branch leaders. Similar to PSPD, to maintain its political independence, DFS has prohibited its leaders from joining a political party and prohibited its committee members and staff activists from holding a political party position (NE Branch 2014, 37).

51. This ministry has witnessed a rather tumultuous history, changing its name multiple times and becoming subject to a controversy for abolition during the 2022 presidential election. Named the Ministry of Gender Equality in 2001, it was renamed in 2005 the Ministry of Gender Equality and Family, then reverted to the Ministry of Gender Equality, and soon to the Ministry for Health, Welfare and Family (2008–2010). This frequent renaming reflects the contentious nature of gender equality in South Korea, and political parties have tried to take advantage of it. In the era of growing political polarization between progressive and conservative social groups, President Yoon Suk-yeol (2022–2026), as a conservative presidential candidate, made a pledge to abolish the ministry to attract support from the younger generation of men.
52. During Lee Myung-bak's rule, the government doubled its financial support for nonprofit civil society organizations. The total number of organizations applying for government funding decreased from 383 (in 2008) to 357 (in 2011), but the total amount of government funding doubled. In addition, there was a noticeable increase in the number of conservative organizations from sixteen in 2010 to over thirty in 2011, and the amount of funding given to them also grew (GY Branch 2011, 3).
53. However, in the aftermath of the 2008 global financial crisis, even middle-class housewives needed to work to cope with escalating economic insecurity. For a detailed discussion, see chapter 5.
54. The "gender mainstreaming" in government policy and budget was formally institutionalized by enactment of the State Finance Act in 2006. This law established a "gender-sensitive budget system," and in the 2010 fiscal year this budget practice was implemented. See Gwan-yeong O, "Seongpyeongdeung, jisokganeungseong, yeondae gachi yesangamsiundonge bangjeom" [The emphasis on the movement to monitor government budget, gender equality, sustainability, solidarity value], in *Hanguk siminsahoeundong 25nyeonsa* [A 25-year history of Korean civil society movements] (Seoul: Citizens' Movement Information Center, 2014), 85–97.
55. There were coalition movements to expand women's political participation, especially as candidates for government office. In 2006, 321 organizations formed the "Women's Solidarity for the 17th General Election and the Women's Network for Clean Politics" and promoted specific "women citizen candidates" (*yeoseongsiminhubo*) (Yeong-il Jeong, "Chongseonyeondaeeseo pulppuriyeondaekkaji," *NGO Times*, May 15, 2006, 2).
56. This is based on my observation during the first round of fieldwork from September 2004 to May 2005 when the public memory of the movement was still vivid.
57. This is based on my survey of their major publications, including the Regular General Meetings and their house organs.
58. Interview with Su-gyeong, July 15, 2015.
59. See their house organs published in the 2000s, *Living and Sharing* for the GY branch and *Open Village Where We Live Together* for the NE branch.
60. GY Branch 2016, 8–9.
61. Moon, "Women's Food Work, Food Citizenship, & Transnational Consumer Capitalism."
62. NE Branch 2019, 91.

63. GY Branch 2018, 59.
64. Information in this section about FOA is based on my fieldwork in 2009 and 2015.
65. See the chronology of FOA's activities at http://blog.naver.com/foasia2002/.
66. Mikyong Cha, "Damunhwa sahoewa 'sahoetonghap' jedoui heohwangdoen kkum" [Multicultural society and a vainglorious dream of "social integration"]. Personal writing given to the author in 2010.
67. For example, its online homepage (https://foa2002.cafe24.com/wp/) posts financial reports for transparency.
68. See FOA members' blogs collected by the author.

3. NEGOTIATING WITH THE MARKET IN NEOLIBERAL SOUTH KOREA

1. See https://www.segye.com/newsView/20220711513296.
2. George Soros, *The Crisis of Global Capitalism* (New York: Public Affairs, 1998); Michael J. Sandel, *What Money Can't Buy: The Moral Limits of Markets* (New York: Farrar, Straus and Giroux, 2012); Ngaire Woods, *The Globalizers: The IMF, the World Bank, and Their Borrowers* (Ithaca, NY: Cornell University Press, 2006); Richard Peet, *Unholy Trinity: The IMF, World Bank, and WTO* (London: Zed, 2009); and Dave Broad and Wayne Andrew Anthony, eds., *Citizens or Consumers? Social Policy in a Market Society* (Halifax, Canada: Fernwood, 1999).
3. Peter Dauvergne and Genevieve Lebaron, *Protest Inc.: The Corporatization of Activism* (Cambridge, UK: Polity, 2014).
4. Edward T. Walker, *Grassroots for Hire: Public Affairs Consultants in American Democracy* (Cambridge: Cambridge University Press, 2014).
5. Dae-yeop Jo, "Gonggongseongui jaeguseonggwa gieobui simingseong" [The restructuring of the public and business corporations' citizenship], in *21-segi hangugui gieopgwa siminsahoe* [Business corporation and civil society in twenty-first-century Korea] edited by Dae-yeop Jo (Seoul: Gutinpomeisyeon, 2007), 51–52.
6. Sang-gyu Hwang, "Gieobui sahoejeok chaegimgwa siminsahoeui gwaje" [Corporate social responsibility and issues for civil society], in *Hanguksiminsahoeundong 25nyeonsa* [A twenty-five-year history of civil society movements in South Korea] (Seoul: Citizens' Movements Information Center, 2014), 99.
7. Although business corporations' donations increased in their absolute amount, their ratio to the total pool of donations remained stagnant. According to a giving index among business corporations measured by Yuhan Kimberly (2004), a rare and exemplary business donor in South Korea, corporate respondents replied that they did not donate money to new public interest foundations because of financial insecurity (68 percent) and distrust of such foundations (47.4 percent) due to news reports about their abuse of public funds (Yeong-il Jeong, "Gibumunhwa hyeonjuso '70:30'" [A current address of donation culture '70 to 30'], *NGO Times* June 24, 2006, 8). Fifteen years later, in 2019 a majority of total donations to charity in South Korea came from individuals (64 percent) rather than from business corporations (36 percent). See National Tax Statistics for 2020 in IUPUI, "Global Philanthropy Indices: South Korea, Country Overview," https://globalindices.iupui.edu/additional-research/digital-for-good/south-korea.html (accessed August 18, 2023).

3. NEGOTIATING WITH THE MARKET IN NEOLIBERAL SOUTH KOREA

8. Yeong-il Jeong, "Siminundong jiwon sahoejeok habui sigeup" [Social consensus on supporting citizens' movements is urgent], *NGO Times*, April 17, 2006, 9.
9. Interview with Yeong-seo, July 2015.
10. Other major examples of public interest foundations include the Human Rights Foundation (1999), the Beautiful Foundation (2000), and the Environmental Foundation (2002). In the mid-2000s, business contributions accounted for roughly 70 percent of their total revenues, and individual contributions accounted for the remaining 30 percent (Yeong-il Jeong, "Gibumunhwa hyeonjuso '70:30,'" *NGO Times*, June 24, 2006, 8). It is noteworthy that employment turnover among full-time activists in these foundations was high due to low pay, overwork, and conflict over their identity as an activist or a partner to a business firm (Jae-hwan Yi and Yeong-il Jeong, "Gongikjaedan gibusiljeok 'deuljjuknaljjuk'" [Donation records among the public-interest foundations are uneven], *NGO Times*, June 24, 2006, 8).
11. Gyeong-hui Kim, "Yeoseongundonggwa gieobui pateuneosip: hangukyeoseongjaedanui sarye" [The partnership between women's movements and business corporations: a case study of the Korea Women's Foundation], in *21-segi hangugui gieopgwa siminsahoe*, 2007, 136.
12. FOA 2019 Gyeolsanbogo [2019 Accounting report]. Goyang, Gyeonggi Province: FOA.
13. Interview of Mr. Kang by author, September 17, 2009 (emphasis added).
14. FOA 2019 Gyeolsanbogo.
15. A long-time activist who personally experienced the transformation of citizens' organizations and social movements since the 1990s shared this recollection:

> From the beginning, like a dictatorial regime in the past, Lee Myong-bak administration was hostile toward people and organizations that voiced different views. . . . There were business corporations which funded and collaborated with citizens' organizations because they were sympathetic to the organizations. Such corporations began to discontinue their support immediately or conveyed their plans to do so. This change did not affect citizens' organizations like the PSPD, which did not receive any financial support from the government and business corporations but it hit hard smaller citizens' organizations focusing on local residents, welfare services, and environmental issues. See Seung-chang Ha, *Naui siminundong iyagi* [My citizens' movement story] (Seoul: Humanist, 2015), 141.

16. Chang-won Yun, "Sahoe gongdongchewa sangsaenggwangye, geurigo saengmyeongnanum" [Social community, symbiotic relations, and sharing of life], in *Korean Civil Society Yearbook* (Seoul: Citizens Movement Information Center, 2017), 347–358, at 353. Rather than working with employees of big business corporations, PSPD has used an intern program for college students who are interested in citizens' movements and organizations. Students can receive academic credit or be provided with a career option, or both (interview with Hyeon-min, July 2015). To give a broader context of this practice, between 2008 and 2015, PSPD used to run a cheongnyeoninteon (Youth Intern) program funded by the Ministry of Labor under the internship support system. The Ministry paid monthly 300,000 to 400,000 Korean won (roughly USD 300 to 400) per intern for their work during the training. In the aftermath of the 2008 Global Financial Crisis, the paid program became very popular and

competitive. Initially fewer than ten interns were hired each year but the number grew to thirty interns by 2012. The acceptance rate became over 1 to 5. Yet the ministry discontinued the intern support system and PSPD turned the paid internship into an unpaid "youth training" program (See PSPD, Chamyeoyeondae 20nyeon hwaldong 100seon, 2014, 533.

17. Sang-hyeon Yi, "Jeongbu, 'jungnipjeok gigu' tonghae mingandanche jiwon neulyeoya" [The government must increase its support for NGOs through a "neutral instrument"], *NGO Times*, July 20, 1998, 19.

18. Hye-jeong Gang, "Ulmyo gyeojameokki 'suiksaeop,' jalhamyon doum" ["Revenue-raising events" are like eating mustard while crying but they can be helpful if done well], *NGO Times*, September 7, 1998, 8, 9.

19. Responding to these negative consequences for what it means to be a human and the sustainability of our collective existence, activists and scholars have explored how and where the capitalist economy can generate impetus and space for resistance. See Roopali Mukherjee and Sarah Banet-Weiser, eds., *Commodity Activism: Cultural Resistance in Neoliberal Times* (New York: New York University Press, 2012); Naomi Klein, *No Logo: Taking Aim at the Brand Bullies* (New York: Picador, 1999); Peter Miller and Nikolas Rose, "Mobilizing the Consumer: Assembling the Subject of Consumption," *Theory, Culture & Society* 14, no. 1 (1997): 1–36. The transnational production, circulation, and consumption of food has turned this universal human necessity into a focal area for exploration. Some scholars analyzed consumer movements for ethical consumption, promoting "fair trade" and "sustainable consumption." See Michael Goodman, "Reading Fair Trade: Political Ecological Imaginary and the Moral Economy of Fair Trade Foods," *Political Geography* 23, no. 7 (2004): 891–915. Others linked food consumption to citizenship and use the term "citizen-consumer." See Cecilia Ricci, Nicola Marinelli, and Lorenzo Puliti, "The Consumer as Citizen: The Role of Ethics for a Sustainable Consumption," *Agriculture and Agricultural Science Procedia* 8 (2016): 395–401; Gill Seyfang, "Ecological Citizenship and Sustainable Consumption: Examining Local Organic Food Networks," *Journal of Rural Studies* 22, no. 4 (2006): 383–95; Cristóbal Gómez-Benito and Carmen Lozano, "Constructing Food Citizenship: Theoretical Premises and Social Practices," *Italian Sociological Review* 4, no. 2 (2014): 135–56; and Stewart Lockie, "Responsibility and Agency Within Alternative Food Networks: Assembling the 'Citizen Consumer,'" *Agriculture and Human Values* 26, no. 3 (2009): 193–201. This notion of citizen consumers and their practices blurs the boundary between the market and civil society. Scholars also explored how consumers became producers through reversing their deskilling and passivity and embracing the concept of "prosumers." See Alvin Toffler, *The Third Wave* (New York: William Morrow, 1980). These hybrid concepts highlight the broader social and political significance of economic activities and urge us to reflect on the destructive consequences of globalized consumption that have threatened the very existence of humanity and the environment.

20. In 1998, the Asia Civil Society Studies Center conducted a survey of twenty-two major citizens' organizations to identify their financial situations. The top three sources of financing included membership fees and donations (41.2 percent), government aid (14.8 percent), and revenue from fund-raising events (12.8 percent). Sang-hyeon Yi, "Jeongbu, 'jungnipjeok gigu' tonghae mingandanche jiwon neulyeoya," *NGO Times*, July 20, 1998, 19.

3. NEGOTIATING WITH THE MARKET IN NEOLIBERAL SOUTH KOREA

21. In 1996, South Korea joined the Organization of Economic Cooperation and Development (OECD). This change of the national status as a developed country led to significant reductions in financial aid from foreign foundations and generated more pressure for financial independence (Byeong-gi Kim, "1cheonyeogae siminundongdanche hyeomnyeok jeonmunhwa hanchang" [Some one-thousand citizens' movement organizations actively pursue the professionalization of their cooperation *NGO Times*, June 1, 1998, 20). The 1997 Asian financial crisis (IMF crisis in South Korea) also aggravated the problem.
22. Dauvergne and Lebaron, *Protest Inc.*, chap. 5.
23. Interview of Gwan-su by the author, October 14, 2009.
24. Chris A. Gregory, *Gifts and Commodities*, 2nd ed. (1982; repr. Chicago: Hau, 2015); Marilyn Strathern, *The Gender of the Gift: Problems with Women and Problems with Society in Melanesia* (Berkeley: University of California Press, 1988); Afke Komter, *Social Solidarity and the Gift* (Cambridge: Cambridge University Press, 2015); and Alice P. Julier, *Eating Together: Food, Friendship, and Inequality* (Champaign: University of Illinois Press, 2013).
25. Karl Polanyi, *The Great Transformation: The Political and Economic Origins of Our Time* (1944; repr. Boston: Beacon, 2001).
26. Miller and Rose, "Mobilizing the Consumer."
27. Komter, *Social Solidarity and the Gift*.
28. Indiana University Lily Family School of Philanthropy and Center on Philanthropy, the Beautiful Foundation, "Digital for Good: A Global Study on Emerging Ways of Giving: South Korea," 20–21 (Indianapolis: IUPUI, 2022).
29. This section relies on my article: Seungsook Moon, "Women's Food Work, Food Citizenship, & Transnational Consumer Capitalism: A Case Study of a Feminist Food Cooperative in South Korea, *Food, Culture & Society* (2021), https://doi.org/10.1080/15528014.2021.1892255.
30. DFS, *Women Going Together*, March/April 2004, 26–27, 46.
31. DFS, *Women Going Together*, May/June 2005, 46.
32. When the public learned of the use of genetically modified soybeans in the production of cooking oil in the early 2000s, the consumption of soybean oil decreased, but usage increased again during the 2008 global financial crisis due to its lower price. In 2014, South Korea imported 1.2 million tons of soybeans, and 80 percent of them were GM soybeans. Korea's soybean self-sufficiency was around 7 percent, and it has relied on massive imports from the United States, Canada, Brazil, and Argentina. As the number one GM crop, 85 percent of soybeans cultivated in the world are genetically modified. See Eung-seo Pak, "Maeil yujeonjabyeonhyeong kong meongneun hangugin" [Koreans who eat GM soybeans everyday], *Science Times*, February 4, 2016.
33. DFS, *Women Going Together*, November/December 2004, 49.
34. DFS, *Women Going Together*, March/April 2005, 8.
35. DFS, *Women Going Together*, September/October 2004, 8.
36. Yang-hui Kim, "Minwuhoe's Life Coop as the Movement for Women Themselves," in *Happy Energy for Twenty Years, Hopeful Synergy for the Future*, Proceedings of the 20th Anniversary Policy Symposium (Seoul: Minwuhoe, Minwu Coop, 2009), 14.
37. Mi-hyeok Kwon, "The Significance of and Issues for Women's Minwuhoe," in *Happy Energy for Twenty Years, Hopeful Synergy for the Future*, Proceedings of the 20th Anniversary Policy Symposium (Seoul: Minwuhoe, Minwu Coop, 2009), 25.

3. NEGOTIATING WITH THE MARKET IN NEOLIBERAL SOUTH KOREA

38. The practice of fair trade began in 2003, when Beautiful Store (*Areumdaungage*), a "social enterprise" established in 2002, imported handicrafts products from other Asian countries. See Hyeong-mi Kim, "Sahoejeokgyeongje 'saengtaegye' mandeulda," [The ecosystem for social economy was made], in *A 25 Year History of Korean Civil Society Movements*, 354.
39. DFS, *Women Going Together*, May/June 2009, 41.
40. DFS, *Women Going Together*, July/August 2011, 42–43.
41. DFS, *Women Going Together*, May/June 2012, 42; Kim, "Sahoejeokgyeongje 'saengtaegye' mandeulda," 354.
42. The term *prefigurative politics* was used by scholars of the 1960s social movements in the United States to refer to activists imagining alternative society or social relations in advance with an aspiration to realize them. See Guilherme Fians, "Prefigurative Politics," in *The Cambridge Encyclopedia of Anthropology* (2022), http://doi.org/10.29164/22prefigpolitics.
43. Interview of In-a by the author, July 2015; emphasis added.
44. Interview of Hye-jeong by the author, September 27, 2009; emphasis added.
45. Interview of Hong-seok by the author, July 2015.
46. Many NGOs are registered with the government as organizations that provide citizens with opportunities for volunteer services. PSPD and FOA have dealt with temporary volunteers who are not dues-paying members but are working for their programs. The role of volunteers has been critical to FOA as a small, resource-scarce organization.
47. PSPD is a larger organization and shows a more noticeable change over time in terms of membership payment. Before its membership grew rapidly in the early 2000s, individuals could become members without pledging the amount of their membership fees. This old system was replaced with a system that requires members to pledge and pay at the time of joining the organization (author's interview with Gwang-bok, October 14, 2009).
48. In 2010, PSPD established its middle-term objectives and direction regarding membership expansion to stabilize its financial base and thereby its sustainability (PSPD, Je17cha jeonggichonghoe [The 17th regular general meeting]. Seoul: PSPD, 2011, 135). During the 2010s, it tried to reach this goal by increasing new members and reducing the number of bracketed members and withdrawers (PSPD, Je19cha jeonggichonghoe [The 19th regular general meeting]. Seoul: PSPD, 2013, 79, 80; Je25cha jeonggichonghoe [The 25th regular general meeting], 2019, 39).
49. Proceedings of Regular General Meeting, which was annually published by each branch during the 2010s, show a recurring gap between a plan to effectively manage members and membership fees and actual practice. For example, GY Branch, Je20cha jeonggichonghoe [The 20th Regular General Meeting], 2020, 47–49; NE Branch, Je20cha jeonggichonghoe [The 20th Regular General Meeting], 2019, 91–92.
50. NE Branch, "Je20cha jeonggichonghoe," 275 (Seoul: NE Branch, 2020).
51. Interview of Ui-pyo by the author, July 2015; emphasis added.
52. Interview of Song-hui by the author, July 15, 2015; emphasis added.
53. Interview of Yeong-nim by the author, July 23, 2015.
54. Georg Simmel theorized about the effects of the money-based economy on the individual, associations of individuals, and culture and suggested that society produces associations or organizations that allow for fleeting or low-intensity involvement.

3. NEGOTIATING WITH THE MARKET IN NEOLIBERAL SOUTH KOREA

He argues that the possession of money, in particular, and the money-based economy, in general, are profoundly individualizing urbanites by unmooring their basic ascriptive ties to local communities, kinship, and finally family. That is, without enduring ties to these human groupings, basic and additional human needs can be satisfied by commodity consumption. See Georg Simmel, *Philosophy of Money*, trans. Tom Bottomore and David Frisby from a first draft by Kaethe Mengelberg (1900; repr. London: Routledge, 2011). See also Karl Marx, "The Meanings of Human Requirements" and "The Power of Money in Bourgeois Society," in *Marx-Engels Reader*, 2nd ed., ed. Robert Tucker (New York: Norton, 1978), 93–101 and 101–5.

55. Interview of Mi-gyeong by the author, July 2015; emphasis added.
56. Interview of Jun-hui, a single thirty-five-year-old high school teacher, by the author, October 4, 2009; emphasis added.
57. Simmel, *Philosophy of Money*, 371–75.
58. Interview of Yeong-sik by the author, July 2015.
59. Min-ho Kim, "Simindanche judo pyeongsaenggyoyuk hwaldong beopjehwaui uimi" [Legislation of the life-long education center established by civil society organizations], *Journal of Lifelong Education* 6, no. 1 (2000): 263–88, at 264.
60. "Kakao Talk" is a mobile messaging application for smartphones and personal computers in South Korea. Created by Kakao Corporation in 2010, it has become widely popular among Koreans not only domestically but also transnationally. It is estimated that 93 percent of smartphone owners in South Korea use the application. See https://en.wikipedia.org/wiki/KakaoTalk (accessed August 9, 2021).
61. Proceedings of PSPD's regular general meeting, published annually during the 2010s, show its enduring and keen interest in professionalizing its publicity work for effective dissemination of its activities and accomplishments; it was eager to translate such publicity to the expansion of membership base, which would strengthen its financial independence and moral authority. In this context, PSPD has used a language of "chamyeoyeondae beuraendeu" [PSPD brand]. See PSPD, Je23cha jeonggichonghoe [The 23rd regular general meeting]. Seoul: PSPD, 2017, 84.
62. PSPD, Je21cha jeonggichonghoe [The 21st regular general meeting]. Seoul: PSPD, 56–57, 61. In order to diversify its publicity tools it began to pay serious attention to social media and "web marketing." Additionally, it is noteworthy that one of the college students I interviewed naturally used the term "brand" in the following way despite her growing critical consciousness of the excessive commercialism on her own college campus. In replying to my question about the perception of PSPD among her peers, she said "the brand image of the PSPD conveys professionalism and a sort of masculine, even though I saw more women than men during my internship program and visits." (Hye-eun, woman in early twenties, interviewed by the author, July 2015).
63. Interview of Gi-yeong by the author, October 14, 2009.
64. Gordon D. Cumming, "French NGOs in the Global Era: Professionalization 'Without Borders'?" *Voluntas* 19 (2008): 372–94; and Samy Cohen, "A Model of Its Own? State-NGO Relations in France" (Washington, DC: Brookings Institution, 2004), 1–5.
65. Proceedings of regular general meetings annually published by each branch during the 2010s show recurring reflection on the persistent problem. For example, GY Branch, Je20cha jeonggichonghoe [The 20th regular general meeting], (Goyang,

3. NEGOTIATING WITH THE MARKET IN NEOLIBERAL SOUTH KOREA

Gyeonggi Province: GY branch, 2020,) 35, 47, 48; NE Branch, Je20cha jeonggichonghoe [The 20th regular general meeting] (Seoul: NE Branch, 2019), 22, 55, 65.
66. Based on interviews with Mr. Kang, September 17, 2009, and Hong-sok, July 2015.
67. Beef imported from the United States began to be a problem in South Korea initially in 2003, when a cow infected with Bovine Spongiform Encephalopathy (BSE) was discovered in Washington State. In response, the South Korean government vacillated between prohibition and permission for beef to be imported from the United States. It was reported in 2007 that Hallmark/Westland Meat Packing Company used electric shocks to process sick cows into its slaughtering system. However, instead of inspecting this practice and verifying whether sick cows were infected with BSE, the U.S. Department of Agriculture drastically cut back on the number of cows inspected for BSE. Similarly, the South Korean government permitted U.S. beef imports without proper regulation under the South Korea-U.S. Free Trade Agreement, which was being negotiated. The MBC television network broadcast a documentary about BSE and its impacts on human beings in its popular show, "PD Pocket Notebook" (PD sucheop), and publicized the problem. See Ha, *Naui siminundong iyagi*, 147, 148; and Wikipedia, "Bovine spongiform encephalopathy," https://en.wikipedia.org/wiki/Bovine_spongiform_encephalopathy#North_America (accessed August 26, 2021). These unfolding events generated public outrage against beef imported from the United States, leading to the massive candlelight protests.
68. YouTube archive, "Candle light protest the first day" shows a mass gathering of citizens of all ages and various walks of life, freely chanting together in the Blue Stream Plaza, displaying pickets that they made to express their personal views, speaking up in front of the gathering, and applauding to show their shared concern for food safety and to demand action from the government and political leaders. The whole gathering conveyed a utopian moment of solidarity energized by a Durkheimian collective effervescence. See https://www.youtube.com/watch?v=Olh45qYO_oo (accessed August 26, 2021).
69. There are classic studies of consumer capitalism and culture that generated and promoted pleasure and entertainment from various political perspectives. From a leftist angle, see Herbert Marcuse, *One-Dimensional Man: Studies in the Ideology of Advanced Industrial Society* (Boston: Beacon, 1964); Neil Postman, *Amusing Ourselves to Death: Public Discourse in the Age of Show Business* (New York: Penguin, 1986); Mike Featherstone, *Consumer Culture and Postmodernism* (Thousand Oaks, CA: Sage, 1991); and Fredrick Jameson, *Postmodernism, or the Cultural Logic of Late Capitalism* (Durham: Duke University Press, 1991). From a conservative angle, see Daniel Bell, *The Cultural Contradictions of Capitalism* (New York: Basic Books, 1976).
70. Zygmunt Bauman, *Liquid Modernity* (Cambridge, UK: Polity, 2000); and Anthony Giddens, *Modernity and Self-Identity: Self and Society in the Late Modern Age* (Stanford, CA: Stanford University Press, 1991).
71. Simmel, *The Philosophy of Money*, chap. 4.
72. Erika Rappaport, *Shopping for Pleasure: Women in the Making of London's West End* (Princeton, NJ: Princeton University Press, 2000); Angela McRobbie, "Young Women and Consumer Culture, *Cultural Studies* 22, no. 5(2008): 531–550; Nancy L. Deutch and Eleni Theodorou, "Aspiring, Consuming, Becoming: Youth Identity in a Culture of Consumption, *Youth & Society* 42:2(2010): 229–254; Judith Mackrell, *Flappers: Six Women of a Dangerous Generation* (New York: Sarah Crichton, 2014).

73. Bryan Turner, "Post-Secular Society: Consumerism and the Democratization of Religion," in *The Post-Secular in Question: Religion in Contemporary Society*, ed. Philip Gorski, David Kyuman Kim, John Torpey, and Jonathan VanAntwerpen (New York: New York University Press, 2012), 135–58, at 143.
74. Turner, "Post-Secular Society," 153.
75. Interview of Gi-yeong by the author, October 14, 2009; emphasis added.
76. Interview of Yeong-sik by the author, July 2015; emphasis added.
77. For example, see PSPD, Je 25cha jeonggichonghoe, 2019, 178, 536.
78. NE Branch, "2014 jeonggichonghoe" [2014 regular general meeting] (Seoul: NE Branch, 2014, 116).
79. For example, what a majority of people like can be determined by the status quo. Hence listening to people is necessary and a sensible beginning, but going along with a majority preference can be problematic without critical reflection and assessment in light of deeper moral values and ethical judgments.
80. Yeong-il Jeong, "Meolgiman han jaechungjeon siminundongga sidae" [Remote possibility of recharging citizen activists in the era of citizens' movement], *NGO Times* June 17, 2006, 10.
81. Yeong-il Jeong, "Siminundong jaesaengsan 'wigigam' paengbae" [Amplification of "a sense of crisis" in the reproduction of citizens' movement], *NGO Times* February 6, 2006, 1.
82. Yeong-il Jeong, "Meolgiman han jaechungjeon siminundongga sidae," *NGO Times* June 17, 2006, 10. PSPD also noticed this change in connection to the relative mainstreaming of civic activism in South Korean society. In the early 2010s, high-school social studies textbooks introduced "siminhwaldongga" (citizen activists) as an occupation and career option. See PSPD, *Chamyeoyeondae 20nyeon hwaldong 100seon* [100 selected activities from the history of PSPD for twenty years], vol. 1 (Seoul: PSPD, 2014), 542.
83. Jae-hwan Yi, "Siminundonggaroseoui sam 'tagworan seontaek" [Living as citizen activists "excellent choice"], *NGO Times* April 24, 2006, 3. Hiring of new full-time staff used to be done through a personal network, but as college student political activism declined on campus in the 1990s, especially after the 1997–98 IMF crisis, staff have been hired through open recruitment (Yeong-il Jeong, "Meolgiman han jaechungjeon siminundongga sidae," *NGO Times*, June 17, 2006, 10).
84. This situation is comparable to the troubled reproduction of religious priests in many societies as the market has become dominant in our private and collective lives.
85. PSPD increased salary of its staff activists and improved their working conditions between 2011 and 2012 after a five-year freeze (PSPD, Je17cha jeonggichonghoe [The 17th regular general meeting], 2011, 103, and PSPD, Je18cha jeonggichonghoe (The 18th regular general meeting), 2012, 25).
86. This overview is based on my in-depth interviews with several staff activists over a decade.
87. Interview of Gwan-su by the author, October 14, 2009; emphasis added.
88. Interview of Mi-gyeong by the author, July 2015; emphasis added.
89. Yeong-il Jeong, "Meolgiman han jaechungjeon siminundongga sidae," *NGO Times*, June 17, 2006, 10.
90. Interview of Yeong-so by the author, July 2015.

91. Various policy projects have been funded by the Women's Foundation, the Seoul Metropolitan government, and the "Gender Equality Fund" from the local ward.
92. NE Branch, Je2ocha jeonggichonghoe, 2019, 91.
93. Interview of Won-jin by the author, July 27, 2015; emphasis added.

4. NEOLIBERAL GOVERNANCE I: COLLABORATIVE LAW AND POLICYMAKING AND UNDERMINING GRASSROOTS PARTICIPATION

1. Hyeong-yong Yi, "Gukka, geobeoneonseuro dijainhada" [The state, designed by governance], in *Hanguksiminsahoeundong 25nyeonsa, 1989–2014* [A twenty-five-year history of Korean civil society movements, 1989–2014], ed. Citizens' Movements Information Center (Seoul: Citizens' Movements Information Center, 2014), 383.
2. Wendy Brown, *Undoing the Demos: Neoliberalism's Stealth Revolution* (Brooklyn, NY: Zone, 2015), 123.
3. Prior to the neoliberal globalization, South Korea was a relatively egalitarian society. Despite rapid economic growth from the late 1960s to the 1980s, South Korea remained relatively egalitarian under tight and extensive control of the developmental state. See Hagen Koo, "Rising Inequality and Shifting Class Boundaries in South Korea in the Neo-Liberal Era," *Journal of Contemporary Asia* 51, no. 1 (2021): 1–19, http://doi.org/10.1080/00472336.2019.1663242. Although the authoritarian state severely suppressed labor and fostered the economic conglomerates as the engines of industrialization at the expense of small and medium businesses, economic expansion for three decades created ample employment opportunities and rising income. In addition, the explosion of labor movements in the late 1980s (connected to the broader democratization movement) enabled workers to achieve significant improvement in their real income and working conditions.

    Ironically, the social condition of relative equality began to change during the 1990s, the decade of democratization, which was accompanied by neoliberal globalization. Even before the 1997 Asian financial crisis, inequality in South Korea began to grow as a confluence of the following structural changes. Deindustrialization shifted the central mechanism of generating wealth from labor-intensive manufacturing to knowledge and capital-intensive industries. This change was facilitated by the accelerated movement of capital through deregulation in the name of liberalization, efficiency, and global competitiveness. As a result, millions of employed people became vulnerable to sudden layoffs and early retirements. Instead of full-time and long-term employment, they were forced to accept temporary and part-time employment. This economic transformation affected even the privileged workforce of middle-class men who enjoyed lifetime employment as family providers. See Bong-jin Jo and Seong-tae Hong, eds., *Hoesagamyeon jungneunda: gyeongjejuui damnonui bipaneul wihan pildsteodi* [If you join a company, you're dead: a field study to criticize economistic discourse] (Seoul: Hyeonsilmunhwayeongu, 1995). Furthermore, the Korean state regressively reduced tax rates for the rich from 70 percent (in the 1970s) to 50 percent (in the 1990s) and further to 35 percent (in the 2000s). See Hong-sik Yoon, *Hanguk bokjigukkaui giwongwa gwejeok 3: Sinjayujuuiwa bokjigukka,1980-nyeonbuteo 2016-nyeong*gaji [The origin and trajectory of the South Korean welfare state. Vol 3.

Neoliberalism and the welfare state—from 1980s to 2016] (Seoul: Sahoepyeongnon Academy, 2019).

Since the two major economic crises, economic polarization in South Korea has been accelerated between the top 10 to 20 percent and the remaining 90 to 80 percent of the population. The superrich or plutocrats at the top 0.1 percent gained tremendously; this social group is composed of large established capitalists (*chaebols*) who own and control major industries and a newly emerging group of CEOs in high technology industries. Below them is the upper-middle class, composed of the top 10 to 20 percent of the population. They are professionals and managers in the expanding medical and financial sectors. There is also internal differentiation in the working class between the "labor aristocracy" consisting of regular blue-collar workers employed by chaebol companies who are well-paid and unionized and the rest of the manual workers. The gap between leading chaebol corporations and the rest is particularly pronounced in larger corporations with more than 300 employees. This is because since the 1990s many smaller companies became subcontractors of the larger firms and subsequently were subjected to unfair and exploitative business relationships with them (see Koo, "Rising Inequality").

Economic insecurity and precarious life experienced by a majority of South Koreans is poignantly reflected in various measurements. Household debt (measured by its share of GDP) in South Korea is higher than it is in the United States, the United Kingdom, and Japan. Buying a house in Seoul has become far more difficult than doing so in other capital cities or major metropolitan cities in industrialized countries. South Korea shows the highest poverty rate among the old (over sixty-six years old) in the OECD countries, which stands at 45.7 percent in 2015. (PSPD, "Jeokjeong nohu sodeuk bojangeul wihae gungminyeongeumi naagaya hal banghyang" [A direction of the national pension to secure an adequate income for the elderly] (December 31, 2018), PSPD website, "Balganjaryo" [Resources issued], https://www.peoplepower21.org/welfare/1604459?cat=931&paged=0.]

"Irregular employment" [bijeonggyujik] among wage workers [imgeumnodongja] has increased over time. According to official statistics, the rate grew from 32.6 percent in 2003 to 38.4 percent in 2021. The OECD average for the rate of irregular employment in 2021 was 11.8 percent but it was 28.3 percent in South Korea. Furthermore, the rate of irregular workers among women was twice as high as that among men. Wages for irregular employment has also decreased in relation to that of regular employment, from 65.2 percent in 2004 to 53 percent in 2021 (Yeong-rim Pak, "Choeageuro ganeun goyonggwa nodong" [Employment and labor racing to the bottom], *Kyunghyang Newspaper*, May 4, 2023, https://m.khan.co.kr/opinion/column/article/202305042241005#c2b).

4. Palma Carvajal and Juan Francisco, *Advocacy NGOs and the Neoliberal Pacification of the Demands of the Street* (London: Palgrave Macmillan, 2021); Feyzi Ismail and Sangeeta Kamat, "NGOs, Social Movements and the Neoliberal State: Incorporation, Reinvention, Critique," *Critical Sociology* 44 (July 2018): 569–77; Bram Verschuere and Joris De Corte, "Nonprofit Advocacy Under a Third-Party Government Regime: Cooperation or Conflict?," *Voluntas: International Journal of Voluntary and Nonprofit Organizations* 26 (2015): 222–41; Peter Dauvergne and Genevieve Lebaron, *Protest Inc.: The Corporatization of Activism* (Cambridge: Polity, 2014); and Edward

4. NEOLIBERAL GOVERNANCE I

T. Walker, *Grassroots for Hire: Public Affairs Consultants in American Democracy* (Cambridge: Cambridge University Press, 2014).
5. Carvajal and Francisco, *Advocacy NGOs*, 6.
6. PSPD, *Chamyeoyeondae 20nyeon hwaldong 100seon* [100 Selected activities from the twenty-year history of PSPD], Seoul: PSPD, 2014; PSPD, *Sesangeul bakkun 15 kiwodeu: 1994–2009 Chamyeoyeondae 15junyeon* [15 Keywords that changed the world: 1994–2009 PSPD's 15th anniversary] 2009, 74–87; PSPD, Chamyeoyeondae 10nyeonui girok, 1994–2004: sesangeul bakkuneun siminui him [PSPD's record of the ten years, 1994–2004], 2004, chap. 2.
7. PSPD, *Sesangeul bakkun 15 kiwodeu*, 2009, 74–75.
8. This new law replaced the Living Protection Law, which was implemented in 1961. The old law approached poverty as an individual trouble, whereas the new one approached poverty as a social issue by clearly designating the state's responsibility for lower-income strata regardless of their capacity for work (PSPD, *Chamyeoyeondae 20nyeon hwaldong 100seon*, 2014, 324–25). PSPD tried to reform the national pension system for the retired by making the management of the pension fund democratic and transparent. This activism is important given that the poverty rate among the elderly in South Korea has been the highest among OECD member countries. However, under the conservative government in the 2010s, the national pension system was altered to reduce the payment from 60 percent of a retiree's income to 40 percent (PSPD, *Chamyeoyeondae 20nyeon hwaldong 100seon*, 2014, 317–19).
9. PSPD, *Chamyeoyeondae 20nyeon hwaldong 100seon*, 2014, 335–36; Byeong-jik Cha, *Sageoneuro boneun siminundongsa: Hyeondaesaui muljulgireul bakkun hanguksiminundong 20 jangmyeon* [A history of citizens' movements seen through events: twenty scenes from citizens' movements that changed major streams of contemporary history in South Korea] (Seoul: Changjakgwabipyeong, 2014), 62–72.
10. National Assembly Discussion Meeting on the Basic Living Protection Law, 11-17-2020, posted in PSPD-issued resources on its website. See https://www.peoplepower21.org/?cat=931&p=1743733&paged=21.
11. Yeon-myeong Kim, "10jang Chamyeoyeondae 'sahoebokjiwiwonhoe' 10nyeonui seonggwawa seongchal" [Ch.10 PSPD's "social welfare committee" a decade of achievement and reflection], in *Chamyeowa yeondaero yeon minjujuuiui sae jipyeong* [A new horizon of democracy opened by participation and solidarity] (Seoul: Areuche, 2004), 226, 228, 229, 232.
12. Hye-jin Mun, "Choejeosaenggyebojangeun naraui uimuda: gungmingichosaenghwalbojangbeop jejeongundong" [Mimimum living protection is the state's responsibility: a movement to legislate the National Basic Living Protection Law], in *Ijagochina bopsida: Chamyeoyeondae gwollyeokgamsiundong 10nyeon* [Let's see if they play by collusion: PSPD's movement to monitor the power for ten years], Byeong-jik Cha, et al. (Seoul: Sigeumchi, 2004), 64–66.
13. PSPD, *Chamyeoyeondae 20nyeon hwaldong 100seon*, 2014, 335–36.
14. Cha, *Sageoneuro boneun siminundongsa*, 62–72.
15. Yoon, *Hanguk bokjigukkaui giwongwa gwejeok 3*, 245.
16. Yoon, *Hanguk bokjigukkaui giwongwa gwejeok 3*, 277.
17. Yoon, *Hanguk bokjigukkaui giwongwa gwejeok 3*, 388.

4. NEOLIBERAL GOVERNANCE I

18. See Sang-jo Kim, "Chamyeoyeondaeui gyeongjeminjuhwaundong" [PSPD's movement to democratize the economy], in *Chamyeowa yeondaero yeon minjujuuiui sae jipyeong* [New horizon of democracy opened by participation and solidarity], ed. Seong-tae Hong (Seoul: Areuche, 2004), 218–20. He argues that small shareholders are highly unlikely to organize themselves into a group to protect their own economic interests because it is easier for them to sell their small shares and exit than to organize themselves and voice their collective interests. More plausible actors for potential activism would be larger institutions that invested in a specific business or, albeit far less likely, organized labor in the form of a labor union that is enmeshed in a specific business.
19. PSPD, *Chamyeoyeondae 20nyeon hwaldong 100seon*, 2014, 211. This response profoundly altered the state's relationship with the economic conglomerates; previously the developmental state had fostered them by granting special favors and privileges at the expense of all other economic and social groups, but now the established big business coalition sought deregulation to maximize their profits at the expense of all other social groups and even that of the state. In addition, shifting the financial loss to the general citizenry was essentially the same mechanism as the U.S. government's bailout of Wall Street with taxpayers' money in the aftermath of the 2008 global financial crisis. The examples of South Korea and the United States, along with a multitude of other countries in the world, revealed that the neoliberal capitalist economy as an economic system siphoned wealth from many ordinary people and redirected that wealth to the few at the very top. See David Harvey, *A Brief History of Neoliberalism* (Oxford: Oxford University Press, 2005).
20. PSPD, *Chamyeoyeondae 20nyeon hwaldong 100seon*, 2014, section IV.
21. Ha-seong Jang, "Gyeraneuro bawireul kkaeda: jaebeolgaehyeok soaekjujuundong" (We break a rock with eggs: small shareholders movement to reform the economic conglomerates), in *Jjagochina bopsida: Chamyeoyeondae gwollyeokgamsiundong 10nyeon*, 44, 48, 49.
22. Kim, "Chamyeoyeondaeui gyeongjeminjuhwundong" 208, 209.
23. Won-seok Pak, "Gyeolko jakji anatdeon 'jageungwollichatgi'" [Finding small rights that was never small), in *Jjagochina bopsida: Chamyeoyeondae gwollyeokgamsiundong 10nyeon*, 187.
24. PSPD "Isyu ripoteu: 1000jowon sosanggongin buchae, munjejeomgwa gaeseonbanghyang" [Issue report: the problem of 1000jowon debts of small business owners and how to improve it] (7-22-2022), PSPD website "Balganjaryo" [materials issued], https://www.peoplepower21.org/?cat=931&p=1898548&paged=8
25. PSPD, *Chamyeoyeondae 20nyeon hwaldong 100seon*, 2014, 248–52.
26. PSPD, *Chamyeoyeondae 20nyeon hwaldong 100seon*, 2014, 289.
27. South Korea has shown a high rate of self-employment among the OECD countries and in the world. In 2014, 27 percent of the Korean labor force was self-employed, and a majority (74 percent) of them were independent contractors without any additional paid employees. The self-employed were heavily concentrated in retail and restaurant businesses. Although self-employment used to be a source of reliable income and upward mobility through hard work, it has become highly insecure employment and comparable to irregular employment. In 2018, the rate of self-employment decreased to 25.1 percent but was still far above the OECD average of 15.3 percent. See Ji-won Yoon and Mira Choi, "Korea's Self-Employment Rate at

4. NEOLIBERAL GOVERNANCE I

25 Percent, 5th Highest in OECD Category," *Maeil Business Newspaper*, September 30, 2019, https://pulsenews.co.kr/print.php?year=2019&no=780684. In 2019, it again decreased to 23.4 percent, which represented 6.66 million Koreans. The steady decline reflected the growth of self-owned microbusinesses crushed by huge debts amid severe competition, whereas its persistent dominance as a form of employment reflected the lack of other viable options. See Yon-se Kim, "Self-Employed in S. Korea Face Strong Headwinds," *Korea Herald*, December 16, 2019, http://www.koreaherald.com/view.php?ud=20191216000230#.

28. PSPD, *Chamyeoyeondae 20nyeon hwaldong 100seon*, 2014, 269–73.
29. This pervasive problem is poignantly portrayed in the film *Parasite*. The husband (Geun-se) of an old housekeeper for the wealthy Park family has been living in the basement bunker to hide from loan sharks who would kill him if they discovered where he was. This is not merely a dramatic exaggeration but a reality for many indigent people who are desperate for money and fall prey to criminal or underground loan sharks willing to kidnap insolvent debtors and harvest their organs for sale. These heinous practices are not limited to South Korea but are the underbelly of the consumer capitalist society. Sean Columb, *Trading Life: Organ Trafficking, Illicit Networks and Exploitation* (Stanford, CA: Stanford University Press, 2020); and Leonard Territo and Rande Matteson, eds., *The International Trafficking of Human Organs: A Multidisciplinary Perspective* (Boca Raton, FL: CRC, 2012).
30. PSPD. *Chamyeoyeondae 20nyeon hwaldong 100seon*, 2014, 279–82.
31. PSPD, *Chamyeoyeondae 20nyeon hwaldong 100seon*, 2014, 279.
32. This implosion of the boundary mirrors the neoliberal economic transformation in the United States, which was marked by the removal of the Glass-Stegall Act during the Clinton administration.
33. PSPD, *Chamyeoyeondae 20nyeon hwaldong 100seon*, 2014, 298–301.
34. This continuity of PSPD activism on the issues of debts among small business owners and financial consumers in recent years is observed in the list of resources on its website.
35. NAFTA became effective in January of 1994 and was replaced by the United States–Mexico–Canada agreement (USMCA) in July 2020.
36. PSPD, *Chamyeoyeondae 20nyeon hwaldong 100seon*, 2014, 201, 457–58; PSPD, *Saerogochim daehanminguk* [Newly repairing the Republic of Korea], 488–98 (Seoul: Imaejin, 2017).
37. PSPD, *Chamyeoyeondae 20nyeon hwaldong 100seon*, 2014, 458–60; PSPD, "HanmiFTAteukwi junggan pyeongga" [KORUR FTA Special Committee mid-term assessment] (11-20-2006), PSPD website, "Balganjaryo," https://www.peoplepower21.org/politics/538750?cat=931&paged=0.
38. PSPD, *Chamyeoyeondae 20nyeon hwaldong 100seon*, 2014, 461.
39. PSPD, *Chamyeoyeondae 20nyeon hwaldong 100seon*, 2014, 469–70.
40. PSPD, *Chamyeoyeondae 20nyeon hwaldong 100seon*, 2014, 471; PSPD, *Saerogochim daehanminguk*, 2017, 38–43; Seung-chang Ha, *Naui siminundong iyagi*, 2015, 147–151.
41. Interview of Tae-seong, a twenty-five-year-old man, by the author, December 9, 2004; emphasis added.
42. Interview of Ho-sang, a man in his early forties, by the author, February 3, 2005.
43. The total number of PSPD members peaked at 14,340 in 2001, reached its nadir of 9,503 in 2005, and bounced back to some 14,000 by 2014 (PSPD, *Chamyeoyeondae*

4. NEOLIBERAL GOVERNANCE I

20nyeon baljachwi [The PSPD's footsteps for 20 years], Seoul: PSPD, 2014, 146). Since then it has maintained this size of membership with the influx of new members and the outflow of existing members.

44. Interview of Ho-sang, by the author, February 3, 2005.
45. In late 1998 and late 1999, there were forty-one and fifty-six full-time staff activists, respectively. Their number grew to a peak of seventy-two in 2002 and decreased to fifty-six in 2005. Since then, their total number has fluctuated between the middle forties and fifties. Regarding the total membership, there were 3,270 members in late 1998 and 6,104 members in late 1999. (See PSPD, *Chamyeoyeondae 20nyeon baljachwi*, 2014, 134, 146).
46. Like any other organization, the character or nature of leadership mattered in this development. According to my interviewees, there was a significant difference between the first director and the second codirectors in terms of their style of leadership. The first paid more attention than the second to individual lay members and staff members and was more experienced in dealing with people with different viewpoints.
47. The centrality of staff activists to advocacy organizations like PSPD seems to be structural, which goes beyond specific social and cultural contexts. A quantitative analysis of local Sierra Clubs in the United States found that the presence of more committed activists was central to their effective outcomes. See Kenneth T. Andrews, Matthew Baggetta, Chaeyoon Lim, Marchall Ganz, and Hahrie Han, "Leadership, Membership, and Voice: Civic Associations That Work," *American Journal of Sociology* 115, no. 4 (2010): 1191–1242.
48. Myeong-ho was a staff activist for five years and then left PSPD to work in a publishing company for several years to support his family after getting married; he then returned to resume his work as an activist. Interview of Myeong-ho, a thirty-four-year-old-man, by the author, October 14, 2009.
49. Interview of Sang-jin, a forty-four-year-old firefighter, by the author, July 2015.
50. Interview of Ye-ji, a woman in her late twenties, by the author, July 2015.
51. Since 2011 PSPD has managed its volunteer activism program more systematically. It regularly surveys its component units for their demands for volunteer activists to identify the total number of such activists and specific tasks in advance and publicize them in its websites. Once volunteer activists are matched to appropriate units, it educates them with basic understanding of citizens' movements and significance of their participation, along with the orientations about specific PSPD units and tasks they will carry out. Prior to this change, PSPD merely assigned individual volunteers to its unit that looked for volunteers (PSPD, *Chamyeoyeondae 20nyeon baljachwi*, 2014, 535, 541).
52. The National Association of Parents for Genuine Education (NAPGE 1989) shows the structural constraint that predisposed citizens' organizations toward professional advocacy groups even when they deal with a mundane issue like children's education. NAPGE envisioned parents as active partners in fostering an appropriate educational environment and making and implementing education policy rather than as passive financial sponsors. Although it relied on unpaid volunteer activities by members, its board of advisors consists mostly of professors, lawyers, and pastors. The headquarters has six full-time staff, and its officers are professors, writers, lawyers, and national assembly members (Hye-jeong Gang, "Hakbumoreul gyoyukjuchero sewotta" [Students' parents are established as the subjects of education.], *NGO Times*,

April 27, 1998, 20–21). Educated members of the middle class in South Korean society have enjoyed high social status stemming from their cultural capital. They also have the professional expertise necessary for legal and policy matters. Hence they have dominated leadership positions in citizens' organizations.

53. Interview of An-su, a forty-one-year-old man, by the author, July 2015.
54. Interview of Min-gyeong, a forty-seven-year-old woman, by the author, July 2015.
55. Simmel's theoretical position is distinct from that of Max Weber, who remained focused on social structures and the macro process of rationalization, including bureaucratization. In contrast, Simmel paid attention to individuals by theorizing how money-based urban society shapes individual behavior and attitudes. See Georg Simmel, *The Philosophy of Money*, trans. Tom Bottomore and David Frisby from a first draft by Kaethe Mengelberg (1900; repr. London: Routledge, 2011), 369–83; and Max Weber, *Economy and Society: An Outline of Interpretive Sociology*, 2 vols., ed. Guenther Roth and Claus Wittich (Berkeley: University of California Press, 1978).
56. Hyeon-mi Kim, Mi-yeon Gang, Su-hyeon Gwon, Yeon-ju Kimgo, Seong-il Pak, and Seung-hwa Jeong, *Chinmiran jeok: Sinjayujuuineun eotteoke ilsangi doeeonna* [An intimate enemy: how did neoliberalism become our routine lives] (Seoul: Ihu, 2010).
57. Interview of Jeon-gil, a thirty-six-year-old man, by the author, July 2015.
58. Interview of Hui-jin, a twenty-one-year-old woman, by the author, July 2015.
59. The South Korean economy since the 1990s has been characterized by the following features that have led to the rapid contraction of good jobs with stability and benefits. First, while the economic conglomerates expanded the manufacturing industry as a major engine of economic growth, they avoided the cultivation of skilled workers, and their growth was the result of aggressively seeking automation and outsourcing. Labor unions failed to resist or reverse this development because they were constrained by multiple factors. Second, the governments, both progressive and conservative, privatized a large number of major public corporations by selling them to transnational business corporations. Third, the governments also generated irregular service jobs in mass by outsourcing social welfare services for care work. See Yoon, *Hanguk bokjigukkaui giwongwa gwejeok*, 260–71, and 412–21.
60. Yoon, *Hanguk bokjigukkaui giwongwa gwejeok*, chaps. 14 and 15.
61. Interview of Yeong-so by the author, July 2015.
62. B. A. Barendregt and F. A. Schneider, "Digital Activism in Asia: Good, Bad, and Banal Politics Online," *Asiascape: Digital Asia* 7, no. 1–2 (2020): 5–19; and Eitan Hersh, *Politics Is Power: How to Move Beyond Political Hobbyism, Take Action, and Make Real Change* (New York: Scribner, 2020).

5. NEOLIBERAL GOVERNANCE II: GRASSROOTS PARTICIPATION THROUGH PRIVATE-PUBLIC PARTNERSHIP AND UNDERMINING CIVIC AUTONOMY

1. Eunju Kim, "Yeoseongjeongchaekgwa yeoseongundong geu hyeonhwanggwa gwaje" [Women's policy and women's movements: their current states and issues], in *Hanguk siminsahoeundong 25nyeonsa* [A twenty-five-year history of Korean civil society movements], ed. Citizens Movement Information Center (Seoul: Citizens Movement Information Center, 2014), 253, 254; author's translation.

5. NEOLIBERAL GOVERNANCE II

2. GY Branch, *Living & Sharing*, monthly house organ vol. 144 (Goyang City, Gyeonggi Province, May 2011), 15.
3. Wendy Brown, *Undoing the Demos: Neoliberalism's Stealth Revolution* (Brooklyn, NY: Zone, 2015), 123.
4. Akihiro Ogawa, *The Failure of Civil Society: The Third Sector and the State in Contemporary Japan* (Albany: State University of New York Press, 2009).
5. Hong-sik Yoon, *Hanguk bokjigukkaui giwongwa gwejeok 3: Sinjayujuuiwa bokjigukka, 1980-nyeonbuteo 2016-nyeong*gaji [The origin and trajectory of the South Korean welfare state, Vol 3. Neoliberalism and the welfare state—from 1980s to 2016] (Seoul: Sahoepyongnon Academy, 2019), 354, 376, 377.
6. GY Branch, "Je10cha jeonggichonghoe" [The 10th Regular General Meeting]. Proceedings of 2010 regular general meeting on January 20, 2010, GY Branch in Goyang City, 96.
7. In 2013, childcare became the major focus of GY branch activism, and it organized a series of public events for grassroots participation. More than a hundred local women came to a three-hour "speaking-up session" to share their experiences of child-rearing and to discuss their ideas about the socialization of childcare. Reflecting the urgency and popularity of this issue among local women raising children, most participants stayed until the end of the meeting and afterwards as well. This initial gathering was followed up with small chatting events for GY branch members for further development of the issue. GY Branch, *Living and Sharing*, vol. 166, September 2013, 16.
8. GY branch has run two other auxiliary centers, including a counseling center and a shelter for survivors of sexual and domestic violence. Each annual proceedings of its regular general meeting shows its organizational scope. For example, see GY Branch, "Je10cha jeonggichonghoe., 2010.
9. Most of the children were primary school students, but there were a few older students from junior high and even high school. It was a co-ed center with a roughly equal ratio of girls and boys.
10. Occasionally, the center offered special education programs reflecting the rapidly changing local context. For example, it organized Vietnamese language instruction as the need to support projects for "multicultural" families increased locally. A total of five classes were taught in partnership with a local General Social Welfare Center in Goyang City. GY Branch, "Je10cha jeonggichonghoe," 2010, 107.
11. GY Branch, "Je18cha jeonggichonghoe" [The 18th regular general meeting. Proceedings of 2018 regular general meeting, January 25, 2018, GY Branch in Goyang City, 178–79.
12. GY Branch, "Je20cha jeonggichonghoe" [The 20th regular general meeting]. Proceedings of 2020 regular general meeting, January 16, 2020, GY Branch, in Goyang City, 31.
13. Examples of public organizations included a town hall, town library, and the center for promoting culture, art, and education; the civil society organizations included Good Neighbors, Publication Cooperative, Physical Education in Life Association, and Green Consumers United. GY Branch, "Je10cha jeonggichonghoe," 2010, 115.
14. GY Branch, "Je12cha jeonggichonghoe" [The 12th regular general meeting]. Proceedings of 2012 regular general meeting, January 12, 2012, GY Branch in Goyang City, 117, 134.

5. NEOLIBERAL GOVERNANCE II

15. The mentoring was done by college students who were paired with individual children (one to one), and each mentor paid a weekly visit to each child at home to assist with academic work and social interaction with conversations and play. GY Branch, "Je10cha jeonggichonghoe," 2010, 93.
16. GY Branch, "Je18cha jeonggichonghoe," 177–88; GY Branch, "Je14cha jeonggichonghoe" [The 14th regular general meeting], Proceedings of 2014 regular general meeting, January 23, 2014, 234–35; GY Branch, "Je12cha jeonggichonghoe" [The 12th Regular General Meeting], 116–24.
17. GY Branch, 2018, 21.
18. The total fertility rate fluctuated between 1.05 and 1.30 during most of the 2010s, but it fell further to 0.98 in 2018 and 0.92 in 2019. The total fertility rate of 2.0 is considered a replacement rate that maintains the current population size. Korean Statistical Information Service (KOSIS), Statistical Database, Daejeon, South Korea, 2020.
19. GY Branch. 2018, 341. In addition, there was an unexpected withdrawal of the initial donation made by an individual, which was instrumental in opening the center in 2007. This was a serious blow to the childcare center. GY Branch 2018, 343.
20. The NE branch applied for the project because women's health has been a major issue for DFS (headquarters and its local branches) as a feminist civic organization. It was chosen through an open competition among applicants from twenty-five autonomous wards in Seoul.
21. The café provided local women with various health programs for physical and mental health. NE Branch, "2013 jeonggichonghoe" [2013 regular general meeting], 63–64.
22. NE Branch, "2013 jeonggichonghoe," 60–64.
23. NE Branch, "2013 jeonggichonghoe," 95.
24. NE Branch, "2013 jeonggichonghoe," 60.
25. NE Branch, "2013 jeonggichonghoe," 103.
26. NE Branch, "2013 jeonggichonghoe," 95–96. This postpartum service job grew in part because this type of personal service (traditionally performed by family members) was rapidly commercialized as central and local governments funded them to encourage women of childbearing age to have children and thus increase the national birth rate.
27. NE Branch, "2014 jeonggichonghoe" [2014 regular general meeting], 78; NE Branch, "2015 jeonggichonghoe" [2015 regular general meeting], 20.
28. NE Branch, "2015 jeonggichonghoe," 73. This extension brought a significant legal change to the NE branch's legal identity. As a local branch of DFS, it had been part of the corporation aggregate. From 2012 to 2014 the NE branch carried out the women's health project on behalf of the DFS headquarters. However, in 2015, when it started to work directly with the metropolitan government for the large-scale project for the next three years, the branch became a corporation to properly handle its resources and responsibilities. NE Branch, 2015, 86. See Byung Chun Park, "Siminsahoedancheui beopjeok jojik hyeongtae" [Legal types of civil society organizations], *Jiyeoksahoeyeongu* [Local society studies] 23, no. 4 (2015): 1–14, for the legal categorization of civil society organizations in South Korea.
29. The metropolitan government selected four wards, including the Dobong Ward, for its showcase project. NE Branch, "2016 jeonggichonghoe," 146.
30. NE Branch, "2016 jeonggichonghoe," 146.

5. NEOLIBERAL GOVERNANCE II

31. NE Branch, "2017 jeonggichonghoe," 41: author's translation.
32. NE Branch, 2016 jeonggichonghoe, 97.
33. NE Branch, 2017 jeonggichonghoe, 41.
34. Troy Stangarone, "COVID-19 Has Widened South Korea's Gender Gap," *The Diplomat*, February 26, 2021, https://thediplomat.com/2021/02/covid-19-has-widened-south-koreas-gender-gap/.
35. GY Branch, Je18cha jeonggichonghoe, 2018, 31.
36. Among restaurant workers, a majority were middle-aged Korean women or migrant foreign women hired by small businesses; they worked longer than ten hours per day and were paid less than the minimum wage, and they had no legal labor protections. GY Branch, *Living and Sharing*, vol. 135 (June 2010), 6, 7.
37. GY Branch, *Living and Sharing*, vol. 166 (September 2013), 8.
38. GY Branch, *Living and Sharing*, vol 135 (June 2010), 6–7.
39. GY Branch, "Je12cha jeonggichonghoe," 36, 183. *Charimsa* conveys an honorific reference to one who arranges in general, and in the context of restaurant services it refers to one who arranges a dining table with various dishes.
40. GY Branch, *Living and Sharing*, vol. 135 (June 2010), 11.
41. GY Branch, *Living and Sharing*, vol. 135 (June 2010), 10.
42. GY Branch, "Je14cha jeonggichonghoe," 2014, 297–99.
43. GY Branch, "Je18cha jeonggichonghoe," 2018, 41, 45.
44. GY Branch, "Je12cha jeonggichonghoe," 2012, 36.
45. GY Branch, "Je14cha jeonggichonghoe," 2014, 297, 300–301.
46. The women's center was founded in 2006 as a public facility in response to a request from local women's organizations and individual women to increase women's participation in society and promote their rights. According to the center's establishment and management laws, its major projects were identified as a women's capacity development project, a childcare project, and a local activism support project. Its ordinances included additional projects such as counseling services and women's welfare promotion as approved by the Ward Chief. See NE Branch, "2018 Dobong Ward Gender Equality Policy Proposal," 2019, 201.
47. This change also influenced the women's center's "lifetime education" by including "effective occupational education" classes. These classes taught marketable skills in cooking and baking, working with computers, arts and crafts, and hairstyling. NE Branch, "2016 jeonggichonghoe," 188. See also Min-Ho Kim, "Simindanche judo pyeongsaenggyoyuk hwaldong beopjehwaui uimi" [Significance of the legislation of the life-long education center led by citizens' organizations], *Journal of Lifelong Education* 6, no. 1 (2000): 263–88, for the legalization of lifetime education in 1999, which increased collaboration between the state and civil society organizations.
48. Funded by the Ministry of Women and Family and the Ministry of Employment and Labor, this new job center gave the women's center additional staff. NE Branch, 2015, 136.
49. NE Branch, 2016 jeonggichonghoe, 2016, 201; and NE Branch, 2017 jeonggichonghoe, 2017, 124.
50. Similar to the Women's Health Network project, during the initial term (2012–2014), the NE Branch was working as a stand-in for DFS headquarters.
51. Funding from multiple government agencies flew into the new job center. The Ministry of Employment and Labor funded a group counseling program serving various

5. NEOLIBERAL GOVERNANCE II

groups of women looking for new employment, and the Locally Tailored Jobs project targeted free training for childcare assistants and professionals and other jobs in demand in the locality. The Ministry of Women and Family funded occupational training programs in accounting and institutional cooking and supported the networking of eleven "women-friendly business firms" in private and public sectors. NE Branch, 2014 jeonggichonghoe, 2014, 110; and NE Branch, 2015 jeonggichonghoe, 2015, 136, 138, 141.

52. NE Branch, Je2ocha jeonggichonghoe, 2019, 24.
53. NE Branch, 2013 jeonggichonghoe, 2013, 112.
54. This coalition was formed in 2002 through a series of local efforts to organize and expand a movement to reform and enact a school meals ordinance that had been underway since the early 2000s. See Kim, "Yeoseongjeongchaekgwa yeoseongundong geu hyeonhwanggwa gwaje." This social movement itself was a societal response to the growing problem of precarious life in the aftermath of the IMF crisis.
55. NE Branch, 2012 jeonggichonghoe, 2012, 10, 36.
56. NE Branch, 2011 jeonggichonghoe, 2011, 47.
57. NE Branch, 2014 jeonggichonghoe, 2014, 99.
58. During the 2010 Municipal Assembly Election in Seoul, the mundane issue of free school meals for children became highly politicized between the conservative ruling party and the progressive opposition party. The opposition party and its supporters promoted environmentally friendly free school meals as a matter of universal welfare. The progressives argued that selective free lunches based on household income would stigmatize recipients and should be replaced with free lunches for all students. The ruling party and its conservative camps opposed free lunches for all as "welfare populism" that could drain the government's budget. In 2011, Se-hoon Oh, then Seoul mayor and a member of the conservative ruling party, proposed a referendum on free school meals for all and promised to step down if he failed to gain a majority in the referendum. The referendum did not materialize due to a lack of electoral participation required for it. He was defeated and immediately resigned. See Jin-geol An, "Hanguksahoe, yanggeukhwa, minsaenge buntohan minsaenghuimangundong yeoksa" [A history of hopeful grassroots life movement that responded to the economic polarization in Korean society], in *Hanguk siminsahoeundong 25nyeonsa* [A twenty-five-year history of civil society movements in South Korea], ed. Citizens Movements Information Center (Seoul: Citizens Movements Information Center, 2014), 295–96; also see, KBS News, "Geuttae geusageon: 2011nyeon Oh Sehoonui 'musanggeupsik' seontaekeun?" [That event back then: Oh Sehoon's choice for "free school meals" in 2011?], November 13, 2014, https://news.kbs.co.kr/news/view.do?ncd=2966268. In October 2011, Won-soon Park, who hailed from PSPD leadership and had decades of experience in civic activism, won the mayoral by-election. Prior to the election, in early 2011, he began the "zero missing meals" (*gyeolsikjero*) movement in response to the budget cut for school meals that the ruling party imposed in the National Assembly meeting in December 2010. The budget cut would stop the provision of school meals for students beginning in 2011. Park initiated a fund-raising campaign to feed those schoolchildren the government refused to feed. As a new mayor, he began his work by signing the budget for free school meals for primary school students. Since November of 2011, free meals have been provided for primary school students in Seoul. See Gyeong-hui Yi,

"'Jeongbuga anhamyeon wuriga handa'... 'gyeolsikadong' mogeum iljuil sae 1eok" ["If the government doesn't, we'll do so"... a fund-raising for "children missing their meals" reached $100,000 in a week], *Pressian*, December 22, 2010, https://www.pressian.com/pages/articles/102899?no=102899&ref=kko#oDKU. Ten years later, in 2021, the environmentally friendly free school meals were extended to cover all K–12 students in Seoul. This would benefit 1,348 schools and 835,000 students. See In-ha 'musanggeupsik' Ryu, "Seoulsi chojunggo chinhwangyeong musanggeupsik jeonmyeonsihaeng... nollan ihu 10nyeonman" [Seoul City implementing the environmentally friendly and free meals for entire primary, middle, and high schools ... ten years after the "free school meals" controversy], *Kyunghyang Newspaper*, February 15, 2021.

59. NE Branch, 2015 jeonggichonghoe, 2015, 22.
60. NE Branch, 2016 jeonggichonghoe, 2016, 78.
61. GY Branch, Je1ocha jeonggichonghoe, 2010, 97.
62. Interview of Sun-gyeong, a thirty-six-year-old woman, by the author, July 15, 2015.
63. Interview of Ji-yeoung, a woman in her mid-fifties, by the author, July 22, 2015.
64. NE Branch, 2015 jeonggichonghoe, 2015, 48–49.
65. NE Branch, 2016 jeonggichonghoe, 2016, 38; emphasis added.
66. GY Branch, Je18cha jeonggichonghoe, 2018, 21.
67. GY Branch, Je18cha jeonggichonghoe, 2018, 342; emphasis added.
68. GY Branch, Je18cha jeonggichonghoe, 2018, 341. Broader cultural changes in schooling since 2010, which stemmed from the liberal reform to increase freedom and choice for children and their parents, ironically undermined the autonomy and discretion of teachers and volunteers at Dream Sprouter in taking care of children. See Seungsook Moon, "Disciplining High-School Students and Molding Their Subjectivity in South Korea: A Shift in Disciplinary Paradigm," in *Challenges of Modernization and Governance in South Korea: The Sinking of the Sewol and Its Causes*, ed. Jae-Jung Suh and Mikyoung Kim (New York: Palgrave Macmillan, 2017), 153.
69. This was in contrast to an earlier practice. Unlike commercial childcare centers, which also received government funding, Dream Sprouter enrolled local children who fell outside the legal definition of children in need, but its teachers believed they should be included on the basis of their discretionary judgment. These "general" children who fell through the formal categorization led to a decrease in government funding for the operational budget, which was calculated on the basis of the number of children legally defined as in need. In the spirit of the local feminist civic organization, Dream Sprouter chose to accept this financial disadvantage. See GY Branch, Je1ocha jeonggichonghoe, 2010, 95.
70. GY Branch, Je18cha jeonggichonghoe, 2018, 339–44.
71. NE Branch, 2013 jeonggichonghoe, 2013, 103.
72. NE Branch, 2017 jeonggichonghoe, 2017, 36.
73. Larissa Fleischmann, "Making Volunteering with Refugees Governable: The Contested Role of 'Civil Society' in the German Welcome Culture," *Social Inclusion* 7, no. 2 (2019): 64–73; Jo Saglie and Karl Henrik Sivesind, "Civil Society Institutions or Semi-Public Agencies: State Regulation of Parties and Voluntary Organizations in Norway," *Journal of Civil Society* 14, no. 4 (2018): 292–310; Mark Chaves, Joseph Galaskiewicz, and Laura Stephens, "Does Government Funding Suppress Nonprofits' Political Activity?," *American Sociological Review* 69, no. 2 (April 2004): 292–316;

and Filip Wijkström, "The Role of Civil Society: The Case of Sweden in International Comparison," paper presented at the First International Korean Studies Workshop on "Civil Society and Consolidating Democracy in Comparative Perspective" held at Yonsei University on May 21–24, 2004.
74. Saglie and Sivesind, "Civil Society Institutions or Semi-Public Agencies."
75. NE Branch, 2015 jeonggichonghoe, 2015, 29.
76. NE Branch, 2017 jeonggichonghoe, 2017, 41.
77. NE Branch, 2015 jeonggichonghoe, 2015, 151.

6. REFUSING NEOLIBERAL GOVERNANCE AND PURSUING PREFIGURATIVE ACTIVISM

1. This is a postscript from the eleventh visit to the Protection Center by a volunteer visitor on August 21, 2020; author's translation. This postscript is part of the collection of writings by FOA members and supporters posted roughly from 2010 to 2020. For identification, I am calling it the Members and Supporters blog. I compiled those writings from FOA's internet sites in January 2021 but this site was removed when FOA updated and cleaned up their home page. I translated all quotations of members' and supporters' words from this collection of writings and in-depth interviews in this chapter unless indicated otherwise.
2. This became obvious from my interviews with a dozen members and supporters of FOA who taught Korean language classes.
3. In-depth interview of Jun-han by the author, October 8, 2009.
4. In-depth interview of Sam-suk, a woman in her early fifties, by the author, October 4, 2009.
5. In-depth interview of Hye-jeong, a woman in her late thirties, by the author, September 27, 2009.
6. Based on my in-depth interview with Sam-suk and conversations with FOA directors.
7. In-depth interview of Chi-hyeon, a man in his mid-forties and a small IT business owner, by the author, September 27, 2009.
8. For critical studies focusing on multicultural families and policy, see Minjeong Kim and Hyeyoung Woo, eds., *Redefining Multicultural Families in South Korea: Reflections and Future Directions* (New Brunswick, NJ: Rutgers University Press, 2022).
9. In the aftermath of the two major economic crises, it became common for college graduates who majored in nonteaching academic fields to reenter teachers' colleges or take teacher employment tests. This trend has recently begun to change as the number of school-age children and teenagers has steadily decreased in South Korea as a result of the rapid decline in child births since the late 1990s (JTBC Evening News, February 19, 2023).
10. Interview of Sam-suk by the author, October 4, 2009.
11. Interview of Chi-heyon by the author, September 27, 2009.
12. Interview of Hye-jeong by the author, September 27, 2009.
13. From my field notes collected in October 2009.
14. This is based on my field notes collected in July 2015, interviews with FOA directors, and its chronology on the website.

15. Interview of Ms. Jang by the author, September 24, 2009. Because FOA is a small local organization, I relied on in-depth interviews with its members rather than formal documents due to their scarcity.
16. See Seungsook Moon, "Multiculturalism in South Korea and the U.S.," in FOA Newsletter, 2009.
17. In-depth interview of Ms. Jang by the author, September 24, 2009.
18. In-depth interview of Ms. Jang by the author, July 2015.
19. According to my conversation with the FOA founder in the summer of 2023, FOA intends to focus on other activities because of its limited capacity and because majung activism has been running regularly and can continue without its involvement.
20. This is based on afternotes by Wu-gyun, July 29, 2018, from the Members and Supporters blog. See Erin Chung, *Immigrant Incorporation in East Asian Democracies* (Cambridge: Cambridge University Press, 2020), for the instrumental roles civic organizations played in incorporating migrants into South Korea, Japan, and Taiwan.
21. A majung activist met both refugees who came to Korea to avoid political and religious persecution and migrants who were detained for a few years even after living in Korea over two decades but were being forced to return to their countries of origin (Wu-gyun, July 2, 2018, Members and Supporters blog).
22. According to the FOA members' blog (https://blog.naver.com/foasia2002/30174660051), majung activism has become one of the most discussed issues since 2016.
23. Members and Supporters blog, May 27, 2016.
24. This fire accident killed ten detainees and injured seventeen detainees. It was caused by a detainee who used a lighter to disable the CCTV and escape. The casualties were high because guards and officers of the Yeosu Protection Center delayed opening its double lock system for fear that detainees would escape as detainees desperately cried for help. In addition, the center did not have fire safety devices such as water sprinklers, and the fire alarm system was not functioning. This tragic accident for the first time exposed the inhumane living conditions in the detention center. See Anonymous, "Hwajaega nado cheolchangeun yeolliji anatta . . . Yeosuchulipgukgwallisamuso chamsa 15junyeon" [When a fire broke out, a steel door didn't open. . . . The fifteenth anniversary of the tragic accident at Yeosu foreigners protection center], *Yeosunet tongnyuseu*, February 11, 2022. https://www.netongs.com/news/articleView.html?idxno=306434.
25. Suk-ja, a volunteer activist, Members and Supporters blog, September 19, 2016; emphasis added.
26. Based on interviews and the Members and Supporters blog.
27. interview of Ms. Jang by the author, September 24, 2009.
28. In-depth interview of Mr. Kang by the author, September 17, 2009.
29. Su-jin on the Members and Supporters blog, May 16, 2015.
30. interview of Jun-han by the author, October 8, 2009.
31. Anonymous, Members and Supporters blog, August 25, 2013.
32. interview of Sam-suk by the author, October 4, 2009; emphasis added.
33. Mr. Kang on the Members and Supporters blog, April 16, 2015; emphasis added.

CONCLUSION: REFLECTING ON THE INTERTWINING OF DEMOCRACY AND NEOLIBERALISM

1. Wolfgang Streeck, *The Delayed Crisis of Democratic Capitalism*, 2nd ed., trans. Patrick Camiller and David Fernbach (London: Verso, 2017).
2. Kyong-Min Son, *The Eclipse of the Demos: The Cold War and the Crisis of Democracy Before Neoliberalism* (Lawrence: University Press of Kansas, 2020).
3. "As liberalism was born through colonial and imperialist wars and occupations, neoliberalism is developed in a postcolonial world order based on its colonial and imperialist legacies and privileges." Masoud Kamali, *Neoliberal Securitization and Symbolic Violence: Silencing Political, Academic, and Societal Resistance* (Cham, Switzerland: Palgrave Macmillan, 2021), 2.

BIBLIOGRAPHY

Adams, Barbara, Ulrich Beck, and Joost Vanloon, eds. *The Risk Society and Beyond: Critical Issues for Social Theory*. London: Sage, 2000.
Adler, Paul, Seok-Woo Kwon, and Charles Heckscher. "Professional Work: The Emergence of Collaborative Community." *Organizational Science* 18, no. 2 (2008): 359–76.
Akçali, Emel, ed. *Neoliberal Governmentality and the Future of the State in the Middle East and North Africa*. New York: Palgrave Macmillan, 2016.
Alexander, Jeffrey C. *The Civil Sphere*. New York: Oxford University Press, 2006.
Alexander, Jeffrey C., David A. Palmer, Sunwoong Park, and Agnes Shuk-mei Ku, eds. *The Civil Sphere in East Asia*. Cambridge: Cambridge University Press, 2019.
Alvarez, Sonia, Jeffrey Rubin, Millie Thayer, Gianpaolo Baiochhi, and Agustin Lao-Montes, eds. *Beyond Civil Society: Activism, Participation, and Protest in Latin America*. Durham, NC: Duke University Press, 2017.
Andrews, Kenneth T., Matthew Baggetta, Chaeyoon Lim, Marchall Ganz, and Hahrie Han. "Leadership, Membership, and Voice: Civic Associations That Work." *American Journal of Sociology* 115, no. 4 (2010): 1191–1242.
Arrington, Celeste L. *Accidental Activists: Victim Movements and Government Accountability in Japan and South Korea*. Ithaca, NY: Cornell University Press, 2016.
Aslam, Ali. *Ordinary Democracy: Sovereignty and Citizenship Beyond the Neoliberal Impasse*. New York: Oxford University Press, 2017.
Aslund, Anders. *How Capitalism Was Built: The Transformation of Central and Eastern Europe, Russia, and Caucasus, and Central Asia*. Cambridge: Cambridge University Press, 2013.
Avenell, Simon Andrew. *Making Japanese Citizens: Civil Society and the Mythology of the Shimin in Postwar Japan*. Berkeley: University of California Press, 2010.
Ayelazuno, Jasper. *Neoliberal Globalization and Resistance from Below: Why the Subalterns Resist in Bolivia and Not in Ghana*. London: Routledge, 2019.

BIBLIOGRAPHY

Barendregt, B. A., and F. A. Schneider, "Digital Activism in Asia: Good, Bad, and Banal Politics Online." *Asiascape: Digital Asia* 7, no. 1–2 (2020): 5–19.
Bauman, Zygmunt. *Liquid Modernity*. Cambridge, UK: Polity, 2000.
Belew, Kathleen. *Bring the War Home: The White Power Movement and Paramilitary America*. Cambridge, MA: Harvard University Press, 2018.
Bell, Daniel. *The Cultural Contradictions of Capitalism*. New York: Basic Books, 1996. First published in 1976.
Biebricher, Thomas. *The Political Theory of Neoliberalism*. Stanford, CA: Stanford University Press, 2018.
Blee, Kathleen M. *Democracy in the Making: How Activist Groups Form*. New York: Oxford University Press, 2012.
Block, Fred, and Margaret R. Somers. *The Power of Market Fundamentalism: Karl Polanyi's Critique*. Cambridge, MA: Harvard University Press, 2014.
Blum, William. *America's Deadliest Export: Democracy and the Truth About US Foreign Policy and Everything Else*. London: Zed, 2013.
Board, Marcus. *Invisible Weapons: Infiltrating Resistance and Defeating Movements*. New York: Oxford University Press, 2022.
Boock, P. J. *Norwegian Social Democracy: From Revolution to Consumerism in the Norwegian Welfare State*. Self-published, 2018.
Bourdieu, Pierre. *Acts of Resistance: Against the Tyranny of the Market*. Trans. Richard Nice. New York: New Press, 1998.
———. "Part III: Symbolic Power and the Political Field." In *Language and Symbolic Power*. Ed. John B. Thompson. Trans. Gino Raymond and Matthew Adamson, 162–251. Cambridge, MA: Harvard University Press, 1991.
Brandtstadter, Susanne, and Hans Steinmuller, eds. *Popular Politics and the Quest for Justice in Contemporary China*. New York: Routledge, 2017.
Broad, Dave, and Wayne Andrew Anthony, eds. *Citizens or Consumers? Social Policy in a Market Society*. Halifax, Canada: Fernwood, 1999.
Brown, Wendy. *Undoing the Demos: Neoliberalism's Stealth Revolution*. Brooklyn, NY: Zone, 2015.
Cahill, Damien, and Martijn Konings. *Neoliberalism*. Cambridge, UK: Polity, 2017.
Carvajal, Palma, and Juan Francisco. *Advocacy NGOs and the Neoliberal Pacification of the Demands of the Street*. London: Palgrave Macmillan, 2021.
Caterino, Brian, and Phillip Hansen. *Critical Theory, Democracy, and the Challenge of Neoliberalism*. Toronto, Canada: University of Toronto Press, 2019.
Chaves, Mark, Joseph Galaskiewicz, and Laura Stephens. "Does Government Funding Suppress Nonprofits' Political Activity?" *American Sociological Review* 69, no. 2 (April 2004): 292–316.
Cheal, David. *The Gift Economy*. London: Routledge, 2017. First published in 1988.
Cherniavsky, Eva. *Neocitizenship: Political Culture After Democracy*. New York: New York University Press, 2017.
Chiavacci, David, and Julia Obinger, eds. *Social Movements and Political Activism in Contemporary Japan: Re-Emerging from Invisibility*. New York: Routledge, 2018.
Cho, Hui-yeon. "14jang Siminundongui segaji saeroun gwaje [Three new challenges to the citizens' movements]. In *Chamyeowa yeondaero yeon minjujuuiui sae jipyeong* [New horizon for democracy that opens through participation and solidarity]. Ed. Seong-tae Hong, 319–49. Seoul: Areuche, 2004.

BIBLIOGRAPHY

Choi, Jang-jip. *Minjuhwa ihuui minjujuui: Hanguk minjujuuiui bosujeok giwongwa wigi* [Democracy after democratization: conservative origin and the crisis of Korean Democracy]. Seoul: Humanitaseu, 2002.

Choe, Paek-sun. "Jinbojeok siminsahoeneun jonjaehaenneunga?" [Did progressive civil society exist?]. *Mirae'eseo on pyeonji* [A letter from the future], September 12, 2014: 53–56.

Chomsky, Noam. *Deterring Democracy*. New York: Hill and Wang, 1991.

Chomsky, Noam, Peter Hutchison, and Jared P. Scott. *Requiem for the American Dream: The 10 Principles of Concentration of Wealth & Power*. New York: Seven Stories, 2017.

Chung, Erin A. *Immigrant Incorporation in East Asian Democracies*. Cambridge: Cambridge University Press, 2020.

Cidam, Cigdem. *In the Street: Democratic Action, Theatricality, and Political Friendship*. New York: Oxford University Press, 2021.

Clemens, Elisabeth S., and Doug Guthrie. "Introduction: Politics and Partnerships." In *Politics and Partnerships: The Role of Voluntary Associations in America's Political Past and Present*. Ed. Elisabeth S. Clemens and Doug Guthrie. Chicago: University of Chicago Press, 2011.

Cohen, Samy. "A Model of Its Own? State-NGO Relations in France," 1–5. Washington, DC: Brookings Institution, 2004.

Collins, Jane L., and Victoria Mayer. *Both Hands Tied: Welfare Reform and the Race to the Bottom in the Low-Wage Labor Market*. Chicago: University of Chicago Press, 2010.

Columb, Sean. *Trading Life: Organ Trafficking, Illicit Networks and Exploitation*. Stanford, CA: Stanford University Press, 2020.

Connolly, William E. *The Fragility of Things: Self-Organizing Processes, Neoliberal Fantasies, and Democratic Activism*. Durham, NC: Duke University Press, 2013.

Copeland, Nicholas. *The Democracy Development Machine: Neoliberalism, Radical Pessimism, and Authoritarian Populism in Mayan Guatemala*. Ithaca, NY: Cornell University Press, 2019.

Crouch, Colin. *The Strange Non-Death of Neoliberalism*. Cambridge, UK: Polity, 2011.

Cumming, Gordon D. "French NGOs in the Global Era: Professionalization 'Without Borders'?" *Voluntas* 19 (2008): 372–94.

Dahlgren, Peter. "Civic Identity and Net Activism: The Frame of Radical Democracy." In *Radical Democracy and the Internet: Interrogating Theory and Practice*. Ed. Lincoln Dahlbert and Eugenia Siapera, 55–72. London: Palgrave Macmillan, 2007.

Dardot, Pierre, and Christian Laval. *Never-Ending Nightmare: The Neoliberal Assault on Democracy*. Trans. Gregory Elliott. London: Verso, 2019.

———. *The New Way of the World: On Neo-Liberal Society*. Trans. Gregory Elliott. London: Verso, 2013.

Das, Ritanjan. *Neoliberalism and the Transforming Left in India: A Contradictory Manifesto*. New York: Routledge, 2018.

Dauvergne, Peter, and Genevieve Lebaron. *Protest Inc.: The Corporatization of Activism*. Cambridge, UK: Polity, 2014.

Della Porta, Donatella, Francis O'Connor, Martin Portos, and Anna Subirats Ribas. *Social Movements and Referendums from Below: Direct Democracy in the Neoliberal Crisis*. Bristol, UK: Policy, 2017.

Deutch, Nancy L. and Eleni Theodorou. "Aspiring, Consuming, Becoming: Youth Identity in a Culture of Consumption." *Youth and Society* 42, no. 2 (2010): 229–54.

Donzelli, Aurora. *Methods of Desire: Language, Morality, and Affect in Neoliberal Indonesia*. Honolulu: University of Hawaii Press, 2019.

Duggan, Lisa. *The Twilight of Equality?: Neoliberalism, Cultural Politics, and the Attack on Democracy*. Boston: Beacon, 2003.

Eckstein, Susan. "Community as Gift-Giving: Collective Roots of Volunteerism." *American Sociological Review* 66, no. 6 (2001): 829–51.

Elias, Norbert. *The Civilizing Process: The History of Manners and State Formation and Civilization*. Trans. Edmund Jepbott. Oxford, UK: Blackwell, 1994. First published in 1939.

Featherstone, Mike. *Consumer Culture and Postmodernism*. Thousand Oaks, CA: Sage, 1991.

Ferrero, Juan Pablo. *Democracy Against Neoliberalism in Argentina and Brazil: A Move to the Left*. London: Palgrave Macmillan, 2016.

Fians, Guilherme. "Prefigurative Politics." In *The Cambridge Encyclopedia of Anthropology*. 2022. http://doi.org/10.29164/22prefigpolitics.

Fleischmann, Larissa. "Making Volunteering with Refugees Governable: The Contested Role of 'Civil Society' in the German Welcome Culture." *Social Inclusion* 7, no. 2 (2019): 64–73.

Foucault, Michel. *The Birth of Biopolitics: Lectures at the Collège de France, 1978–1979*. Ed. Michel Senellat. New York: Palgrave Macmillan, 2008.

Francisco, Juan, and Palma Carvajal. *Advocacy NGOs and the Neoliberal Pacification of the Demands of the Street*. Cham, Switzerland: Palgrave Macmillan, 2021.

Gang, Myeong-kwan. *Joseonhugi yeohangmunhak yeongu* [A study of yeohang literature in late Joseon Dynasty]. Seoul: Changjakkwabipyeong, 1997.

———. *Joseonui dwitgolmok punggyeong* [The landscape of back allies in Joseon]. Seoul: Pureunyeoksa, 2003.

George, Cherian. "Neoliberal 'Good Governance' in Lieu of Rights: Lee Kuan Yew's Singapore Experiment." In *Speech and Society in Turbulent Times: Freedom of Expression in Comparative Perspectives*, 114–30. Cambridge: Cambridge University Press, 2018.

Gerbaudo, Paolo. *The Mask and the Flag: Populism, Citizenism, and Global Protest*. New York: Oxford University Press, 2017.

Giddens, Anthony. *Modernity and Self-Identity: Self and Society in the Late Modern Age*. Stanford, CA: Stanford University Press, 1991.

Giroux, Henry A. *Terror of Neoliberalism: Authoritarianism and the Eclipse of Democracy*. New York: Routledge, 2018.

Giugni, Marco, and Maria T. Grasso. *Street Citizens: Protest Politics and Social Movement Activism in the Age of Globalization*. Cambridge: Cambridge University Press, 2019.

Go, Seok-gyu. "18, 19segi Seourui waljjawa sangeopmunhwa: siminsahoeui ppuriwa gwallyeonhayeo" [Waljja and commercial culture in Seoul during the eighteenth and nineteenth centuries: concerning the root of civil society]. *Seoul Studies* 13 (July 1999): 45–86.

Gómez-Benito, Cristóbal, and Carmen Lozano. "Constructing Food Citizenship: Theoretical Premises and Social Practices." *Italian Sociological Review* 4, no. 2 (2014): 135–56.

Goodman, Michael. "Reading Fair Trade: Political Ecological Imaginary and the Moral Economy of Fair Trade Foods." *Political Geography* 23, no. 7 (2004): 891–915.

BIBLIOGRAPHY

Gregory, Chris A. *Gifts and Commodities*, 2nd ed. Chicago: Hau, 2015. First published in 1982.
Grodsky, Brian K. *Social Movements and the New State: The Fate of Pro-Democracy Organizations When Democracy Is Won*. Stanford, CA: Stanford University Press, 2012.
Gross, Michael L. *Ethics and Activism: The Theory and Practice of Political Morality*. Cambridge: Cambridge University Press, 1997.
Habermas, Jürgen. *The Theory of Communicative Action. Volume 2, Lifeworld and System: A Critique of Functionalist Reason*. Trans. Thomas McCarthy. Boston: Beacon, 1985.
Haddad, Mary Alice. *Building Democracy in Japan*. Cambridge: Cambridge University Press, 2012.
Harvey, David. *A Brief History of Neoliberalism*. Oxford: Oxford University Press, 2005.
Hersh, Eitan. *Politics Is Power: How to Move Beyond Political Hobbyism, Take Action, and Make Real Change*. New York: Scribner, 2020.
Hong, Nansook. *In the Shadow of the Moons: My Life in the Reverend Sun Myung Moon's Family*. Written with Boston Globe reporter Eileen McNamara. New York: Little, Brown, 1998.
Honig, Bonnie. *Public Things: Democracy in Disrepair*. New York: Fordham University Press, 2017.
Hopkin, Jonathan. *Anti-system Politics: The Crisis of Market Liberalism in Rich Democracies*. New York: Oxford University Press, 2020.
Hvenmark, Johan, and Filip Wijkström. "The Popular Movement Marinade: The Dominant Civil Society Framework in Sweden." In SSE/EFI Working Paper Series in Business Administration 2004:18, Stockholm School of Economics.
Hwang, Sang-gyu. "Gieobui sahoejeok chaegimgwa siminsahoeui gwaje" [Corporate social responsibility and issues for civil society]. In *Hanguksiminsahoeundong 25nyeonsa* [A twenty-five-year history of civil society movements in South Korea], 99–111. Seoul: Citizens' Movements Information Center, 2014.
Ikegami, Eiko. *Bonds of Civility: Aesthetic Networks and the Political Origins of Japanese Culture*. New York: Cambridge University Press, 2005.
Im, Hyug Baeg. "Authoritarian Developmentalism, Democratic Neoliberalism, and Economic Growth in Korea: Economic Growth in Different Policy Regimes." In *Growth, Crisis, Democracy*, 196–221. London: Routledge, 2017.
Indiana University Lily Family School of Philanthropy and Center on Philanthropy, the Beautiful Foundation. "Digital for Good: A Global Study on Emerging Ways of Giving: South Korea." Indianapolis: Indiana University-Purdue University Indianapolis (IUPUI); and Seoul: the Beautiful Foundation, 2022.
Ismail, Feyzi, and Sangeeta Kamat. "NGOs, Social Movements and the Neoliberal State: Incorporation, Reinvention, Critique." *Critical Sociology* 44 (July 2018): 569–77.
Jameson, Fredrick. *Postmodernism, or the Cultural Logic of Late Capitalism*. Durham, NC: Duke University Press, 1991.
Jasper, James M. *The Art of Moral Protest: Culture, Biography, and Creativity in Social Movements*. Chicago: University of Chicago Press, 1997.
———. "Cultural Approaches in the Sociology of Social Movements." In *Handbook of Social Movements Across Disciplines*. Ed. Bert Klandermans and Conny Roggeband, 59–109. Cham, Switzerland: Springer, 2010.

Jeong, Cheol-hee. *Hanguksiminsahoeui gwejeok: 1970-nyeondae ihu siminsahoeui donghak* [The trajectory of civil society in South Korea: the dynamics of civil society since the 1970s]. Seoul: Areuche, 2003.

Jeon, Jeong-hwan. *Geundaeui chaegilgi: Dogjaui tansaenggwa hanguk geundaemunhak* [Modernity and reading: The birth of readership and Korean modern literature]. Seoul: Pureuyeoksa, 2003.

Jeong, Sang-dae. *Bareugesalgiundongeul tonghae bon hangugui siminsahoeundong* [Civil society movements in South Korea seen through the Right Living Movement]. Seoul: Sehong, 2013.

Jeong, Sang-ho. "Siminsahoe yeonguui gwaje: Gongikjeok siminundongeul neomeoseo" [A problem in studies of civil society: moving beyond the citizens' movements focusing on public interests]. *Economy and Society* 60 (Winter 2003): 175–94.

Jeong, Seon-tae. "Dongnipsinmunui Joseon, Joseoninnon: geundaegyemonggi 'minjok' damnonui hyeongseonggwa gwallyeonhayeo" [The discourse of Korea and Koreans in *Independence Newspaper*: concerning the formation of the discourse of "nation" during the modern enlightenment period]. In *Geundaegyemonggi jisiggaenyeomui suyonggwa geu byeongyeong* [The adoption of knowledge and its modified use during the modern enlightenment period]. Ed. Ewhayeodae hangungmunhwayeonguwon [Ewha Womans University Korean Culture Studies Center]. Seoul: Somyeongchulpan, 2005.

Jeong, Tae-seok. "Gieobui siminsahoe jibae: Siminsahoeui gieopsahoehwa" [Business corporations' rule of civil society: corporatization of civil society]. *Miraegongbang* 5 (2008): 141–64.

———. "Minjuhwa ihu hanguksahoeui byeonhwawa chamyeoyeondae" [Social change after democratization and the PSPD in South Korea]. *Civil Society & NGO* 11, no. 2 (2013): 3–39.

Jeong, Yong-in. "A Quarter Century of Citizens' Movements with Glory and Opprobrium: Can Its Heyday Be Returned?" *Weekly Kyunghyang* 1136 (July 28, 2015): 33.

Jo, Bong-jin, and Seong-tae Hong, eds. *Hoesagamyeon jungneunda: gyeongjejuui damnonui bipaneul wihan pildsteodi* [If you join a company, you're dead: a field study to criticize economistic discourse]. Seoul: Hyeonsilmunhwayeongu, 1995.

Jo, Dae-yeop. *Hangugui siminundong* [Citizens' movements in South Korea]. Seoul: Nanam, 1999.

Jo, Dae-yeop, Sang-cheol Yun, Taek-myeon Yi, Gil-seong Pak, and Gyeong-hui Kim. *21segi hangugui gieopkkwa siminsahoe* [Business corporation and civil society in twenty-first-century Korea]. Seoul: Kutinpomeisyeon, 2007.

Jo, Myeong-rae. "Hanguk siminundongui wichiwa seonggyeok byeonhwa: gukka-siminsahoe gwangyereul jungsimeuro" [Changes in the position and nature of citizens' movements in Korea: Focusing on the state-civil society relation]. In *Hanguksiminsahoeundong 25neyonsa* [A twenty-five-year history of civil society movements in Korea], 27–39. Seoul: Citizens Movements Information Center, 2014.

Jo, Yong-seung. "'Gwollyeokkamsi' naesewotteon chamyeoyeondae museoun gwollyeok geu jachero 'baljeon'" [The PSPD vocal about "monitoring the power" has "developed" into the power itself]. *Hanguknondan* (January 2011): 74–81.

Johnston, Hank, and Bert Klandermans, eds. *Social Movements and Culture*. Minneapolis: University of Minnesota Press, 1995.

Jones, Bryn, and Mike O'Donnell, eds. *Alternative to Neoliberalism: Towards Equality and Democracy*. Bristol, UK: Polity, 2017.

BIBLIOGRAPHY

Ju, Seong-su. *Hanguksiminsahoesa: minjuhwagi 1987-2017* [A history of Korean civil society]. Seoul: Hakmin, 2017.
Julier, Alice P. *Eating Together: Food, Friendship, and Inequality*. Champaign: University of Illinois Press, 2013.
Junker, Andrew. *Becoming Activists in Global China: Social Movements in the Chinese Diaspora*. Cambridge: Cambridge University Press, 2019.
Kamali, Masoud. *Neoliberal Securitization and Symbolic Violence: Silencing Political, Academic, and Societal Resistance*. Cham, Switzerland: Palgrave Macmillan, 2021.
Kärrylä, Ilkka. *Democracy and the Economy in Finland and Sweden Since 1960: A Nordic Perspective on Neoliberalism*. Cham, Switzerland: Palgrave Macmillan, 2021.
Kim, Dong-choon. "Growth and Crisis of the Korean Citizens' Movement." *Korea Journal* 46, no. 2 (2006): 99–128.
Kim, Eun-ju. "Yeoseongjeongchaekgwa yeoseongundong geu hyeonhwanggwa gwaje" [Women's policy and women's movements: their states and issues]. In *Hanguk siminsahoeundong 25nyeonsa* [A twenty-five-year history of Korean civil society movements]. Ed. Citizens Movement Information Center. Seoul: Citizens Movement Information Center, 2014.
Kim, Gyeong-hui. "Yeoseongundonggwa gieobui pateuneosip: hangukyeoseongjaedanui sarye" [The partnership between women's movement and business corporations: a case study of the Korea Women's Foundation], In *21segi hangugui gieopgwa siminsahoe* [Business corporations and civil society in Korea in the 21st century]. Ed. Dae-yeop Jo, 133–58. Seoul: Gutinpomeisyeon, 2007.
Hyeon-mi Kim, Mi-yeon Gang, Su-hyeon Gwon,Yeon-ju Kimgo, Seong-il Pak, and Seung-hwa Jeong, *Chinmiran jeok: Sinjayujuuineun eotteoke ilsangi doeeonna* [An intimate enemy: how did neoliberalism become our routine lives]. Seoul: Ihu, 2010.
Kim, Hyung Chul. "Simindancheui seongeochamyeohwaldong pyeonggawa hwalseonghwa bangan: 2016 chongseonsiminneteuwokeureul jungsimeuro" [The evaluation of citizens' organizations' electoral participation movement: focusing on the Citizens' Network for 2016 general election]. *Election Studies* 8 (2018): 153–81.
Kim, Hyung Chul, and Kyung Sun Hong. "Seongeoundongui jayuwa gongjikseongeobeop gaejeong bangan: simindancheui seongeobeop wibansaryereul jungsimeuro" [Freedom of election campaign and the revision of the public officials election law: focusing on the cases of violation of the law by citizens' organizations]. *Comparative Democracy Studies* 14, no. 2 (2018): 5–43.
Kim, Jeong-hun. "Chamyeoyeondaereul tonghae bon hangugui siminundongui byeonhwa: 'daeuiui daehangeseo 'jinbojeok gongnonjangui hyeongseongjaro" [Change in citizens' movement in South Korea seen through the PSPD: from "the representative of general will" to "a maker of progressive public discourse"]. *Memory & Prospect* 26 (Summer 2013): 8–49.
Kim, Min-ho. "Simindanche judo pyeongsaenggyoyuk hwaldong beopjehwaui uimi" [Significance of the legislation of the life-long education center led by citizens' organizations]. *Journal of Lifelong Education* 6, no. 1 (2000): 263–88.
Kim, Minjeong, and Hyeyoung Woo, eds. *Redefining Multicultural Families in South Korea: Reflections and Future Directions*. New Brunswick, NJ: Rutgers University Press, 2022.
Kim, Samuel S., ed. *Korea's Globalization*. Cambridge: Cambridge University Press, 2000.

Kim, Sang-jo. "Chamyeoyeondaeui gyeongjeminjuhwaundong" [PSPD's movement to democratize the economy]. In *Chamyeowa yeondaero yeon minjujuuiui sae jipyeong* [New horizon of democracy opened by participation and solidarity]. Ed. Seong-tae Hong, 218–20. Seoul: Areuche, 2004.

Kim, Sun-Chul. *Democratization and Social Movements in South Korea: Defiant Institutionalization*. New York: Routledge, 2016.

Kim, Sun-mi. "Siminundong wigi damrongwa baljeon bangan: Siminsahoe jihyeongbyeonhwawa gwallyeonhayeo" [The discourse of citizens' movements in crisis and a suggestion for solution: concerning the changing context of civil society]. *Damnon201* 10, no. 3 (2008): 143–73.

Kim, Yeon-myeong. "10jang Chamyeoyeondae 'sahoebokjiwiwonhoe' 10nyeonui seonggwawa seongchal" [Ch. 10 PSPD's 'social welfare committee' a decade of achievement and reflection]. In *Chamyeowa yeondaero yeon minjujuuiui sae jipyeong* [A new horizon of democracy opened by participation and solidarity], 226–32. Seoul: Areuche, 2004.

Kim, Young Soon. "Minjuhwa ihu 30nyeon, hanguk bokjigugga baljeonui juchewa gwollyeokjawon byeonhwawa jeonmang" [The main actors in the development of the welfare state and their power resources in post-democratization Korea]. *Simingwasegye* [Citizen & the World] 31, no. 2 (2017): 1–44.

Kingstone, Peter. *The Political Economy of Latin America: Reflections on Neoliberalism and Development After the Commodity Boom*. New York: Routledge, 2011.

Klein, Naomi. *No Logo: Taking Aim at the Brand Bullies*. New York: Picador, 1999.

———. *The Shock Doctrine: The Rise of Disaster Capitalism*. New York: Picador, 2007.

Komter, Afke. *Social Solidarity and the Gift*. Cambridge: Cambridge University Press, 2015.

Koo, Hagen. "Rising Inequality and Shifting Class Boundaries in South Korea in the Neo-Liberal Era." *Journal of Contemporary Asia* 51, no. 1 (2021): 1–19. http://doi.org/10.1080/00472336.2019.1663242.

Kwon, Hui-yeong. *Hangugsawa jeongsinbunseok* [Korean history and psychoanalysis]. Seoul: Chimmundang, 2001.

Lea, David. *Neoliberalism, the Security State, and the Quantification of Reality*. Lanham, MD: Lexington, 2017.

Lee, Jae-cheol. "Hanguksahoeui yanggeukhwawa segyehwa geurigo siminsahoe" [Polarization, globalization, and civil society in South Korea]. *21segi jeongchihakhoebo* [21-Century Political Science Association Journal] 19, no. 2 (2009): 237–58.

Lee, Namhee. "From *minjung* to *simin*: The Discursive Shift in Korean Social Movements." In *South Korean Social Movements: From Democracy to Civil Society*. Ed. Gi-Wook Shin and Paul Y. Chang, 41–57. New York: Routledge, 2011.

———. *Memory Construction and the Politics of Time in Neoliberal South Korea*. Durham, NC: Duke University Press, 2022.

Lee, Yoonkyung. *Between the Streets and the Assembly: Social Movements, Political Parties, and Democracy in Korea*. Honolulu: University of Hawai'i Press, 2022.

Lemke, Thomas. *Foucault's Analysis of Modern Governmentality: A Critique of Political Reason*. Trans. Erik Butler. London: Verso, 2019.

Lewis, David. "Nongovernmental Organizations, Definition and History." In *International Encyclopaedia of Civil Society*. Ed. Helmut K. Anheiner and Stephan Toepler, 1–10. New York: Springer, 2009.

BIBLIOGRAPHY

Liu, Jan. *Shifting Dynamics of Contention in the Digital Age: Mobile Communication and Politics in China*. New York: Oxford University Press, 2020.

Lockie, Stewart. "Responsibility and Agency Within Alternative Food Networks: Assembling the 'Citizen Consumer.'" *Agriculture and Human Values* 26, no. 3 (2009): 193–201.

Mackrell, Judith. *Flappers: Six Women of a Dangerous Generation*. New York: Sarah Crichton, 2014.

Macpherson, C. B. *The Political Theory of Possessive Individualism: Hobbes to Locke*. Oxford: Oxford University Press, 1962.

Madariaga, Aldo. *Neoliberal Resilience: Lessons in Democracy and Development from Latin America and Eastern Europe*. Princeton, NJ: Princeton University Press, 2020.

Marcuse, Herbert. *One-Dimensional Man: Studies in the Ideology of Advanced Industrial Society*. Boston: Beacon, 1964.

Marwell, Nicole P. "Privatizing the Welfare State: Nonprofit Community-Based Organizations as Political Actors." *American Sociological Review* 69, no. 2 (2004): 265–91.

Marx, Karl. "The Meanings of Human Requirements" and "The Power of Money in Bourgeois Society." In *Marx-Engels Reader*, 2nd ed. Ed. Robert Tucker, 93–101 and 101–5. New York: Norton, 1978.

McRobbie, Angela. "Young Women and Consumer Culture." *Cultural Studies* 22, no. 5 (2008): 531–50.

Miller, Peter, and Nikolas Rose. "Mobilizing the Consumer: Assembling the Subject of Consumption." *Theory, Culture & Society* 14 (1997): 1–36.

Minkoff, Debra C. "The Emergence of Hybrid Organizational Forms: Combining Identity-Based Service Provision and Political Action." *Nonprofit and Voluntary Sector Quarterly* 31, no. 3 (2002): 377–401.

Moon, Seungsook. "Buddhist Temple Food in South Korea: Interests and Agency in the Reinvention of Tradition in the Age of Globalization." *Korea Journal* 48, no. 4 (Winter 2008): 147–80.

———. "Carving Out Space: Civil Society and the Women's Movement in South Korea." *Journal of Asian Studies* 61, no. 2 (May 2002): 473–500.

———. "Disciplining High-School Students and Molding Their Subjectivity in South Korea: A Shift in Disciplinary Paradigm." In *Challenges of Modernization and Governance in South Korea: The Sinking of the Sewol and Its Causes*. Ed. Jae-Jung Suh and Mikyoung Kim, 143–68. New York: Palgrave Macmillan, 2017.

———. "The Interplay Between the State, the Market, and Culture in Shaping Civil Society: A Case Study of the People's Solidarity for Participatory Democracy in South Korea." *Journal of Asian Studies* 69, no. 2 (2010): 479–505.

———. "Local Meanings and Lived Experiences of Citizenship: Voices from a Women's Organization in South Korea." *Citizenship Studies* 16 (February 2012): 49–67.

———. *Militarized Modernity and Gendered Citizenship in South Korea*. Durham, NC: Duke University Press, 2005.

———. "Overcome by Globalization: The Rise of a Women's Policy in South Korea." In *Korea's Globalization*. Ed. Samuel S. Kim, 126–46. Cambridge: Cambridge University Press, 2000.

———. "Women's Food Work, Food Citizenship, & Transnational Consumer Capitalism: A Case Study of a Feminist Food Cooperatives in South Korea." *Food, Culture & Society*, 2021. https://doi.org/10.1080/15528014.2021.1892255.

Morris-Suzuki, Tessa. *Japan's Living Politics: Grassroots Action and the Crisis of Democracy*. Cambridge: Cambridge University Press, 2020.

Mouffe, Chantal, ed. *Dimensions of Radical Democracy: Pluralism, Citizenship and Community*. London: Routledge, 1992.

Mukherjee, Roopali, and Sarah Banet-Weiser, eds. *Commodity Activism: Cultural Resistance in Neoliberal Times*. New York: New York University Press, 2012.

Norris, Pippa. *Democratic Phoenix: Reinventing Political Activism*. Cambridge: Cambridge University Press, 2010.

O, Gwan-yeong. "Seongpyeongdeung, jisokganeungseong, yeondae gachi yesangamsiundonge bangjeom" [The emphasis on the movement to monitor government budget, gender equality, sustainability, solidarity value]. In *Hanguk siminsahoeundong 25nyeonsa* [A twenty-five-year history of Korean civil society movements], 85–97. Seoul: Citizens' Movement Information Center, 2014.

Ogawa, Akihiro. *The Failure of Civil Society: The Third Sector and the State in Contemporary Japan*. Albany: State University of New York Press, 2009.

Pak, Eung-seo. "Maeil yujeonjabyeonhyeong kong meongneun hangugin" [Koreans who eat GM soybeans everyday]. *Science Times*, February 4, 2016.

Pak, Yeong-seon. "Chamyeoyeondae naebuuisagyeoljeonggujo yeongu" [A study of the internal decision-making structure of the PSPD]. *Civil Society and NGO* 12, no. 1 (2014): 35–71.

Park, Byung Chun. "Siminsahoedancheui beopjeok jojik hyeongtae" [Legal types of civil society organizations]. *Jiyeoksahoeyeongu* [Local society studies] 23, no. 4 (2015): 1–14.

Park, Sang-pil. "A Framework for Assessing the State Governance." *Journal of NGO Studies* 9, no. 2 (2014): 1–24.

Paker, Hande. *Cosmopolitan Democracy Revisited in a World of Rising Populism, Deepening Polarization, and Rampant Neoliberalism*. Istanbul, Turkey: Istanbul Policy Center, 2017.

Passy, Florence, and Gan-Andrea Monsch. *Contentious Minds: How Talk and Ties Sustain Activism*. New York: Oxford University Press, 2020.

Peet, Richard. *Unholy Trinity: The IMF, World Bank, and WTO*. London: Zed, 2009.

Pekkanan, Robert. *Japan's Dual Civil Society: Members Without Advocates*. Stanford, CA: Stanford University Press, 2006.

Piketty, Thomas. *Capital in the Twenty-First Century*. Cambridge, MA: Harvard University Press, 2014.

Polanyi, Karl. *The Great Transformation: The Political and Economic Origins of Our Time*. Boston: Beacon, 2001. First published in 1944.

Postman, Neil. *Amusing Ourselves to Death: Public Discourse in the Age of Show Business*. New York: Penguin, 1986.

Putman, Robert D. *Bowling Alone*. New York: Simon & Schuster, 2000.

Ram Saran, Dave., ed. *Contradictory Existence: Neoliberalism and Democracy in the Caribbean*. Kingston, Jamaica: Ian Randle, 2016.

Ranis, Peter. *Co-ops Confront Capitalism: Challenging the Neo-Liberal Economy*. London: Zed, 2016.

Rancière, Jacques. *Hatred of Democracy*. Trans. Steve Corcoran. New York: Verso, 2014. First published in 2005.

BIBLIOGRAPHY

Rappaport, Erika. *Shopping for Pleasure: Women in the Making of London's West End.* Princeton, NJ: Princeton University Press, 2000.

Ricci, Cecilia, Nicola Marinelli, and Lorenzo Puliti. "The Consumer as Citizen: The Role of Ethics for a Sustainable Consumption." *Agriculture and Agricultural Science Procedia* 8 (2016): 395–401.

Richard, Analiese. *The Unsettled Sector: NGOs and the Cultivation of Democratic Citizenship in Rural Mexico.* Stanford, CA: Stanford University Press, 2016.

Rockhill, Gabriel. *Counter-History of the Present: Untimely Interrogations Into Globalization, Technology, Democracy.* Durham, NC: Duke University Press, 2017.

Saad-Filho, Alfredo, and Lecio Morais. *Brazil: Neoliberalism Versus Democracy.* London: Pluto, 2018.

Saglie, Jo, and Karl Henrik Sivesind. "Civil Society Institutions or Semi-Public Agencies: State Regulation of Parties and Voluntary Organizations in Norway." *Journal of Civil Society* 14, no. 4 (2018): 292–310.

Sandel, Michael J. *What Money Can't Buy: The Moral Limits of Markets.* New York: Farrar, Straus and Giroux, 2012.

Schwartz, Nelson D. *The Velvet Rope Economy: How Inequality Became Big Business.* New York: Anchor, 2021.

Seyfang, Gill. "Ecological Citizenship and Sustainable Consumption: Examining Local Organic Food Networks," *Journal of Rural Studies* 22, no. 4 (2006): 383–95.

Shin, Gi-wook, and Paul Y. Chang, eds. *South Korean Social Movements: From Democracy to Civil Society.* London: Routledge, 2011.

Shin, Kwang-yeong, Don-mun Jo, and Eun Cho. *Hanguksahoeui gyegeumnonjeok ihae* [Understanding the Korean society through the theory of social class]. Paju: Hanulacademi, 2003.

Simmel, Georg. *The Philosophy of Money.* Trans. Tom Bottomore and David Frisby from a first draft by Kaethe Mengelberg. London: Routledge, 2011. First published in 1900.

Skocpol, Theda. "Advocates Without Members: The Recent Transformation of American Civic Life." In *Civic Engagement in American Democracy.* Ed. Theda Skocpol and Morris P. Fiorina, 461–509. Washington, DC: Brookings Institution Press, 1999.

———. *Diminished Democracy.* Norman: University of Oklahoma Press, 2003.

Slobodian, Quinn. *Globalists: The End of Empire and the Birth of Neoliberalism.* Cambridge, MA: Harvard University Press, 2020.

Son, Kyong-Min. *The Eclipse of the Demos: The Cold War and the Crisis of Democracy Before Neoliberalism.* Lawrence: University Press of Kansas, 2020.

Soros, George. *The Crisis of Global Capitalism.* New York: Public Affairs, 1998.

Stangarone, Troy. "COVID-19 Has Widened South Korea's Gender Gap." *The Diplomat,* February 26, 2021. https://thediplomat.com/2021/02/covid-19-has-widened-south-koreas-gender-gap/.

Stephan, Rita, and Mounira M. Charrad, eds. *Women Rising: In and Beyond the Arab Spring.* New York: New York University Press, 2020.

Stern, Alexandra Minna. *Eugenic Nation: Faults and Frontiers of Better Breeding in Modern America.* Berkeley: University of California Press, 2016.

Strathern, Marilyn. *The Gender of the Gift: Problems with Women and Problems with Society in Melanesia.* Berkeley: University of California Press, 1988.

Streeck, Wolfgang. "Citizens as Consumers: Considerations on the New Politics of Consumption." *New Left Review* 76 (July–August 2012): 27–47.

———. *The Delayed Crisis of Democratic Capitalism*, 2nd ed. Trans. Patrick Camiller and David Fernbach. London: Verso, 2017.

Taft, Jessica K. *The Kids Are in Charge: Activism and Power in Peru's Movement of Working Children*. New York: New York University Press, 2019.

Taylor, Marilyn, and Joanna Howard. "Citizen Participation and Civic Activism in Comparative Perspective." *Journal of Civil Society* 6, no. 2 (2010): 145–64.

Territo, Leonard, and Rande Matteson, eds. *The International Trafficking of Human Organs: A Multidisciplinary Perspective*. Boca Raton, FL: CRC, 2012.

Thompson, Michael. *Twilight of the Self: The Decline of the Individual in Late Capitalism*. Stanford, CA: Stanford University Press, 2022.

Tilly, Charles. "From Interactions to Outcomes in Social Movements." In *How Social Movements Matter*. Ed. Marco Giugni, Doug McAdam, and Charles Tilly, 253–70. Minneapolis: University of Minnesota Press, 1999.

Toffler, Alvin. *The Third Wave*. New York: William Morrow, 1980.

Toplišek, Alen. *Liberal Democracy in Crisis: Rethinking Resistance Under Neoliberal Governmentality*. London: Palgrave MacMillan, 2019.

Turner, Bryan S. "Post-Secular Society: Consumerism and the Democratization of Religion." In *The Post-Secular in Question: Religion in Contemporary Society*. Ed. Philip Gorski, David Kyuman Kim, John Torpey, and Jonathan VanAntwerpen, 135–58. New York: New York University Press, 2012.

United Nations, "Agenda 21." In Report of the United Nations Conference on Environment and Development, convened in Rio de Janeiro, June 3–14, 1992. New York: United Nations, 1993.

Verschuere, Bram, and Joris De Corte. "Nonprofit Advocacy Under a Third-Party Government Regime: Cooperation or Conflict?" *Voluntas: International Journal of Voluntary and Nonprofit Organizations* 26 (2015): 222–41.

Vormann, Bons, and Christian Lammert. *Democracy in Crisis: The Neoliberal Roots of Popular Unrest*. Philadelphia: University of Pennsylvania Press, 2017.

Walker, Edward T. *Grassroots for Hire: Public Affairs Consultants in American Democracy*. Cambridge: Cambridge University Press, 2014.

Walker, Edward T., John D. McCarthy, and Frank Baumgartner. "Replacing Members with Managers? Mutualism Among Membership and Nonmembership Advocacy Organizations in the United States." *American Journal of Sociology* 177, no. 5 (2011): 1284–1337.

Weber, Max. "Class, Status and Party." In *From Max Weber: Essays in Sociology*. Trans. and ed. H. H. Gerth and C. Wright Mills, 180–95. Boston: Routledge & Kegan Paul, 1974. First published in 1948.

———. *Economy and Society: An Outline of Interpretive Sociology*, 2 vols. Ed. Guenther Roth and Claus Wittich. Berkeley: University of California Press, 1978.

Wei, Ran, ed. *Mobile Media, Political Participation, and Civic Activism in Asia: Private Chat to Public Communications*. New York: Springer, 2016.

Wijkström, Filip. "The Role of Civil Society: The Case of Sweden in International Comparison." Paper presented at the First International Korean Studies Workshop on "Civil Society and Consolidating Democracy in Comparative Perspective," Yonsei University, May 21–24, 2004.

BIBLIOGRAPHY

Williams, Michelle, and Vishwas Satgar, eds. *Destroying Democracy: Neoliberal Capitalism and the Rise of Authoritarian Politics*. Johannesburg, South Africa: Wits University Press, 2021.

Wolin, Sheldon. *Democracy Incorporated: Managed Democracy and the Specter of Inverted Totalitarianism*. Princeton, NJ: Princeton University Press, 2010.

Woods, Ngaire. *The Globalizers: The IMF, the World Bank, and Their Borrowers*. Ithaca, NY: Cornell University Press, 2006.

Wright, Stuart A., ed. *Armageddon in Waco: Critical Perspectives on the Branch Davidian Conflict*. Chicago: University of Chicago Press, 1995.

Wuthnow, Robert. *Loose Connections: Joining Together in America's Fragmented Communities*. Cambridge, MA: Harvard University Press, 1998.

Xu, Bin. *The Politics of Compassion: The Sichuan Earthquake and Civic Engagement in China*. Stanford, CA: Stanford University Press, 2017.

Yi, Se-Jeong. "Bogeon uiryobunya jeongchaekgyeoljeong ipbeopgwajeongeseo simindancheui yeokhalgwa chamyeo hwakdae bangan" [A study of how to increase roles and participation of citizens' organizations in the policymaking decisions and legislation in the field of health and medicine]. *Beopjeyeongu* [Journal of Legislation Research] 45 (2013): 39–66.

Yilamu, Wumaier. *Neoliberalism and Post-Soviet Transition: Kazakhstan and Uzbekistan*. Cham, Switzerland: Palgrave Macmillan, 2018.

Yoon, Hong-sik. *Hanguk bokjigukkaui giwongwa gwejeok 3: sinjayujuuiwa bokjigukka, 1980-nyeonbuteo 2016-nyeonggaji* [The origin and trajectory of the South Korean welfare state. Vol 3, Neoliberalism and the welfare state—from 1980s to 2016]. Seoul: Sahoepyeongnon Academi, 2019.

Yoon, Min-jae. *Minjuhwa ihu hanguksahoewa sinjayujuui: daetongnyeong rideosipgwa tongchiseong* [Korean society after democratization and neoliberalism: presidential leadership and governmentality]. Seoul: Oreum, 2017.

Yun, Chang-won. "Sahoe gongdongchewa sangsaenggwangye, geurigo saengmyeongnanum" [Social community, symbiotic relations, and sharing of life]. In *Korean Civil Society Yearbook*, 347–58. Seoul: Citizens Movement Information Center, 2017.

Youngs, Richard. *Civic Activism Unleashed: New Hope or False Dawn for Democracy?* New York: Oxford University Press, 2019.

Yu, Seok-chun, and Hye-suk Wang. *Chamyeoyeondae bogoseo* [PSPD Report]. Seoul: Jayugieopwon, 2006.

Zhiping, Liang. "Rethinking Civil Society in China: An Interpretative Approach." In *The Politics of Affective Relations: East Asia and Beyond*. Ed. Hahm Chaihark and Daniel A. Bell, 169–99. Lanham, MD: Lexington, 2004.

KOREAN PRIMARY SOURCES

An, Jin-geol. "Hanguksahoe, yanggeukhwa, minsaenge buntohan minsaenghuimangundong yeoksa" [A history of hopeful grassroots life movement which responded to the economic polarization in Korean society]. In *Hanguk siminsahoeundong 25nyeonsa* [A twenty-five-year history of civil society movements in South Korea]. Ed. Citizens Movements Information Center, 289–303. Seoul: Citizens Movements Information Center, 2014.

Baek, Cheol. "Gwanbyeondanche subaegeok hyeolse eonjekkaji julgeongayo" [Until when do you grant to pro-government organizations millions of bloody tax money?]. *Weekly Kyunghyang* 1134 (July 14, 2015): 25–27.

Cha, Byeong-jik. "Giuttunghan gyunhyeongeul chajaseo: 2000- jeongchijeok jungnipseong nonjaeng" [Looking for a Tilted Balance: Since 2000 the Political Neutrality Controversy]. *Chamyeosahoe* [Participatory Society] 206 (January 2014): 20–25.

———. *Sageoneuro boneun siminundongsa: Hyeondaesaui muljulgireul bakkun hanguksiminundong 20 jangmyeon* [A history of citizens' movements seen through events: twenty scenes from citizens' movements that changed major streams of contemporary history in South Korea]. Seoul: Changjakkwabipyeong, 2014.

Choe, Paek-sun. "Jinbojeok siminsahoeneun jonjaehaenneunga?" [Did progressive civil society exist?], *Miraeeseo on pyeonji* [A letter from the future] 20 (September 12, 2014): 53–56. Seoul: Labor Party House Organ.

Citizens Movement Information Center. *Hanguk siminsahoeundong 25nyeonsa* [A twenty-five-year history of Korean civil society movements. Seoul: Citizens Movement Information Center, 2014.

DFS (Democratic Friends Society). *Je21cha jeonggichonghoe* [The 21st regular general meeting]. Proceedings of 2008 regular general meeting. Seoul: Korea DFS Headquarters, 2008.

KOREAN PRIMARY SOURCES

———. *Je30cha jeonggichonghoe* [The 30th regular general meeting]. Proceedings of 2017 regular general meeting. Seoul: Korea DFS Headquarters, 2017.

———. "*Je32cha jeonggichonghoe* [The 32nd regular general meetings]. Proceedings of 2019 regular general meeting. Seoul: Korea DFS Headquarters, 2019.

———. *Hamkkeganeun yeoseong* [*Women Going Together*], house organ of the DFS headquarters.

FOA (Friends of Asia). Collection of writings by FOA members from 2010 to 2020. Compiled by Seungsook Moon, January 2021, from public FOA website.

———. 2019 Gyeolsanbogo [Accounting report].

GY Branch. *Salimgwa nanum* [Living and sharing], house organ, Goyang City, Gyeonggi Province: GY Branch. Vol. 131 (February 2010), Vol. 135 (June 2010), Vol. 140 (December 2010), Vol. 144 (May 2011), Vol. 160 (December 2012), Vol. 166 (September 2013), Vol. 170 (May 2014), Vol. 175 (March 2015), Vol. 180 (January 2016), Vol. 185 (November 2016), Vol. 194 (May 2018).

———. *Je10cha jeonggichonghoe* [The 10th regular general meeting]. Proceedings of 2010 regular general meeting, January 20, 2010. Goyang City: GY Branch.

———. *Je12cha jeonggichonghoe* [The 12th regular general meeting]. Proceedings of 2012 regular general meeting, January 12, 2012.

———. *Je14cha jeonggichonghoe* [The 14th regular general meeting]. Proceedings of 2014 regular general meeting, January 23, 2014.

———. *Je16cha jeonggichonghoe* [The 16th regular general meeting]. Proceedings of 2016 regular general meeting, January 21, 2016.

———. *Je18cha jeonggichonghoe* [The 18th regular general meeting]. Proceedings of 2018 regular general meeting, January 25, 2018.

———. *Je20cha jeonggichonghoe* [The 20th regular general meeting]. Proceedings of 2020 regular general meeting, January 16, 2020.

Ha, Seung-chang. *Naui siminundong iyagi* [My citizens' movement story]. Seoul: Humanist, 2015.

Han, Hyewon. "Hanchongni 'gungmintonghap hyeopchi apjangseogetta . . . iljalhaneun yuneunghan chaegimjeongbu,'" [Prime minister Han "I will lead the integration of citizens and governance . . . a competent government of responsibility"], *Yonhap News*, May 23, 2022.

Hong, Su-yeong. "DJ-No jeongbu banmyeongyosa 10nyeon <5> Kwollyeoge muldeun simindanche" [DJ-Roh administrations reactionary ten years: <5> citizens' organizations colored by political power]. *Dong-A Daily*, January 4, 2008. https://www.donga.com/news/View?gid=8529887&date=20080104.

Jang, Ha-seong. "Gyeraneuro bawireul kkaeda: jaebeolgaehyeok soaekjujuundong" [We break a rock with eggs: small shareholders movement to reform the economic conglomerates]. In *Jjagochina bopsida: Chamyeoyeondae gwollyeokgamsiundong 10nyeon* [Let's see if they play with collusion: PSPD's movements to monitor the power for ten years]. Ed. Byeong-jik Cha, 43–58. Seoul: Sigeumchi, 2004.

Jang, Mi-gyeong. 2008. "Damunhwa sahoewa 'sahoetonghap' jedoui heohwangdoen kkum" [Multicultural society and a vainglorious dream of "social integration"]. Personal writing given to Seungsook Moon.

Jeong, Gyu-ho, Seong-su Ju, Seon-mi Yi, and Seong-mi Jo. *Araerobuteoui siminsahoe: siminhwaldongga 30inege deunneunda* [Civil society from below: Listening to thirty citizen activists]. Seoul: Changjakgwabipyeong, 2008.

KOREAN PRIMARY SOURCES

Jeong, Yong-in. "A quarter century of citizens' movements with glory and opprobrium: Can its heyday be returned?" *Weekly Kyunghyang* 1136 (July 28, 2015): 31–33.

Jo, Heung-sik, and Ji-yeon Jang, eds. *Pyeonghwawa bokji, Gyeonggyereul neomeo: Pyeonghwabokjigukkaui jongchijeok jogeongwa juchereul chaja* [Peace and welfare, crossing the boundary: In search for political conditions and subjects of the peace and welfare state], Seoul: Imaejin, 2014.

Jo, Jaeyeon. "Gwollyeok pyeonseunghamyo jeongchidanche byeonjil . . . Moon jeong-buseon 'mansachamtong' yegikkaji" [Changing into a political organization by riding on the political power . . . even like a "free pass" in Moon's administration]. *Munhwa Daily*, March 19, 2020. http://www.munhwa.com/news/news_print.html?no=2020031901031727328001.

KBS News. "Geuttae geusageon: 2011nyeon Oh Sehoonui 'musanggeupsik' seontaekeun?" [That event back then: Oh Sehoon's choice for 'free school meals' in 2011?], November 13, 2014. https://news.kbs.co.kr/news/view.do?ncd=2966268.

Kim, Hyeong-mi. "Sahoejeokgyeongje 'saengtaegye' mandeulda," [The ecosystem for social economy was made.] In *A Twenty-Five Year History of Korean Civil Society Movements*, 349–358. Seoul: Citizens' Movement Information Center, 2014.

Kim, Jung-bae. "Undongui noegwaneul chajara" [Find out the movement's detonator]. In *Ijagochina bopsida*, 274–79. Seoul: Sigeumchi, 2004.

Kim, Sang-jo. "9. Chamyeoyeondaeui gyeongjeminjuhwaundong" [Ch. 9 PSPD's movement to democratize the economy]. In *Chamyeowa yeondaero yeon minjujuuiui sae jipyeong* [New horizon of democracy opened by participation and solidarity]. Ed. Seong-tae Hong, 199–221. Seoul: Areuche, 2004.

Kim, Yang-hui. "Yeoseongdeurui dangsajaundongeuroseoui yeoseongminwuhoe saenghyeop" [Minwuhoe's Life Coop as the movement for women themselves]. In *20nyeonui haengbokeneoji mirae hyanghan huimang sineoji* [Happy Energy for Twenty Years, Hopeful Synergy for the Future]. Proceedings of the 20th Anniversary Policy Symposium, 7–23. Seoul: Minwuhoe, Minwu Coop, 2009.

Kim, Yeon-myeong. "10jang Chamyeoyeondae 'sahoebokjiwiwonhoe' 10nyeonui seong-gwawa seongchal" [Ch. 10 PSPD's 'social welfare committee' a decade of achievement and reflection]. In *Chamyeowa yeondaero yeon minjujuuiui sae jipyeong* [A new horizon of democracy opened by participation and solidarity]. Ed. Seong-tae Hong, 223–37. Seoul: Areuche, 2004.

Kim, Yeon-se. "Self-Employed in S. Korea Face Strong Headwinds." *Korea Herald*, December 16, 2019. http://www.koreaherald.com/view.php?ud=20191216000230#.

Kwon, Mi-hyeok. "Yeoseongminuhoe saenghyeobui uiuiwa gwaje" [The significance of and issues for women's Minwuhoe]. In *Happy Energy for Twenty Years, Hopeful Synergy for the Future*, 24–30.

Mun, Hye-jin. "Choijeosaenggyebojangeun naraui uimuda: gungmingichosaenghwal-bojangbeop jejeongundong" [Mimimum living protection is the state's responsibility: a movement to legislate the National Basic Living Protection Law]. In *Ijagochina bopsida*, 59–68. Seoul: Sigeumchi, 2004.

NE Branch. "2011 jeonggichonghoe" [2011 regular general meeting]. Proceedings of the regular general meeting, January 20, 2011. Seoul: NE Branch.

———. "2012 jeonggichonghoe" [2012 regular general meeting." Proceedings of the regular general meeting, February 2, 2012.

———. "2013 jeonggichonghoe" [2013 regular general meeting]. Proceedings of the regular general meeting, January 29, 2013.

———. "2014 jeonggichonghoe' [2014 regular general meeting]. Proceedings of the regular general meeting, January 22, 2014.

———. "2015 jeonggichonghoe" [2015 regular general meeting]. Proceedings of the regular general meeting, January 28, 2015.

———. "2016 jeonggichonghoe" [2016 regular general meeting]. Proceedings of the regular general meeting, January 28, 2016.

———. "2017 jeonggichonghoe" [2017 regular general meeting]. Proceedings of the regular general meeting, January 19, 2017.

———. "Je20cha jeonggichonghoe" [The 20th regular general meeting]. Proceedings of the regular general meeting, January 25, 2019.

NE Branch. "2018 Dobonggu seongpyeongdeungjeongchaek jean [2018 Dobong Ward Gender Equality Policy Proposal]. In Je20cha jeonggichonghoe, 196-201. Seoul: NE Branch, 2019.

NGO Times, from May of 1993 to January of 2007.

NGO Press, from April of 2007 to December of 2009.

Pak, Won-seok. "Gyeolko jakji anatdeon 'jageungwollichatgi'" ["Finding small rights" that were never small]. In *Jjagochina bopsida*. Ed. Byeong-jik Cha, 185–210. Seoul: Sigeunchi, 2004.

Park, Won-sun. *Sesangeun kkumkkuneun saramdeurui geosida: Chamyeoyeondae silcheongyeongyeongnon.* [The world belongs to those who dream: Notes from practical management of People's Solidarity for Participatory Democracy]. Seoul: Nanam, 2004.

Participatory Society Studies Center. "Jwadam: Chamyeoyeondae 20nyeon, dojeongwa seongchal geurigo saeroun mosaek" [PSPD twenty years, challenge, reflection, and new exploration]. Publication of the talk on June 10, 2014. Seoul: PSPD.

PSPD (People's Solidarity for Participatory Democracy). *Chamyeoyeondae 10nyeonui girok, 1994-2004: Sesangeul bakkuneun siminui him* [PSPD's record of the ten years, 1994-2004: Citizens' power that changed the world]. Seoul: PSPD, 2004.

———. *Sesangeul bakkun 15 kiwodeu: 1994-2009 Chamyeoyeondae 15junyeon* [15 Key words that changed the world: 1994-2009 PSPD's 15th anniversary]. Seoul: PSPD, 2009.

———. "Chamyeoyeondae je17cha jeonggichonghoe: Ttatteutan yeondae salmannaneun sesang" [PSPD 17th regular general meeting: Warm solidarity and world worthy of living]. Seoul: PSPD, 2011.

———. "Chamyeoyeondae je18cha jeonggichonghoe: Siminui himeuro" [PSPD 18th regular general meeting: with citizens' power]. Seoul: PSPD, 2012.

———. "Chamyeoyeondae je19cha jeonggichonghoe: Gonggamgwa haengdong" [PSPD 19th regular general meeting: empathy and action]. Seoul: PSPD, 2013.

———. "Chamyeoyeondae je20cha jeonggichonghoe" [PSPD 20th regular general meeting]. Seoul: PSPD, 2014.

———. *Chamyeoyeondae 20nyeon hwaldong 100seon* [100 selected activities from the twenty-year history of the PSPD]. *Chamyeoyeondae 20nyeonui girok, 1994-2014* [The PSPD's record for twenty years, 1994-2014] vol. 1. Seoul: PSPD. 2014.

———. *Chamyeoyeondae 20nyeon baljachui* [The PSPD's footsteps for twenty years]. *Chamyeoyeondae 20nyeonui girok, 1994-2014*, vol. 2. Seoul: PSPD. 2014.

———. *Chamyeoyeondae 20nyeon jaryo* [PSPD's resources for twenty years]. *Chamyeoyeondae 20nyeonui girok, 1994-2014*. vol. 3., Seoul: PSPD. 2014.

KOREAN PRIMARY SOURCES

———. *Chamyeoyeondae 20junyeon hwaldongbogoseo* [PSPD 20th anniversary activities report]. Seoul: PSPD, 2014.
———. "Chamyeoyeondae je21cha jeonggichonghoe: Haengbokhan chamyeo ttatteutan yeondae" [PSPD 21st regular general meeting: happy participation warm solidarity]. Seoul: PSPD, 2015.
———. "Chamyeoyeondae je22cha jeonggichonghoe: Siminui him" [PSPD 22nd regular general meeting: "people power"]. Seoul: PSPD, 2016.
———. "Chamyeoyeondae je23cha jeonggichonghoe: Siminui him" [PSPD 23rd regular general meeting: "people power"]. Seoul: PSPD, 2017.
———. *Saerogochim daehanminguk* [Newly repairing the Republic of Korea]. Seoul: Imaegin, 2017.
———. "Chamyeoyeondae je24cha jeonggichonghoe: Ttuieora Chamyeoyeondae narara minjujuui" [PSPD 24th regular general meeting: run PSPD fly democracy]. Seoul: PSPD, 2018.
———. "Chamyeoyeondae je25cha jeonggichonghoe: Haengdonghaneun simin hamkke-haneun Chamyeoyeondae" [PSPD 25th regular general meeting: PSPD together with acting citizens]. Seoul: PSPD, 2019.
———. "Chamyeoyeondae 2019 hwaldongbogoseo" [PSPD 2019 annual activities report]. Seoul: PSPD, 2020.
Right Society Citizens Meeting. "Toron: 'Gyowonui jeongchijeok jungnipseonge bichwo bon 'jeongyojoui jeongchitujaeneul malhada!" [Discussion: speaking about the National Teachers' Union's political struggle in light of "school teachers' political neutrality"]. Proceedings of the meeting April 7, 2016.
Ryu, In-ha. "Seoulsi chojunggyo chinhwangyeong musanggeupsik jeonmyeonsihaeng... 'musanggeupsik' nollan ihu 10nyeonman" [Seoul City implementing the environmentally friendly and free meals for entire primary, middle, and high schools . . . in ten years after the 'free school meals' controversy]. *Kyunghyang Newspaper*, February 15, 2021.
Yi, Gyeong-hui. "'Jeongbuga anhanmyeon wuriga handa' . . . 'gyeolsikadong' mogeum iljuil sae 1eok" ["If the government doesn't, we'll do so" . . . a fund-raising for "children missing their meals" reached $100,000 in a week]. *Pressian*, December 22, 2010. https://www.pressian.com/pages/articles/102899?no=102899&ref=kko#0DKU.
Yi, Hyeong-yong. "Gukka, geobeoneonseuro dijainhada" [The state, designed by governance]. In *Hanguksiminsahoeundong 25nyeonsa, 1989–2014* [A twenty-five-year history of Korean civil society movements, 1989–2014], Ed. Citizens' Movements Information Center, 383–88. Seoul: Citizens' Movements Information Center, 2014.
Yi, Sang-jun. "Chamyeoyeondae jeongbuui wiheomseong. Nomuhyeon jeongbuwa dejabu" [Danger of the PSPD government. Déjà vu with Roy Moo-hyun government]. *Deilian* April 10, 2018. https://dailian.co.kr/printPage2.html.
Yoon, Ji-won, and Mira Choe. "Korea's Self-Employment Rate at 25 Percent, 5th Highest in OECD Category." *Maeil Business Newspaper*, September 30, 2019. https://pulsenews.co.kr/print.php?year=2019&no=780684.

INDEX

Italicized page numbers indicate photos.

accelerated wealth accumulation, 179, 181, 214
activism: actors involvement in, 8–9, 15; internet-based, 7; marketing to members and supporters technique, 89, 108–111, 244n61; professionalized, 211–214; protests against U.S. beef importation and mad cow disease, 63, 72, 111, 139, 145, 150, 237n42; traditional compared to civic for institutional or social change, 40; West market framework for, 88. *See also* civic activism; paid activists and reproduction; volunteer members and activists
activism for institutional and social change, by DFS, 237n39; auxiliary research center for, 79, 81; campaign against sexual violence, 72, 73, 74, 99, 170, 254n8; for environmental issues, 73, 74–75; with food co-op, 73, 74–75; for gender equality in family, 73, 74; mass media monitoring by, 73; social services provision of, 21, 73–74, 81, 154–155; volunteer, 82; for women's bodies and health, 73, 75–76, 76
activism for institutional and social change, by PSPD, 60, 61, 62; on electoral politics reform, 61–63; for mobile phone charges reduction, 64; to reform use of Seoul Plaza, 63–64, 94; to restore small rights by, 64, 133
activism for institutional and social change, of FOA, 85, 86, 195–199; investigations of migrant issues, 81; for native South Koreans and migrants personal interactions, 81, 182–195
actors: activism involvement by, 8–9, 15; capital and, 9; citizens' organizations as, 25; collaborative ruling of nonstate, 27, 124–152; for democratization, 15; nonstate, 13, 14, 27, 206; PSPD mobilization of, 133, 140; YMCA as Independence Movement major, 41
administered mass organizations (AMOs): Kim Young-sam and, 32–33, 226n33; removal of special favors given to, 32

INDEX

advocacy organizations: citizens' organizations growth and, 28–29; in U.S., 28–29, 224n17, 233n5

Ahn, Chang-ho, 41

AMOs. *See* administered mass organizations

anticommunism: as New Right ideology, 38; NTU and, 41

Anti-Discrimination Law (2022), PSPD enactment support of, 62

archival and field research (2004–2020), of author, 18; *NGO Times* use for, 19

Asia Civil Society Study Center: on citizens' organizations financial situations, 241n20; on NGOs financial instability, 34–35; on NGOs volunteer members, 43–44

Asia Education and Culture Studies Center, 195–196

Asian financial crisis (1997–1998): cultural fever for investment after, 221n44; Kim Dae-jung and, 2–3; neoliberal governance spread after, 36, 247n3

authentic education, 41, 229n68

auxiliary research center, for DFS activism for institutional and social change, 79, 81

Bauman, Zygmunt, 11, 13

Beautiful Foundation, 240n10; crowdfunding of, 95; FOA indirect corporate funding from, 90

Blee, Kathleen M., 6

Bourdieu, Pierre, 6, 144, 220n25; on cultural/symbolic capital, 46; theory of social space and political fields, 8–9

Brown, Wendy, 11, 124, 220n35

business corporations, 11, 12; citizens' organization independence from, 90; social contribution programs of, 88, 90–93

capital: actors and, 9; of political authority, 9–10; politics maximization of accumulation of, 26

capital accumulation. *See* wealth accumulation

capitalism: financialization of, 11–12; mode of ruling and economic system of, 11; neoliberal, 2, 22, 26

CCEJ. *See* Citizens Coalition for Economic Justice

Central Association of Consumers Cooperatives, 42

charitable activities: paternalism of, 42; volunteer activists for, 91–92

childcare center project, of DFS, 155, 158; Dream Sprouter after-school childcare center of GY Branch, 156–157, 169, 171–172, 176, 258nn68–69; Infants and Toddlers Care Act and, 156; Low Birth and Aging Society Basic Law, 156; Roh Moo-hyun childcare privatization and, 156; Unlimited Carework Project and, 156

Cho, Hui-yeon, 29

citizens' activities support center foundation, 45

Citizens Coalition for Economic Justice (CCEJ), 26, 30–31, 36–37

citizens' movement organizations (*siminundongdanche*), 28; civil society through democratization of, 24; democratization movement of 1980s and, 23; Kang on, 31; of middle-class reformative activism, 17, 30

Citizens' Movements Information Center: *Korean Civil Society Year book of*, 26; *Korean NGOs Directory* of, 26; leading citizens' organizations establishment of, 26

citizens' organizations (*simindanche*): as actors, 25; Asia Civil Society Study Center on financial situations of, 241n20; from comparative historical perspective, 46–48; demands on ruling elite from, 46; democracy and neoliberalism contradictory relationship, 22; democratic civic identity of, 42; democratic social change through, 4, 16, 24; democratization in 1990s

INDEX

and, 19; development of, 19–20; diversification of, 7, 49; East Asia Institute on public trust of, 230n79; economic crises as precipitating events for, 19–20; equality and solidarity promotion and pursuit by, 20; financial and political independence from state by, 20; funding denials for, 35, 227n42; funding lack since NPO Support Act, 35; individual donations decrease for, 227n41; institutional and social change focus of, 20; moral codes of, 20, 25, 31–46; neoliberal globalization in 1990s and, 19; older form of NGOs and, 25; political neutrality perception for, 37; professional middle-class leadership in, 24; rapid growth in 1990s and 2000s, 24; social change democratization by, 7; transformation of, 240n15; transnational advocacy organizations and, 28–29

citizens' playground project, of PSPD, 66–67

Citizens' Solidarity for the General Election, PSPD and, 62–63

Citizens United for the Environment, 26

civic activism, 4–6; for democratization, 21; of DFS food co-ops, 96; market facilitation and constraint of, 203–205; market ethos and reenvisioning for fun, enjoyable, sustainable, 89, 111–116; of middle class, 48; neoliberal governance enabling and undermining of, 206–211; neoliberalism democratizing of, 214–216; politics of status distinction and, 24; study research methodology, 16–19; as symbolic and political actions, 7–10; traditional activism compared to institutional or social change, 40

civic identity politics, DFS and, 171–176; as movement organization, 195–199; small groups for, 168–170; stagnant membership problem for, 170

civic identity politics, FOA and, 195, 197–199; religious organizations for migrant support centers, 196

civic identity politics, PSPD and: of college students, 148–149; division of labor in, 140; grassroots participation challenge in, 141–142; mobile communication technology and, 150–151; of older-generation, 149–150

civil society: citizen's movement representation of, 24; democratization and study of, 221n40; NGO discourse of, 27–28; *NGO Times* discourse of, 25–26; as public place for social movements, 31; studies of Korean history of, 47

civil society organizations (*siminsahoedanche*), 39, 229n64; Jeong on role of, 40; Kim Dae-jung financial assistance to, 34; *Korean NGOs Directory of 2006* on, 38, 229n63; Lee Myung-bak funding to, 35, 80, 238n52; multiculturalism of, 181, 191, 200; nonprofit nature of, 28

Civil Society Organizations' Common Policy Council, 32

Cold War: capitalism victory over communism with end of, 2; globalization with neoliberal capitalism and procedural democracy after, 26; neoliberal globalization and, 217n3

collaborative law and policymaking, of PSPD, 21, 72, 124; civic identity politics, 140–151; movements to expand social welfare, 126–130; movements to protect small business owners and citizen financial consumers, 126, 133–137; movements to reform big business, 126, 130–133; movements to stop KORUS FTA, 58, 125, 126, 137–140; political and economic powers monitoring, 126–140

collaborative ruling, of nonstate actors, 21, 27, 124–152

INDEX

Collection of Donation Prohibition Law (1951), 33
commercial culture, positive affirmation of, 113
Committee to Promote Wholesome Development of National Territory, 33
community-based organizations, grassroots participation for, 45
conservative administration (2008–2017), 19
conservative government, of South Korea, 3; political neutrality and, 234n16; PSPD conflict with, 60
conservatives, progressives culture war with, 234n16
co-op. *See* food cooperative
corporatization of activism: Dauvergne and Lebaron on, 88; global trend of, 89
Council for Dealing with Foreign Workers' Human Rights, 230n69
Council for the Second National Construction, Kim Dae-jung launch of, 58
Council of Democratic Press Movements, 40–41
Council of Doctors Practicing Humanism, 40
credit cards, proliferation of, 12, 135–136
crowdfunding, of Beautiful Foundation, 95
cultural fever investment, after Asian financial crisis, 221n44
cultural projects education about migrants, of FOA, 181, 192, 198–199; to overcome ignorance and prejudice, 189; participatory events for, 190–191
cultural/symbolic capital, Bourdieu on, 46
culture: commercial positive affirmation, 113; conservatives and progressives war, 234n16; neoliberalism transformation of, 2

Dardot, Pierre, 11, 220n35; on political nature of debt, 12
Dauvergne, Peter, 88

democracy: as branded product in West, 15; civic activism and, 5–6; instrumentalization of, 15, 17; as mode of ruling, 45; neoliberalism relationship with, 13–16, 202–216; political participation monopoly situation in, 9; as value and product, 5–6, 15, 26, 30
democratic appropriations, of neoliberal governance, 29–30; moral code of diversity, 38–40; moral code of grassroots participation, 42–46; moral code of independence from state, 31–37; moral code of movements for institutional and social change, 40–42
Democratic Friends Society (DFS): on employment insecurity, 22, 162–166, 178; feminist medium size organizations of, 16, 21, 55–56, 67–78; on free school meals for children, 153, 166–168, 257n58; local nature of, 78; marketing to potential and current members and supporters, 111; mass media monitoring by, 73; membership fees as support for, 103, 105–106; membership of, 67, 78, 104, 236n38, 237n41; moral code of, 55; motto of, 51; neoliberal governance enabling and undermining of, 207–209; nonprofit food co-op of, 67, 67–68; political party participation prohibition by, 237n50; reenvisioning fun, enjoyable, sustainable civic activism of, 115; social services provision of, 21, 73–74, 154–155. *See also* activism for institutional and social change, by DFS; civic identity politics, DFS and; financial and political independence from government, of DFS; Goyang Branch, of DFS; grassroots people participation, of DFS; Northeast Branch, of DFS; private-public partnerships and grassroots participation, of DFS
Democratic Lawyers' Group, 41
democratic social change, through citizens' organizations, 4

INDEX

democratization: actors for, 15; citizens' movement organizations and, 23, 24; citizens' organizations and, 7, 19; civic activism for, 21, 214–216; neoliberal globalization and civic activism, 25; neoliberal transformation in, 2, 3; progressive social groups push for, 30; public administration and civil society studies of, 221n40
deregulation, 125, 127, 132, 247n3, 250n19; high interest rates and, 136–137
DFS. *See* Democratic Friends Society
differentiation, Bourdieu on social world and principle of, 8–9
diversity: as citizens' organization moral code, 25; of citizens organizations, 7; of civic activism, 7
Doing-Together Citizens' Action, 45
Dream Sprouter after-school childcare center, of GY Branch, 156–157, 169, 171–172, 176, 258nn68–69

East Asia Institute, on citizens' organizations public trust, 230n79
Ebert Foundation Fund, for DFS women employment projects, 162
economic growth and export expansion, of Roh Moo-hyun, 137
economic inequality, 247n3; neoliberal globalization and, 10, 125; PSPD small shareholders movement and, 126, 130–133, 250n18
Economic Planning Board, 227n42
economic polarization, 247n3
economy: Joseaon Dynasty prospering of, 47; Simmel on money-based, 243n54
education: authentic, 41, 229n68; for credentials and certificates, 12; DFS events about feminism, 75–76, 76; DFS on free school meals for children, 153, 166–168, 257n58; FOA cultural projects about migrants, 181, 189–192, 198–199; global leaders through reformative, 1–2; NE Branch women lifetime, 256n47; promotion of democratic citizenship, 32; PSPD program for citizens', 109; social status and, 20
egalitarian society, of South Korea, 247n3
Election Law, 61–62; prohibition of NGOs election campaign involvement, 63; PSPD reform of, 63
electoral politics: NE and GY branches participation in, 73; PSPD on reform of, 61–63
employment insecurity, DFS on, 22, 162–166, 178
Environmental Foundation, 240n10
environmental issues, DFS activism for, 73, 74–75
equality: civic activism constraint for, 20; mode of ruling practice of, 5. *See also* gender equality

family, DFS activism for gender equality in, 73, 74
Family Law, DFS activism to reform, 73
Federation of Freedom United, 33
feminist organizations, of DFS, 16, 21, 55–56, 67–78
financial and political independence from government, of DFS, 72, 85, 154–155, 237n45; food co-op stores for, 67, 67–70, 70; gender equality and women's human rights promotion, 68; government funding and, 70–71; pop-up restaurant for fund-raising, 69, 69; volunteer activists in, 79
financial and political independence from government, of FOA, 56, 85; bank contribution end and, 91; government funding rejection, 79–80; through membership fees and donations, 79, 107; moral code of, 79
financial and political independence from government, of PSPD, 57, 85; conflict with conservative government, 60; General Election Campaign of 2000 led by, 59; government positions of, 58–59; Kim Dae-jung launch of Council for the Second National Construction, 58; KORUS FTA opposition by,

financial and political independence from government (*continued*) 58, 125, 126, 137–140; political neutrality violation by, 59–60, 233n12; progressive government cooperation with, 58, 60; during Roh Moo-hyun's government, 58

financial dimension, of independence from state: AMOs special favors removal, 32; Civil Society Organizations' Common Policy Council for, 32; civil society organizations financial assistance and, 34; on law revisions for fundraising activities restrictions, 33; NGOs financial instability, 34–35; Nonprofit Organization Support Act on funding, 34

financialization, of capitalism, 11–12

FOA. *See* Friends of Asia

food cooperative (co-op), of DFS, 67, 67–70, 70; activism for, 73, 74–75; commercial stores weakening of, 99–100; efforts for women farmers as suppliers, 97; food product imports, 97–98; grassroots participation in, 77–78; GY and NE social relations market alternative of, 89, 93, 95–100; KORUS FTA and campaign for, 96; on organic food products, 96–97

France, NGOs in, 223n5

free market: with liberal democracy, 15; market fundamentalism belief in doctrine of, 88; West promotion of, 2

Free Trade Agreement (FTA), 30; Lee Myung-bak ratification of, 138; NAFTA, 137, 251n35; as mechanism of neoliberal globalization, 137; PNMH to stop, 138–139. *See also* South Korea-U.S. Free Trade Agreement

Friends of Asia (FOA): Beautiful Foundation and Human Rights Foundation indirect corporate funding, 90; investigative research of, 80; Korean language class of, 100–102, 181–189, 197–198, 200, 259n2; marketing to potential and current members and supporters, 111; membership fees as support for, 79, 107; membership of, 79, 104; on migrant issues, 22, 78–79, 81; moral code of, 55; motto of, 51; as movement organization, 195–199; neoliberal governance enabling and undermining of, 209–211; paid activists constraints for, 121; physical location of, 54, 54–55; prefigurative practice of migrant solidarity building, 89, 93, 100–102, 122; profit-earning project of, 93; reenvisioning fun, enjoyable, sustainable civic activism of, 115–116; small, local organization of, 16; social change movement with government partnership, 22. *See also* activism for institutional and social change, of FOA; civic identity politics, FOA and; financial and political independence from government, of FOA; grassroots people participation, of FOA

FTA. *See* Free Trade Agreement

funding. *See* government funding

fund-raising activities: of DFS pop-up restaurant for, 69, 69; GY and NE Branches Women's Foundation campaign, 90; law revisions for restrictions on, 33; mass media criticism of PSPD, 90; professionalization of, 92

GATT. *See* General Agreement on Tariffs and Trade

gender equality, 238n51; DFS activism for family, 73, 74; DFS promotion of, 68; mass media on, 73, 76; South Korea low level of, 236n37

General Agreement on Tariffs and Trade (GATT), 27, 225n19

General Election Campaign (2000), PSPD leading of, 59

gift economy of donations, 89, 93–95, 122, 239n7

global leaders, through reformative education, 1–2

INDEX

governance: collaborative ruling of nonstate actors and, 21, 27, 124–152; government, business, civil society partnership in, 11; of state, 11. *See also* neoliberal governance
governmentality, Foucault concept of, 220n35
Government Cooperation Forum, on partnership and new governance, 124
government funding: citizens' organizations denial of, 35, 227n42; DFS financial and political independence from government and, 70–71; FOA rejection of, 79–80; Lee Myung-bak nonprofit civil society organizations, 35, 80, 238n52; in mode of ruling, 34
Goyang (GY) Branch, of DFS, 16; beginning in 1996, 68; childcare focus of, 254n7, 255n19; counseling center and domestic and sexual violence shelter, 72, 73, 74, 99, 170, 254n8; Dream Sprouter after-school childcare center, 156–157, 169, 171–172, 176, 258nn68–69; electoral politics participation by, 73; local government cooperation by, 71–72; membership of, 78, 104, 236n38, 237n41; on mentoring, 255n15; paid activists constraints for, 119–121; physical location of, 53, *53*; public funding for, 71; public organizations of, 254n13; restaurant workers, 256n36; self-employment and, 163; Women's Foundation fundraising campaign for, 90
Goyang City Local Childcare Centers United, 157
grassroots people participation, 211–214; as citizens' organization moral code, 25; by citizens organizations, 20; civic identity politics and, 140–151; collaborative law and policymaking and undermining of, 21, 27, 124–152; practice of, 5; volunteer activists in, 43–44
grassroots people participation, of DFS, 22; education events about feminism, 75–76, *76*; in food co-op work, 77–78; small group gatherings for, 76–77, *77*, 167–168, 178. *See also* private-public partnerships and grassroots participation, of DFS
grassroots people participation, of FOA, 81, 83, 83–84, *84*; migrant marriage focus of, 82; moral code of, 82
grassroots people participation, of PSPD, 21, 55–56, 64, *65*, 85; citizens' playground project and, 66–67; civic identity politics challenge to, 141–142; lay members decision-making and officers, 66; MG small gatherings, 65. *See also* collaborative law and policymaking, of PSPD
Gross, Michael L., 6
GY. *See* Goyang Branch

Hatred of Democracy (Rancière), 202
hierarchy, 20, 21
Human Rights Foundation, 90, 240n10
Hwaseong Foreigners Protection Center: FOA majung visits to, 181, 192–195, 198, 260n21; migrants detained in, 180, 181; unhealthy living conditions at, 193–194

IMF. *See* International Monetary Fund
In, Myong-jin, 230n69
Independence Movement, YMCA as major actor in, 41
independence from state, as citizens' organizations moral code, 25
individualization/fragmentation of human actions, in market framework, 20
Infants and Toddlers Care Act (2004), 156
institutional and social change: as citizen's organization moral code, 25, 36–37, 40–42; citizens' organizations focus on, 20; moral code of movements for, 25, 36–37, 40–42. *See also* activism for institutional and social change, by DFS; activism for institutional and social change, by PSPD; activism for institutional and social change, of FOA

instrumentalization, of democracy, 15, 17
international development promotion by UN, IMF, WB, WTO funding of, 27
International Monetary Fund (IMF), 217n5; Kim Dae-jung acceptance of rescue package of, 2–3, 30, 36, 131; neoliberal economic restructuring and, 26; UN international development funded by, 27
internet-based activism, 7
investment, cultural fever after Asian financial crisis, 221n44

Jeong, Chan-yong, 40
Jin, Jung-gwon, 234n16
Joseon Dynasty: economic prosperity during, 47; middle strata in, 24

Kang, Mun-gyu, 31
K Bank advertising campaign, 87
Kim Dae-jung (1998–2003): Asian financial crisis and, 2–3; citizens' organization proximity to government with, 37; civil society organizations financial assistance, 34; Council for the Second National Construction launched by, 58; IMF rescue package acceptance by, 2–3, 30, 36, 131; National Basic Living Protection Law established by, 128–129; NPO Support Act established by, 28; NTU legalization under, 41; office for civil affairs of, 228n53; PSPD collaboration with, 128; PSPD officers in administration of, 233n12; social welfare system of, 129–130; women's policy institutionalization under, 72
Kim Young-sam (1993–1998): AMOs and, 32–33, 226n33; neoliberal economic restructuring of, 29–30; neoliberal globalization pursuit by, 2; new big business policy of, 131; *NGO Times* publication during administration of, 26; NTU persecution by, 41; PSPD officers in administration of, 233n12; project of worldification promotion by, 2, 30

Korea: state-society relations in traditional, 24; studies of history of civil society in, 47
Korean Citizens' Organizations Council, National Citizens' Organizations Conference of, 36
Korean Federation of YMCA, Kang on citizens' movement of, 31
Korean language classes, of FOA, 100–102, 181–182, 188, 197–198, 259n2; migrant worker enrichment through, 189; migrant worker profiles in, 184–185; student volunteers for, 183; volunteer activists for, 183, 185–187, 200–201
Korean NGOs Directory, 2006: on civil society organizations, 38, 229n63; on NGOs diversity, 39
Korean Progressive Coalition, Lee Myung-bak funding denial for, 35
Korea Telecommunications (KT), PSPD lawsuit against, 64
KORUS FTA. *See* South Korea-U.S. Free Trade Agreement
KT. *See* Korea Telecommunications

labor market, 2, 253n59
labor movement, 17, 247n3
Laval, Christian, 11, 220n35; on political nature of debt, 12
law: Anti-Discrimination Law, 62; Collection of Donation Prohibition Law, 33; Election Law, 61–63; Family Law, 73; Infants and Toddlers Care Act, 156; Low Birth and Aging Society Basic Law, 156; Multicultural Family Support Act, 190–191; National Basic Living Protection Law, 128–130, 249n8; NPO Support Act, 28, 34, 35
Lebaron, Geneviève, 88
Lee Myung-bak (2008–2013): civil society organization funding, 35, 80, 238n52; election of, 38; FTA ratification bill of, 138; neoliberal globalization and, 30; Seoul Plaza use restrictions by, 63–64

INDEX

liberal democracy: free market identification with, 15; global promotion of, 22; neoliberal economic restructuring as precondition of, 3–4; neoliberalism impact on, 13
Liberal Democracy in Crisis (Toplišek), 202
Lifetime Education Act and Ordinance (1999), 109
local government, GY and NE cooperation with, 71–72
Local Health Ecosystem project, 173
Low Birth and Aging Society Basic Law (2004), 156

mad cow disease, protests against U.S. beef importation and, 63, 72, 111, 139, 145, 150, 237n42
majung visits to Hwaseong Foreigners Protection Center, of FOA, 181, 192–195, 198, 260n21
market framework: of activism in West, 88; citizens organizations resistance to, 20; economic activities tool of, 20; human actions individualization/fragmentation in, 20; for neoliberalism, 3, 20–21, 87–123; New Right on importance of, 38; paid activists and reproduction constrained by, 21, 116–121; for politics and society organization, 87–88; profit maximization in, 20
marketing: global trend of branded good sales and joint, 92–93; to potential members and supporters, 89, 108–111, 244n61; web, 244n62
market model of activism, in West, 88
market techniques, 122; activism marketing to members and supporters, 89, 108–111, 244n61; membership fees as commitment indicator, 89, 103–108, 243n48; reenvisioning civic activism as fun, enjoyable, sustainable, 89, 111–116
mass media: DFS monitoring of, 73; on gender equality, 73, 76; National Neo-Conservatism United and, 38; PSPD fund-raising criticism by, 90; social movements led by, 58; social services recruitment use of, 43–44
Members' Gathering (MG), of PSPD, 65, 141
membership: of DFS, 67, 78, 104, 236n38, 237n41; of FOA, 79, 104; of PSPD, 57, 104, 251n43, 252n45
membership fees, as market technique, 89, 103–108; citizens' organizations membership base cleaning up, 103–104; of DFS branches, 103, 105–106; FOA and, 79, 107; as individual capacity extension, 105–107; PSPD and, 103–107, 243n48
MG. *See* Members' Gathering
middle-class: CCEJ on ordinary citizens represented by, 31; citizens' movements reformative activism by, 17, 46–47; citizens' organizations professional leadership by, 24; civic activism of, 48; literary works publication by, 48
migrants. *See* Friends of Asia
militant street protests, 7
military dictatorship, people's movement against, 23, 223n3
minjungundong. *See* people's movement
mobile communication technology: PSPD activism to reduce phone charges, 64; PSPD civic identity politics and, 150–151
mode of ruling: capitalist economic system and, 11; democracy as, 45; equality, self-determination, grassroots people participation practices in, 5; global spread of neoliberal, 14; government funding in, 34; neoliberalism as, 10–13, 27
money-based economy, Simmel on, 243n54
moral code, of diversity, 25, 40; civil society organizations list, 38–39; National Neo-Conservatism United and, 38; New Right and, 38
moral code, of grassroots participation, 25; citizens' activities support center foundation for, 45; citizens'

moral code (*continued*)
  organizations decline, 44–45; citizens' organizations democratic civic identity, 42; community-based local organizations for, 45; internal and external criticism of, 43, 49, 66; on law and policy reforms, 43; procedural democracy promotion in, 44–45; Progressive Network for internet users, 43; volunteer activists and, 43–44
moral code, of independence from state: activism directed toward government, 32; citizens' organizations enter into institutional politics, 25, 36–37; democratic citizenship education promotion and, 32; financial and political dimension of, 32; on law revisions for fund-raising activities restrictions, 33; of PSPD, 57–60; registration system and, 36; Song on, 32; UN promotion of NGOs and, 31–32
moral code, of movements for institutional and social change, 25, 36–37; NTU and, 41; paternalism of charitable activities and, 42; professional organizations for, 40–41; YMCA and, 41
moral codes, of citizens' organizations, 89; diversity, 25, 38–40; grassroots participation, 25, 42–45, 49, 66; independence from state, 25, 32–37, 57–60; institutional and social change movements, 25, 36–37, 40–42
movement organization, FOA meanings of, 195–199
Multicultural Family Support Act (2008), 190–191
multiculturalism: appropriation by government of, 79, 182, 190; of civil society organizations, 181, 191, 200; FOA prefigurative activism and, 181–182, 186

NAFTA. *See* North America Free Trade Agreement
National Association of Parents for Genuine Education (NAPGE), 252n52

National Basic Living Protection Law, 249n8; Kim Dae-jung establishment of, 128–129; Park Geun-hye attempt to undo, 128; PSPD support of, 130
National Citizens' Organizations Conference, of Korean Citizens' Organizations Council, 36
National Neo-Conservatism United. *See Sinbosujuui jeongukyeonhap*
National Network for School Meals, 166
national pension system, 249n8
National Teachers' Union (NTU), 41
NE. *See* Northeast Branch
neoliberal capitalism: Cold War globalization with, 26; flexible labor under, 2; neoliberal governance and, 22
neoliberal economic restructuring, 250n19; credit card debt crisis and, 12, 135–136; deregulation and high interest rates, 136–137; financialization of economy in, 135–136; of Kim Young-sam, 29–30; as liberal democracy precondition, 3–4; NGOs and, 10; WB, IMF and WTO on, 26; worldification project and, 2, 30
neoliberal globalization, 1; Cho on, 29; economic inequality and, 10, 125; flexible labor under, 2; FTA mechanism for, 137; hierarchical division of labor and, 21; Kim Young-sam pursuit of, 2; mobile transnational capital and, 10; South Korea in 1990s shaped by, 2; West promotion of, 217n3
neoliberal governance, 14; Asian financial crisis spread of, 36, 247n3; civic activism enabled and undermined by, 206–211; collaborative law and policymaking undermining grassroots participation, 21, 27, 124–152; democracy undermined by, 24; democratic appropriation of, 29–46; FOA and, 22; GY and NE branches of DFS and, 21; hierarchy and, 21; multiculturalism and, 191; neoliberal capitalism challenge from, 22; PSPD and, 21

INDEX

neoliberalism: democracy relationship with, 13–16, 202–216; democratizing civic activism and, 214–216; as destructive force, 13–14; development of, 261n3; liberal democracy impacted by, 13; market framework for, 3; as mode of ruling, 10–13, 14; as political rationality, 10–13; political rationality of, 3; professionalized activism and grassroots participation, 211–214; transformation of state power, 11
neoliberal resilience, Madariaga study on, 14
neoliberal transformation: citizens' movement and, 17; culture from, 2; democratization with, 2, 3; Madariaga study on, 15; political nature of, 3; of state, 11, 28; in U.S. of markets ascendance, 3
New Job Women's Internship, 165
New Right: anticommunism as ideology of, 38; on market importance, 38; moral code of diversity and, 38
New Social Movements, racial, ethnic, sexual minorities empowerment and, 28–29
New Village Movement Association, 33, 226n33, 229n68
NGO Press, *NGO Times* replaced by, 26
NGOs. *See* nongovernmental organizations
NGO Times: archival research use of, 19; citizens' organizations publication of, 26; civil society discourse of, 25–26; *NGO Press* replacement of, 26; president sexual harassment scandal, 26, 224n7; UNDP conference sponsored by, 23
nongovernmental organizations (NGOs): Asia Civil Society Movement Research Center on volunteer members for, 43–44; Asia Civil Society Study Center on financial instability of, 34–35; citizens' organizations and older form of, 25; civil society discourse of, 27–28; Election Law prohibition of election campaign involvement by, 63; in France, 223n5; government funding of, 34; *Korean NGO Directory of 2006* on diversity of, 39; neoliberal economic restructuring and, 10; role in participatory democracy, 23; tax exemptions and tax benefits preference for, 35; UN partnership with, 27; UN revival of, 26–27; volunteer activists in, 243n46; Yang on sales of goods during fund-raising campaigns, 92
Nonprofit Organization (NPO) Support Act (1998), 34; citizen's organizations lack of funding since, 35; Kim Dae-Jung establishment of, 28
nonstate actors, 13, 14, 27, 206
North America Free Trade Agreement (NAFTA), 137, 251n35
Northeast (NE) Branch, of DFS, 16; beginning in 1992, 68; electoral politics participation by, 73; financial support for, 237n48; lifetime education for women of, 256n47; local government cooperation with, 71–72; membership of, 78, 104, 236n38, 237n41; new job center of, 256n51; paid activists constraints for, 119–121; physical location of, 53; postpartum service job, 255n26; public funding for, 71; Support Center for Elderly Care Workers of, 165–166; women's health focus of, 255n20, 255n28; women's center of, 256n46; Women's Foundation fund-raising campaign for, 90
NPO. *See* Nonprofit Organization Support Act
NTU. *See* National Teachers' Union

OECD. *See* Organization of Economic Cooperation and Development
Oh, Gwan-yeong, 45
100 Voters' Committee, 63
Organization of Economic Cooperation and Development (OECD), 242n21, 247n3; country self-employment rate, 250n27

paid activists and reproduction constraints, 21, 116; alternative career options and, 117; for DFS GY and NE branches, 119–121; for FOA, 121; for PSPD, 117–118

Pan-National Movement Headquarters (PNMH), to stop FTA, 138–139

Park Geun-hye (2013–2017): attempt to undo National Basic Living Protection Law, 128; citizens' organizations funding denial by, 35

participatory democracy: NGOs role in, 23; of Roh Moo-hyun, 35, 190–191

paternalism, of charitable activities, 42

people's movement (*minjungundong*): citizens' movement and, 30, 225n22; middle-class professional as leaders of, 23–24; against military dictatorship, 23; workers, farmers, urban poor in, 24; workers, peasants, marginalized social groups focus of, 17, 30

People's Solidarity for Participatory Democracy (PSPD), 16, 26, 233n7; actors mobilized by, 133, 140; Anti-Discrimination Law support by, 62; business corporation donations indirect link to, 90; central citizens' organization position of, 232n3; citizens' education program of, 109; Citizens' Solidarity for the General Election and, 62–63; on Election Law reform, 63; gift economy of donations for, 89, 93–95, 122, 239n7; lay members as volunteer members, 142–144, 252n51; local branches creation reluctance, 232n4; marketing to potential and current members and supporters, 109–111, 244n61; mass media criticism on fund-raising by, 90; membership fees as support for, 103–107, 243n48; membership of, 57, 104, 251n43, 252n45; moral code of, 55; motto of, 51; neoliberal governance enabling and undermining of, 206–207; paid activists constraints for, 117–119, 246n85; physical location of, 51–52, 52; policy reform and, 21, 85, 125–126, 130–133; on public interests, 125; publicity efforts of, 110–111; as quasi-political party, 126; reenvisioning fun, enjoyable, sustainable civic activism of, 113–114; social minorities protection and support by, 16; on South Korea naval vessel *Cheonan* sinking, 235n18; on staff activists professionalization, 146–148; Youth Intern program of, 240n16. *See also* activism for institutional and social change, by PSPD; civic identity politics, PSPD and; collaborative law and policymaking, of PSPD; financial and political independence from government, of PSPD; grassroots people participation, of PSPD

Philosophy of Money, The (Simmel), 87

PNMH. *See* Pan-National Movement Headquarters

policy reform, PSPD and, 21, 85, 125–126, 130–133

political actions, civic activism as, 7–10

political authority, capital of, 9–10

political dimension, of independence from state, 32

political nature of debt, Dardot and Laval on, 12

political neutrality: conservative government and, 234n16; PSPD controversy of, 59–60, 233n12

political participation, democracy monopoly situation of, 9

political rationality: Brown, Dardot and Laval on, 220n35; of neoliberalism, 3, 10–13

prefigurative activism, of FOA, 259n1; cultural projects education about migrants, 181, 189–192, 198–199; Korean language classes, 100–102, 181–189, 197–198, 200–201, 259n2; majung visits to Hwaseong Foreigners Protection Center, 181, 192–195, 198, 260n21; multiculturalism and, 181–182,

INDEX

186; neoliberalism enabling and constraining of, 199–200
prefigurative practices, 243n42; of FOA for migrant solidarity building, 89, 93, 100–102, 122
private-public partnerships and grassroots participation, of DFS, 153–154, 169–179; childcare center project, 155, 156–158; GY childcare focus, 254n7, 255n19; women's employment projects, 155, 162–166; women's food work for children, 155, 166–168; women's health networks, 155, 158–161
privatization, 10, 125, 127; Roh Moo-hyun public childcare, 156; wealth accumulation and, 19, 147, 148, 204, 214
procedural democracy, 5; grassroots promotion of, 44–45; neoliberalism facilitation of, 14, 223n3; South Korea military dictatorship replaced with, 16–17
professionalization, 20; of fund-raising, 92; PSPD on staff activists, 146–148
professionalized activism, 211–214
profit maximization, in market framework, 20
progressive administration (1998–2007), 19; PSPD cooperation with, 21, 58, 60
Progressive Network, for internet users, 43
progressive political parties, 236n33; conservatives culture war with, 234n16
PSPD. *See* People's Solidarity for Participatory Democracy
public administration, democratization and study of, 221n40
publicity efforts, of PSPD, 110–111
public resources: civic activism to promote and protect, 6; neoliberalism destruction of, 14

quasi-political party, PSPD as, 126

racial, ethnic, sexual minorities empowerment, New Social Movements and, 28–29

Rancière, Jacques, 5, 202
reform-oriented activism, 24
registration system, citizens' organizations request for, 36
reinvestment practices, 12
research methodology, of author: archival and field research from 2004 to 2020, 18; interviews in, 18; *NGO Times* archival research, 19; PSPD, DFS, FOA organizations in, 16–17; publication review for, 18–19
Residents' Welfare Centers, 191
Right Living Movement (RLM), 33, 228n51
Roh Moo-hyun (2003–2008): citizens' organizations KORUS FTA opposition funding denial, 35; citizens' organizations proximity to government under, 37; on economic growth and export expansion, 137; impeachment efforts against, 229n59; KORUS FTA and, 3, 35; neoliberal globalization and, 30; NTU and, 41; participatory democracy of, 35, 190–191; PSPD during, 58; public childcare privatization by, 156; suicide of, 63; women's policy institutionalization under, 72

self-employment, 117; GY Branch and, 163; South Korea rate of, 250n27
Seoul Plaza, PSPD activism to reform use of, 63–64, 94
sexual violence, DFS campaign against, 72, 73, 74, 99, 170, 254n8
simindanche. *See* citizens' organizations
siminsahoedanche. *See* civil society organizations
siminundongdanche. *See* citizens' movement organizations
Simmel, Georg, 87, 108, 253n55; on money-based economy, 243n54
Sinbosujuui jeongukyeonhap (National Neo-Conservatism United), 38
small group gatherings, for DFS grassroots participation, 76–77, 77, 167–168, 178

small rights, PSPD activism to restore, 64, 133
small shareholders movement, PSPD and, 126, 130–133, 250n18
social change: as citizens' organization moral code, 25; citizens' organizations democratization of, 4, 7, 16, 24; citizens' organizations focus on, 20, 230n79; middle-class citizens contribution to, 31. *See also* institutional and social change
social contribution programs, of business corporations, 88, 121; for FOA, 90–91; global trend of joint marketing and branded goods sales in, 92–93; GY and NE branches of DFS indirect link to business donations, 90; professionalization of fund-raising, 92; PSPD indirect link to donations, 90
social movements: civic activism old and new forms for, 7; civil society as public space for, 31; identity-based service provision of, 233n5; internet-based activism as new form of, 7; mass media leading of, 58; militant street protests as new form of, 7; neoliberalism as external to, 7; New Social Movements, 28–29; Tilly on, 231n87; transformation of, 240n15
social relations market alternatives: food co-op, 89, 93, 95–100, 122; gift economy of donations, 89, 93–95, 122, 239n7; prefigurative practice of migrant solidarity building, 89, 93, 100–102, 122
social services: DFS activism for provision of, 21, 73–74, 81, 154–155; mass media use for recruitment, 43–44; volunteer activists for, 91–92
social status, education and cultivation for, 20
social world, Bourdieu on differentiation principles of, 8–9
sociocultural factors, neoliberal restructuring in, 14
Song, Wol-ju, 32

South Korea: economy since 1990s features, 253n59; as egalitarian society, 247n3; fertility rate in, 255n18; food safety in, 237n42; low level of gender equality in, 236n37; NGOs significance in, 27–28; OECD joined by, 242n21; population density in, 232n2; PSPD on naval vessel *Cheonan* sinking, 235n18; self-employment rate in, 250n27; UN membership in 1992, 23
South Korea-U.S. Free Trade Agreement (KORUS FTA): DFS campaign for food co-op products and, 96; protests against beef imports and mad cow disease, 63, 71, 111, 139, 145, 150, 237n42; PSPD opposition to, 58, 125, 126, 137–140; Roh Moo-hyun funding denial for citizens' organization opposing, 35; Roh Moo-hyun signing of, 3
state: citizens organizations financial and political independence from, 20; logic of financial markets and business enterprises of, 11, 12; moral code of independence from, 31–40; neoliberal transformation of power of, 11, 28; Tilly on civic activism and, 8
"State, Designed with Governance, The" (Yi), 124
state-society relations, in traditional Korea, 24
substantive democracy, 5; neoliberalism facilitation of, 14; neoliberalism undermining of, 14, 22
Support Center for Elderly Care Workers, of NE Branch, 165–166
symbolic actions, civic activism as, 7–10

theory of social space and political fields, of Bourdieu, 8–9
Tilly, Charles, 8; on social movements, 231n87
Toplišek, Alen, 202
traditional activism, civic activism for institutional or social change compared to, 40

INDEX

transnational capital, neoliberal globalization and mobile, 10

UN. *See* United Nations
UN Conference on Environment and Development: NGOs active involvement in, 27
Undoing the Demos (Brown), 124
UNDP. *See* United Nations Development Programme
United Nations (UN): Agenda 21, 23; global standards of NGOs by, 27; NGOs partnership with, 27; NGOs revival by, 26–27; promotion of NGOs moral codes, 24, 49–50; South Korea membership in 1992, 23
United Nations Development Programme (UNDP), *NGO Times* sponsoring of, 23
United States (U.S.): advocacy organizations in, 28–29, 224n17, 233n5; protests against mad cow disease and beef importation from, 63, 72, 111, 139, 145, 150, 237n42. *See also* South Korea-U.S. Free Trade Agreement; West
Unlimited Carework Project, 156
U.S. *See* United States

value, of democracy, 5–6, 15, 26, 30
volunteer members and activists, 79, 228n52, 230n76; Asia Civil Society Movement Research Center on NGOs and, 43–44; of DFS for institutional and social change, 82; for FOA Korean language classes, 183, 185–187, 200–201; in grassroot people participation, 43–44; in NGOs, 243n46; PSPD lay members as, 142–144, 252n51; for social service or charity organizations, 91–92

WB. *See* World Bank
wealth accumulation, 87, 125, 127, 132, 137, 212; accelerated, 179, 181, 214; politics maximizing of, 26; privatization and, 19, 147, 148, 204, 214
Weber, Max, 8, 220n26

web marketing, 244n62
West: democracy as branded product in, 15; free market promotion by, 2; market model of activism in, 88; neoliberal globalization promoted by, 217n3
women: coalition movements to expand political participation of, 238n55; DFS activism for bodies and health of, 73, 75–76, 76; DFS feminist organization for, 16, 21, 55–56, 67–78; DFS promotion of human rights for, 68; Kim Dae-jung and Roh Moo-hyun institutionalization of policies for, 72
women's employment projects, of DFS, 22, 155, 178; to address insecure employment, 162; Ebert Foundation Fund for, 162; of GY Branch, 162–165; of NE Branch, 165–166; self-employment in, 163; SM One Fence meetings for, 164
women's food work for children, of DFS, 155, 178; on free school meals for children, 153, 166–168, 257n58; National Network for School Meals and, 166
Women's Foundation, GY and NE branches indirect business donations link from, 90
Women's Health Project, of DFS, 177; local health ecosystem project expansion, 160–161, 173; NE Branch management of, 155, 158–161; project diversity in, 160; women health leaders for, 159–160
Women's New Job Center, 174–175
workers, peasants, marginalized social groups, people's movement focus on, 17, 30
World Bank (WB), 217n5; neoliberal economic restructuring and, 26; UN international development funded by, 27
worldification: Kim Young-sam promotion of, 2, 30; project of neoliberal economic restructuring, 30

World Trade Organization (WTO), 217n5; establishment of, 30; formation of, 225n19; neoliberal economic restructuring and, 26; UN international development funded by, 27

Yank, Yeong-hui, 92
Yeosu Protection Center, 80, 194, 260n24

Yi, Hyeong-yong, 124
Young Men's Christian Association (YMCA), 26; Ahn as founder of, 41; civic activism for social change of, 41–42, 230n70; social issues attention from, 41
Youth Intern program, of PSPD, 240n16